Charleston and Savannah

Charleston and Savannah

The Rise, Fall, and Reinvention of Two Rival Cities

THOMAS D. WILSON

The University of Georgia Press | Athens

A Wormsloe
FOUNDATION
PUBLICATION

© 2023 by the University of Georgia Press
Athens, Georgia 30602
www.ugapress.org

Designed by Melissa Buchanan
Set in Adobe Caslon Pro

Most University of Georgia Press titles are
available from popular e-book vendors.

Printed digitally

Library of Congress Control Number: 2022948285
ISBN 9780820363219 (hardcover)
ISBN 9780820363196 (paperback)
ISBN 9780820363202 (ebook)

CONTENTS

Additional details and discussion relevant to the material covered in this book is available at https://ugapress.manifoldapp.org /projects/charleston-and-savannah/.

ILLUSTRATIONS

TABLES

PREFACE

Dickens's *A Tale of Two Cities* is an account of London and Paris leading up to and during the French Revolution. A notable parallel between this tale and the story of Charleston and Savannah is that both are about resurrection and reinvention. London and Paris, in the Dickens novel, saw "long ranks of the new oppressors . . . risen on the destruction of the old." Paris became particularly abysmal as the promise of the Revolution sank into the Terror. Across the Atlantic during the period spanned by the novel, the United States gained its independence and became a republic. But for Charleston and Savannah, long ranks of new oppressors, a constellation of petty tyrants, obtained the constitutional means for exercising their bizarre notion of liberty for a small wealthy and privileged minority.

A Tale of Two Cities famously begins, "It was the best of times, it was the worst of times, it was the age of wisdom, it was the age of foolishness, it was the epoch of belief, it was the epoch of incredulity, it was the season of Light, it was the season of Darkness, it was the spring of hope, it was the winter of despair." Those words also describe the plight of the oppressed in Charleston and Savannah during the Revolutionary era and again, to an even greater degree, during the Civil War and Reconstruction era that followed. Hope held by the oppressed majority for the arrival of a just society rose and fell repeatedly as tenacious oppressors thwarted reform again and again and held tight the reins of government across the South.

The prospect of social equity—fair, just, and equitable treatment by the political system—would not rise again until nearly three hundred years after the founding of Charleston. It was in the mid-twentieth century that the civil rights movement, "the second Reconstruction," brought new hope. But again it was the best of times and the worst of times, the spring of hope and the winter of despair. Pervasive social inequity and racism proved durable. Yet in many places, Charleston and Savannah among them, equity and justice began arriving, one monumentally difficult step at a time. For once, all their citizens could finally say, as Dickens's character Carton did before his selfless submission to execution, "I see a beautiful city and a brilliant people rising from this abyss, and, in their struggles to be truly free, in their triumphs and defeats, through long years to come, I see the evil of this time and of the previous time of which this is the natural birth, gradually making expiation for itself and wearing out."[1]

The "deep map" of Charleston and Savannah that follows was largely completed in 2020, the year of the 350th anniversary of the founding of Charleston. This exceptional time was called the Year of Reckoning across the nation, the year in which all the promises of the past have come due, a "third Reconstruction." The subtitle of this book acknowledges that cities are projects in progress. They are places that create opportunity, wealth, wisdom, culture, and justice. In their lifespan they rise and fall and may rise and fall again. Great cities will ultimately achieve a capacity for self-awareness that will allow them to consciously reinvent themselves. Charleston and Savannah are once again reinventing themselves with the benefit of renewed enlightenment bursting forth.[2]

Savannah is the younger of the two cities, inspired in its founding sixty-three years after Charleston by core principles of the Enlightenment. It remained in the older, wealthier city's shadow for decades before earning its own wealth and notoriety. It gained a few advantages on Charleston in the eighteenth century, but it was not until the 1830s, a century after its founding, that it moved to the fore as arguably the South's most technologically progressive city.[3]

Charleston held the distinction for more than a century of being the only mature city in the southern tier of the Thirteen Colonies. An old fable tells of a traveler nearing his destination in Savannah and stopping to ask how much farther he had to go:

> "How far is it to the city?" he inquired.
> "Ninety-five miles, sir," a local man replied.
> "What? Ninety-five miles to Savannah? Surely not!" gasped the traveler.
> "No, sir," explained the local man. It ain't but five miles to Savannah, but it's ninety-five miles to the *city*."[4]

This anecdote, related in 1937, was of a much earlier time, a time that could have been anywhere between 1733 and the 1840s, when Charleston's superior status began to wane and, in the public imagination, Savannah became more of an equal.

The story of Charleston and Savannah that follows is a tale of two cities that are geographic neighbors but have been very far apart more often than not in their character and outlook. The story is told from various perspectives and contains multiple themes and threads, or through lines. The ultimate purpose is to portray the richness of character of both cities, the interrelatedness of their character, and the reinvention of both cities as an ongoing struggle begun in the 1960s.

Charleston and Savannah

INTRODUCTION

Charleston and Savannah are a mere ninety miles apart, but today they hardly know each other. Occasionally, professionals in fields such as tourism, port operations, and city planning meet to discuss specific issues, but there is little recognition of an entwined past, shared engrained character traits, and an interdependent future. One of several reasons for this book is to make the case that the two cities with so much in common should become reacquainted.

Leaders, residents, and the many admirers of Charleston and Savannah stand to benefit from such self-reflection. Lessons from a shared past can shed light on the path to an inclusive and sustainable future. Both cities attract visitors and new residents by preserving the historic built environment, cultivating an atmosphere that mingles past and present, and confronting a heritage that can simultaneously elicit shame and warrant pride. Preservation-oriented growth comes with the risk of losing authenticity and killing the goose that laid the golden egg.

The *principal* reason for this book is to provide a comprehensive and analytical comparison of Charleston and Savannah. In a single volume, the reader will find an assessment of the cities' history, geography, environment, economy, political culture, racial division, and other dimensions. A rich array of books on the two cities is available that focuses on specialized topics—the Civil War, plantations, and architecture, to name three—but few books offer a comprehensive and integrated perspective on both cities.[1]

Rise, Fall, and Reinvention

The rise of Charleston and Savannah is defined here as the long period of population growth, economic expansion, and increasingly forceful projection of political influence that spanned much of the colonial and antebellum eras. In the case of Charleston, that period began in the early 1700s and ended with the Civil War. For Savannah, it began in the 1750s and also ended with the Civil War. Rice plantations were the backbone of the economy, creating more wealth than any other crop or industry, and slavery was the backbone of rice production. Enslaved people not only provided the labor for rice production but also brought with them much of the technology that created aristocratic and oligarchic prosperity. The more essential enslaved Africans and their descendants became to the prosperity of European Americans, the more refined became the methods of oppression, a subject essential to understanding the genetic coding of both cities.

The Civil War ended legalized slavery and destroyed the agrarian model for growth that had spanned six generations. Reconstruction brought with it the prospect of a new model for growth, one that placed greater emphasis on small family farms, including those of formerly enslaved people. The new model was resisted and eventually overcome by Whites, who reclaimed much of their former race-based privilege. The South's largest concentration of former slaves and their descendants was excluded from full participation in the economy. Charleston and Savannah suffered economically, in large part from being immersed in an exclusionary society, while steadily declining in size relative to other cities. The long rise had ended, and a precipitous fall had begun.

The civil rights movement presented Charleston and Savannah with an opportunity for reinvention. Progressive mayors in Charleston advanced reforms, overcoming considerable White-majority resistance. In Savannah, where there was a modest Black majority, mayors came in fits and starts, some advancing reforms, some catering to White fear. More enlightened business interests learned that there was profit in diversity and inclusion. Both cities gradually reinvented themselves, presenting to the world a rich mix of cultural attributes, even though at home racism persisted, hidden behind the smile of southern hospitality.

In both cities, historic preservation became central to economic growth. Professional preservationists generally understood the history of racism and the limitations it placed on the preservation movement and its linkages to economic development. They helped broker advances in social equity, thereby inventing a more inclusive new model for the economy.

The year 2020 put the advancement of the new model economy under the microscope and found many advances wanting. Elitism had spun up a new kind of economy, one that consumed the historic core of each city and is on the verge of creating a massive underclass, excluded from the heart of their own city. Once again preservationists are situated at the fulcrum of change. The preservation movement has grown beyond protecting old buildings and now includes advocates for cultural preservation, social equity, environmental justice, and environmental protection. This new alliance of varied interests has conceived a new level of reinvention, and the strength of the new alliance will determine whether Charleston and Savannah can attain what they envision or whether a new generation of oligarchs and elites will prevail.

Colonial Cities and Incipient Southern Character

Charleston assumed a leading role in the creation of southern political culture, and Savannah had a supporting role. Note that "the South" did not exist as a cultural region when the cities were established during the colonial era. The South did not exist then and would not come into being until after ratification of the U.S. Constitution. An *incipient* South existed in the Tidewater region of Virginia and Maryland since 1619, and in Carolina later in the seventeenth century, but no one called themselves a "southerner" until the newly created United States consciously divided itself into free states and slave states, reifying the division acknowledged in the Constitution.

Although Charleston was founded fifty-one years after slavery was introduced into Virginia, it would become the insipient South's only real city *Charleston* of the early colonial period. As a result, it became a focal point for self-awareness and justification of an emerging society fundamentally dependent on slavery.

The idea of the South as a distinct place entered an incipient or emergent stage in the 1780s. When Pennsylvania adopted a law for the gradual abolition of slavery in 1780, its action gave regional meaning to the Mason-Dixon Line, a boundary survey completed in 1767. After 1780, the states were divided de facto into slaveholding states to the south of the line and free states to the north of it. Yet no people at that point considered themselves northerners or southerners. People thought of themselves as residents of their respective states, and colonies before that, nothing more.[2]

It was not until 1789, following the adoption of the U.S. Constitution, that the Continental Congress confronted the new nation's regional identity. James Madison made the distinction in a speech to Congress on June 29, 1789, in response to debate over the balance of power between small and large states. He asserted that the principal difference was not small and large but slave and non-slave—that is, North and South.

Mason Dixon line — completed in 1767

[Madison] contended that the States were divided into different interests, not by their difference of size, but by other circumstances; the most material of which resulted partly from climate, but principally from the effects of their having or not having slaves. These two causes concurred in forming the great division of interests in the United States. It did not lie between the large and small States. It lay between the Northern and Southern; and if any defensive power were necessary, it ought to be mutually given to these two interests.

Madison argued that the houses of Congress were divided in such a way as to recognize the differing interests of the slaveholding states and the free states: "By this arrangement, the Southern scale would have the advantage in one House, and the Northern in the other." Madison's term for the two distinct areas, "scale," would eventually be replaced with "section" and the more modern term "region."[3]

Although "the South" did not exist in the minds of the colonials who lived in the Tidewater area and farther south, regional political cultures were well formed by the time of independence. Charlestonians, in particular, had created a distinct culture that was different from that of the colonies to the north. Elements of that culture were forged on the frontier through the interactions of the colonists with Indigenous Americans and enslaved Africans as well as the geopolitical challenges presented by the Spanish and French. But there were also elements traceable to the various cultures of the British Isles.

At the time of Savannah's founding in 1733, several other towns in the southern tier of colonies were well established. As the sparsely populated southeastern colonies became the incipient South, Savannah was a colonial capital, a busy port city, a commercial beneficiary of being near the established city of Charleston, and a planned city, which imparted many advantages. During the antebellum era, it arguably became one of the South's earliest industrialized cities.

The issue of southern regional identity coupled with the use of the geographic term "the South" is inextricably tied to slavery. While independent variables such as climate are now associated with regional character, it was slavery and associated variables, such as settlement patterns and agricultural systems, that initially gave rise to regional identity. Further, regional identity subsequently changed the concept of slavery. Before the Revolutionary era, as the economic historian Jacqueline Jones has written, "the fiction of race played little part in the origins and development of slavery." Pre-Revolutionary motivations for the enslavement of Africans, and for a time Native Americans, were power and profit. Carolinians and Virginians began to reflect on the institution of slavery and develop an ideology for its existence. Concepts of White supremacy and societal paternalism emerged as core principles, and rhetorical clichés were invented and deployed for justification. The thread of slavery and White supremacy is woven into later chapters and the conclusion of this book.[4]

Scope of the Book

There are six parts to this book, each examining Charleston and Savannah from different but overlapping perspectives. Part 1 examines character, culture, and geography. Part 2 contains a short history, or "biography," of each city. Part 3 describes how the two cities began with elaborate plans that distinguished them as the only comprehensively planned cities in British America. Part 4 focuses on the early economic foundations of the two cities and the centrality of chattel slavery to both. Part 5 examines the cultural economy produced over generations of strain between the slaveholding plantation elite and an oppressed, enslaved labor force that constituted a majority of the population. Part 6 follows the decline and reinvention of the two cities. Finally, a conclusion draws together threads, or through lines, identified in the preceding twelve chapters, comparing and contrasting the two cities since the founding of Savannah in 1733. This conclusion also ventures a look to the future, speculating that growth trends will ultimately bring the cities closer together, forming a loosely bound Lowcountry metropolis.

An afterword wraps up a discussion begun in the preface regarding realities confronted in both cities as a result of the intense, consciousness-raising events of 2020. In writing about the present, an author risks making observations that might quickly become irrelevant. The risk is accepted here because the national discussions on race and social equity are very much those that have challenged Charleston and Savannah since the era of the civil rights movement. In that regard, this project is intended to have contemporary relevance and influence.

Finally, the wealth of material comparing and contrasting the two cities made it impractical to include all of it in this book. For additional evidence and continuing discussion, see the online supplement at https://ugapress .manifoldapp.org/projects/charleston-and-savannah/.

Charleston streetscape with
the city's unique side-yard
house in foreground.
(Photo by author)

Savannah streetscape illustrative of
the city's famous urban forest.
(Photo by author)

Character, Place, and Culture

Nearly all cities possess character elements derived from a mixture of the natural environment, the built environment, and the cultures of the inhabitants, a concoction of traits that makes most cities sui generis. Visitors instantly sense something different in Charleston and Savannah, a feeling that for many is more profound than what one senses in most cities. Part I delves into the attributes of the two cities that account for their strange attraction.

The early Enlightenment poet Alexander Pope applied the ancient Roman concept of genius loci, the spiritual character of a place, to landscape design, writing to Richard Boyle, Earl of Burlington, "Consult the genius of the place in all." Since establishing that principle, the idea that places have a distinctive atmosphere, a spirit of the place, has spread to other disciplines and has guided this work.

[handwritten annotations: "sui generis" (margin), "genius loci — spiritual character of a place"]

CHAPTER ONE

Historic City Character Study

The allure of Charleston and Savannah is unique in the United States. They are the only two cities in the nation where the richness of the colonial past resides side by side with present-day urban complexity. One can walk a mile in a straight line through either city and take in centuries-old streetscapes amid the bustle of a modern economy. A walk of merely an hour or two in either city can take one through several intimate neighborhoods and past hundreds of different doors with hundreds of interesting stories lying behind them.

The experience is one that is distinctly different from anything possible in this nation's other historic cities. In cities such as Key West or New Orleans one may take similar walks, but they are cities that were founded and developed later. There are older historic cities, such as Santa Fe, where one can walk a mile through history, but here one doesn't experience hundreds of doors in tight proximity. And there are larger colonial cities, such as Boston and Philadelphia, but the scale of their business and housing demands necessitates larger buildings and a greater separation of land uses, interrupting the continuity of the historic transect.

The central business districts in the historic cores of Charleston and Savannah, and the cities' smaller commercial districts, preserve historical character by maintaining compact, fine-grained (tight-knit) development patterns and rarely permitting large-footprint structures that are out of scale with their surroundings. Similarly, new residential developments (e.g., condominiums and apartments) often take the form of repurposed historic buildings or historically compatible designs that respect scale as well as architecture. Modern buildings that diminish historical character are anomalies.

One reason for the rich detail of colonial cities was their compactness. People of that era walked nearly everywhere, so houses and businesses were close together, and the fabric of life was woven more finely than in today's world. Entire cities were seldom more than a square mile in size, a natural limit to growth when people traveled about town on foot. When cities reached that limit, they grew *inward* by subdividing larger lots typically into two or three smaller ones and increasing the height of buildings from one or two stories to three or four. Through the process of growing inward, they became even more complex, compact, and richly mixed in their land-use patterns.

While other cities built over and around old urban patterns, erasing them or isolating them into historic enclaves, Charleston and Savannah built within their original city plans. Charleston retained its colonial and antebellum built environment essentially by default, as investors and industrialists left it behind and moved capital to strategic transportation hubs such as New Orleans and Atlanta, freezing existing conditions in place. Savannah adapted somewhat better to the new industrial era. It had a proud tradition of city planning dating to its founding, and it retained its identity largely by choice, even while losing some of its luster.

And so the strange and wonderful commingling of past and present in these two cities is a result of their early rapid development, followed by a long period of stagnation and decline and inadvertent preservation. The preservation ethic, present in Savannah since the antebellum era, and later a potent force in nostalgic Charleston, became the second necessary condition for creating the seamless *timescape*—the cityscape in which the dimension of time is prominent—that makes one feel one is living in history.

The captivating and exotic timescape of Charleston stems from a potent visual concoction of narrow streets, historical architecture, segregated living spaces, intimate public spaces, secretive private gardens, and subtropical sultriness. Time and space mingle everywhere. Streets are virtually medieval, unrestrained, and organic in places, dating to the seventeenth century but seeming to have older roots. The original city plan became less and less evident as colonists and the colony's far-away founders gradually parted ways. The city's architecture is that of the nineteenth century but with considerable eighteenth- and twentieth-century contributions. Public spaces take all forms and come in surprising places—public squares, linear promenades, waterfront parks—spaces created at different times in the city's history. Private gardens often barely visible from the street are seemingly haunted by ghosts of the past centuries while being maintained by their present owners. The surface materials of these places—mostly brick, plaster, and oyster shell tabby—are aged and softened, tempting those walking past to reach out and touch a moldy brick wall to feel its history.[1]

Where the city was once economically stuck in the past, it now preserves the past with purpose and perseverance. It does so not for the exclusive or even primary purpose of drawing tourists but because those who live there would have it no other way. They expect nothing less than a modern, vibrant urban environment with a complex economy, situated within the context of a time long past, a long-gone time when their city was the deeply flawed jewel of the South. Whether its success will collapse under the weight of tourism and outside investment is a subject taken up in the conclusion.

The South's Wealthiest City

Charleston was a politically and economically powerful city in colonial and antebellum America as well as the South's earliest vibrant city. In a through line in its story arc, South Carolina would learn to magnify and project its colonial power, and later its state power, through political rhetoric and brinksmanship cultivated by Charleston and its plantation hinterland, the Lowcountry. That ability was made possible through Charleston's size and centrality in the lives of South Carolinians, a feature that created a hive of intellectual and economic activity with disproportionate impact on the southeastern region and eventually the entire nation.

Charleston was the English-speaking southern region's most populous city from 1720 until New Orleans captured that distinction in 1820. The first census of the United States was conducted in 1790 as required by the U.S. Constitution, which had been ratified two years earlier. The census confirmed Charleston's early stature as one of the new nation's principal cities, its fourth largest (it would drop to fifth in 1800). Charleston, with its valuable exports, was by all accounts the nation's most prosperous city through most of the eighteenth century and well into the nineteenth century. At present, Charleston's population has fallen to 191st among U.S. cities, but its character and notoriety have continued to grow.

Few of the nation's major cities have a longer or richer history. Virginia was settled well before the founding of Charleston, and it enjoys the distinction of being the South's first colony. But as the South's mother colony it failed over two centuries to produce a city as vibrant as Charleston. Even with a much larger

U.S. City Population Rank, 1800–2000		
Year	Charleston	Savannah
1800	5	21
1850	15	44
1900	68	69
1950	174	88
2000	243	161

Source: U.S. Census

population, Virginia manifested its economic and intellectual vitality during the colonial and Revolutionary periods through its plantations and aristocratic networks. It was an unplanned colony of widely dispersed plantations and little urban life. Jamestown and Williamsburg, the colony's early capitals, never achieved anything approaching the social, cultural, or economic prominence attained by Charleston. Thomas Jefferson, who was famously anti-urban, saw only advantages in Virginia's agrarian development pattern.

One reason Charleston flourished long before other southern cities is that it was a planned city, intentionally designed to connect efficiently with surrounding towns and plantations. Another reason behind its rapid rise to prominence was that it was perfectly situated to take advantage of established Atlantic trade routes. Charleston was thus the capital of a compact and efficiently organized colony that was able to rapidly marshal the political will and organize the resources to expand its export economy and prosper—even in the face of disputes among its settlers and infamous lapses in leadership.

Charleston's Source of Wealth

No matter how well planned, Charleston could not have prospered and would not be what it is today had it not been able to take advantage of well-established transatlantic trade routes. Ships sailing from Africa with cargos of enslaved people and African goods had supplied European colonies in the Caribbean since the early 1500s. Charleston's position on the North Atlantic Gyre, described in the next chapter, opened up the southeastern coast of North America to expanded trade. With rice production beginning in the 1690s, the Lowcountry found its niche in the powerful Atlantic economy. Charleston's image today to a great extent channels this early history of elite city mansions amid a vast landscape of sprawling plantations.

The eighteenth century was a period of growth and prosperity for Lowcountry planters and Charleston merchants. Plantation owners grew rich producing rice through forced labor, and merchants grew rich exporting rice, importing enslaved Africans to cultivate and process rice, and importing consumer goods to meet growing demand in the prosperous colony. At the same time, inland traders also fueled the economy by selling rum and European manufactured goods to Native Americans and purchasing hides and other Indigenous products for export.

A culture arose amid the spectrum of activities that blended European, African, and Indigenous American influences on Lowcountry terrain. Like the terroir that makes a wine the unique product of environmental conditions, Charleston's character was formed out of that complex set of cultural and natural interactions.

The extreme concentration of wealth and power in Carolina during the colonial and antebellum periods requires an appropriate vocabulary if it is to be described accurately. The wealthy upper class thought of themselves as both an aristocracy and a patriarchy and adopted unusual titles conferred by the Lords Proprietors through the colony's constitution (see chapter 5). But a more contemporary vocabulary is needed for an objective discussion of those periods. The terms "aristocracy" and "oligarchy" are both accurate and objective, with the former placing emphasis on a social upper class and the latter placing emphasis on a ruling class of wealthy and powerful individuals. Some writers use the term "slavocracy" to describe the late-colonial and antebellum southern way of life, but the term "slave society" is more common. Other terms commonly used are "plantation elite," "slaveholder elite," and "political elite."

Historians and other scholars typically study their subject matter by examining the actions and consequences of the elite classes and high-profile historical figures. Fortunately, a new approach is emerging in which historical subject matter is explored through the lens of the greater body of people who lived through a particular period, including those who were disenfranchised or oppressed, for whom an appropriate vocabulary is also required. From this new perspective, terms such as "mechanic" (a skilled laborer or artisan) have been rediscovered and applied to the working classes. In this example, the use of appropriate terminology promotes an understanding of how the antebellum elite classified the people they saw as beneath them in the social hierarchy, as well as how those tiers of society conceived of themselves. There is also value in using a new, modified vocabulary when it offers a more accurate perspective on historical periods. An example is the use of the term "enslaved person" rather than always using the word "slave," to emphasize that slavery was an unnatural and forced condition. Words matter, and care is taken here to select those that most accurately describe all segments of society.[2]

Carolina's Formative Plan and the Character of Charleston

Charleston, originally styled Charles Town (or Towne), was founded in 1670 with the arrival of two shiploads of colonists from England, Ireland, the Bahamas, and Barbados. The colonists initially settled on the west bank of the Ashley River and completed a relocation across the river to the present site on the peninsula between the Ashley and Cooper Rivers by 1680. At the original site, the State of South Carolina maintains Charles Towne Landing State Historic Site, which opened in 1970 to commemorate the state's tercentenary (often called a "*tricentennial* commemoration").

A comprehensive plan for the development of Carolina was prepared in advance of settlement. Anthony Ashley Cooper, the wealthy and influential English politician who is considered the colony's founder, was the leader of its eight Proprietors and the prime mover behind its plan. The Ashley and Cooper Rivers were named for him. This man with two last names, as Oliver Cromwell called him, retained the services of a young surgeon from Oxford, John Locke, to assist in drafting the plan for the colony, which became known as the Grand Model. Ashley Cooper and his protégé Locke, who later rose to fame as a philosopher, put an indelible stamp on the colony by designing its initial settlement pattern, system of governance, and social hierarchy.[3]

While the Grand Model was never fully implemented, its influence never completely dissipated. Several authorities on early South Carolina history have concluded that land allocation and social hierarchy, in particular, shaped the cultural economy and political culture of the colony. The story of this period is told in greater detail in chapters 3 and 5, but it is essential in discussing the character of Charleston to note that it took form at a time that predated the Enlightenment and the concepts of natural equality and modern democracy. Aristocracy, oligarchy, patriarchy, and slavery were embedded in Charleston's genetic code, so to speak, remaining there to shape its character for generations.[4]

A lack of understanding of the Lowcountry environment proved to be one of the first great hurdles to settling the colony according to plan. The climate caught planners and settlers alike by surprise. It was much harsher than expected, the region's heat was far worse than most Englishmen had ever experienced, and even those who had worked in the tropical Caribbean sun were accustomed to a degree of relief from the prevailing southeast trade winds. The region is also subject to hard winter freezes, which many Mediterranean crops such as citrus cannot well tolerate. Colonists reported freezes so hard that chamber pots froze overnight.[5]

The Grand Model set forth principles of site selection dating to the Greco-Roman city planner Vitruvius, who set standards that endured into the eighteenth century. Those standards included locating cities on high ground, orienting the street grid to benefit from prevailing winds, and avoiding building on sites near extensive wetlands. The initial siting of Charleston grossly violated the ancient planning principles prescribed by the Grand Model. The new site for the city, across the Ashley River, was more conforming to plan but still imperfect from a Vitruvian perspective.

As a result of its less-than-ideal location, Charleston is vulnerable to extreme damage from hurricanes, frequent flooding, and various diseases transmitted by mosquitoes that breed in the low-lying areas common in and around the city (a problem largely resolved once modern public health measures were put in place, as described below).

The historic preservationist Christina Rae Butler documented the history of physical alteration on the Charleston Peninsula since colonial times in *Lowcountry at High Tide: A History of Flooding, Drainage, and Reclamation in Charleston, South Carolina.* In addition to showing how the city grew by filling wetlands and extending river banks to increase buildable land, she drew the connection between topography and epidemiology in the low-lying city. Marshes, flood-prone areas, and construction sites were breeding grounds for mosquitos. Affluent residents of the city often filled and raised their property, allowing runoff to drain into poor sections of the city.[6]

Butler shows that for the first two centuries of its history, Charleston was left to address public health within the framework of the miasma theory, the belief that "bad air" was chiefly responsible for most disease (the word "malaria" means "bad air" in old Italian). Since bad air supposedly emanated from wetlands, the practice of filling low-lying areas as a public health measure began in the 1690s and continued to the early twentieth century. Modern public health practices acquired traction in the mid-1800s as the causes of diseases were better understood, but filling wetlands remained the principal method of fighting malaria and other diseases that were linked to mosquitos through the century. Advanced drainage practices finally replaced extensive filling in the early twentieth century.[7]

Structures built in the eighteenth and nineteenth centuries to control drainage often had the perverse effect of trapping stormwater runoff in the city and worsening hurricane-related flooding while also expanding the breeding areas of disease-carrying mosquitos. Trapped water contaminated freshwater supplies and caused fires by compromising cooking facilities. Charleston's many narrow streets (which stand in sharp contrast to those of Savannah) further increased the city's vulnerability to the rapid spread of disease and fire.

After-the-fact adaptations to poor site planning are reflected in Charleston's architectural heritage today. The famous Charleston single house, or side-yard house, normally has a piazza that faces west or south toward the yard, while the narrow side of the house faces the street, allowing more air to move across the porch and between structures. The main level of the house is elevated to minimize flood damage, and larger windows on the upper floors allow substantial cross-ventilation to efficiently dry out a storm-damaged house.

piazza

A Frontier Town in the Lowcountry

An English shipmaster named Martin described Charles Town in verse, vividly encapsulating the city's demographics, climate, economy, and vulnerabilities.

> Black and white all mixed together
> Inconstant, strange, unhealthful weather
> Burning heat and chilling cold
> Dangerous for both young and old
> Boisterous winds and heavy rains
> Fevers and rheumatic pains
> Houses built on barren land
> No lamps or lights, but streets of sand
> Everything at a high price
> But rum, hominy, and rice.[8]

Diseases that regularly afflicted the Lowcountry were malaria, yellow fever, smallpox, cholera, and dysentery. Charleston, surrounded by the constant flow of tidal waters and offshore air, was considered healthful in comparison to most Lowcountry plantations. But truly healthful it was not, and many among the aristocracy summered in cooler climates, with Newport, Rhode Island, being a favorite retreat. Physicians described the Lowcountry as a paradise in the spring but hell in the summer and a hospital in the fall.[9]

The watery environment of the Lowcountry made travel difficult in the early colonial decades. Coastal travel was usually conducted by small, single-masted sloops and even smaller oar boats, called pettiaguas. When roads were eventually constructed, they swung inland to avoid wetlands, often adding greatly to the distance of point-to-point travel compared to waterways. The physical geography of peninsulas and waterways around Charleston was, nevertheless, helpful in partially implementing the Grand Model and its prescription for compact development. While regional development around Charleston is not as compact as that of Savannah (founded sixty-three years later), it was more compact than was the case in Virginia (founded sixty-three years earlier), where longer rivers invited deeper inland migration.

Most early Carolina plantations were located as close as possible to the capital (or other planned towns such as Beaufort and Georgetown) in order to minimize the complications of travel in the Lowcountry. Settlers took advantage of the pattern of rivers around Charleston, locating plantations where they could reach the city by water in no more than a few hours. The Ashley, Cooper, Stono, and Wando Rivers led directly to the capital, and tributaries such as Goose Creek provided convenient access as well.

Many of the "rivers" of the Lowcountry are tidal flows between islands or along peninsulas rather than actual rivers that drain upland watersheds. The Ashley River flows past the western side of the Charleston Peninsula, draining inland swamps before it widens into tidal estuary. The Cooper River on the other side of the peninsula is also primarily a tidal river with bidirectional flow. Both are actual rivers in the sense that they have a drainage basin, but they each are primarily tidal bodies of water within a larger estuarine environment.

These two rivers are essential elements of Charleston's character, creating working waterfronts and water views on either side of the city. The bridges that span the rivers today are also character elements in themselves. The Arthur Ravenel Jr. Bridge over the Cooper River is particularly noteworthy. The eight-lane bridge, which opened in July 2005, replaced two obsolete cantilever truss bridges that terrified many crossers. The new bridge has a span of 1,546 feet, making it the third-longest cable-stayed bridge in the Western Hemisphere. Its pedestrian path is an intensively used public space, with expansive city and harbor views.

A twenty-two-mile segment of the Ashley River with the largest concentration of historic plantations in South Carolina is designated a state scenic river. Plantations on the river that are open to the public include Drayton Hall, Middleton Place, and Magnolia Plantation. Anthony Ashley Cooper's original plantation (which he never occupied but managed from England) is now a site of archaeological research. A section of South Carolina Highway 61 that follows the river past the plantations is a designated scenic route.

Charleston Becomes a City

The 350-year history of Charleston began with a rapid rise during its first century from frontier town to America's wealthiest city. Its rise faltered during the antebellum era as New Orleans and other cities farther west became new magnets for growth. The enormous Mississippi Valley boomed with prosperity from cotton and became the nation's largest economic region as steamboats and railroads connected it with the Midwest and increased connectivity within the Southwest (then perceived as Arkansas, Louisiana, and Texas), leaving Charleston in decline as the nation expanded. The city's arc faded further after the Civil War as the South struggled to regain its economic footing.

Charleston eventually benefited from federal investment in naval facilities and the attendant dredging of its shipping channels, but it would be a long time before it would regain a measure of its past vitality. The city hit bottom as the Jim Crow regime of White elitism and Black structurally enforced subservience encountered the civil rights movement. Despite deeply entrenched attitudes, the city responded to the new era of equality with sustained attempts at reinvention. Much of its reinvention had to do with the leadership of mayors J. Palmer Gaillard and Joseph P. Riley Jr. The latter, who served from 1975 to 2015, was particularly committed to a new paradigm of racial equality while being equally committed to renewing the city's prosperity.

One of Mayor Riley's notable achievements (which are discussed more fully in subsequent chapters) was launching the annual Spoleto Festival USA, a major international performing arts event. The composer Gian Carlo Menotti, in seeking a partner for the *Festival dei Due Mondi* (The Festival of Two Worlds) in Spoleto, Italy, found one in Charleston, which he described as "intimate, so you can walk from one theatre to the next." "It has Old World charm in architecture and gardens. Yet it's a community big enough to support the large number of visitors to the festival."[10]

Charleston hosts other festivals year-round that reinforce the city's image as a literary, artistic, and creative city. There are several music festivals, as well as multiple culinary, ethnic, and other cultural festivals. Other events include house and garden tours, an annual antique show, and maritime heritage events. The city's rich cultural heritage together with its present support for the arts is on virtually continuous display throughout the year.

A community's principal institutions—churches, colleges, museums, military installations, and others—can define the dimensions of its character. Historic cities can range from sedate and stately to artsy and intellectual or raucous and honky-tonk in character. Often the institutions of a city engage with the natural environment to enrich attributes of character. In New Orleans, bars, jazz, and sultry weather meld into a single, character-defining institution (one of many in that complex city) that is part of its individuality.

Charleston was once well known for the diversity of its churches and a tradition of religious tolerance, which led to the nickname Holy City. Its many places of worship remain significant architectural and historical statements, but three institutions of higher learning contribute far more now to the vibrancy and character of downtown Charleston. The College of Charleston, the Medical University of South Carolina, and the Citadel collectively add more than thirty thousand students, faculty members, and research professionals to the eight-square-mile peninsula.[11]

The modern economies and major institutions of Charleston and Savannah are discussed in general terms in chapter 12. Their rebirth and prosperity, as well as the many new challenges they face, are also the subject of chapter 12 and the conclusion that follows.

Savannah Created from a Modified Template

When Savannah was conceived, Charleston was still a frontier city but one with three generations of experience. Even though often eclipsed by Charleston in the early decades, Savannah emerged as one of the South's earliest fully functional cities. After its near-century-long struggle in Charleston's shadow, it would become one of the region's most industrial cities and Charleston's principal economic rival.

Eventually the two cities would grow old together, making way for younger cities like Atlanta to build their careers. They were, as Scarlett O'Hara described them, "like aged grandmothers fanning themselves placidly in the sun." The pair were rare southern cities with a rich colonial legacy, and, though at times battered by hurricanes, ravaged by disease, and consumed by fires, they bequeathed a complex built environment that now fascinates admiring visitors.[12]

On the surface, Savannah and Charleston appear similar. Both have large but walkable historic districts. Their eighteenth-century streetscapes are lined with many nineteenth-century structures. They project an ambiance too old to feel familiar to many Americans, yet they are filled with modern activity. To the casual observer they look much the same, yet there is an intangible gestalt about each that is different.

Notable among their differences is that Savannah, according to many observers, presents a more European appearance than Charleston or virtually all other American cities. Its formal streets, most with wide, tree-shaded sidewalks and many with landscaped medians, readily evoke the streets and boulevards of London and Paris. The relationship between buildings and streets in places resembles that of Paris after it was rebuilt in the mid-1800s by prefect Georges-Eugène Haussmann for Emperor Napoleon III. Its network of squares is like the pattern seen in many European cities, but it is notably anomalous in English-speaking North America.[13]

In Savannah, public space is on par with private space: both realms offer a unique, rich experience. The city's squares present an opportunity for everyone entering them, from every vantage point, to view the surrounding built environment, while those in the buildings that adjoin city squares and green spaces take in a view of public activity. The design that permits this reciprocal experience is part of the city's genetic code, one might say, inherited from the egalitarian urban plan formulated by city founder James Edward Oglethorpe (1696–1785).

Not only is Savannah's public realm alluring to visitors and residents alike for its historical attributes, it is enchantingly forested as well. Twenty-one of the city's twenty-two squares are covered in oak canopies. Each square is connected to others by tree-lined streets and tree-shaded sidewalks. To the north of the city's squares, verdant parks line the riverfront area, and city sidewalks to the south flow seamlessly through a twelve-acre botanical garden. In the words of John Berendt, author of *Midnight in the Garden of Good and Evil*, historic Savannah is like "a giant parterre garden."[14]

From the Savannah River along Bull Street to Forsyth Park, where the city maintains a botanical garden in the fountain area, is a distance of one mile. The walking route is one of several remarkable transects of the city. It takes the walker through five squares offering two hundred linear feet or more of green space. Each square has a monument, including a towering statue of Oglethorpe midway along the route. The architecture is predominantly of the mid- to late-nineteenth century.

The sense of being in a vibrant urban forest is fundamentally different from Charleston's more gothic or medieval vibe. In Savannah, one often looks up and around, whereas in Charleston one tends to look at the next remarkable specimen of architecture and perhaps peer into its accompanying private garden. Yet the dominant feeling for most visitors is the same in both cities: the distant past (in American terms) is still alive in ways seldom seen in the nation's other cities.

City planners extol the virtues of both Savannah and Charleston. Both have walkable urban environments of a sort that many modern cities lack. Sidewalks are sufficiently wide to accommodate pedestrian traffic, buildings abut sidewalks to create interest and tacit participation in city life, and trees and architectural features such as arcades offer shade from the hot sun and shelter from rain. Pedestrians have parks and squares in which to gather, and strong preservation movements in both cities offer a wide array of museums and historic buildings to entertain and inform the public. A fine-grained mix of uses—residential, commercial, and civic—adds complexity to the urban scene, pleasantly challenging the senses.

Historic cities faced a challenge when engineers were put in charge of city planning after World War II. It was a time when Americans rapidly exited urban areas for the suburbs, and the principal concern of those officials was infrastructure, in particular road-building needed to accommodate the postwar boom. Most Americans living today grew up in the suburban, car-oriented environment engineers created. Visitors to Charleston and Savannah experience a glimpse of life as it was before the automobile dominated the modern landscape. The historic city experience of easy walking, accessibility, and human-scale proportionality comes as a novel and often pleasant surprise to Americans accustomed to suburbia.

Most people can readily understand the paired virtues of accessibility and ease of walking. A short, pleasant walk to get coffee, mail a package, pick up a prescription, and buy a bottle of wine readily seems like a desirable arrangement to all but the most ardent car-oriented suburbanite. Proportionality of urban design, on the other hand, is a more subliminal feature of historic cities and modern urban planning. Ancient Greeks and Romans were deeply concerned with it, a concern that was revived during the Renaissance and in the Enlightenment. But appreciation of its importance all but disappeared in post–World War II America. The suburban tide began slowly turning in the late twentieth century as urban and landscape design movements reapplied old principles in new contexts. Now, even in some cases in the suburbs, design principles of proportionality are recognized enhancements to the built environment.

Classical design principles of human-scale proportionality are generally present in Savannah to a greater extent than in Charleston. One such principle is the ratio of street width to building height. Generally, ratios in the range of 1:1 to 1:3 are considered ideal, with the higher end of the range more appropriate for narrower streets. Pedestrians experience a comforting sense of enclosure, as opposed to a sense of *exposure*, in spaces that achieve those ratios. That sense is maintained to a greater extent throughout the original planned area of Savannah than in comparable areas of Charleston.

Another principle of human-scale proportionality where Savannah stands out is in its civic realm, particularly in its twenty-two squares. The proportions and other details are discussed in chapter 6, but the bottom line is that the city's squares frame a place where cars, bicycles, and pedestrians can safely and comfortably share the streets. Additionally, Savannah's sidewalks are generally wider, which also reduces the intrusion of vehicular traffic on pedestrian consciousness. Savannah benefited greatly from conscientiously preserving the proportions of its original design as the city grew and modernized.

Savannah's Contrasting Character

Savannah has an image of being a quirky place. Like Charleston, it has the odd mix of aspiring newcomers, white- and blue-collar workers, college students, eccentrics, a substantial creative class, and pretentious locals with unreconstructed antebellum attitudes. John Berendt's local guide when he first arrived in Savannah was Mary Harty, an elderly woman who had much to say about the uniqueness of her city. "We're not at all like the rest of Georgia," she said. "If you go to Atlanta, the first question people ask you is, 'What's your business?' In Macon, they ask, 'Where do you go to church?' In Augusta, they ask your grandmother's maiden name. But in Savannah, the first question people ask you is 'What would you like to drink?'"[15]

Social lubrication peaks on St. Patrick's Day, which effectively begins at dawn as locals and visitors alike bring their coolers and folding chairs to prime spots along the city's parade route. Savannah stages one of the largest St. Patrick's Day parades in the nation, a four-to-five-hour extravaganza involving every niche of society. Government offices and businesses that do not sell food, alcohol, or memorabilia close for an informal holiday. Politicians wave at the throngs from floats and convertibles, bands march, military convoys roll, and all manner of people flow from Forsyth Park (Savannah's Central Park) through its squares and down its wide avenues. The revelry continues into the night, concentrated along River Street, where alcohol is most plentiful. Savannah is one of those rare cities that allows people to move about town with open containers of alcohol, and tens of thousands of revelers take advantage of that liberty.

More events occur in the public realm in Savannah than in Charleston. Its squares, wide tree-lined avenues, and green spaces are natural venues for art and food festivals, concerts, holiday celebrations, outdoor markets, parades, and open-air private events such as weddings. At Christmas, squares are decorated by the residents and businesses that surround them, giving each one a uniquely festive look. In Charleston, most notable events occur in Marion Square, the city's central focal point. But in Savannah there are dozens of venues where events of all kinds and sizes continuously take place.

Savannah largely resisted the devastating effects of decentralization that ravaged historic city centers during the urban renewal period of the mid-twentieth century. Suburbanization initially depressed the downtown area, but City of Savannah and Chatham County public officials chose to retain their administrative headquarters in the city center, as did many institutions and businesses. The Historic Savannah Foundation established a preservation movement in the 1960s that saved and improved historic structures. It partnered with the tourism industry, which featured the city's historical character and in time made Savannah not only an attraction for tourists but an attraction for people living in the metropolitan region as well. The relationship between tourism and historic preservation is a related through line in the story of both cities.

Next to tourism, perhaps the greatest impact on historic Savannah came from higher education. Savannah has three major institutions of higher learning: Georgia Southern University's Armstrong Campus, Savannah State University, and Savannah College of Art and Design (SCAD). The total student body population of the three institutions in 2020 was over twenty thousand. SCAD is the largest of the three institutions, with nearly twelve thousand students. The SCAD campus is spread across downtown Savannah and contiguous historic districts. It operates in over seventy historic buildings and newer, compatible structures. SCAD's impact on downtown Savannah is comparable to that of the College of Charleston, with a student population of similar size.

The area referred to here as "downtown" Savannah has essentially the same boundaries as the city's National Historic Landmark District. It is ninetenths of a square mile and encompasses all twenty-four squares laid out by the city, twenty-two of which still exist as public spaces. It is within this six-hundred-acre area that downtown residents, tourists, office workers, college students, and others mingle in a vibrant urban environment. The downtowns of Savannah and Charleston and their various historic districts are compared and contrasted in chapter 12 and in the subsequent conclusion.

Beyond downtown Savannah lie twelve other historic districts, most of them contiguous. The Victorian District is immediately south of the Landmark District, and beyond that is the Thomas Square Streetcar Historic District, which was laid out when the mobility offered by streetcars allowed residents to live farther from the downtown area. Other historic districts such as Ardsley Park Historic District were laid out even farther from downtown at the dawn of the automobile era. These twelve additional historic districts, which extend three miles south of the river and over four miles southeast, offer a rich diversity of architecture, neighborhood form, and cultural diversity.

One aspect of the site chosen by Oglethorpe to build Savannah that proved disadvantageous was the presence of wetlands on both sides of the town, which turned out to be breeding areas for disease-carrying mosquitoes. In the 1850s, the problem was worsened when rice cultivation moved into those wetlands and planters impounded free-flowing water. The problem was not addressed until 1917.

Before continuing with the often interrelated, sometimes tangled, story of Charleston and Savannah, it should be pointed out what is meant by "Charleston" and "Savannah." The names are elastic since both cities were never static. During the colonial period, both occupied a walkable area of only about a square mile. Between the Revolutionary period and the Civil War, they both grew to a still-walkable size of about three square miles. In the late 1800s and through the early 1900s, when streetcars enhanced mobility, they increased in size to around five square miles. With the advent of the automobile, growth accelerated dramatically. Presently, both cities have a land area of over one hundred square miles within their municipal boundaries. The image they project today is that of historic cities, but in reality they contain far more area that is suburban in character than area that is urban or historic.

Nevertheless, an area of about four to five square miles still defines Charleston and Savannah, and it is generally that dense, vibrant core area that is referenced throughout, not the residential suburbs, commercial corridors, shopping meccas, or industrial parks. It is in discussing contemporary conditions that name usage becomes especially elastic. For some statistical purposes, the city names may refer to municipality, county, or metropolitan area. In the end, however, as the discussion of the two cities boils down to their essence, it returns to their historic cores. It remains *that* area—not jetliner manufacturing or Panamax ships—that defines each city's character and purpose.

CHAPTER TWO

Transatlantic Culture in the Lowcountry Landscape

Charleston and Savannah owe much of their celebrated history and character to geography. They were strategically positioned from their founding to become major players in transatlantic trade. The wealth from that trade, the cultural whirlpool that resulted, and the sultry climate of the Lowcountry created two of America's most charming and intriguing cities.

The Lowcountry backdrop for the story of Charleston and Savannah is a 150-mile stretch of South Carolina coastline that extends from the lower Savannah River on the south to the Pee Dee River just beyond Georgetown to the north. Much of the topography is estuarine, with tidal waters interspersed with lowlands, often in equal proportions. The expansive swath of land and water extends inland about forty miles on average from the Sea Islands lining the coast to the edge of higher terrain. While the coastal region extending from Wilmington, North Carolina to Jacksonville, Florida is topographically uniform, the Lowcountry stands out with its concentration of cultural attributes.

Lowcountry author Pat Conroy wrote in *Lords of Discipline*, a novel about the Citadel, "You can never completely escape the sensuous, semitropical pull of Charleston and her marshes." Most of his other novels, from *The Water is Wide* to *South of Broad* portray a fusion of characters with their environment. The sultry Lowcountry atmosphere of Savannah was captured in John Berendt's *Midnight in the Garden of Good and Evil* and equally well in Clint Eastwood's movie of the same title. Culture and natural landscape are so thoroughly blended in the Lowcountry that it is impossible to separate them.[1]

The Lowcountry is situated due west of the Sargasso Sea, which lies in the middle of the North Atlantic Ocean and is the world's only sea bounded entirely by water. Popularized in literature as the sea that covers mythical Atlantis and as a watery graveyard of sailing vessels, this sea within an ocean left many ships becalmed and adrift in its doldrums before navigators learned to avoid it. Much of the lore about the Sargasso Sea began with the account of the first voyage of Christopher Columbus to America. The *Niña*, *Pinta*, and *Santa Maria* were becalmed there for days, and the crews grew fearful of becoming entangled in its seaweed (*Sargassum*) and running aground on some previously undiscovered and inhospitable land.

While the sea itself is generally calm, it forms a large hub around which winds and ocean currents flow in a massive clockwise motion. That swirling pattern, known as the North Atlantic Gyre, was the world's most dynamic engine of commerce for more than three centuries. It drove the Atlantic triangular trade, a maritime trading system that made Charleston the wealthiest city in North America, rich enough to temporarily remake neighboring Savannah in its image after the younger city ended its formational twenty-year utopian experiment.

In the fifteenth century, Europeans began harnessing the flow around the Sargasso Sea to explore the larger world and ultimately to create intercontinental maritime trade routes. The Portuguese were the first to navigate the winds and currents rotating around the sea. Initially, in the early 1400s, they discovered the Azores and Madeira islands and explored the Atlantic coast of North Africa. By mid-century they had reached tropical West Africa, made contact with indigenous nations, and established insipient trade relations. And by the end of the century, they discovered South America and were establishing transatlantic trade routes. They were followed by Spain, Holland, France, Britain, Denmark, and Sweden in building wealth-generating transatlantic trade empires.

The Sargasso Sea is bounded on the east by the Canary Current, named after the Canary Islands, which, together with northeasterly trade winds, drove European sailing vessels south toward Africa. The Portuguese were ideally suited geographically, facing the Sargasso Sea from the east, to be the first to take advantage of winds and currents to explore Africa from the sea.

South of the Sargasso Sea, the North Atlantic Equatorial Current flows from Africa toward the Caribbean, reinforced by the northeasterly trades, which become more westerly off the coast of West Africa. Columbus's third and fourth voyages to America fully exploited this combination of ocean current and prevailing winds while avoiding the earlier entrapment in the Sargasso Sea.

West of the Sargasso Sea, the Gulf Stream flows northeast from the Caribbean, past Florida, Georgia, and the Carolinas, eventually bending toward and warming the British Isles. Midway across the Atlantic, the Gulf Stream

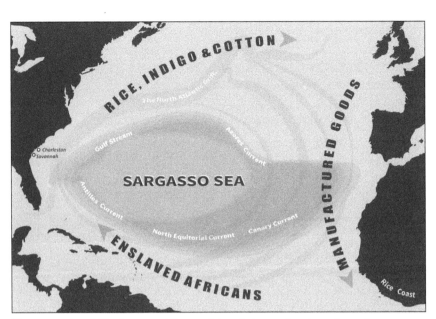

The geography of Charleston and Savannah in relation to the triangular trade and North Atlantic currents. *(Map by Teri Norris)*

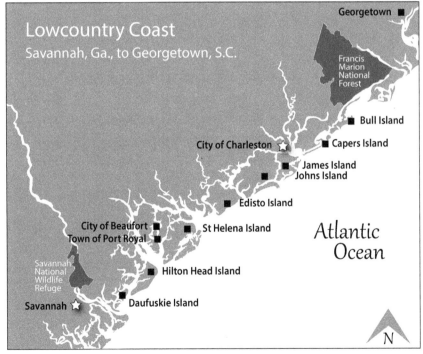

The Lowcountry coast from Savannah to Georgetown. *(Map by Teri Norris)*

becomes known as the North Atlantic Current, or North Atlantic Drift, where the current is reenergized by the westerlies, a global pattern of higher-latitude winds that includes a flow from North America toward Europe. This combination of currents and winds became essential to treasure-laden Spanish fleets for their return to home port.

England, France, the Netherlands, and other northern European nations gradually absorbed the knowledge of Atlantic winds and currents first acquired by the Portuguese and Spanish. Ships sailing from England rode the westerlies and the Canary Current for the voyage to Africa. At African ports, they initially traded European manufactured goods for a range of indigenous African products, including high-quality iron implements and textiles as well as gold and agricultural products. Later, as the demand for labor in America soared, the slave trade came to dominate African export commerce. Ships departing Africa caught trade winds and the Equatorial Current in sailing west toward the Caribbean. There they sold cargoes of enslaved people and purchased sugar and rum.[2]

Charleston and Savannah were founded in 1670 and 1733, respectively, during the peak of Caribbean engagement in transatlantic trade. They became the first ports of call visited by many English ships returning home from the Caribbean by way of the Gulf Stream. By the 1690s, the stage was set for Charleston to become a major player in transatlantic trade. Savannah would not reach that point until 1752, when it effectively became a satellite of Charleston. But the South's second city was destined to soon become a competitor of its wealthy neighbor.

Charleston began exporting rice in the 1690s and within a few decades became the richest city in North America by selling the commodity through English merchants, who in turn supplied British and European markets. It retained an essential place in transatlantic trade for over a century, with a continuing demand for enslaved workers and exports of rice along with substantial secondary products such as indigo, animal skins, naval stores (pine resin products used to seal ships), and Sea Island cotton (*Gossypium barbadense*, high-quality cotton with a silky texture). Caribbean rum was imported and traded to Native Americans, in defiance of objections from their leaders.

Rice production was labor-intensive, and the African slave trade supplied all the labor Carolina planters required. Recent scholarship has shown that enslaved Africans provided much of the technical expertise for successful coastal rice cultivation, a subject taken up in detail in chapter 7. Slave ships began sailing directly from African ports to Charleston by mid-century, and the city became the largest importer of enslaved Africans in North America. Savannah soon afterward became the second-busiest slave port on the continent.

The founders of Charleston did not envision a future economy based almost entirely on African enslaved labor. They certainly foresaw an important role for slavery in a diversified, exporting economy, but the Carolina Colony was not envisioned to become a "slave society" (a term scholars apply to societies built on a foundation of slavery). It was only after much of the Carolina Lowcountry began producing rice and then became dominated by plantation owners from Barbados, who had decades earlier become dependent on slavery, that the colony was transformed into a slave society. The Georgia Colony, with its early, formal prohibition of slavery, stood in stark contrast, but Charlestonians soon after the founding of Savannah began plotting to convert Georgia from a colony of yeoman farmers to one of large plantations made more productive by enslaved labor.

Before Charleston and Savannah existed, their planners looked to *latitude* in imagining their future economies. The hinterlands of the two cities were expected to grow the kinds of crops typically found in Mediterranean climates of similar latitude, such as grapes (for wine) and olive, orange, and nut trees. The scientifically sophisticated plan for the Georgia Colony, developed with assistance from the Royal Society, even included a provision for an experimental garden in which plants from around the world would be tested for viability in its supposed Mediterranean climate.

Cities of the Mediterranean with a similar latitude include Athens, Algiers, Barcelona, Beirut, Jerusalem, Valencia, and Tunis. Other cities within the typical Mediterranean band of latitude include Los Angeles and San Diego in the Northern Hemisphere, and Cape Town, South Africa, Perth, Australia, and Santiago, Chile in the Southern Hemisphere. Regions at that latitude, both north and south of the equator, typically have a mild climate, and, while they tend to be dry, they can be highly productive agriculturally if they have a water supply.

Planters found, however, that Charleston and Savannah had an entirely different sort of climate. Mediterranean climates (outside of the Mediterranean) are typically found along *western* coasts where cold currents influence climatic conditions. The Lowcountry and coastal Georgia, lying on

Lowcountry Latitude

	Degrees	Minutes
Charleston	33	47
Savannah	32	8

Subtropical range: 23.5–35 degrees

the eastern continental coast, face a warm current, the Gulf Stream, that has relatively little effect on the local climate. The first settlers in the region, unable to cultivate land as they had in Europe, or apply methods suitable for Mediterranean climates, were forced to learn by trial and error. The easiest method, as it turned out, was to apply techniques learned in the Caribbean and in Africa—parameters that would shape the history and character of the region.

In present-day terminology, the southeastern United States has a humid subtropical climate, quite different too from the temperate climate of northern Europe. Much of the region experiences alternating weather patterns. Moisture-laden air flowing from the Gulf of Mexico brings warm, humid weather and rain. Frequent cold fronts coming in from the north bring drier and cooler air. Each winter, cold fronts will typically bring several hard freezes to both cities.

The fluctuations in those weather patterns are caused by variability in the polar and subtropical jet streams that flow west to east across North America. The two jet streams are closely associated with latitude: polar jets form around 60°N; subtropical jets form around 30°N. Being on the eastern side of North America, the polar jet can bring frigid continental air masses down on the Lowcountry, or, just as likely, the subtropical jet can bring balmy tropical weather, even in midwinter. While the two jet streams can bring mild or severe weather to Charleston and Savannah in the summer and winter, the spring and fall typically bring mild weather. Although today both cities have year-round tourism, those two more predictably mild seasons are the busiest.

The Lowcountry Context

Charleston and Savannah share a unique geographical setting on the southeastern coast of the United States. Separated by only ninety miles of marshy coast, they first appear remarkably similar but then, upon closer examination, seem worlds apart. Each city has a complex character steeped in a rich blend of physical geography, economic history, and cultural legacy, but differences in details such as elevation and founding plans yield notable differences.

Charleston is the centerpiece of the Lowcountry, a seven-county area that also includes the historic coastal cities of Beaufort, Port Royal, and Georgetown, as well as many Sea Island communities, including Sullivan's Island, Hilton Head, and St. Helena, home of the Gullah culture. What these towns and island communities have in common, in addition to climate and topography, is a unique blend of African and European cultures born in an era of vast rice plantations cultivated by an enslaved labor force.[3]

The Ashley and Cooper Rivers that define the Charleston Peninsula, along with their numerous coastal tributaries, formed a natural transportation network for early settlers that linked the city to surrounding plantations. The historical area of the city from the tip of the peninsula to its "neck" is four miles in length and averages about two miles in width. Much of the city is less than ten feet above mean sea level, leaving it vulnerable to flooding from hurricanes and other severe storms.

Although Savannah and Charleston are virtually identical in physical geography, the word "Lowcountry" is seldom applied to the Georgia coast. The present-day term for that area is "Coastal Empire." Historically, however, the two cities were part of the same coastal region dominated by tidal wetlands and rice plantations. Therefore, in discussing Charleston and Savannah together in historical context, Lowcountry is a fitting name for the region encompassing both cities.

Savannah is located on the south side of its namesake Savannah River, fifteen miles upstream from the Atlantic coastline. The name "Savannah" most likely came from the Spanish *sabana*, which in turn came from the Taino word *zavana*, meaning marshy or low-lying ground. However, the Savannah Indians, a branch of the Shawnee, inhabited the Savannah River area, either giving the river their name or acquiring their own name from the Spanish or Taino name.[4]

The founder of Savannah, James Oglethorpe, chose a site for the city that was navigable yet sufficiently inland to be located on high ground. The site was on a coastal ridge nearly fifty feet above mean sea level where it would not be subject to flooding. The ridge was of sufficient width and depth to allow the town to grow to its planned size.

Once the town was built out according to plan, it extended along the river for nearly one mile and inland exactly one mile. That original planned square mile is now designated a National Historic Landmark District. The Savannah River, which Savannah's historic downtown faces, forms (with a few exceptions) the modern state line between Georgia and South Carolina.

Historically, the length and navigability of the Savannah River offered Savannah more inland trade opportunities than the Ashley or Cooper Rivers provided Charleston. The Savannah River is 301 miles long, beginning at the confluence of the Seneca and Tugaloo Rivers, which in turn have their headwaters in the Blue Ridge Mountains of the southern Appalachian mountain range.

Lowcountry terrain is composed of tidal waters, marsh, and lowlands.
(Photo by Teri Norris)

The river was historically navigable by dugout canoes and other small trade boats, which were used throughout its entire length. Indian trails ran parallel to the river on the Georgia side, and settlements and trading posts were established at numerous locations on both sides. Larger pole boats were used by European settlers and traders from the early 1700s, with a rapid increase in activity after the founding of Savannah in 1733 and Augusta in 1736. The river is navigable for deeper draft vessels to Augusta, which lies at the fall line (where the foothills meet the coastal plain) two hundred miles from Savannah.

The Lowcountry and the neighboring region south of Savannah are interspersed with estuaries and maritime forests of live oaks, pines, and palmettos. The overall appearance of this unique landscape is that of a verdant water wonderland where one is never quite sure where the land ends and the sea begins. The effect is particularly stunning at high tide when vast areas are inundated with glistening Atlantic waters.

Estuaries are brackish bodies of water partially enclosed by sea islands (technically termed barrier islands and back-barrier islands) and the mainland. They are tidally influenced, and rivers associated with them carry tidal waters many miles inland in various places. Such is the case for Charleston and Savannah, where the tidal range is typically over six feet and can run as high as ten feet (particularly in the spring). Tides flow in and out every six hours, so tidal waters move rapidly in the rivers around the two cities, rising and falling between one and two feet per hour.

Both cities have major ports, with Savannah ranking among the top fifty container ports in the world. Charleston's port facilities on the Cooper River and its tributaries extend inland fifteen miles; port facilities on the Savannah River extend inland twenty-four miles. Ships ride the tides in and out at high water, maximizing channel depth while moving with the tidal flow. Historically, tides were especially important to shipping since vessels otherwise had to rely solely on wind for propulsion; the greater depth at high tide reduced the chances of running aground or hitting obstacles such as sunken vessels.

There are two kinds of rivers in the Lowcountry. Most coastal rivers drain watersheds, joining other streams as they progress toward the sea. Principal rivers of that type in the Lowcountry are the Savannah, the Great Pee Dee, the Santee, the Ashepoo, the Combahee, and the Edisto. The shorter Ashley and Cooper Rivers that merge at Charleston are vital to the city's maritime industry. The other type of river more common to this region than elsewhere is the tidal river. Rather than having a drainage basin, these rivers flow in and out of inlets and between large coastal islands. The Stono River near Charleston, the Moon River in Savannah, named in honor of the Johnny Mercer song, and the Broad River in Beaufort County between the two cities are a few examples of the many that exist in the Lowcountry.

Vast areas of marsh grass punctuated by countless islands constitute the serene, defining look of the Lowcountry and coastal Georgia. Marsh grasses—known as cordgrass or spartina—grow over six feet out of a bed of "pluff mud," as it is called locally. The coastal marsh habitat surrounding Charleston and Savannah is a highly productive marine nursery for many species of fish and shellfish, notably shrimp, that live within the spartina ecosystem—one of the most productive fisheries on earth. Coastal marshes are also important because they buffer land areas from storm surges, thereby reducing coastline erosion and property damage.

The serenity of the salt marshes coupled with the sultriness of the long summers imparts a unique feel to Charleston and Savannah. The climate of the two neighboring cities, of course, is nearly identical. Both are famously hot and humid in the summer, weather that persists from May through September with high temperatures averaging well over eighty degrees. Savannah has slightly warmer average temperatures year-round, only by about one degree.

The first naturalists to comprehensively study the Lowcountry were the botanists William Bartram (1739–1823) and Andre Michaux (1746–1802). Bartram, a Quaker from Pennsylvania, traveled the Southeast with his father, the famous botanist John Bartram, in the 1760s and then on his own from 1773 to 1777. The acclaimed account of his explorations, known as *Bartram's Travels*, was published in 1792. Michaux also traveled the region and published influential books on American flora. He settled for about eleven years near Charleston and during that period befriended Bartram. Later he explored the Savannah River, following an earlier trek upriver by Bartram. Michaux wrote the authoritative descriptions for 188 species of flora native to the Carolinas. He also exported thousands of species to Europe, while importing others to the Lowcountry, including the camellia, crepe myrtle, mimosa, parasol tree, sweet olive, and ginkgo. Michaux's work is celebrated today with a mural at Charleston International Airport, which covers the site of his botanical garden. The knowledge of botany and the ethic of gardening common in the Lowcountry and essential to its character can be traced to the work of Bartram and Michaux.[5]

Charleston averages fifty-one inches of rainfall a year, while Savannah averages forty-nine inches. There is no distinct wet or dry season: monthly amounts for both cities vary from a low of between two and three inches in November and a high of just over six and a half inches in August. Rain associated with hurricanes can bring much greater rainfall totals, with ten to twenty inches not being uncommon in a single storm event. Heavy rainfall coupled with storm surge and exceptionally high tides associated with hurricanes periodically cause catastrophic flooding.

The first severe hurricane reported by Carolina colonists occurred in 1686, sixteen years after Charleston was founded. All hurricanes on record known to have damaged the city have struck in late summer and early fall. Nearly all of them were followed with fire and outbreaks of disease. Some hurricanes were utterly devastating. Hurricane Hugo is an example in recent memory, but there were earlier storms that were even worse. The two hurricanes of September 1752 wrought such devastation that it took Charleston four years to fully recover.

Charleston is slightly more hurricane-prone than Savannah, as evident in the records, yet it is relatively sheltered geographically compared with the Outer Banks to the north and Florida to the south. The North American coast between Maine and Florida is concave (nearly boomerang-shaped), with the innermost part located along the Georgia Bight. Hurricanes are often deflected from the South Carolina and Georgia coasts by continental high pressure, causing them to veer out to sea or make landfall farther north.

Fourteen hurricanes have made landfall near Charleston over the past three hundred years, compared to nine that have made landfall near Savannah. Approximately ninety hurricanes have affected the Lowcountry during that period, most offshore, producing at least minor damage. Charleston is northeast of Savannah, a little closer to the more common hurricane tracks that so often strike the Outer Banks of North Carolina. Savannah is tucked farther into the Bight of Georgia (also known as the Atlantic Embayment) that extends from Outer Banks to Cape Canaveral.

While Savannah's subtropical climate is virtually identical to that of Charleston, its exposure to hurricane damage is lessened by virtue of its location on a high bluff sixteen miles up the Savannah River. As a rule, most hurricane damage is caused by flooding rather than winds, so being fifty feet above sea level has accrued to its benefit.

While hurricane season officially extends from June through November, most hurricanes occur in August, September, and October. The Saffir-

Hurricane Landfalls Near Charleston

1686	September
1700	September
1713	September
1728	August (a direct hit)
1752	September (two)
1797	October
1800	October
1813	September
1874	September
1878	September
1885	August
1940	August
1959	September (Gracie)
1989	September (Hugo)
2016	September (Matthew)

Sources: Fraser, *Lowcountry Hurricanes*; National Hurricane Center

Hurricane Landfalls Near Savannah

1804	September
1871	August
1881	August
1885	August
1893	September (two)
1896	August
1898	September
1911	August
1940	August
1947	October
1979	September (David)

Sources: Fraser, *Lowcountry Hurricanes*; National Hurricane Center

Simpson hurricane wind scale classifies hurricanes into five categories. Category 4 and 5 storms will generally produce catastrophic damage. Hurricane Hugo was a category 4 storm that struck just north of Charleston in September 1989. It was one of the most destructive storms to strike the United States mainland in more than a century of record-keeping.

A newer threat to Charleston and Savannah is that of rising sea level associated with climate change. Charleston, with its lower elevation of barely ten feet above sea level, is particularly vulnerable. Sea level there has risen about eight inches since 1900, and the rate is increasing. Scientists predict the oceans could rise by as much as 4.3 feet by the end of this century. Such an increase would have a dramatic impact on the city. In 2021, Charleston began addressing the threat by allowing historic homes to be elevated, a bold move for a city committed to historic preservation.[6]

Although Savannah is less directly vulnerable to the impacts of sea level rise by being built on a ridge, its relatively low-lying suburbs and neighboring municipalities face the same threat as Charleston. Planners in both cities now realize that the current rate of climate change and sea level rise vastly exceeds historical rates. This realization will necessitate moving from their current "threat assessment" posture to actual capital improvements planning and budgeting for flood prevention systems that may include dikes, pump stations, and potentially even mass relocations.[7]

Ancient sea level rise and fall—a more gradual process than that occurring now—is responsible for creating some of the Lowcountry's notable topographic features that add to its distinctive character. Coastal ridges of the Lowcountry are ancient shorelines created during epochs when sea levels were higher. Many of the towns of the Lowcountry, and the roads that connect them, were prudently built on ridges to avoid flooding.

Indigenous Habitation and European Exploration

Hunter-gatherer artifacts dating back twenty thousand years have been found along the Savannah River, and evidence of permanent settlement dates back to 2000 BC. The earliest culture known to have settled permanently in or near the Lowcountry are the Mississippian people who arrived about one thousand years ago. One of the earliest cities in the extended region is the Ocmulgee site located in present-day central Georgia, where large earthen structures characteristic of the Mississippian people are preserved today in Ocmulgee Mounds National Historic Park. The Ocmulgee River, a tributary of the Altamaha River, became a conduit for inland Mississippian people to reach the coast near the Lowcountry. As settlement moved north, the Savannah River became an ever-greater corridor for Indigenous trade and development.

William Bartram was the first Anglo-American to thoroughly inventory Indigenous cities throughout much of the region. *Bartram's Travels* identified ancient cities of the region and described Bartram's visits to the ruins of some. The region was extensively populated and to a great extent culturally unified until it was dramatically depopulated of Indigenous people by disease, war, genocide, encroachment, displacement, and forced resettlement.

The Creek Nation, which constituted the largest of the Indigenous nations with boundaries reaching into the Lowcountry, may have formed from the earlier Mississippian mound builder cultures of the region. More information on Indigenous nations present when the Lowcountry was settled by Europeans can be found in chapter 10.

The first Europeans to reach the Lowcountry arrived in the 1500s. Ponce de Leon, Hernando de Soto, Tristan de Luna, Juan Pardo, and Pedro de Salazar all explored the region north of Florida, with Salazar in 1515 probably being the first to arrive in the Lowcountry and interact with Native Americans. The first European settlement in North America was likely San Miguel de Gualdape, established in 1526 and located sixty miles from present-day Savannah. It was also the first year enslaved Africans were introduced in territory that would become the United States. Later that year a more permanent settlement was founded in Port Royal Sound, midway between Charleston and Savannah. Its name, Santa Elena, has been in continuous use since then, though now rendered in English as St. Helena. The settlement is older than St. Augustine, Florida, which was established in 1565, the latter being credited, however, as being the oldest continuously inhabited European city in what is now the United States.[8]

The French Huguenot explorer Jean Ribault arrived at the abandoned town of Santa Elena in 1562 and began constructing the new town of Charlesfort on the same site. He named the large natural harbor Port Royal before sailing back to France for reinforcements. Charlesfort was abandoned the next year by its twenty-two residents before Ribault could return. Near starvation, they built a makeshift vessel and sailed for France. One of the survivors of that desperate voyage, Martin Atinas, later returned to again sail the disputed coast of what was to become Carolina and Georgia, this time with English privateer John Hawkins, the first of the English slave traders.

The Spanish admiral based in St. Augustine, Pedro Menendez, reestablished his nation's presence at Santa Elena, ordering the construction of the town of La Ciudad de San Salvador in 1566 before he temporarily returned to Spain. Captain Juan Pardo was sent to build Fort San Felipe to protect the town. Pardo then began extensive exploration of the interior, reaching the Appalachian Mountains. In 1571 Santa Elena became the capital of La Florida, which the Spanish believed to be a large island encompassing most of the present-day southeastern United States. Resistance by Indigenous people forced the Spanish to evacuate the city in 1576.[9]

Even though the Spanish relocated the capital of La Florida back to St. Augustine following another temporary abandonment of Santa Elena, Spain's interest in the region quickly transformed into a territorial claim that was largely ignored by the English when they settled the Lowcountry. Charles II, king of England when the Province of Carolina was founded in 1670, leaned toward Catholicism, and his Catholic brother James II, who succeeded Charles in 1685, were unlikely to go to war with France or Spain over such a fledgling and remote colony.

James II was overthrown in 1688 in the Glorious Revolution, which brought the Protestant joint monarchs William and Mary to power. This set the stage for rising tensions in the southeastern region of North America. Carolina was becoming a profitable colony and one that would compete for territory with the Spanish in Florida and the French in Mississippi. The geopolitical competition and conflict that ensued was not settled until James Oglethorpe, the founder of Georgia, repelled the Spanish at the Battle of Bloody Marsh in 1742.

The Sargasso Sea was a defining element in the geopolitical power struggle among England, Spain, and France. Whereas the Portuguese, who began the transatlantic slave trade in the fifteenth century, were primarily sailing the mid-Atlantic equatorial region as they settled Brazil, their later rivals were plying the North Atlantic as they colonized North and Central America, with the Spanish routing their colonization of South America through that region.

The western edge of the Sargasso Sea, defined by the Gulf Stream, became a particularly acute geographic focus of international rivalry. England, Spain, France, and the Netherlands depended on the Gulf Stream for their return route to Europe. With Charleston and later Savannah strategically situated opposite this critically important ocean corridor, England was poised to gain dominance in the southeastern region and the Caribbean.

Formative Cities in the Southern Cultural Region

[margin: entrepôts]

Charleston and Savannah were, in sequence, American frontier settlements, colonial capitals and entrepôts, militarily strategic cities in a grand geopolitical power struggle, powerful cities shaping nationhood, and ultimately small cities in an enlarged South (although at times, in the case of Charleston, exerting outsized influence).

When Charleston was founded in 1670 there was still no South in a political or cultural sense. No people thought of themselves as southerners. There were only the Tidewater colonies of Virginia and Maryland, and then Carolina. Neither of the two areas initially had much in common, and as noted in the introduction it would not be until 1788 at the Constitutional Convention that the newly created slave states would begin seeing themselves as *the South*.

[margin: 1788 Constitutional Convention]

Over the course of the eighteenth century a cultural economy that would become the South emerged as large-scale, slave-based plantations became the backbone of a unifying cultural and political identity from Maryland to Georgia. It was during this century that Charleston became the largest city south of the Potomac River. Towns in Virginia as well as Annapolis, Maryland, and New Bern, North Carolina, among other settlements, were founded before Charleston, but they remained very small towns rather than becoming cities through the colonial and Revolutionary periods.

By 1680, Charleston had reestablished itself in its permanent location at the tip of the peninsula on the east side of the Ashley River, a site known as Oyster Point. An elaborate master plan for the settlement of Carolina (described in the next chapter) ensured that Charleston would become a major city by prohibiting disorderly, decentralized growth and by promoting centralized development.

Although Virginia had been settled more than sixty years earlier than Charleston, and more than a century before Savannah, the colony lacked a master plan to encourage the formation of towns, a deficiency that allowed its population to scatter. At the time of the first census of the United States in 1790, Charleston (which by then had adopted the modern spelling of its name) was the new nation's fourth-largest city, whereas Virginia, the largest of the colonies, had no town with a population of more than four thousand.[10]

Population comparisons during the colonial era are tricky because censuses were not conducted simultaneously throughout the colonies. It is clear, however, that Charleston was the *only* substantial city south of the Potomac right up to the first census of the United States in 1790. Moreover, it had become a dynamic central place that met the criteria to be called a city: It was Caro-

Principal Cities of
the United States
FIRST CENSUS IN 1790

Philadelphia	42,444
New York	33,131
Boston	18,038
Charleston	16,359

Sources: U.S. Census,
historical reports

lina's officially designated capital. It had a population over twenty-five hundred. It was compact and vibrant. And it was an entrepôt with a harbor that was thriving with import and export activity.[11]

Savannah's rise to importance as a competitor with Charleston did not occur until the later colonial era. The Virginia towns of Richmond (also founded in 1733), Norfolk, Petersburg, and Alexandria were approximately the same size as Savannah in the late colonial and post-Revolutionary periods (1740 to 1790), but they lacked the urban form, political character, and import and export entrepôt functions that were present in Savannah. Savannah's relationship with Charleston was strong during this period, thereby leveraging a prominent role in transatlantic trade and magnifying its economic influence.

To the west, New Orleans, another planned city (although far less comprehensively so), was founded in 1718 and soon afterward became the capital of New France. Its population may have exceeded that of Savannah at times during the colonial period, and it exceeded that of Savannah in 1788 when a census enumerated 5,321 residents. But New Orleans did not become part of the United States until it was acquired in the Louisiana Purchase of 1803. Long before that, Savannah was an integral part of the emerging cultural region that would become known as the South. Along with Charleston, Savannah was laying the foundation for a cultural economy that defined the South until Emancipation forced structural changes on southern slave society. New Orleans, by contrast, was an outpost of foreign powers (France and Spain) during that formative period.[12]

Contrasts and Similarities

Charleston and Savannah are now approaching the three-century mark in their entwined relationship as neighbors on the southeastern Atlantic coast. Their often-strange relationship began cooperatively in 1733 as Charleston aided the new town of Savannah in laying out its street grid and building its first houses. In exchange, Charleston acquired a strategic partner to protect its southern flank from multiple threats posed by the Spanish in Florida, the French in Louisiana, the Native American allies of those two adversaries, and a host of Indigenous nations and subgroups that might challenge Britain's *strategic defense partnership* presence in the region.

The strategic defense partnership held, but the relationship deteriorated in every other aspect. Georgia's planners envisioned a slave-free, socially level society of yeoman and gentry family farmers living cooperatively with their Indigenous neighbors. Carolina's planners envisioned a well-ordered, neo-feudal ("gothic," as they likely called it, since "feudal" was not yet in use) society with an enslaved labor class, royalty, and various social strata in between. And while Carolina's founders also envisioned good relations with Native Americans, they had no authority in the colony capable of enforcing the policy. In Georgia, by contrast, Oglethorpe was present to vigorously pursue good relations with Indigenous people during his tenure in the colony. Differences over slavery and Native American relations escalated, fracturing the relationship between the two colonies for two decades. When Georgia became a royal colony in 1752, conflict and competition between the two colonies temporarily abated.[13]

As a royal colony, Georgia came within Carolina's orbit, and Savannah increasingly came to resemble Charleston, with a slaveholding aristocracy holding the reins of power. Yet the two cities had different genetic coding inherited from their creators, and the more egalitarian plan for Savannah kept it from becoming at heart a city of oligarchs. As the city grew after the American Revolution, it once again became independent of Charleston's influence. The Savannah River became vitally important to the city's economy, especially after the introduction of steamboats in the early nineteenth century, and Savannah rose to again become a rival of Charleston.

Charlestonians realized during the 1820s that its smaller neighbor had grown up and become a competitor. Lacking river access deep into Carolina's *Railroads* interior, it was forced to look to a major innovation, railroads, as a way of competing with Savannah. In 1829 it began operating the first major railroad in the United States. Not to be outdone, Savannah vigorously entered the Railroad Age soon after Charleston and arguably became the most industrial city in the South by mid-century. Leaders in both cities eventually grasped that a growing economy meant a larger pie for everyone and agreed to link their ports by railroad.

The Civil War was another watershed in the evolving relationship between the two cities, putting an end to their rising economic prospects and a brief era of cooperation. Following Reconstruction, both reinstituted the traditional social hierarchy predicated on White superiority, and they reinforced each other in restoring one-party control of government. At the turn of the twentieth century, Jim Crow laws governed both cities, and neither possessed an economic model that prepared it for the inevitable reckoning that was to come during the era of the civil rights movement.

In the 1960s, as Whites in South Carolina and Georgia began leaving the Democratic Party over its newly aggressive support for civil rights, they found welcome arms in the Republican Party, which abandoned Lincolnesque original principles favoring civil rights for a new initiative, eventually called the Southern Strategy, aimed at winning over White southern voters. But Charleston and Savannah increasingly bucked the trend and began embracing civil rights for all, equality, and a heritage of diversity. Led by forward-thinking mayors, Charleston was the first of the two cities to become politically progressive and better-suited for a modern, service-sector economy, particularly tourism. Savannah vacillated between parties and did not fully commit to civil rights for all until the 1990s, when it elected its first African American mayor. Forms of the racist past persist, less overt than before, but major advancements came out of the civil rights movement.

While civil rights reforms have enabled Charleston and Savannah to build thriving economies based on historical and cultural tourism, the heritage of transatlantic trade remains a potent force. Both remain major seaports on global trade routes, often in direct competition with one another for container traffic. The Port of Savannah passed the Port of Charleston in 2003 to become the fourth busiest container port in the nation.[14] But Charleston has grown its relationship with the industrial Upcountry region around Greenville and Spartanburg, and it remains a strong competitor in global commerce. The diversified economies of both cities—with strong transportation, tourism, education, and health services industries—easily weathered the Great Recession of 2007–9, exemplifying the greater resilience of the reinvented southern city. As this is written, both cities are facing the COVID-19 pandemic, which will hurt their economies but not permanently alter them. The racial justice reckoning of 2020 will likely have longer-term consequences.

The next two chapters of this book are short "biographies" of Charleston and Savannah. Since many histories of the two cities have been written that cover the Revolutionary War and the Civil War in great detail, those subjects are covered only broadly. For the same reason, many of the political machinations related to sectionalism are covered only to the extent necessary to complete the story of the two cities. The following chapters place

2020 census

Charleston and Savannah Current Demographic Profiles

	Charleston	Savannah
City population	150,227	147,780
County population	408,235	295,291
Metro population	799,636	404,791
White	74%	39%
Black	22%	55%
Median age	34.4	32.3
Median income	61,400	39,400
Voting age population	105,848	109,545
Employed labor force	70,777	64,369
Service-sector labor force	13,486	16,432
Non-vehicular commuters	14.7%	10%
Public transit commuters	1.2%	4.4%

Sources: U.S. Census (city, county, and metro populations are from the 2020 census); other data from the American Community Survey, 2017. Non-vehicular commuter number is the percentage of workers who walk or bicycle to work or work at home.

more emphasis on the evolution of a unique political culture and the cultural economy it supported, formative aspects of the Lowcountry that gave it the exceptional character it possesses today.

Before proceeding with the entwined story of Charleston and Savannah, statistically minded readers may wish to peruse the table titled "Charleston and Savannah Current Demographic Profiles," which illuminates some of their present similarities and differences. Their populations are nearly the same, although Charleston's metropolitan area is notably larger. Savannah is a Black-majority city, while Charleston has a relatively small African American population. Savannah is younger and less affluent on average, with a much larger percentage of its population engaged in generally lower-paying service-sector jobs. Both cities have large numbers of people who walk or bicycle to work compared to the national average of 3.4 percent, an indicator of the livability of their downtowns and adjoining neighborhoods. The economic and demographic characteristics of the two cities are introduced in chapter 12, with additional detail provided in the online supplement: https://ugapress .manifoldapp.org/projects/charleston-and-savannah/.

A 1938 image of a vestigial Lowcountry rice field. Traces of rice cultivation remain visible across the Lowcountry landscape at present. The photo was taken by Frances Johnston (1864–1952), a photo-journalist known for her images of southern architecture.
(Prints and Photographs Division, Library of Congress)

PART II

Historical Legacies

Charleston and Savannah share complex legacies rooted in the transatlantic slave trade: an enslaved majority Lowcountry population; a wealthy oligarchy comprising merchants and plantation aristocrats; a rich cultural blend of African, European, and Indigenous American traditions; a long succession of struggles between those holding power and the oppressed seeking social equity; and a sense of being under siege, initially from being situated on an exposed and dangerous frontier and later from the enemies made within and without over slavery.

While the two cities have much in common, they also have many differences. Charleston began as the capital of a gothic or feudal society that permitted slavery, whereas Savannah began as an egalitarian society. Charleston abandoned its city plan, but Savannah maintained and revered its original plan. Charleston is an aged and weathered city, while Savannah has a more ordered appearance. Today Charleston is a White-majority city, and Savannah is a Black-majority city.

This section examines how history shaped each city, producing similarities and differences while making each a jewel among the nation's colonial legacy cities.

Savannah—egalitarian society that permitted slavery

CHAPTER THREE

A Brief Biography of Charleston

The story of Charleston, like that of many cities, can be described as an arc extending from its initial struggle to find an economic footing, to a period of rapid growth, followed by maturity and slower growth, eventual decline, and then reinvention and renewal. As with all frontier towns by their very nature, Charleston's initial trajectory was uncertain. But the chances of its story arc soaring toward prosperity were greater than most. The large land grants offered by the Lords Proprietors created motivated self-interest. There was the added benefit of potentially becoming a member of the nobility if one were willing to endure initial hardship. On top of that, the Grand Model prepared for the colony ensured that Charleston would be at the center of a hive of activity in a compact and geographically well-organized region. Finally, above all else, the city was geographically well positioned to become a player in transatlantic trade. *transatlantic trade*

The six periods comprising Charleston's story arc are examined in the sketches that follow. Each sketch is a short biographical story rather than a conventional history and as such features the distinctive plot elements that formed the city's *character* rather than a full accounting of historically noteworthy people and events. Taken as a whole these sketches provide a story arc that captures threads, or through lines, of identity that link past to present while revealing an often entwined relationship with neighboring Savannah.

Periods in Charleston's Story Arc	
1670–1729	Early colonial period
1730–1788	Later colonial and Revolutionary period
1789–1861	Post-Revolutionary and antebellum period
1861–1877	Civil War and Reconstruction
1878–1962	Jim Crow era
1963–present	Modern era

Early Colonial Period

The first period of the Charleston story arc occurred between the founding of Carolina and its establishment as a royal colony. It was during this period, which includes the Proprietary period (1670–1721), that Charleston established its economic foundation and grew from a frontier outpost to a city on the cusp of prosperity.[1]

The expedition that led to the founding of Charleston was organized and financed by eight English noblemen who had been awarded a charter in 1663 by Charles II to settle the Province of Carolina. The king designated these eight men Lords Proprietors of Carolina. The territory encompassed by their charter included present-day North and South Carolina and an unbounded area extending to the west. There was no formal English presence in the Lowcountry at the time the charter was drafted, and there was no substantial English settlement for nearly 350 miles to the north of the coastal peninsula that would become Charleston.

The king's motivation in granting the charter to the Lords Proprietors was twofold. First, it was to reward them for their roles in restoring England's monarchy in 1660. Charles's father, Charles I, had been executed in 1649 during the English Civil War, after which the Commonwealth of England was established as a republic without a monarch. The Lords Proprietors were men who concluded that the republican experiment had failed and were instrumental in restoring the monarchy, an event known as the Restoration.

The second reason for the appointment was to settle the colony through men who had the means and abilities necessary to expand England's footprint in North America at a time when the nation was poised to become a major transatlantic power. Some of the Proprietors already had investments in Barbados, a highly profitable sugar-producing Caribbean colony. Their business acumen and experience in the Americas would be invaluable in serving the interests of the Crown.

The initial leader of the Lords Proprietors was likely Sir John Colleton, a wealthy plantation owner with property in Barbados. Colleton died in 1666, and leadership fell to Anthony Ashley Cooper, the Earl of Shaftesbury from 1672, who is now considered the founder of North and South Carolina. Ashley Cooper was a rather notorious figure in English politics, having switched sides from the monarchy to those who overthrew the king during the English Civil War, then back to the monarchy, only to finally turn on the monarchy once again, for which he was twice imprisoned in the Tower of London before fleeing to exile in Amsterdam in late 1682.[2]

For generations, Ashley Cooper's actions were perceived as self-serving. However, modern historians have reexamined that legacy and found that in changing allegiances he was steadfastly holding to his republican principles.

The Grand Model (Carolina's amalgamated constitution and development plan) that Ashley Cooper prepared for Carolina, with John Locke's assistance, reflected those long-held convictions.[3]

When the Interregnum (the period without a king) ended with the Restoration in 1660, Charles II officially named Carolina for his executed father. The name Carolina is derived from Carolus, the Latin equivalent of Charles. The Lords Proprietors expressed their gratitude for having been awarded the Carolina charter by naming Charleston (Charles Town) for Charles II.

The Grand Model for Carolina specified that the Lords Proprietors, as the colony's hereditary nobility, would each be granted a tract of fifteen thousand acres as well as a large lot in Charleston. Other tracts of the same size would be granted to lesser nobility and groups of small farmers. Rather than allowing landowners to claim their tract of land anywhere in the colony, tracts were allocated in a regular and contiguous manner, to the extent terrain would allow it, and they were situated within the orbit of Charleston or other future planned towns. While this practice sometimes made grants less than optimal from the individual landowner's perspective, it created a *synergy of proximity* that ultimately benefited everyone while creating a stronger capital city than would have emerged from a more scattered pattern of development.

Much of the first period of Lowcountry history has been aptly described as "the grim years." European settlers, indentured servants, and enslaved Africans and Native Americans often labored together in a common struggle for survival. The patriarchy, class distinctions, and racism so characteristic of South Carolina in later periods had not yet rigidified. Over the first two decades, cattle grazing and trade with nearby Indigenous nations were the primary sources of income for the early settlers. Although rice cultivation began on a large scale in the 1690s, it would be another decade before cultivation techniques were sufficiently refined to make it highly profitable.[4]

Charleston grew steadily, considering the harshness of conditions, and reached about one thousand inhabitants by the end of its first decade. By 1680, the settlement was relocated from the west side of the Ashley River to Oyster Point, the tip of the peninsula at the confluence of the Ashley and Cooper Rivers. The new site was an ideal location to build port facilities along both rivers amid a deepwater natural harbor.

Some of the ships then frequenting the new port city were from Africa by way of the Caribbean, bringing enslaved workers, rum, and more settlers. In 1685 or thereabouts, depending on the account, a ship from Africa left a bag of rice that would shape the future of the colony as a major player in the system of Atlantic triangular trade and slavery that forever altered Europe, Africa, and America.

The Carolina Colony encroached on territory considered part of La Florida by the Spanish, and Charleston came close to being sacked and burned in 1686. It escaped that fate when a hurricane drove back the Spanish attackers. The Carolina coast to the 37th parallel had long been claimed by Spain. Spanish fleets had been sailing in the Gulf Stream current for a century and a half before the arrival of English settlers, and it would be three generations before Britain's claim to Carolina was secured.

Many of the early settlers who came to Charleston were from the Caribbean. The new colony was a particularly attractive destination for sugar planters in Barbados. Although the Caribbean island was England's first highly profitable colony, its small size (166 square miles) limited growth potential for prosperous planters. Ashley Cooper had owned an interest in a plantation on the island, as had John Colleton, and those investments informed their vision for Carolina. Colleton's son Peter, who took his father's place as an active Carolina proprietor, retained large holdings in Barbados. With that connection to the new colony of Carolina, word of its potential spread quickly among Barbadian landowners.[5]

The most influential Barbadians were those wealthy planters who brought their enslaved workforce to the new colony. A class of "plantation elite," as some historians call wealthy and influential slaveholders, came to dominate affairs in Carolina, as they had in Barbados. Many others also came from Barbados, including small farmers, merchants, artisans, sailors, and servants. The effect was to make Carolina a unique colony among those on the American mainland, one that was very diverse in its makeup and much more like the islands to the south than the colonies to the north.[6]

Charleston began to resemble Bridgetown, the capital of Barbados, in both form and atmosphere. As a temporary home to sailors and fortune-seeking adventurers, it was a bawdy town. The African influence was also palpable, despite the repressive efforts of slaveowners. The lilt of the Lowcountry Gullah dialect heard then and still today originated, many believe, in the Bajan creole of Barbados. Other nationalities and ethnicities were also part of the Lowcountry's diverse population. Scots were among the earliest settlers, establishing themselves Stuart Town soon after their arrival in June 1684; the population was dispersed by a Spanish surprise attack in August 1686. French Huguenot refugees were also among the early settlers; as merchants and artisans, they tended to stay in Charleston. Sephardic Jews from the Iberian

Peninsula came by way of London, where they had earlier found refuge from the Inquisition. Eventually, with Ashkenazi Jews emigrating from Central Europe, the Jewish community would become among the largest in North America.[7]

Barbados was well established when Carolina was founded. Its sugar exporting economy dated to the 1630s before Jamaica was taken from the Spanish in 1655 and surpassed it as Britain's largest sugar producer. Barbadians thus brought a mature plantation system to Carolina, one that relied entirely on the use of enslaved African labor. The refined methods for controlling such a large labor force fundamentally hostile to the goals of those profiting from it were transferred to Carolina.

In Carolina, rice rather than sugar eventually became the principal export product and primary source of wealth. The story of rice, sorted out in chapter 7, may seem like a singularly bland subject, but it is a key piece in the puzzle of not only Charleston's biography but American history as well. The word "puzzle" is used intentionally because, as scholars now fully admit, the understanding of American history became scrambled after Reconstruction by a confusing mix of historical fact and cultural (particularly "Lost Cause") mythology. The story of rice helps to sort fact from fiction and shines a bright light on the emergence of an early era of southern prosperity and the political culture that emerged from it.[8]

When the Lowcountry began cultivating rice on a large scale in the 1690s, more enslaved workers were needed to implement the Barbadian economic model. Native Americans were initially the primary source of forced labor. Nations of the Southeast had an existing practice of slavery (raiding enemies and enslaving captives) that was readily merged with the system imported by Europeans. According to the historian Alan Gallay, "trade in Indian slaves was the most important factor affecting the [Southeast] in the period 1670 to 1715." Eventually Native American enslavement was complicated by the victims' familiarity with the region and ties to its cultures.[9]

In contrast to inevitable complications that developed with Native American slave trading, there were virtually no constraints on either the supply of or politics regarding enslaved Africans, who were a vast distance from their homelands. By 1710 Africans were not only the larger body of enslaved workers, they were a majority population in the colony.

Carolina's enslaved population tripled to twelve thousand between 1710 and 1720 as rice cultivation expanded. Rice exports from the Lowcountry increased from ten thousand pounds annually in the late 1690s to more than

Year in Which Enslaved Africans Became the Majority Population	
1660	Barbados (approx. 25,000 enslaved)
1708	Carolina (approx. 4,000 enslaved)

twenty thousand pounds in 1730, then skyrocketed to sixty million pounds per year in the 1770s. At the beginning of the Civil War, one hundred thousand enslaved people cultivated about 180,000 acres for sixteen hundred Lowcountry plantations, making Charleston one of the wealthiest cities in the world.[10]

For most of two centuries thereafter, up until the 1920s, African Americans were the majority population in South Carolina. The percentage declined only after six million African Americans left the South during the Great Migration. The political and cultural heritage of the Lowcountry, and by extension the Deep South, cannot be understood without grasping the formative, structuring influence of rice, race, and slavery.

Although slaveholder prosperity was well within sight at the end of the seventeenth century, the vulnerability of Charleston was never clearer than in 1698–99. The prospect of revolt suddenly seemed all too real with the increasing African population, and added to that fear there was a sobering realization that environmental threats were unrelenting. In less than two years, the city was damaged by earthquake, fire, and hurricane and ravaged by yellow fever and other diseases. This vulnerability is a thread in the city's story from its founding to the present, one it shares with Savannah.

Prosperity Arrives

Charleston took center stage in the Carolina economy as agriculture boomed. The Lowcountry's large plantations, and later the plantations of the Midlands that produced short-staple cotton, were in some respects self-sustaining entities, but they needed the port city and its merchants to reach world markets. They also needed the legal and regulatory protection it could offer as the seat of government in matters related to the control of their increasingly valuable "property in slaves," and they needed the city to marshal colonial defenses in a hostile region.

The pressing demands of owning a large plantation, as well as the need to retreat from those plantations during the summer season of disease, meant that slaveholders necessarily spent considerable time in the city. While many wealthy slaveholders increasingly sailed north to escape the oppressive Lowcountry summer, they spent ample time in Charleston conducting essential business and enjoying the city's expanding cultural offerings. The amount of time spent in Charleston required the plantation elite to either rent or own accommodations, which created a demand-supply growth cycle. By the end of the early colonial period, the demand for housing, services, and cultural amenities was such that only a mature city could offer it all, and Charleston had sufficiently matured to meet nearly all demands.[11]

While the Lowcountry was becoming established and prosperous, migrants were beginning to populate the Midlands and Upcountry. However, a plan to create a protective ring of new towns and prevent a dispersal, as had occurred in Virginia, was not working at the end of the Proprietary period. Newly settled areas remained largely ungovernable from Charleston, just as was distant North Carolina, which gained autonomy from South Carolina in 1712. The Lowcountry was thus a world unto itself, and its plantation and merchant elite puffed themselves up to impress their external adversaries (European and Indigenous) while tightening the reins of control within their supposedly paternalistic slave society.

The lack of protection from external threats emanating from Spanish Florida and nearby Native American nations became unacceptable with the Yamasee War of 1715–17, which ravaged much of the colony. A settler rebellion broke out against the Proprietors in 1719 over their unresponsiveness to colonial demands, and the Charleston government petitioned the Crown for independence in that year. The British government responded by appointing a royal governor for South Carolina in 1720. By 1729 the Proprietors were almost entirely bought out, and their diminished role in the colony ended entirely.[12]

As the early colonial period neared an end, a visitor wrote that

Notable Dates in Charleston's Early Colonial Period	
1670	Charles Town founded
1680	Relocation to Oyster Point completed
1708	Enslaved population becomes a majority
1712	North and South Carolina separated
1715	Yamasee War begins
1719	Charles Town renamed Charlestown
1721	Proprietary period ended

increasingly wealthy Charlestonians were "trained up in luxury" and were the "greatest debauchers in nature." Charleston's destiny was to be an edgy place of excessive rhetoric and pretentious lifestyles.[13]

Later Colonial and Revolutionary Period

The second period in the city's story arc was its advance from the capital of a newly minted royal colony to a force in the Revolutionary War era. The city's elite would become wealthier, more cultured, and even more pretentious. They came to expect gentility from not only their peers but their minions as well. A model for southern politeness formed in Charleston, one that spread across the South, and a new political culture and cultural economy formed that would spread westward with it.

In 1729 an initiative was taking shape in London that would influence the city's future. James Oglethorpe concluded a parliamentary investigation of English prison conditions and recruited nearly thirty members of the investigations committee to form a bold new initiative. The investigation had laid bare the horrendous conditions faced not just by English prisoners but also by the larger population to which they belonged, the nation's urban poor people, and Oglethorpe's initiative aimed to establish the new colony of Georgia between South Carolina and Spanish Florida that would become a place of fresh opportunity for England's "worthy poor."

Georgia's humanitarian raison d'être was, by itself, insufficient to convince George II, Parliament, and wealthy backers to support founding a new colony. Georgia was thus also promoted as a much-needed buffer colony protecting South Carolina from the Spanish as well as the French in Mississippi. Settlers would be trained to serve in militia units under a system devised by Oglethorpe, a formally trained military officer.

The Lowcountry elite welcomed the advent of a new colony on its lower border, not realizing at first that the egalitarian principles on which it was conceived were antithetical to those of a slave society. By the time Georgia was founded in 1733, Carolinians were fully convinced that enslaved African labor was essential to the success of their plantation economy. Africans were thought to be better adapted to the climate than European indentured servants, and enslaved workers were less expensive than servants, who had to be fed, clothed, mollified, and eventually compensated. Additionally, enslaved people lacked legal recourse for abuses, whereas servants theoretically enjoyed the legal rights of British citizens.

Carolinians soon found the new colony's egalitarian orientation incompatible with their way of life. They argued with Georgia officials for nearly two decades over slavery, attempting to divert them from their plan for a slave-free colony of yeoman farmers. Such a utopian colony next door would challenge the entire basis of their economy and would prevent the acquisition of new land by the Lowcountry aristocracy and the expansion of their slavocracy.

Initially, it had appeared that South Carolina and Georgia would have the mutually beneficial, symbiotic relationship hoped for in Charleston. The former would aid the latter in building Savannah and laying out farmlands, eventually shipping its products abroad through the established system of transatlantic trade. The latter would shield it from attack and become a partner in prosperity. But the fundamental disparities between the social and economic foundations of the two colonies quickly led to deteriorating relations. Georgia's founders had been inspired by the new ideals of the Enlightenment. Their vision was one of "agrarian equality" through yeoman family farms, not vast plantations worked by an enslaved labor force. Carolina was steeped in an earlier, gothic or feudal age, one that was incompatible with Enlightenment ideals.

In 1730, when Georgia was a mere notion in Oglethorpe's mind, South Carolina provincial governor Robert Johnson conceived a plan to establish nine towns in the Midlands frontier region. The scheme would create a protective ring of White settlements. It would also attract more European settlers and increase the proportion of Whites in the colony at a time when enslaved people outnumbered them by a two-to-one ratio and external threats abounded as well. Additionally, the ring of settlements would encircle and contain fugitive slaves and become part of a comprehensive plan to quell slave rebellions. Johnson's plan for the orderly establishment of new towns was generally consistent with the former policy of the Lords Proprietors. The location and orientation of towns, their street grids and lot patterns, the allocation of parcels for civic uses, and other design elements were planned in advance of settlement. Although many of the towns never grew as planned, their layouts reflect a high value placed on city planning during early American settlement.[14]

The mortal danger to the Carolina aristocracy created by enslaving a labor force vastly larger than itself became apparent with the Stono Rebellion of 1739, in which nearly eighty enslaved people rebelled and attempted to flee to

Spanish Florida. During the conflict, over ninety people were killed, about half enslaved people and half White. The rebellion solidified the resolve of many in Georgia to resist following the Carolina model, but it intensified efforts in Charleston to overturn the Georgia Trustees' plan for a more egalitarian society.

Merchants and land speculators in Charleston worried over their diminished prospects in Georgia, while some colonists in Georgia eyed the wealth of the Lowcountry elite and wanted large plantations and enslaved workers of their own. In addition to their fundamental differences over slavery, the colonies differed in their policies on Native American trade. Oglethorpe insisted on what he viewed as equanimity in trade, which required regulation, and Carolina traders insisted on continuing their unregulated trade that extended into Georgia territory along the Savannah River. Where Oglethorpe sought to prohibit trading rum (a staple of Atlantic triangular trade) at the request of Native American leaders, the Carolinians insisted upon continuing to sell it.

A review of articles and letters in the *South Carolina Gazette* from its inception in 1732 reveals an abrupt change in attitude toward Georgia, and Oglethorpe in particular, starting in 1735. On January 29, 1736, the newspaper published notice of a new publication by the colony's legislative body, the South Carolina General Assembly, titled "Report of the Committee Appointed to Examine into the Proceeding of the People of Georgia, with Respect to the Province of South-Carolina, and the Disputes Subsisting between the Two Colonies." Some of the disputes were subsequently arbitrated in London, while others lingered unresolved.[15]

The battle between Georgia and South Carolina over slavery, in particular, was eventually taken up by the British Parliament in the early 1740s and became the first public debate over slavery in the English-speaking world. This set up moral arguments against slavery that arose later in the eighteenth century—a significant event in the evolution of the abolitionist movement. South Carolina ultimately prevailed, of course, and by 1750 slavery had clandestinely crept into Georgia and had become virtually unstoppable. When the Georgia Trustees returned their charter to the Crown in 1752, the lid came off, and Georgia largely adopted the South Carolina socioeconomic model, putting on a fast track to becoming a slave society.

With expanding markets in Georgia, the Midlands, and the Piedmont Upcountry, Charleston's oligarchy grew larger and wealthier. The merchant

Peter Manigault (1731–73) was well on his way to becoming the wealthiest man in North America at mid-century. Others were also politically powerful, including Henry Laurens (1724–92), who succeeded John Hancock as president of the Continental Congress. Laurens operated the largest slave-trading house in North America, selling more than eight thousand enslaved people in the 1750s.

The value of exports from Carolina reached a peak in the 1740s with mean annual values averaging approximately £187,000, more than three times the value in 1720. The colony's total population more than doubled over a two-decade period, from approximately twenty-five thousand in the mid-1720s to approximately fifty-two thousand in the mid-1740s. The Black share of population remained at 65 percent through the period.[16]

The wealth produced by the slave trade and rice plantations solidified a sense of entitlement among the Lowcountry elite in the mid-1700s, but it took subsequent generations to refine the myth of White superiority and natural Black servitude. While Oglethorpe's assault on the morality of slavery between 1734 and 1743 raised awareness in Britain and America of the inequity of slavery, South Carolina ultimately prevailed, and there was little need through the later colonial period to defend the morality of the institution from external attack.

A new period of economic expansion began in 1752 in which Charleston capital moved into Georgia. Lowcountry-model rice plantations were rapidly established in Georgia, eventually encircling Savannah, replacing the small family farms of the Georgia Trustee period.

When the British Stamp Act of 1765 provoked White Charlestonians to fly a flag with the word LIBERTY on it, enslaved people in Charleston echoed their call for liberty. But rather than prompting any sort of reflection on the future of slavery, as occurred in Virginia, the act only reinforced the sense that a slave society had to be rigidly regulated. Usage of the words "liberty" and "freedom" would subsequently take a peculiar course in Carolina and across the South, taking on meanings quite different from anywhere else.[17]

There were few breaks in the ranks of those who accepted slavery as an appropriate economic system for the Lowcountry. But there were notable exceptions. John Rutledge (1739–1800), a Charleston lawyer and the second chief justice of the U.S. Supreme Court, claimed to dislike slavery but convinced the Constitutional Convention to preserve the institution. His wife

Elizabeth, however, emancipated her enslaved workers, and his nieces, Sarah Grimké (1792–1873) and Angelina Grimké (1805–79) would become the first prominent female abolitionists and advocates of women's rights.

The Charleston elite were so wealthy that entire families summered with their northern aristocratic peers in select places such as Newport, Rhode Island. They sent their children to northern schools and to schools in Europe, providing favored institutions with endowments while ignoring education at home. When over two centuries later, in 2003, Rhode Island's Brown University came to terms with its "historical relationship to slavery and the transatlantic slave trade," it cited not only the school's ties to Rhode Island slave-trading families but also the Charleston aristocracy. Likewise, in 2021, the College of Charleston confronted its more obvious past connections to slavery in the video *If These Walls Could Talk*, in which it was admitted, "This was a campus devoted to white supremacy."[18]

Wealthy, elite Charleston families became well established during the early decades of the eighteenth century, and in one way or another they dominated public affairs until the modern era. Even today their presence is felt in the city. Names currently found in parcel records for the exclusive and historic South of Broad neighborhood include many from the colonial and Revolutionary periods, such as Laurens, Rutledge, Middleton, Rhett, Rivers, Hammond, Boykin, Quattlebaum, and Ravenel.[19]

The *South Carolina Gazette*, which began publishing in 1732, documented the rise of wide-ranging cultural pursuits among the wealthy planter and merchant class, including clubs and societies, as well as private instruction in dancing, drawing, music, and languages, including French, Latin, and Greek. The social graces were emphasized throughout all such activities.[20]

Charleston's elite evolved from successful frontier planters and traders to self-styled aristocrats of high culture. As wealthy second- and third-generation families reflected on their origins, they convinced themselves that they were inherently deserving of their social status as descendants of English Cavaliers, the royalist supporters of the monarchy that included the Lords Proprietors. As such, they maintained that they were uniquely prepared by breeding to erect and lead biblical patriarchy, which they believed to be the highest form of civilization ever attained in human history.[21]

The gentility and manners long associated with the South began in and around Charleston with the Lowcountry elite, who increasingly viewed society as a rigidly structured class pyramid. Maintaining order in and among classes in the pyramid required each class to understand and respect the system, particularly toward those who viewed themselves as the aristocratic class. A scripted, "domestic charade" emerged in which each class exhibited the behaviors expected of it, particularly in the eyes of aristocrats.[22]

Any breach of civility in a society with an enslaved majority, as was the case in Carolina for a century and a half, was an indication of potential trouble that might require corrective action. Thus, the emphasis on culture and manners not only reinforced aristocratic sensibilities but also established a subtle line of defense against rebellion. It was (and is) understood that disrespect for authority might occur, but as long as it was confined to interactions within a particular class and directed unnoticed toward another class, order could still be maintained. Those not of African descent participated in the charade to maintain social acceptance by the elite. Jews managed to retain a cultural identity while also adhering to strong normative influences. The first synagogue, Beth Elohim, was formed in 1749.

Although Charleston fashioned itself as cultured, genteel, and circumspect, cities throughout the colonies were often seen by the general populace as breeding grounds of corruption and debauchery. The idea of urban wickedness, dating to Oglethorpe's reformism of the 1720s and uniquely American reactions such as the Regulator Move-

Capital Cities of South Carolina	
Columbia	1786–present
Charleston	1670–1786

ment, led many of the first thirteen states to relocate their capitals to new towns far from established urban centers. South Carolina was one of the first to do so, moving its capital to Columbia in 1786. Charleston, however, remained the largest city and the center of power until the Civil War. In some respects, it retains power disproportionate to its population even today.[23]

Wealthy Charlestonians were not prime candidates for revolution against Britain. They saw themselves as a branch of English aristocracy and valued that tradition. The Stamp Act had been an insult they might have endured. The Townshend Acts that followed in 1767, however, went too far for many loyalists. That series of acts aggressively taxed the colonies to pay the salaries of royal administrators and secure their loyalty. The Charleston elite were forced to join in opposition with the White laboring classes, thus becoming "reluctant revolutionaries."[24]

After the signing of the Declaration of Independence, South Carolina was an independent state, loosely joined with the other twelve independent former British colonies. The new government disestablished the Anglican Church and turned toward the separation of church and state to avert the "infringement of liberty." Charleston remained the capital for another decade and was allotted more seats in legislature than proportional to its population, thus keeping power at the traditional center.[25]

The Coercive Acts of 1774, which Americans called the Intolerable Acts, strained relations between Britain and her American colonies beyond acceptable limits. The first three acts were directed at Massachusetts in response to the Boston Tea Party. The fourth act, the Quartering Act, applied to all colonies. The act authorized senior officers to determine suitable quarters for soldiers, who would be quartered at colonists' expense.

The British strategy to isolate and punish Massachusetts backfired and served to unify previously disparate colonies. The First Continental Congress met in September to organize the colonies' first unified response to the British government, after much debate between northern and southern colonies agreeing to ban exports to Britain, Ireland, and the British West Indies. At this point, South Carolina was committed to taking action, short of war, but Georgia held back and did not attend. Because of the shock that it would cause to the economy of South Carolina in particular, it was given one year in which to find new export markets for rice.

The Second Continental Congress was convened on May 10, 1775, in Philadelphia, again without Georgia. This time the congress was responding to military aggression against the colonies in the Battles of Lexington and Concord. It set the stage for potential independence by adopting the Declaration of the Causes and Necessity of Taking Up Arms. The following year Georgia joined the congress and signed the Declaration of Independence. South Carolina, however, was not unified in its commitment to go to war. It was divided nearly evenly between loyalists and patriots.

The Revolutionary War that followed created a complicated pattern of loyalties in the Lowcountry. Most Blacks, free and enslaved, supplied labor in support of the war effort. Twenty-five thousand Blacks escaped slavery and left with the British and loyalists or took refuge in the Lowcountry wilderness.[26]

In the Siege of Charleston from March to May 1780, General Benjamin Lincoln surrendered the city to the British army, and many residents willingly pledged allegiance to the king. American forces under General Nathanael Green moved to recapture Charleston and succeeded in doing so in December 1782, ending two and a half years under the British authority. In August 1783 Charles Town was incorporated as Charleston, and the city was divided into thirteen wards. The city's old class divisions were restored after the war, continuing the elitist through line in its story arc.

Charleston's economy was in ruins after the war. Despite the affluence of the elite, Charleston was "notoriously crowded and dirty," a problem that created a demand for more-healthful suburbs. As the city recovered economically in the 1780s, speculators laid out the new neighborhoods of Cannonsborough, Mazyckborough, Radcliffborough, Wraggsborough, extending the city to the narrow portion of the peninsula known as the Neck.[27]

The College of Charleston was founded in 1770, a century after the city's founding. The new college signaled greater interest in local higher education among the elite, who had previously sent their children north or abroad for higher learning. The College of Charleston presently claims to be the oldest educational institution south of Virginia and the oldest municipal college in the United States.[28]

South Carolina returned to rice cultivation in its recovery, while also planting a new crop, cotton. The state grew, and the center of its population moved toward the new capital in the Midlands, but Charleston and its Lowcountry elite remained powerful, keeping the state's *political* center of gravity near the coast. Charlestonians would hold on to the reins of power through the Civil War and into modern times, another though line in its story arc.

Notable Dates in Charleston's Second Period	
1739	Stono Rebellion near Charlestown
1749	Beth Elohim Synagogue established
1770	College of Charleston established
1780	British Siege of Charlestown
1783	Charleston incorporated, adopting the modern version of its spelling
1786	State capital moved to Columbia

The Post-Revolutionary and Antebellum Period

The third period of the story arc was the era between the formal establishment of the United States in 1788, with the ratification of the U.S. Constitution, and the election of Abraham Lincoln in 1860, which encompasses the antebellum era dating from 1812 to the Civil War. Five generations of Charlestonians had contributed to building Charleston at the beginning of this period, and by the end another three generations had left their mark.

The Rhett family, from which Margaret Mitchell derived the name Rhett Butler for the novel *Gone with the Wind*, was one that was quintessentially Charlestonian in the antebellum era. Rhett paternal lineage dated to Thomas

Smith, a landgrave (a member of the Carolina royalty established under the Grand Model) minted by the first generation of Lords Proprietors. He also had the distinction of being the owner of Oyster Point, the tip of the peninsula where Charleston became permanently situated in 1680. Male members of the Smith family changed their name to Rhett five generations later in the antebellum period to honor ancestor William Rhett as well as to take for their own what they believed was a more distinguished name. The Rhett name reinforced the sense of aristocratic heritage that through the generations had become increasingly important to Charlestonians.[29]

Robert Barnwell Rhett (1800–1876), one of three Smith brothers who changed their name, was the great-great-grandson of landgrave Thomas Smith. Rhett epitomized the Lowcountry elite, with a law practice in Charleston and two Lowcountry plantations with more than one hundred enslaved people in total. While Rhett shared the same aristocratic belief system as others among the Lowcountry elite, he was also among the more vocal defenders of the South's "peculiar institution" of slavery. As a group, these men were known as Fire-Eaters for the intensity of their arguments. Rhett's pro-slavery rhetoric was at times even too extreme for South Carolina, typically the most extremist of the slaveholding states. When Rhett was not steering political events, he was shaping political discourse.

Rhett had a central role in the third period of Charleston's history. The period was characterized by the ultimate refinement of southern social structure and its enabling philosophy. That peculiar philosophy was overtly anti-Enlightenment, declaring that "abstract justice and equality" were misguided ideals and arguing instead that "passion" had merit that was at least equal to that of reason. Rhett argued that slavery was "sanctioned by Christianity and best for the race over whom it prevails."[30]

Rhett had a talent for appropriating the "language of liberty" from colonial times to bolster his argument for southern rights. His peculiar concept of "liberty" ultimately became ingrained in southern politics, eventually influencing national political discourse. Rhett and his contemporaries saw no contradiction in demanding liberty and freedom for themselves and their aristocratic class while debasing and enslaving others.

Other South Carolina Fire-Eaters included J. D. B. De Bow, publisher of the influential *De Bow's Review*, a pro-slavery journal of agriculture; William Porcher Miles, designer of the Confederate battle flag; John C. Calhoun, vice president of the United States and senator from South Carolina; Laurence M. Keitt, a U.S. congressman and Confederate congressman; Louis Wigfall, later of Texas, where he served as a Confederate senator; William Lowndes Yancey, later of Alabama, where he served as a Confederate senator; and Maxcy Gregg, author of the manifesto, "An Appeal to the State Rights Party of South Carolina" and later a general in the Confederate army. Charlestonian Christopher G. Memminger, who had been a moderate over nullification (states' rights to nullify federal laws) and during the early debates on secession, joined the Fire-Eaters in advocating secession after the election of Abraham Lincoln in 1860. Memminger became the first Confederate States secretary of the treasury.

The antebellum belief system of the South Carolina aristocracy, which Rhett articulated at every opportunity, can be summarized as follows.

Antebellum Beliefs of the Lowcountry Elite
- The highest form of civilization is one led by an elite aristocracy.
- The Carolina aristocracy is composed of natural leaders descended from English Cavalier stock.
- The natural form of social organization is patriarchy.
- Africans are incapable of civilization, and paternalistic enslavement is a benefit to them.
- The patriarchal class system of which slavery is a part is biblically ordained and justified by historical evidence.

The assault on patriarchy and slavery delivered by the Age of Enlightenment had an enormous influence on America's Founders. The beginning of the Enlightenment coincided with, and was reinforced by, publication in 1689 of John Locke's *Two Treatises of Government*, a book that departed radically from *The Fundamental Constitutions of Carolina* that he coauthored twenty years earlier. In the first treatise, Locke demolished the idea of patriarchy as the natural form of social organization. Then, in the second treatise, he constructed the new idea that leadership in social organizations such as governments derives its authority through the mechanism of a contract or compact (he used both terms) between the people and those who govern them.

Tenets of the Enlightenment are enshrined in the Declaration of Independence and the U.S. Constitution. And while the Upper South never lost touch with those principles, the Deep South never accepted them. Virginians Jefferson, Madison, and Monroe recognized the tension between the ideals of the Enlightenment and the South's peculiar institution of slavery, and they found it troubling. South Carolinians never struggled with any such introspection, and the slave society model developed in Barbados and refined in the Lowcountry spread across the cotton-growing South, unrestrained by any qualms over slavery.

Charleston was at the center of the American alternative view to the Enlightenment. That view, articulated by men like Rhett, De Bow, and Keitt, saw democracy as "mobocracy" (a gothic view also held by Ashley Cooper) and cited the French Revolution as proof. Their alternative was a strongly patriarchal system in which aristocratic men, bred and brought up to be leaders, were the glue that held society together as well as the intellectual force that drove civilization forward. The aristocrats of the South, in that view, were connected to the land and to the people that worked the land. The barons of industry in the North, by contrast, were connected only to banks and trade merchants and had little regard for those who labored in their factories.[31]

The long-established Lowcountry elite skillfully advanced the political philosophy of states' rights beginning in the 1820s as a means of blunting the threat to southern slavery posed by northern abolitionism. As the cotton-growing Midlands elite rose in power, they joined in this effort. The first formal meetings on "state rights," as it was first called, were held in Charleston. Rhett (then still Smith) warned of becoming "the vassals and slaves of a consolidated empire" led by northern states. Sectionalism intensified, along with an accompaniment of supporting rhetoric. Early calls suggesting a secession option were made by Rhett, who said "give me disunion rather than a consolidated government. . . . Under such a government I would rather be a slave, ruled despotically [under] the fell spirit of bigotry."[32]

Southern views toward slavery and the prospect of secession began hardening in the 1820s as the Fire-Eaters vigorously defended the South's peculiar institution from both internal and external threats. Earlier in the antebellum period, South Carolinians were less radicalized. The U.S. Constitution, ratified in 1788, had secured a place for southern slavery, the internal threat of slave rebellion was at low ebb, and external challenges from abolitionists were not deemed an existential threat. Southerners were able to convince themselves that their system was stable and sustainable. Even in South Carolina, with its enslaved majority, Whites usually felt comfortably in control. In Charleston, Black and mulatto freemen became part of the middle class while enslaved people moved about the city with relative ease, presumed to be in dedicated service of their masters.

rice → cotton

The Lowcountry economy boomed between 1800 and 1820 as rice production increased and cotton became an established crop. Mechanization arrived with the cotton gin and steam-powered rice milling, increasing productivity and profits. Charleston's role as the political and cultural center of the elite became even more pronounced during this period, especially during summers when the plantations were particularly unhealthful places to reside and the city was bustling.

The illusion shared among White Charlestonians that all was well in their slave society came to an abrupt end in June 1822. Authorities became aware of a planned rebellion potentially involving thousands of enslaved people in Charleston and throughout the Lowcountry. Meticulous planning for the rebellion had been in the works for some time, and weapons had been hidden away for the purpose of killing plantation owners and liberating their enslaved labor force. Following the liberation, the freed people of Carolina would unite with those of Haiti, who had been liberated in 1804.

A court of seven White judges took testimony from Whites and Blacks who had gained knowledge of the plot, as well as from the accused plotters themselves. Upon adjournment in August, a total of 131 accused conspirators had been jailed, and 35 sentenced to death. The convicted leader of the plot was Denmark Vesey, a free Black carpenter who had a family and a successful business in Charleston. Having the means, the education, and the ability to lead, the multilingual Vesey made it his mission to orchestrate the rebellion, or so the evidence suggested. *Denmark Vesey*

Governor Thomas Bennett argued that the conspiracy had been exaggerated, and innocent people may have been arrested and executed, including three enslaved members of his household. Bennett wrote that "humanity wept" over the court's actions, and he asserted that the entrenched evil of slavery had caused Whites to act with horrible injudiciousness.[33]

Few Whites were as introspective as Bennett. Most reacted with horror and suddenly became mistrustful of African Americans whether enslaved or free. Secretary of War John C. Calhoun reacted by sending troops to Charleston to aid "in quelling the disturbances." Charleston officials petitioned the state for additional protection through the establishment of an arsenal, or "citadel," to augment local forces. The citadel was built in 1825, and in 1841 it became the military academy commonly known as The Citadel. The campus of The Citadel, The Military College of South Carolina (its full name) relocated two miles northwest to a site on the Ashley River in 1922, and the original centrally located citadel on Marion Square was subsequently converted to a hotel.[34] *The Citadel*

Another landmark event in South Carolina history is attached to Denmark Vesey's legacy. He was one of the founders of Emanuel African Methodist Episcopal Church ("Mother Emanuel") in Charleston in 1818. Vesey had become a member of the AME Church in Bermuda before arriving in Charleston. When the city's Black residents became dissatisfied with discrimination experienced in White Methodist churches, nearly two thousand of them followed Morris Brown (a free Black Charlestonian who had learned of the AME Church when he visited Philadelphia), Vesey, and others in establishing the new denomination. The church had taken root there after its formal establishment in Philadelphia in 1816.[35]

During the antebellum period preceding the Vesey incident, there had been an easing of the sense of siege from internal and external threats among White South Carolinians. That era was gone forever following exposure of the conspiracy. Whites saw Blacks in a different light, and they worried that increasing *moral* opposition to slavery from abolitionists would ignite new threats. At the same time, *political* opposition to slavery was building in Congress, heightening concern in the slaveholding South over state sovereignty.

The Nullification Crisis of 1828–32 was a confrontation over sovereignty between South Carolina and the federal government during the Jackson administration. South Carolina unilaterally declared the federal tariffs of 1828 and 1832 null and void within the sovereign state. Protective tariffs sheltered northern industries, but they were thought to hurt South Carolina's agricultural economy. While the tariffs were blamed for the economic slowdown, the issue also provided a useful constitutional lever for South Carolina to pull in objecting generally to northern political power exercised through the federal government. The crisis clarified the need for political discourse on the necessity of secession should state sovereignty be violated by federal actions. (See chapter 10 for further discussion of nullification as a constitutional crisis.)

The voices of South Carolina nullifiers would resonate with those of the Fire-Eaters until the state seceded in 1861. They included the Calhoun associates George McDuffie, Robert Y. Hayne, James Henry Hammond, William Campbell Preston, Francis W. Pickens, Andrew P. Butler, Warren Davis, Armistead Burt, and Waddy Thompson, most of whom were from the Midlands. Hammond amplified their voices through the *Southern Times*, while Henry L. Pinckney gave Lowcountry nullifiers a voice through the *Charleston Mercury* (later owned by Robert Barnwell Rhett).[36]

To the nullifiers and the Fire-Eaters alike, slavery was a first principle, the "domestic institution" at the base of the patriarchy, the human system that mirrored God's ordained hierarchy. Tariffs, the pro-slavery elite argued, would reduce the value of "slave property," which would lead to emancipation and the destruction of southern society. Slavery was "interwoven," as Robert Y. Hayne (a South Carolina senator, governor, and mayor of Charleston) put it, into the fabric of the southern cultural economy. While the oligarchs behind nullification had the loudest voices, *unionists* accused the "disunion party" of representing a society of "only masters and slaves" while ignoring the plight of non-slave-owning Whites.[37]

As White southerners faced increasingly distressing criticism of their "domestic institution," they honed new rhetoric in its defense. The idea of benevolent patriarchs providing a meaningful Christian life to people who would otherwise live in savagery was refined to include "scientific" evidence of *polygenesis*, the hypothesis that "races" have separate origins. Proponents of polygenesis such as Josiah C. Nott (1804–73), a South Carolina physician and a founder of the Medical College of Alabama, used the hypothesis to defend the enslavement of Blacks as a form of benevolent rescue from innate savagery. Nott, an "owner" of enslaved people, coauthored two polygenesis-promoting books in the 1850s, *Types of Mankind* and *Indigenous Races of the Earth*, that became influential justifications for slavery. It was not until Charles Darwin published *The Descent of Man* in 1871 that polygenesis lost momentum, and it was not fully discredited until the Human Genome Project, completed in 2003, brought about a paradigm shift undercutting long-prevalent concepts of race.[38]

Charleston's economy experienced several cyclical swings during the antebellum period, exposing vulnerability behind the confident claims of the oligarchs, self-deceptions that ultimately blinded the Fire-Eaters to secession pitfalls. While world markets generally enriched Charleston and all of the South in the first half of the nineteenth century, those expanding markets stimulated supply competition to meet the growing demand that would eventually challenge the dominant position of the South. New sources of cotton were emerging elsewhere in the world, and it became apparent that the South would not dominate the world supply indefinitely. Nevertheless, sectional pride and confidence in cotton production swelled as the antebellum South became the wealthiest agricultural region in the world.

South Carolina's economy slumped in the 1850s, with the rice-producing coast hit the hardest. Many South Carolinians looked to Mississippi and the Southwest as the new land of opportunity. During the decade, seven thousand Whites with seventy thousand enslaved people relocated from South Carolina to the newer Mississippi Valley states. The boom in the Southwest drove up the price of an enslaved person from about $925 in the 1830s and 1840s to $1,658 in the late 1850s, an increase of 79 percent in the South's principal capital investment. Upper South slaveholders took advantage by exporting their "property" to the Lower Mississippi, a transaction known as "selling them down the river."[39]

Intraregional competition also presented a challenge for Charleston. Savannah's economy was growing, fueled in part by industrialization, but it was becoming a competitor in the new cotton market. Charleston confronted the challenge by forming the South Carolina Canal and Railroad Company (SCC&RR), chartered in 1827 and financed by private interests. The SCC&RR would offer service between Charleston and Hamburg (now North Augusta), a 136-mile route that would provide efficient transportation of cotton from the interior to the port of Charleston. The SCC&RR was the nation's first railroad offering passenger and freight service, and it briefly had the additional distinction of being the longest rail line in the world.

The historian Aaron W. Marrs in *Railroads of the Old South* maintains that southern investors and leaders were forward-thinking about railroads and new technology, even as they remained determined to maintain the system of slavery supporting an agrarian economy. Some even believed that their embrace of railroads could bridge the growing divide between North and South by knitting together the two sections with an efficient transportation system. While the divide was never bridged, railroads gave the South a sense of near parity with the North in the Industrial Age.[40]

The SCC&RR began service with four passenger engines and five freight engines. The passenger engines pulled four passenger cars and additional baggage-and-freight cars. By the end of 1834, SCC&RR owned twelve locomotives, four built in New York, four built in England, three built in South Carolina, and one built in Philadelphia. Initially trains traveled at ten to fifteen miles per hour, depending on the number of freight and passenger cars. In 1839 passenger train speeds were increased to a maximum of twenty-five miles per hour, while freight trains were limited to sixteen miles per hour.[41]

The availability of the new train service from the South Carolina interior to the coast replacing limited stagecoach service for passengers and siphoned cotton shipments and other freight services from the steamboat carriers that operated on the Savannah River between Augusta and Savannah. Charleston and Savannah were in an intense period of competition for trade during the antebellum period, and at this point the former had gained a distinct advantage.

The SCC&RR opened a new line to Columbia, the state capital, and nearby Camden in 1842. Two years later the railroad merged with the Louisville, Cincinnati, and Charleston Railroad Company, forming the South Carolina Railroad (SCRR). In 1851 the new company owned thirty-seven locomotives. Its Charleston backers miscalculated, however, in failing to finance a line from the central depot in Camden, South Carolina, to Wilmington, North Carolina. The Wilmington and Manchester Railroad filled that void in 1853, transporting cotton and other products from Manchester, in the heart of South Carolina's agricultural interior, to the port of Wilmington, bypassing Charleston altogether.[42]

In 1834, in its first full year of operation, the SCC&RR carried 13,575 passengers. Passenger volume increased to 29,279 in 1840 and then nearly fourfold to 117,351 in 1850, then operating as the SCRR. Other railroads began tying into the SCRR network to reach Charleston or began serving the city directly. By 1860 five railroads were serving the city.[43]

For a time, Charleston enjoyed the benefits of economic diversification coupled with industrial innovation, at least as applied to agricultural production. Rice cultivation remained profitable, and cotton growing expanded inland from its original home on the Sea Islands. When one crop was down in price, the other became a source of economic stabilization. At the state level, the vulnerability of monoculture was temporarily and partially mitigated. For the most part, however, overreliance on a single economic sector is a through line in the story of both cities.

By the mid-1850s it was clear not only that Charleston would continue to face stiff competition from Savannah but also that cities to the west were rapidly surpassing the mother city in both population and economic vitality. After the war, Atlanta would emerge as a major transportation hub by virtue of its strategic location at the foot of the Appalachians, and Charleston would falter for a century before reinventing itself.

Although Charleston was losing ground economically in the 1850s, both to neighboring Savannah and to the Southwest, it remained red hot politically, becoming the hearth of pro-slavery and secession rhetoric that was leading the South toward the Civil War. While not everyone agreed with Carolina's Fire-Eaters, most of the elite were convinced that the establishment of the anti-slavery Republican Party in 1854 and the election of Lincoln in 1860 required strong countermeasures, and they were fully prepared to use hyperbolic secession rhetoric as a bluff in advancing their political agenda.

Fearing what could be in store, Charleston was prepared to advance secession rhetoric when it hosted the first of three Democratic National Conventions between April 23 and May 3, 1860. Fire-Eaters from Charleston and other slaveholding states made *Dred Scott*—the Supreme Court decision that denied the rights of citizenship to Black people—a litmus test for the presidential nomination. The decision was unpopular in the North, thus splitting the party. Senator Stephen A. Douglas of Illinois, the front-runner for the Democratic nomination, had advocated a doctrine that opposed Supreme Court authority to impose pro-slavery ruling over the will of a people in a territory. This "Freeport Doctrine," which addressed the *Dred Scott* decision, in particular, was seen by the Fire-Eaters as too moderate on slavery. They split the convention, literally, by leaving Institute Hall for an alternative venue, St. Andrews Hall on Broad Street. The convention adjourned without a candidate and was forced ultimately to reconvene in Baltimore to finish the business of nominating a candidate. Some have suggested that the Fire-Eaters intentionally sabotaged the Charleston convention to provoke southern secession.[44]

The violent rhetoric at times became physical. Such violence came to the halls of Congress on May 22, 1856, when South Carolina congressman Preston Brooks brutally caned Massachusetts senator Charles Sumner in retaliation for an antislavery speech in which Sumner verbally attacked Brooks's cousin, Senator Andrew Butler, who was an advocate of the Kansas-Nebraska Act. Brooks returned home to adulation and was reelected, but he had brought on the wrath of many northerners.

Charleston's role in U.S. history as a cauldron of conservative, neo-feudalistic bombast dating to the early Fire-Eaters was derived entirely from a small minority that lorded over the populace. A mere 155 families owned half of the city's wealth in 1860, and a visitor from England observed that there was "no middle class; only rich and poor." That was a distortion, to be sure, as there was a distinct mechanic or tradesman class, but the showiness of the upper class and their minions dominated society. The outsized influence of a few Charleston oligarchs and their Midlands cohorts steered the South into secession and brought on a catastrophic war.

The demographics of Charleston have always been diverse. Charleston had a larger Black population than most other southern cities. In the eighteenth century and during the antebellum period, Charleston also had the largest

Jewish population [handwritten annotation]

Jewish population of any city in the United States. The stratification of society during the colonial and antebellum periods was particularly painful for those at the bottom of the class pyramid, although most Whites were oblivious to it, but it also had the perverse effect of enriching the city's cultural legacy. What one sees now in Charleston in its narrower streets, its architecture, its cuisine, and in its names and faces is the legacy of that rich blend of cultures, a legacy it now finally embraces.[45]

Notable Dates in Charleston's Antebellum Period

1816	Emanuel AME Church founded
1822	Denmark Vesey's alleged slave rebellion
1832	Nullification Crisis begins
1842	Citadel chartered
1861	Battle of Fort Sumter

Civil War and Reconstruction

Civil War & Reconstruction [handwritten annotation]

The fourth period of the city's story arc began with the Civil War and continued through Reconstruction, a short but impactful and consequential sixteen years. Secession rhetoric had been churning in the city for decades, radiating outward to South Carolina's sister states across the Deep South as well as its cousin slaveholding states of the Upper South.

It was fitting, then, that the Civil War began in Charleston. South Carolina issued its declaration of secession from the United States on December 20, 1860, just weeks after Abraham Lincoln was elected president of the United States. It then demanded that the U.S. Army remove its forces from facilities in Charleston Harbor. Soon afterward, the U.S. Army secretly relocated troops stationed on Sullivan's Island to the more defensible Fort Sumter in Charleston Harbor. The newly constituted Confederate army began building up its forces in Charleston to take the fort by force if necessary. The war began on April 12, 1861, when the Confederates bombarded the fort.

The core issue that led to secession was slavery. Lincoln and the Republican Party opposed the expansion of slavery, northern abolitionists were attacking it on moral grounds, and opposition to slavery within Congress threatened the South's future stability. North-South relations were being tested regularly through both intense debate and open hostility. The worst of the latter occurred in "Bleeding Kansas" between pro-slavery "Border Ruffians" such as Benjamin F. Stringfellow, author of *Negro Slavery, No Evil*, and anti-slavery "Free-Staters" such as John Brown.

Lost Cause mythology spun after the war created and honed alternative explanations for the conflict based on higher, constitutional principles. The reasons for the war were easy to obscure for generations, despite the efforts of scholars, until document digitization and the internet made primary source materials easily accessible to anyone researching the war's causes. Formal state declarations, newspaper articles, speeches, and correspondence provide ready proof that slavery was the overarching concern, a concern that emanated most intensely from Charleston.

That said, the sectional divide over slavery progressed side-by-side with South Carolina's objections to protective tariffs, which dated back to 1790 when Senator Pierce Butler warned the tariffs might eventually destroy the union. Forty years later the Nullification Crisis might have proven his concern justified. But if the pure constitutional issue of nullification and states' rights was the core issue, the South was guilty of inconsistency by pressing for passage of the Fugitive Slave Act of 1850, which required the federal government to compel northern states to return southern "property."

The broad cultural issue of slavery and the narrower issue of tariffs should be viewed in the larger context of the evolution of southern political culture. The Carolina Colony faced multiple internal and external threats throughout its history—slave revolt, lower-class disloyalty, tensions and wars with Native Americans, geopolitical competition with Spain and France, Enlightenment ideals, and abolitionists. Charleston became the seedbed for framing and planning opposition to such threats. Eventually the Charleston paradigm became the model for the Deep South economy and political culture as Carolinians forged westward and settled in the Mississippi Valley.

Suspicions of a strong central government and a dominant North had existed since colonial times. Many South Carolinians believed the North had not aided the South in the Revolutionary War, an erroneous belief (Washington's army was in Virginia in 1781) that contributed to incipient sectionalism. The Constitutional Convention of 1787 also highlighted sectional differences over slavery. Rhett believed Charles Pinckney was the "father of the Constitution" rather than Madison, promoting a sense that the Constitution was a creation of the Deep South and presumably subject to interpretation in the lower tier's best interests.[46]

Given Charleston's long history of suspicions, grievances, and secessionist rhetoric, it was to be expected that the Civil War would begin in that city. When Union forces surrendered Fort Sumter to the Confederates, the North's military strategists immediately began planning to retake Charleston, the cradle of secession and the prime symbol of southern intransigence.

Charleston after bombardment during the Civil War siege, as seen from
the Circular Congregational Church, 150 Meeting Street. Daguerreotype
photography was new technology first introduced in 1838.
(Prints and Photographs Division, Library of Congress)

Before Union forces attacked, a devastating fire destroyed 575 homes and
many other structures. Union forces began attacking the weakened city by
sea and land in 1863. It held Charleston under siege longer than any city and
spared no effort in finally taking it. Confederate forces were equally determined, and they withstood the long assault almost to the end of the war.

When General William T. Sherman's army entered South Carolina en
route to Columbia in early 1865, the defending forces finally retreated, surren-
dering Charleston to Union control. The city was left in ruins and described
by some as looking like ancient Athens. A visitor described the wharves as
appearing "as if they had been deserted for half a century. . . . No imagination can conceive of the utter wrecks, the universal ruin, the stupendous
desolation."[47]

The war, of course, was not fought entirely on land. In a notable example of
the naval war, the *H. L. Hunley* became the first combat submarine to sink a

warship during the siege period. A forty-foot-long vessel built in Mobile, the *Hunley* was shipped by train to Charleston in August 1863. In her only action in the war, the submarine attacked and sank the 1,240-ton sloop USS *Housatonic* in February 1864. The *Hunley* went missing after the attack and is now presumed to have been sunk by shock waves from its own torpedo. The lost submarine was located and recovered in 1995 and is preserved and exhibited at the Warren Lasch Conservation Center in North Charleston.

After the war, federal forces occupied Charleston and remained in the city through Reconstruction. The city was economically devastated, but African Americans enjoyed new opportunities as freed people. Their participation in governance increased, institutions such as churches were revitalized, and, with increased purchasing power, they began shaping a new economy.

Reconstruction held great promise for African Americans, but White southerners resisted, still very much attached to a belief in racial superiority. During Reconstruction, 1863 to 1877, six African Americans were elected to Congress from South Carolina, more than in any other southern state. Across the South, sixteen formerly enslaved men were elected to Congress, more than eight hundred were elected to state offices, and more than one hundred were elected to city and county offices.[48]

Violence became common across the South as Whites silenced Black officials and suppressed others who sought upward mobility through farm or business ownership. According to Eric Foner, an authority on Reconstruction, no Black official was free from an ever-present threat of violence. Beatings of African Americans by members of the Ku Klux Klan and the White League were common, justified by their "impudence" to run for office against a White man. Ridiculed by Whites as incompetent and corrupt, most Black officials were in fact capable officeholders who understood the issues facing them and effectively pursued the best interests of their constituents.[49]

The postbellum South and the Jim Crow period that followed Reconstruction are sometimes compared with the forty-five-year apartheid regime of South Africa. Invoking the comparison occurs with sufficient frequency to warrant a brief digression. While South Africa did not have legalized slave labor, apartheid laws like those in the South enforced racial division and unequal justice. In South Africa, however, apartheid ended with a reconciliation and reconstruction process that remade the country. In 1992 local elections were held in which Africans participated as equals with Whites. Whites generally accepted the new, democratic society. The author was there at the time and observed White city planners anxiously leaving a meeting to take African language classes, recognizing that understanding was a two-way process. With the election of Nelson Mandela as president in 1994, a New South Africa (as it was then styled) was created.

The South following the Civil War could not have been more different. Whites clung to the belief in White superiority and the expectation of Black servitude. Fear of Black freedom and accompanying social unrest were pervasive in White society. Reconstruction was a White southerner's nightmare forced on the South by the North. The implicit invitation to become part of a modern liberal democracy was spurned.

The enormous chasm dividing southern Whites and Blacks is evident in the contrast between Robert Barnwell Rhett and Robert Smalls (1839–1915), an African American born into slavery in Beaufort, a few blocks from where Rhett was born. Rhett's prewar rhetoric of southern White superiority and cultural destiny, cited earlier, persisted into Reconstruction. His son Alfred, editor of the *Charleston Mercury*, amplified his father's voice of resistance to change. The message was that Whites had to maintain their position of authority, and Blacks should never be able to assume any meaningful role in government.

Robert Smalls proved otherwise, but Rhett would never allow himself to see it. Smalls had been an enslaved African American who rose in freedom to become a ship's pilot, sea captain, and congressman. During the war, he had seized a crucial moment to free himself and his crew and families on May 13, 1862, commandeering a Confederate ship in Charleston harbor and sailing it to Union-controlled waters. His action came to the attention of Lincoln and reinforced his decision to enlist African Americans in the army and navy. Smalls was elected to Congress in 1874 and ultimately served five terms in office. He was one of the longest-serving African American congressmen in the Reconstruction and Jim Crow eras.

Smalls and other African American leaders faced insurmountable odds after Reconstruction. Whites gerrymandered congressional districts and created legal roadblocks to Black voters. Southern states began rewriting history, literally erasing the record of advances made during Reconstruction. A period of legal maneuvering and terrorism followed, and by the 1890s African American political representation was reduced to a fraction of what it had been in the 1870s and 1880s. Next, southern states began passing laws requiring racial segregation, once again securing a regime of White superiority.

Although the Charleston elite restored White political supremacy after Reconstruction and returned African Americans to the bottom of the class pyramid, they were unable to regain the prosperous prewar agrarian economy. Wetland rice cultivation declined rapidly with the advent of an emancipated labor force, however constrained; Sea Island cotton cultivation was devastated by the boll weevil; and other southern cities had grown larger and were better adapted to the emerging industrial economy.

Growth in the South increasingly shifted westward to the Mississippi Valley during the nineteenth century. By 1860 New Orleans was the largest southern city and had more than four times the population of Charleston. It was the fifth-largest city in the nation. Charleston went from being the nation's sixth-largest city in 1800 to the sixty-eighth in 1900, followed by Savannah in sixty-ninth. The combined populations of Charleston and Savannah in 1900 only barely exceeded the population of Memphis, another rising powerhouse on the Mississippi River.[50]

Another competitor to the west also rose rapidly during the nineteenth century. St. Louis was ideally situated as both a railroad center feeding the American West and a Mississippi port city specialized in transshipping agricultural products from the Midwest's powerful agricultural economy. At the beginning of the twentieth century, St. Louis had become the largest city in the South (albeit a North-South edge city) and the fourth-largest city in the nation. In response to Charleston being eclipsed by newer cities, South Carolina passed legislation in 1866 that encouraged the immigration of Whites to offset the Black majority.

The Port of Charleston was key to the city's recovery as well as its long-term future. After the war, the channel and harbor were littered with sunken ships, and port facilities were bombed-out ruins. The federal government undertook the rehabilitation of the Charleston Navy Yard beginning in 1869, but it would take three decades to complete the work.[51]

Notable Dates in Charleston's Fourth Period

1860	South Carolina secedes from the Union on December 20
1861	War begins in Charleston on April 12
1863	Emancipation Proclamation read on New Year's Day in Port Royal between Charleston and Savannah
1863	Siege of Charleston Harbor begins in July
1865	Union troops occupy the city
1874	Robert Smalls elected to the House of Representatives
1877	Reconstruction ends

The Post-Reconstruction and Jim Crow Era

The fifth period of Charleston's story arc began with the end of Reconstruction in 1877 and ended with the beginning of the "second Reconstruction," the civil rights movement of the 1960s. Reconstruction ended slavery, but it failed to end racism, patriarchy, and enforced legalized inequality. The second Reconstruction succeeded in ending legalized inequality and beginning the slow process of building broader social equity and acceptance of diversity.

Much of this period is commonly called the Jim Crow era, the time when Jim Crow laws were adopted to counter and limit the constitutional rights of African Americans. "Jim Crow" was a term used by White southerners in the nineteenth and early twentieth centuries. It was derived from a White actor's blackface character that became popular in the 1830s.

*Jim
Crow*

After the withdrawal of all federal troops from the South by 1877, political power in South Carolina was split between the "old gentry class" and new "demagogues" who built a power base of "impoverished and demoralized Whites," a base that was resentful and fearful of the future. In an area of agreement over race, the two power blocs created a segregated society that enacted a voter suppression law in 1882 and produced the Constitution of 1895, which terminated political access for Black citizens. The new political architecture would support White privilege until the 1960s. Until then, segregation of nearly all public-use facilities was enforced by law.[52]

Atlanta

Atlanta was among the few cities in the Deep South to prosper after Reconstruction, and it left Charleston, and to a lesser extent Savanah, in its shadow. Originally named Terminus for its position as a rail center, Atlanta was perfectly situated in the rolling terrain south of the Appalachian Mountains to dominate the region in the new age of railroads. Eventually Atlanta would surpass all other southern cities to become the economic capital of the South, an achievement that solidified in the twentieth century with the rise of air travel and interstate trucking. Charleston's trajectory went in the opposite direction after Reconstruction. Nevertheless, it remained an important port city and a feeder for landlocked Atlanta.

Freed people and farmers were especially hard hit by the war. General Sherman's "Forty Acres and a Mule" policy for freed people of coastal Georgia and the Lowcountry was reversed by President Andrew Johnson before it could be significantly implemented. Johnson ordered all land under federal control to be returned to its previous owners. Although they regained their land, farmers and the plantation elite alike lacked a labor force. The system of sharecropping, seldom used earlier, became a common means of farming. Sharecropping enabled poor Blacks and Whites to make a living by farming portions of land owned by large landowners and splitting the harvest.

The breakup of large plantations and the loss of an enslaved labor force also required farmers to find new ways to increase yields on smaller holdings. One way to do so was through the use of fertilizers, and the Lowcountry to its advantage had large deposits of phosphate-rich marl (chalky limestone deposits). Marl was discovered in the Lowcountry in the 1870s, with particularly rich deposits found along the Ashley and Cooper Rivers near Charleston. Demand for fertilizer was increasing not only in the postwar South but also nationally and internationally, creating an enormous market.

The Charleston Mining and Manufacturing Company was formed in 1868 and soon purchased land to begin mining and processing marl to obtain phosphates for fertilizer. Both crude phosphates and processed superphosphates were exported from Charleston in the 1870s through the 1890s. Many other phosphate mining companies followed their lead, investing heavily along the Ashley River and elsewhere in the Lowcountry. By 1884 twenty-five land and river mining companies and eleven fertilizer manufacturing companies had processed 409,000 tons of product, and they employed thousands of workers. In the mid-1880s, Charleston handled about half of global production. The new industry attracted African Americans, who saw the industry as a better-paying alternative to sharecropping, even though the work was difficult and dangerous. The Charleston earthquake of 1886 damaged production facilities and marked the beginning of the decline in the phosphate industry along the Ashley River. Industrialization of the aesthetically pleasing river with its immaculate plantations had shocked and dismayed Charlestonians, so they were not inclined to rescue and perpetuate the industry. Toxic waste sites exist along Charleston-area rivers to the present day.[53]

South Carolina remained predominately agricultural through the remainder of the nineteenth century, and cotton was its principal crop. Ten percent of the nation's cotton crop was shipped through the Port of Charleston, with the Port of Savannah being its principal competitor. Crabbing, shrimping, and other fisheries also constituted a sizable industry. Seafood-loving Charlestonians reportedly consumed hundreds of pounds of shrimp daily in the typical May through December season.[54]

Charleston was destined to remain a port city in the midst of an agricultural and fisheries economy. As the Upcountry began rapidly industrializing in the 1880s with cotton textile manufacturing, relatively little manufacturing came to the Lowcountry. A primary reason was that it lacked the railroad connectivity of Atlanta in the era of railroads.

The federal Naval Appropriation Act of 1916 allocated funds to dredge the channel to a depth of thirty feet at widths of six hundred to one thousand feet. But while the federal government was pumping money into infrastructure, railroads with stronger ties to Savannah were strangling the Port of Charleston. A study completed in 1921 found: "Charleston failed to get railroad connection with the Middle West. Southeastern railroads were consolidated into systems, whose interests lay in developing Norfolk, Savannah, Mobile, and New Orleans." The report contained fifty-five findings and recommendations for improving port performance. The study confirmed the need to bring all port-related functions under a municipal authority.[55]

The transition led to a boom in the 1920s, aided by the roaring national economy. Gross tonnage doubled in 1922 and peaked at over three million tons in 1926. Trade began to decline in 1927 and crashed with the Great Depression in 1929.[56]

In 1941 a committee was created to "investigate the cause of the shrinkage of waterborne commerce through the Port of Charleston and to recommend legislative or executive action to remove such causes." The Shrinkage Report, as it came to be called, led to the conclusion that the city alone could not compete with state-operated ports. Enabling legislation creating the State Ports Authority was enacted in 1942. The chairman of the SPA board in 1943 envisioned "Charleston becoming to South Carolina what Savannah already was to Georgia, Jacksonville to Florida, and Norfolk to Virginia."[57]

It was not until after World War II that the SPA acquired sufficient resources to implement a plan to improve facilities and compete in the global marketplace. Locomotives, lift trucks, cranes, and other necessary equipment were assembled, some of it coming from the federal government. On December 10, 1945, the SPA officially handled its first ship.[58]

Acquiring the North Charleston Terminal from the federal government following the war was the next step. One of the officials who helped make that happen was General Miles Sherman Reba, liaison between the Pentagon and Congress. Upon discovering that General Reba was the grandson of General William Tecumseh Sherman, one SPA official was described as horrified, saying, "My God, we're sunk, Sherman's grandson! He'll never do anything for Charleston." General Reba, however, got on board and facilitated the acquisition of the terminal.[59]

One of the first specialized cargoes courted by the SPA was bananas. Dow

Chemical Company was another early source of cargo. Coffee and tea came next, along with grain exports, and soon the port was booming again. But its true heyday would not arrive until it was transformed by containerization.[60]

Containerization was first put into practice in the North Atlantic in 1955, pioneered by Malcolm McLean and Land-Sea Services, a division of McLean Industries. Standardized containers revolutionized efficiencies in intermodal (truck-train-ship) transfer of cargo. Containers came in twenty-foot equivalent units, or TEU, now an international standard. The transition to containers at the Port of Charleston began in 1966.[61]

Charleston's population increased from 49,984 in 1880 to 54,955 in 1890, a 10 percent increase largely attributable to the phosphate boom. Building construction during boom times can be haphazard and unsafe, which may explain the devastating effects of natural catastrophes that struck the city during the decade.[62]

Charleston contended with back-to-back natural disasters in 1885 and 1886. On August 24, 1885, a hurricane of probable Category 2 strength made landfall near Charleston, causing flooding, severe damage, and a high death toll. The aforementioned earthquake, which occurred on August 26, 1886, was as damaging as any of the worst hurricanes. The intraplate earthquake, the less common type associated with the interior of a tectonic plate, was likely amplified by liquefaction of subsurface sedimentary strata, which can increase surface movement. Modern mapping of subsurface liquefaction has revealed a high-risk factor for earthquake damage throughout much of the Lowcountry.[63]

Sixty to ninety people died in the earthquake (accounts vary), and most of the city's masonry structures were severely damaged. Many structures had to be demolished, and those that survived were reinforced with a system of bolts joining opposing walls. The magnitude of the earthquake is estimated at 6.9–7.3 on the Mercalli seismic intensity scale, a level classified as an extreme event.

The next hurricane to strike the area came on August 27, 1893, arriving at high tide and bringing a sixteen-foot storm surge to Charleston as well as Savannah. The hurricane caused around two thousand deaths in the Lowcountry. A second hurricane, probably at Category 3 force, made landfall just north of Charleston on October 12 in the same year.

A major boost to Charleston came from the routinely maligned federal government during World War I. The war footing brought about an expansion of the Navy Yard and with it a stimulus to the economy. The Charleston Neck became navy headquarters for the Southeast. Over seven thousand officers and enlisted personnel and twenty-five thousand recruits were based there, and civilian employment reached a wartime peak of five thousand.[64]

Charleston's economy seesawed, with advances coming in the form of activity at the naval station or the Port of Charleston, and setbacks often occurring in the regional agricultural economy. In 1919 most of the Sea Island cotton crop was destroyed by the boll weevil, and no other crop would rise in value to replace it. Then there was the lingering burden of Jim Crow, isolating and limiting the African American participation in the economy and weighing down the city's growth potential.

Accessibility and connectivity were also factors that negatively affected both Charleston and Savannah. Most newer, rapidly growing cities during this period were major railroad hubs or river ports. While both cities were early adopters of transportation technology, many other cities enjoyed comparative advantages as transportation hubs. As the new era of the automobile dawned in the 1920s, the two cities fared no better. The first national highway spanning the east coast, U.S. Route 1, was planned in 1925, allowing federal funding for modern road construction. The route followed the fall line to avoid the wetlands of the coastal plain, passing through Columbia, two hundred miles inland from Charleston, and bypassing Savannah at a similar distance. U.S. 17, known as the Coastal Highway, was planned subsequently and routed through Charleston and Savannah, with paving completed in 1930. The route was secondary to U.S. Route 1 for servicing long-haul East Coast traffic, leaving both cities underserved by the new national highway network and only marginal beneficiaries of the new age of interstate automobile traffic.

Charleston was deeply afflicted with poverty, despite the jobs created by the naval installation. It was blighted with some of the worst slums in the nation; 49 percent of its houses had no indoor toilet, compared to the national average of 18 percent. Homicide rates were extremely high between the late 1930s and the 1970s, reaching twice the national average. Yet, with all its problems, the city was wealthier than the rest of South Carolina, with a per capita income nearly three times the state average, due in large part to its port and naval installations.[65]

Jim Crow was a way of life in Charleston throughout this period. African Americans constituted a majority population in the city and in South Carolina until 1930 and remained a large minority over the remainder of the period. The disenfranchisement of such a large segment of the population had a crippling effect on the economy in terms of creative contributions and growing markets. With internal economic stagnation and the rise of other southern cities, Charleston dropped out of the top one hundred largest cities in the nation in 1920, and it fell behind Savannah, which remained in the top one hundred for another forty years.

Jim Crow held a powerful grip on South Carolina until federal court actions and civil rights legislation finally ended it. As late as 1944, the General Assembly passed 147 laws in six days aimed at effecting voter suppression, in part by privatizing primaries. In 1947 the state's last mob lynching occurred, and defendants in a closely watched trial were all acquitted. That same year, the all-White Democratic primary was ruled unconstitutional. Then, in 1954, the *Brown v. Board of Education* decision by the U.S. Supreme Court overturned state-sponsored segregation in effect since the court's infamous *Plessy v. Ferguson* decision in 1896. However, the final blows to the long reign of Jim Crow would not be delivered until the passage of the Civil Rights Act of 1964 and the Voting Rights Act of 1965.[66]

The level of resistance to change in Charleston is exemplified in the reactions to the decisions of Judge Julius Waties Waring (1880–1968), a Charlestonian in the thick of early legal battles over segregation. From 1942 to 1952, Waring was a federal judge in the U.S. district court in Charleston, where he heard several pivotal civil rights cases. His decisions influenced the U.S. Supreme Court in *Brown*. Judge Waring's view of segregation as base inequality and his decisions dismantling the Jim Crow system led to his ostracism from Charleston society. Waring maintained that South Carolinians were "obsessed" with White supremacy, and he was forced to leave his hometown when he retired in 1952.[67]

Charleston establishment views were reflected in the opinions of *News and Courier* editor Tom Waring, who promoted the old view of the South and vowed like Robert Barnwell Rhett a century before to support armed rebellion to resist federal intervention. When Black students held sit-ins across South Carolina calling for an end to segregation, Waring warned of "a world conspiracy" and advised law enforcement officers to use whips and guns or whatever necessary to preserve order. Waring's steadfast segregationist views were eventually challenged in 1963 when five hundred demonstrators gathered in front of the *News and Courier* (predecessor to the *Post and Courier*) to sing freedom songs in protest of the paper's policies. Police arrested sixty-eight people and charged them with rioting. But the protests continued, leading Mayor J. Palmer Gaillard Jr. (1920–2006) to appoint a biracial committee

to examine race relations. The committee called on Tom Waring to end in- *mayor Gaillard*
flammatory rhetoric, but it was to no avail.[68]

During Mayor Gaillard's tenure, Charleston more than tripled in area
through annexation, growing from five to eighteen square miles. Between 1970
and 1976, the number of visitors increased by 60 percent, rising to 3.4 million
tourists in the mid-1970s. Improvements in race relations made the city less
stigmatized, improving its national image. The first Black cadet graduated
from The Citadel in 1970 in a highly visible sign of racial progress (Clemson
and the University of South Carolina desegregated in 1964 and 1965). Yet only
a handful of Whites attended Judge Waring's funeral in 1968, whereas an estimated two hundred African Americans were in attendance.[69]

The city's historic preservation movement, initially steeped in Old South *Susan Pringle Frost*
nostalgia, began during this period. In 1920 real estate broker Susan Pringle
Frost called a meeting of the city's elite to discuss how to halt plans for the
demolition of historic homes. They founded the Charleston Society for the
Preservation of Old Dwellings, later becoming the Preservation Society of
Charleston. Frost was the organization's first president. In 1929 the city adopted a zoning ordinance to protect the historic district. The following year,
history-minded Charlestonians published *The Carolina Low-Country*, a nostalgic look at the Old South that imagined a
virtuous hierarchical society of beneficent
aristocrats and "grateful slaves."[70]

Later generations would build on the
more progressive of the initiatives to remake Charleston into a new kind of city.
In doing so, they would reject the old
premises about class and segregation,
creating a new, more inclusive concept
of historic preservation that would benefit all of Charleston. (For more detail
on historic preservation and tourism, see
chapter 12.)

Notable Dates in Charleston's Fifth Period	
1877	End of Reconstruction
1886	Earthquake
1920	Society for the Preservation of Old Dwellings
1947	Historic Charleston Foundation established
1969	March 20: Charleston Hospital Strike begins

Charleston in the Modern Era   *Modern Era*

The sixth period of Charleston's story arc began with an opportunity for reinvention following the civil rights upheaval of the 1960s. The city faced up
to the failure of Jim Crow and Lost Cause mythology, acknowledged its fac-

tual history, and reconceived itself as a mosaic of cultural influences that was greater when taken in as a whole than when featured in its separate parts. As this new era dawned, Charlestonians pivoted from romantic self-reverence to an outward, *shared* reverence that invited the world to participate in and enjoy its unique qualities. The stage was set for the new, modern period of the city's story during the administration of Mayor Gaillard. It was subsequently secured with the election of Mayor Joe Riley in 1975. At his inauguration, Riley quoted the Declaration of Independence tenet "All men are created equal" and emphasized "unity" and "racial harmony."[71]

While Charleston had begun the process of shedding its Jim Crow past in the 1960s, Riley's election definitively moved the city into a new age. He became a transformational figure, not only for Charleston but also for the entire urban South. He hired an African American, Jewish police chief, Reuben M. Greenberg, brought African Americans to the table when making political decisions, supported African American candidates for public office, and continued to lead the effort to make the birthday of Martin Luther King Jr. a state holiday. At the same time he harnessed historic preservation to the economy through city planning in a manner that respected and enlarged upon the existing, deeply nostalgic sense of place.

When Riley was elected in 1975, Charleston was still steeped in antebellum tradition. According to his biographer, "a person's worth and identity was measured by their ancestors." The city was sharply divided and going nowhere economically, yet it was ready for change. As Riley altered the city's course, he struggled to alter the status quo, even as his approval rating as mayor rose to 85 percent.[72]

Before becoming Charleston's mayor, Riley served three terms in the state legislature. The experience equipped him to negotiate political accommodations between progressives and rural conservatives whose attitudes had changed little since the Civil War. Governor Olin Johnson rebuked the civil rights movement, saying, "God didn't see fit to mix them and I am tired of people agitating social equity of races in our state." Men like Olin and the powerful Speaker of the House Sol Blatt represented the state's entrenched, rural power structure that had no interest in leaving the Jim Crow era.[73]

Riley knew that the old political establishment would not support new ideas of equality. But he knew they would support economic initiatives that would indirectly further equality. The best way to satisfy both old and new thinking was to hitch his city's economic wagon to its growing tourism economy, with more than four million visitors a year when he took office. By successfully building on that economic base, he correctly believed that he could bring the city's old elitist social order into the modern world while creating a more democratic and diverse urban society.

In 1975, the year Riley was elected, the Army Corps of Engineers approved deepening of the Cooper River channel to forty-two feet to accommodate larger vessels, essential to the city's economic future. The SPA's planned Wando Terminal was another essential ingredient in building a more dynamic port. Long delays to the project, however, began to limit the port's growth by 1980. The terminal finally opened in 1982, stimulating new interest from shipping lines. At the time, the terminal was considered one of the most efficient and productive in the United States.[74]

The container revolution accelerated in the 1980s as railroads began upgrading their intermodal facilities. Both major regional railroads, CSX and Norfolk Southern, were serving Charleston at maximum efficiency. The closing of the Charleston Naval Shipyard in 1996 was a blow to the economy, but by then the new service economy was booming, and the Port of Charleston was the fourth-largest container port in the United States. The navy property became new real estate for expansion of those sectors. In 2002, an aggressively expanding Port of Savannah surpassed Charleston in container traffic, but the growth of the Port of Charleston continued, fueled to a great extent by the demands of industry in the South Carolina Upcountry, particularly the automotive industry concentrated in the Greenville area.[75]

One of Mayor Riley's development strategies was to annex large expanses of the city's unincorporated suburbs to expand the tax base for reinvestment in the urban core, as well as to coordinate planning initiatives essential for the city's modernization. The apparent success of large-scale annexation may, however, entail a day of reckoning since city planning lagged behind new development. More permissive development standards in those areas appear to have accelerated congestion, contributed to flooding, and assaulted Lowcountry aesthetics. The cumulative impact may be to drown out the positive image projected by the reinvented urban core. While Charleston continues to be defined positively by its historic core, it may ultimately find itself projecting a negative image of a traffic-clogged city that failed to manage growth.

Following the retirement of Mayor Riley, John J. Tecklenburg was elected mayor, assuming office in January 2017. Mayor Tecklenburg has continued most of his predecessor's progressive policies. The city continues to project an image of reinventing itself through tolerance, inclusion, diversity, and social equity. Gentrification is being addressed head-on; a national forum on reparations for slavery was held in the city in November 2019; and Charleston-area historic sites are increasingly telling the entire story of the Lowcountry's past, even as some visitors tell guides they prefer not to hear about slavery.[76]

In 2020 the need to address issues of social equity boiled over across the nation. On June 24, "amid a chorus of cheers and songs," the most conspicuous symbol of the city's racist past was removed. The twelve-foot bronze statue John C. Calhoun, which stood atop a 115-foot pedestal, had towered over Marion Square since 1896.[77]

The city now faces the challenge of structural changes necessary for a renewal of the goals of the civil rights movement, the "second Reconstruction." Many Charlestonians are hopeful that 2020 will mark the beginning of such a renewal, a *third* Reconstruction.

Notable Dates in Charleston's Modern Period

1975	Joseph P. Riley Jr. elected mayor
1977	Spoleto Festival USA launched
1989	Hurricane Hugo strikes
1996	Naval Shipyard closes
2015	Massacre at Emanuel AME Church
2015	Mayor Riley retires
2020	350th anniversary; removal of the Calhoun Monument

The preceding "biography" of Charleston contains various threads, or through lines, that run through multiple periods and contribute unique features to its composite character. First among those threads is Charleston's founding as a planned city. Although the plan, or Grand Model, was not fully implemented, it left an indelible physical and cultural imprint on the city and the Lowcountry.

A second thread is the emergence of a rigid, aristocratic class structure, a feature that emerged from the interaction between the Grand Model and the ad hoc model for a slave society acquired largely from Barbados. When wealth came from rice, oligarchy was spun up from aristocracy. The result was a potent mix of economic power and cultural authoritarianism wielded by the Lowcountry elite.

A third thread is the development of monolithic defenses in the face of internal and external threats. The Lowcountry elite learned to adopt strategies necessary to defend their way of life. They began by implementing increasingly repressive methods to control an enslaved majority. From there, they progressed to well-honed, vitriolic rhetoric (not unlike that of the abolitionists) directed at their opponents. Next, they developed a polygenesis-based framework for white superiority, and finally they developed a biblical, *patriarchal* rationale to justify their medieval, gothic class structure to a liberalizing world.

White supremacist racism endemic in the city and across the South required a Civil War to end its legal status. The toll taken on enslaved people and the hold of racism on many White Americans remained through Reconstruction and the civil rights era (the second Reconstruction). And explicit white supremacism spilled out from containment, spreading as fast as the coronavirus pandemic of 2020, requiring a reckoning with truth and a corrective third Reconstruction, a reset to original principles.

A fourth thread, entwined with the previous three, is that Charleston had an outsized role in shaping the social mores and political culture of the South. It brought intensity born of necessity in a slave society in spreading its cultural economy west across the Deep South. With its progeny influencing the political culture of other states, Charleston leveraged its power to achieve secession and new forms of racial repression.

A fifth thread is that of the challenging environmental conditions affecting life in the Lowcountry. Charlestonians were perpetually confronted by tropical diseases in the long, hot summer, while other diseases were caused by sanitation deficiencies, fires, and hurricanes. In the face of environmental threats, all tiers of the social pyramid learned to cooperate on a basic level to survive and rebuild following catastrophe. Charleston could be one society when necessary, exhibiting a strange and perverse unity that in the modern era enables it to thrive as a city steeped in class, cultural, and ethnic diversity. In addition to cultural influences, the Lowcountry environment also brought into being an exceptional architectural palette, one of sophistication yet openness and airiness essential to its environmental context.

A sixth thread is the surprising depth of cultural diversity in a city that for three centuries suppressed the notion that it was a blended society. Charleston aristocrats preferred to believe that they were the pinnacle of civilization while the world around them was conforming, as best it could, to their model. They believed it was their paternalistic "domestic institution" that brought civility to ruffians and savages. Yet under the surface there was a simmering stew of cultures, one cooked to its present deliciousness by environmental conditions and by the rich cultural milieu the aristocracy could never destroy—and perhaps secretly never wanted to.

A final thread is the entwined relationship between Charleston and Savannah. The two cities share a creation story and have a common history. While the relationship has been ignored for many decades, it is currently being brought to the forefront by the plight facing both cities over their entwined future. The historic core of each has attained a luxury-elite status that is expelling its residents after a long period of attracting them back downtown and back into historic neighborhoods. A time of reckoning has arrived in which the reinvention begun in the 1960s must either be sustained or left to be smothered by a new elitism.

CHAPTER FOUR

A Brief Biography of Savannah

Savannah's story begins with its founding as the capital of the new British colony of Georgia, the thirteenth of those that would collectively declare independence from the mother country forty-three years later. The new, planned city was, in a sense, the offspring of Charleston, a parent that soon found its young one insufferable. The story arc of the two cities' relationship is complicated. Charleston went from proud mother city to postpartum rejection, and then at various times it became a rival, a partner, a sister city, or a distant relative. Their story is one of a relationship that shifted between cooperation to competition at least four times.

Today, as well at various times past, despite being separated by barely ninety miles, the two cities are worlds apart. Savannah's biography is nevertheless entwined with that of Charleston far more than most residents of either city now realize, and its story arc composed of six distinct periods contains numerous points of tangency with its neighbor.

Periods in Savannah's Story Arc

1733–1743	Early colonial Trustee period
1744–1788	Later colonial and Revolutionary period
1788–1860	Antebellum era
1861–1877	Civil War and Reconstruction
1878–1962	Jim Crow era
1963–present	Modern era

Early Colonial Trustee Period

The first period in the city's story arc is a short but formative span of twenty years. During that period, Savannah was a political vortex within which Enlightenment and gothic thinking collided, causing debate that at times spiraled out into the larger world. The city was the capital of an experimental colony conceived by James Oglethorpe with scientific, philosophical, humanitarian, and political dimensions. Slavery was prohibited early in the experiment, first by practical design and later as a moral imperative. Debate over the colony's central tenets swirled in London and reverberated in the halls of Parliament among supporters and detractors.

The colony provoked debate on other grounds as well. Relations with Indigenous nations were scrutinized on moral grounds on both sides of the Atlantic. The relationship between civil administration and the church was debated when the colony kept those institutions separate at a time when it was uncommon to do so. Large landholdings were prohibited, provoking the ire of the Lowcountry elite and their partners in Britain. The form of representative government appropriate to replace initial, frontier administration was debated among the colonists and contained elements of new political thinking that blossomed in 1776. In essence, Savannah was a hub of Enlightenment discourse, a precursor of the emergence of liberal democracy. The new colony altered regional geopolitics as well, and it leveraged the nation's emergence as the prevailing power in most of North America and much of the Caribbean.

Savannah was founded on February 12, 1733, as the capital city of the Province of Georgia. The city's founder, James Edward Oglethorpe, was a reform-minded member of the British Parliament who had created the Trustees for the Establishment of the Colony of Georgia in America two years earlier as an instrument to achieve various goals. It was formally chartered on April 21, 1732. Oglethorpe had chaired a parliamentary committee on prison reform, and his first goal for the colony was to create a place of fresh opportunity for the "worthy poor" released from debtors' prisons. Within a year, Oglethorpe formulated additional goals, overshadowing the initial goal, after consulting with social reformers, philanthropists, scholars, and politicians.

Three additional goals for Georgia were codified in its charter. It was intended to offer a new home to Europe's persecuted Protestants, a personal concern of King George II, to expand British mercantile opportunities in America, and to create a buffer colony between the prosperous Province of South Carolina and the geopolitically ambitious Spanish colony of La Florida. In addition to those explicit goals, Oglethorpe and many of his closest associates envisioned creating a new kind of society based on the principle of "agrarian equality." It was a vision of an equitable society of yeoman farmers similar to that envisioned by Thomas Jefferson fifty years later.

Charlestonians had long felt threatened by the Spanish in Florida and welcomed the new colony for the protection it would offer and the new markets it would open. As discussed in the preceding chapter, they did not initially see Georgia's egalitarian design as a threat to their slave society. In fact, the tighter network of family farms in Georgia would mean more friendly eyes to prevent both Spanish invasion and enslaved people escaping to Flor-ida. But it was not long before the Lowcountry elite realized that their new neighbor posed a significant challenge to their way of life.

Oglethorpe and forty families, sufficient to complete both a *ward* of forty houses in the predesigned town of Savannah and occupy four square miles of surrounding family farms, set sail from Gravesend near London on the frigate *Anne* in November 1732 and reached Charleston on January 13, 1733. Oglethorpe went ashore without the colonists, met briefly with South Carolina's leaders, and then returned to the ship to sail to a staging area in Port Royal Sound. After depositing the colonists in new barracks at Fort Frederick, about thirty linear miles from the Savannah River, he ventured south with local scouts to select the site for Georgia's first city and capital. Oglethorpe selected a site sixteen miles upriver on a high bluff that offered room to build the town and lay out a grid for farms and outlying villages.

With the benefits Georgia had to offer firmly in mind, Charlestonians gladly provided several forms of support in carving out the new town of Savannah in the southern wilderness on the Savannah River, sending surveyors and carpenters to help build the town and supplying food and cattle to sustain it through its infancy. Oglethorpe wrote to the Trustees with a description three weeks after his arrival,

> I fixed upon a healthy situation about ten miles from the sea. The river there forms a half-moon, along the south side of which the banks are about 40 foot high and upon the top a flat which they call a bluff. The plain ground extends into the country five or six miles and along the riverside about a mile. Ships that draw twelve-foot water can ride within ten yards of the bank. Upon the riverside in the center of this plain, I have laid out the town.[1]

Oglethorpe had received formal military training and studied siting and design principles applied by Roman armies in establishing colonial towns. His knowledge of those principles bequeathed Savannah a more viable town plan than the one created by John Locke for Charleston.

About an hour after setting foot on the ridge where they would build the town of Savannah, colonists were heartened by a welcoming reception from their Indigenous neighbors. A Yamacraw delegation from the only village in the area, located about a quarter-mile away, emerged from the woods and performed ceremonial dancing and singing. The impressive greeting included a brandishing of white feathers signifying peaceful relations, and Chief Tomochichi and his small delegation shook hands with Oglethorpe. The two leaders then spoke through an interpreter for about fifteen minutes, after which the Yamacraw returned to their village.[2]

That evening, several of the colonists, not yet having tents put up in which to sleep, went to a trading post beyond the village to spend the night. The trading post was owned by half-Creek Mary Musgrove (1700–1765), or Coosaponakeesa, and her husband John, both of whom served as interpreters. The Yamacraw made a bonfire and danced around it in continuing celebration of the new friendship. One of the colonists, an older man, became intoxicated, danced wildly, and had to be escorted away before he created a bad impression.[3]

Good relations with Indigenous Americans was a high priority for Oglethorpe. He found three culturally distinct Indigenous nations inhabiting Georgia, the Lower Creek, or Muskogee (including the Yamacraw on the Savannah River), the Upper Creek, also part of the Creek Confederacy, and the Euchee (or Yuchi). The Choctaw, who spoke a Muskogean language, held strategically important land immediately to the west of the Creek people in present-day Alabama and Mississippi. The Cherokee of the southern Appalachian area were also a factor in regional geopolitics, although weakened during the 1730s by an epidemic of smallpox. Indigenous cultural diversity had been significantly reduced by disease and war since the founding of Carolina nearly sixty years earlier.

Oglethorpe's rapport with Native Americans created allies out of potential adversaries. Tomochichi and other Native Americans served with British forces in later campaigns against the Spanish. The Lower Creek were strategic allies against both the Spanish and the French, while the Choctaw on Georgia's de facto western frontier were an important buffer against the French.

Oglethorpe led with moral authority and stoic discipline, traits instilled in him since childhood. He slept in a tent while others moved into houses, he worked late into the night, and he was the first to rise in the morning. Nevertheless, it became apparent in the first year that instilling a pious attitude and strong work ethic in the colonists would be a challenge, even though they had been interviewed for those traits by the Trustees and had entered into a contractual obligation to fulfill a commitment to the settlement project. Oglethorpe wrote to the Trustees on August 24 that he had returned from a trip to Charleston to find that "the people were grown very mutinous and impatient of labour and discipline." He attributed the "petulancy" to drinking rum and said some of them were willing to trade "wholesome food for a little rum punch."[4]

Despite such difficulties, Oglethorpe remained firm in his optimism, writing at the end of the first year, "I cannot but congratulate you upon the great success your designs have met with, being not only approved of by all America but so strongly supported by His Majesty and the Parliament of Great Britain. Providence itself seems visible in all things to prosper [fulfill] your designs calculated for the protection of the persecuted, the relief of the poor and the benefit of mankind."[5]

In the same letter, Oglethorpe reported that three and a half wards had been assigned to colonists, out of six planned to constitute the town. Fifty houses were built, and the remaining lots were either being cleared or houses already under construction on them. The Savannah population stood at 259, including ten families each in the "out-villages" of Hampstead and Highgate. The following month he wrote that the population of Savannah alone had reached 259, and there were 178 more in the villages and other settlements, for a total of 437 in the colony.[6]

In February, the Trustees received the first shipment of exports from Georgia, consisting of rice and deerskins. Two weeks later, Peter Gordon arrived from the colony and presented the Trustees with a drawing of Savannah as it stood at the beginning of the year. His account of progress was powerful testimony to the early successes of the colony and Oglethorpe's effective leadership.

Oglethorpe left Savannah for Charleston on March 12, 1734, to arrange material support for the new colony and discuss administrative matters with Carolina authorities. He concluded his mission in Charleston and sailed for England on April 26, 1734. Early in 1735, following Oglethorpe's advice, the Trustees approved three new regulations that would strengthen existing policies: an act prohibiting slavery; an act prohibiting of importation and consumption of rum; and an act for maintaining peace with "Indian Nations" (to use Oglethorpe's term) in the province.

Oglethorpe remained in England most of the year to secure funding from Parliament and to address security on the colonial frontier. Increasingly he saw both the Spanish and the French in Mississippi as existential threats to the colony. The colonial militia was necessary but not sufficient for defense, and Oglethorpe wanted regular army soldiers posted on the southern frontier. He was granted a contingent of Scots Highlanders and made provisions for them to settle on the Altamaha River, the southern boundary of the colony. Once there, they established the towns of Darien and Frederica (named after Frederick, Prince of Wales). A new fort was constructed at the latter settlement on St. Simon's Island in the disputed territory south of the Altamaha River.

Oglethorpe had arranged for Tomochichi, his family, and an entourage to follow him to Britain for what amounted to a state visit. John Musgrove accompanied them to serve as their interpreter, although it proved challenging to keep him sufficiently sober to translate effectively. Oglethorpe by that time was personally close to Tomochichi, then ninety years old, and deeply respectful of the man and his culture. He sincerely wanted his Yamacraw friend to see his country, and he also knew that his contingent would draw needed attention to the colony and bolster support for it. The tactic worked. They had audiences with not only the Trustees but also with members of Parliament and the king and queen, who received them at Kensington Palace on August 1, 1734. The Yamacraw entourage returned to their native land by year end, arriving in Savannah on December 27, 1734.[7]

Mary Musgrove, who had stayed behind to manage the trading post, facilitated communication and trade with Indigenous nations in the hinterland. She wrote to Oglethorpe in July to report that the young colony's officers, with assistance from Colonel William Bull of South Carolina, invited the Upper Creek and the Choctaw to meet to discuss peace and trade, "which is more than ever Carolina could do to get them down before."[8]

The model society that Oglethorpe envisioned promoted the new ideals of the Enlightenment, which were antithetical to those of the Lowcountry elite. The concept of natural equality, that "all men are created equal" (conceived by Locke but not imparted to Carolina), was inherent in those ideals and a precept of the Declaration of Independence that would be writ-

equality

ten forty-two years later. But any broadly construed idea of equality could not have been more foreign to Charleston, which by then had become a society in which a majority population was enslaved by a minority. Other fundamental differences undermined the initial harmony between the two colonies, including their respective relations with the Indian nations, as they were called.

Taking advantage of Oglethorpe's absence, merchants in South Carolina who had been disappointed at the lack of opportunity to sell rum and enslaved people in Georgia, began an effort to undermine Trustee authority. They nurtured a relationship with a disaffected group in Savannah that envied the slaveholding Carolina model. The Savannah group, which became known as the Malcontents, continuously petitioned first the Trustees, then the government, for enslaved workers and more generous land grants. They were rebuked by Oglethorpe and the Trustees repeatedly, but they persisted and ultimately took their case to Parliament. The Trustees prevailed, and for a while the matter seemed to be settled.

Malcontents

Oglethorpe departed England in November 1735 with 257 new colonists, including brothers John and Charles Wesley, both ministers, and the Scots Guards bound for Darien and Frederica. They reached Savannah on February 5, 1736. Oglethorpe was received as a hero when he returned from England. Not only was he the colony's much-respected founder and leader, he was also seen as the one person who could resolve the many problems besetting the early colonists.

Restoring order in Savannah and implementing new military defense plans were top priorities. Once those matters were settled, Oglethorpe ventured deep into western interior regions to secure treaties with Native Americans. It was a grueling five-hundred-mile trek on horseback that few Englishmen would have been capable of undertaking successfully. Oglethorpe had to overcome severe illness on the trek to achieve his goals of peace and mutual respect.

Oglethorpe returned to Savannah to handle lingering administrative matters before heading south to Frederica, seventy miles down the coast. With matters in the north largely resolved, he departed on February 12. Relocating his base of operations to Fort Frederica left Savannah vulnerable to greater influence from Charleston. To counter that and to improve communications, Oglethorpe began construction of a road connecting the northern and southern settlements, thereby significantly reducing travel time. He wrote to the Trustees that he had a hundred workmen assigned to the road project. Nevertheless, some Trustees were uncomfortable with Oglethorpe's expansion of the colony, believing order should be established in Savannah and its immediate hinterlands before settling the frontier region south of the Altamaha River.[9]

The years 1735 and 1736 were among the busiest for the Trustees and colonial officials in Savannah, with the population increasing to around two thousand settlers. The growth was largely enabled by a grant from Parliament in support of settlement and defenses. Obtaining parliamentary support was a remarkable achievement since first minister Robert Walpole was not entirely on board and colonies were generally conceived as largely self-supporting mercantile ventures.

One of the reasons Georgia was able to sustain government support was its embrace of persecuted European Protestants, a high priority for George II, who was born in northern Germany. Several Protestant sects that had been hemmed in and increasingly persecuted in predominantly Catholic Europe ultimately found refuge in Georgia. They included Salzburgers, from the borderlands between present-day Austria and Germany; Moravians from Bohemia and later Saxony (aided by the charismatic Count Nikolaus Zinzendorf, a friend of Oglethorpe's); Palatinates from a region of southwest Germany then within the Holy Roman Empire; Swabians, from a region southwest of present-day Bavaria; and the French-speaking Vaudois, from the western canton of Vaud in Switzerland. Most of these groups eventually dispersed to other colonies, with the Moravians notably migrating to Pennsylvania. The Salzburgers, however, remained, and their legacy in Georgia is preserved by the Salzburger Society headquartered at the site of their original settlement of Ebenezer, twenty-five miles upriver from Savannah.[10]

The officers and colonists in Savannah who remained loyal to Trustee administration prevailed over the Malcontents in 1736, although the fracture gradually became more pronounced with continued meddling from Charleston. Savannah continued to grow through the year, and the amount of land under cultivation increased considerably. By November there were "upwards of 300 houses, beside huts" in Savannah. A sea captain returning from Georgia in May reported that most of the garden lots had been cleared and that the people were busy clearing their forty-five-acre farm lots.[11]

The Wesley brothers assumed multiple duties. In addition to educating Native Americans on Christianity, John was the minister in Savannah and

John & Charles Wesley

Charles served as Oglethorpe's secretary, a duty he came to resent. Charles resigned his position in July 1736 and returned to England, where he met with the Trustees and gave them a lengthy account of conditions in Georgia, increasing their apprehensions.

A year after Charles's departure, John became interested in a young parishioner named Sophie Hopkey. When she rejected him for another man, he became embroiled in a feud with her family. Suddenly, in early December 1737, he slipped away in the middle of the night, making his way to Charleston from whence he was able to sail home. Despite the early strains, the Wesleys would remain lifelong friends of Oglethorpe.[12]

Late in 1736, Oglethorpe planned a second trip to England, the chief focus of which would be on colonial defense. *colonial defense* He continued to believe the colony was threatened by Spanish forces in Florida and French forces to the west, and he thought that British dominance in the region might be in jeopardy. He may also have believed that an emphasis on increasing the nation's military presence would constitute a more effective means of funding the colony than reliance on mercantile and philanthropic motives.

Oglethorpe left Georgia on October 24, reaching Wales in early January 1737. By January 7, he was back in London, in good health, and meeting with other Trustees. His report was encouraging: colonists had become more industrious, the stores were full, and a treaty with the Spanish at St. Augustine had prevented war. He also managed to assuage the concerns of most Trustees over expanding settlement to the south.[13]

While in England, Oglethorpe received a letter from Samuel Eveleigh, a South Carolina merchant, claiming that the Spanish were planning to attack Georgia and South Carolina and that the Spanish had promised freedom to enslaved people who did not aid their masters during the attack. A month later the Trustees received another letter warning of an impending attack, this one from Thomas Broughton, lieutenant governor of South Carolina. Such warnings supported Oglethorpe's request to Parliament for funding and a regiment of seven hundred men under his command to be based at Frederica.[14]

The Trustees remained wary of Oglethorpe's plan to strengthen and populate the southern frontier, feeling that he would become too distracted to communicate regularly with them. To enhance communications, they appointed a permanent secretary to Savannah. William Stephens, a former member of Parliament who had recently been to South Carolina on business, was hired for the position. Arriving on November 1, 1737, while Oglethorpe was in England, Stephens immediately began sorting out the feuding factions and conflicting reports about the colony. His correspondence with the Trustees was extensive, and it left an invaluable record of early Georgia history. Stephens, then in his sixties, was an able and loyal officer until he retired to his Georgia estate at the end of the Trustee period. He worked closely and effectively with Oglethorpe, even as his son, Thomas Stephens, joined the Malcontents.[15]

In 1738, as Oglethorpe prepared to return to Georgia, relations with Spain were becoming increasingly tense. Spain had two points of contention with Britain. First, they claimed territory to 33°50' based on the Anglo-Spanish treaty of 1670 (the Treaty of Madrid), a claim that encompassed most of British South Carolina. Second, they contended that Oglethorpe's establishment of a military presence at Fort St. George on the St. John's River, which he ordered to be built in 1736, was an incursion into their territory. With potential conflict brewing, Oglethorpe and a portion of his regiment sailed from Southampton in May 1738.[16]

Two major engagements with Spanish forces occurred during Oglethorpe's remaining four years in the colony. The Siege of St. Augustine took place in June and July 1740. It was part of the larger conflict between Britain and Spain known as the War of Jenkins's Ear. Oglethorpe's forces captured several forts near St. Augustine before laying siege to the Castillo de San Marcos. The siege was ultimately unsuccessful in dislodging the Spanish from the region, and British forces under Oglethorpe's command returned to Georgia and South Carolina.

The Battle of Bloody Marsh took place on July 7, 1742, when Spanish forces outnumbering Oglethorpe's troops five to one invaded St. Simon's Island. Oglethorpe was forced to withdraw from Fort Frederica, but his troops managed to ambush the pursuing army and subsequently trick the Spanish into thinking their numbers were much greater. The Spanish withdrew from Georgia and never returned.

An interesting meeting of utopian visionaries occurred during Oglethorpe's final months in the colony. At about the same time Oglethorpe conceived and implemented the utopian plan for the Georgia Colony, a German by the name of Christian Gottlieb Priber conceived his own plan for a New World utopian society in the Georgia and Carolina Appalachians. Priber crossed the Atlantic to Charleston and set out for the Appalachians. He took up residence with the Cherokee, learning the language and adopting their customs. After gaining their confidence, Priber set about establishing an ideal society that he called "The Kingdom of Paradise." The new nation would counter the advance of European domination, quarantining Old World cultural infection within the coastal plain. Priber's utopian society would welcome people of all races and circumstances who accepted the premises of human equality and communal living.[17]

Priber's ideals were a product of the Enlightenment, as were those of Oglethorpe. Both men sought to create a more equitable and just society, they both believed in preserving the dignity of ordinary people, and they both offered a home to debtors and others who needed new opportunities. They sought to achieve their vision of a new society through scientific rationalism and experimentalism. They differed, however, in the means by which they pursued an end. Priber envisioned a revolutionary break from existing authority. Oglethorpe envisioned a more subtle revolution, one that did not directly challenge established authority, in which the frontier would become a focus of national renewal.

Priber became a threat to South Carolina authorities when it became apparent that he was advocating a new nation, founded with Native Americans, to challenge European authority. He was arrested in early 1743 and transported to Frederica, where he was turned over to Oglethorpe, the designated military commander in the region. Six months later, Oglethorpe returned to England for the final time. One may speculate about conversations between the two idealists, both of whom welcomed intense philosophical discussion, but no record of any such exchange has been discovered. Priber died the following year while still in custody in Frederica.[18]

At the time of Oglethorpe's final departure for England on July 22, 1743, his utopian vision was faltering. He and other Trustees held firm for several more years on the prohibition of slavery and the ideal of agrarian equality. But with Oglethorpe out of the way, the Charleston elite began chipping away at Georgia's foundational principles. Williams Stephens reported to the Trustees that enslaved people were being slipped into the colony to labor on secretly enlarged landholdings. The Trustees ordered him to crack down, and he initially complied. By 1750, however, Stephens reported that he could no longer contain the intrusion of the Carolina model. The Trustees, with

**Notable Dates in Savannah's
Early Colonial Period**

1733	Founding of Georgia
1735	Slavery prohibited
1742	Battle of Bloody Marsh
1743	Oglethorpe returns permanently to Britain
1750	Prohibition of slavery rescinded
1752	End of the Trustee period

Oglethorpe no long attending meetings, relented and allowed the "importation and use of Negroes," subject to provisions for humanitarian treatment and religious instruction.[19]

The experimental, utopian phase of the Georgia Colony formally ended in 1752 when the Trustees transferred authority to the Crown and held a final meeting on June 28. A new era began in which Savannah would come under the sway of Charleston and Georgia would become a slave society.

The Georgia experiment failed to establish an alternative society, but the idealism behind it lives to this day. Thanks primarily to Oglethorpe, chattel slavery came to be seen as a moral issue for the first time. The idea of natural equality articulated by Locke gained more adherents through the debate over the Georgia plan. And the design of Savannah, with its various aesthetic, functional, and egalitarian components, is a continuing inspiration.

Later Colonial and Revolutionary Period

The second period of the story arc begins with the close of the Trustee period in 1752. Georgia officially became a royal colony in 1754, and a succession of three royal governors attempted to refine the local administrative apparatus and strengthen Britain's hold on the region. The royal governors took slavery for granted, and two owned enslaved people themselves, even though questions over the morality of slavery had arisen on both sides of the Atlantic little more than a decade earlier.

Without Trustee opposition, slavery would inevitably expand in Georgia. At the time of transition, however, vestiges of the original plan for the colony were still evident. The pattern of small, yeoman farms dominated the landscape. Blacks and Whites were welcomed to integrated church services in Savannah by Rev. Bartholomew Zouberbuhler. Whites still outnumbered Blacks by more than two to one (4,500 to 1,855), in sharp contrast to the lopsided ratio of enslaved people to Whites in Carolina.[20]

But the shift to oligarchic "slavocracy" was coming. Just as Carolina had once been a colony of the colony of Barbados (in some basic ways), Georgia too was becoming a colony of South Carolina. Carolinian Jonathan Bryan, one of first Carolina planters to expand into Georgia, introduced rice cultivation in 1752. Unlike his father, Hugh Bryan, who had warned slaveholders that they faced the wrath of God, the younger Bryan was an advocate of the "Carolina way" (as Georgians called it) of large-scale plantations and a vast, enslaved labor force. At the same time, James Habersham began promoting the slave trade as part of the chain of wealth linking together the Lowcountry elite in a prosperous oligarchy.[21]

The land use pattern of small farms and settlements around Savannah was transformed into one resembling Charleston's surroundings. Small farms were bought up and consolidated into larger plantations. Wetlands on either side of the ridge where Oglethorpe built the city, which had been unusable as family farms, were ideal for large-scale rice production. A compact pattern of large plantations within easy reach of the city took form, making Savannah wealthier and more sophisticated.

While Savannah took on some of the characteristics of Charleston, it also differentiated itself from its wealthy neighbor during the period. The historian Paul M. Pressly provides a detailed account of Savannah's emergence as a transatlantic player in *On the Rim of the Caribbean*. Pressly shows that Savannah established a closer economic relationship with the Caribbean than Charleston, exporting lumber and foodstuffs to the islands in exchange for enslaved people, rum, and sugar. Exports of longleaf pine increased from 307,000 feet of lumber in 1761 to 2.1 million feet in 1768.[22]

As Savannah's trade ties to the Caribbean strengthened, the character of the city changed. With half of its shipping directed toward the islands, compared to less than a quarter of Charleston's, it was inevitable that Savannah would acquire some of the island vibe. Merchants, artisans, sailors, privateers, and enslaved people from throughout the Caribbean arrived in Savannah, bringing the city a new, more vibrant atmosphere.[23]

Georgia's Slave Code of 1755 ensured "due subjugation and obedience" but contained provisions to prevent the more heinous practices endemic in South Carolina. Georgians remained, at least to a small degree, under the sway of the humanitarian regime of the Trustees. Before the period ended, however, Georgia's oppression of enslaved people would match that of South Carolina.

As the number of enslaved people increased in Savannah, White artisans came to fear competition from skilled Black artisans, as had happened in Charleston. From the perspective of the Lowcountry oligarchy, racial tension was preferable to class tension, and it could even be beneficial. Bacon's Rebellion in Virginia in 1676 was precedent-setting for the plantation elite throughout the incipient South: better to cultivate racial resentment, and suffer whatever tensions that might entail, than face working-class solidarity.

James Wright became Georgia's third and last royal governor, serving in office from 1760 to 1776. Georgia prospered during Wright's administration and became the fastest-growing colony in British America. Wright was archetypal of the Lowcountry elite, owning a dozen plantations and over five hundred enslaved people. Early in the Revolutionary period, he fled Georgia on a British warship that had been anchored off Tybee Island. He returned, however, leading the British forces that retook Savannah. At the beginning of Wright's administration, Whites outnumbered Blacks two to one. But Black and White populations had reached parity by the end of his administration in 1782.

The French and Indian War of 1755 to 1763 (the American theater of the Seven Years' War) concluded with Britain's victory over France and Spain, which had joined France's side near the end. In 1764, with Britain in full control of the region, Wright's jurisdiction was enlarged. The boundaries of Georgia were fixed at the St. Mary's River on the south (the current state border) and the Mississippi River to the west. Most of present-day Alabama and Mississippi lay within the colony's western boundary, while newly minted British Florida extended northwest along the coast of the Gulf of Mexico to Louisiana.

Under Wright, Georgia was slow to join calls for independence. The colony did not attend the first Continental Congress in 1774. But there were meetings in Savannah, centering around Peter Tondee's Tavern, where the fire of revolutionary spirit first began flickering. By the time of the Second Provincial Congress in 1775, Savannahians were enthusiastic about the emerging independence movement.

Each of the colonies formed a committee of correspondence to coordinate resistance to British policies. Three Savannahians who served on the Georgia committee were John Houstoun, Noble Wimberley Jones, and Archibald Bulloch. Houstoun, who married Jonathan Bryan's daughter, served two terms as governor during the Revolutionary period. Bulloch, the great-great-grandfather of Theodore Roosevelt and great-great-great-grandfather of Eleanor Roosevelt, was an attorney who moved from Charleston to Savannah in 1764. He became close to John Adams while serving in the Continental Congress and served a term as governor of Georgia at the start of the Revolution. Noble Wimberley Jones, perhaps the best known today of Savannah's second generation of leaders, was the son of Noble Jones, who had served as the Oglethorpe's surveyor in Savannah. Part of the family's Wormsloe estate is now a Georgia historic site.

None of the three, as fate would have it, went on to become signers of the Declaration of Independence. Three other Georgians gained that distinction: Button Gwinnett, George Walton, and Lyman Hall. Gwinnett drafted Georgia's first constitution and became governor after Archibald Bulloch. Walton became a successful attorney in Savannah after moving from Virginia at an early age; he served as senator, acting governor, and chief justice after the Revolution. The third signer, Lyman Hall was one of the few Revolutionary leaders who was not a Savannahian. Hall initially settled in Liberty County, south of Savannah, but eventually became a prominent planter in Burke County, near Augusta. A granite monument in Augusta memorializes the three signers.

While revolutionary fervor had not built as quickly in Savannah as in Charleston (to Charleston's dismay), when it did arrive Savannah became a full partner in opposing the motherland's taxes and remote governance. Hostilities began when Noble Wimberly Jones and others raided the British magazine in Savannah, as Charlestonians had already done in their city.

In response to such actions, the British military seized Savannah in late 1778 and occupied Charleston in early 1780. British loyalists were then placed firmly in control of local governmental institutions. The Continental army and local militias fled Savannah and regrouped in mid-1779 with a plan to retake the city.

In September, American and French forces attacked British defenses in Savannah. The ensuing Siege of Savannah was one of the bloodiest battles of the war. Casimir Pulaski, a young Polish nobleman, died in fierce fighting. Pulaski had fought for Polish independence and then joined Washington's Continental army. He distinguished himself by forming the army's first cavalry unit and later saving Washington's life in a daring charge.

Pulaski is one of the most commemorated war heroes in the United States as well as in Poland. A monument honoring General Pulaski was erected in Monterey Square in 1853. Pulaski Square, laid out in 1837, was also named for the general. Remains under the monument in Monterey Square were exhumed in 1996 to test the long-held belief that it was Pulaski's skeleton. Initial results were positive, but it was not until 2019 that the Smithsonian Institution confirmed that it was Pulaski's remains through testing mitochondrial DNA from his grandniece. An interesting aspect of the test results is that Pulaski appears to have been female or intersex (i.e., having mixed-gendered genetic characteristics).[24]

The Siege of Savannah is commemorated in Haitian history, since free Haitian soldiers fought on the side of American forces. Their experience in the American Revolution may have contributed to the success of the Haitian Revolution twelve years later. In the first decade of the twenty-first century the City of Savannah erected a monument to those Haitians in Franklin Square. Words at the base of the monument read, in part, "In the fall of 1779, over 500 Chasseurs Volontaires sailed from Saint Domingue, the modern island of Haiti. The City of Savannah honors the Les Chasseurs Volontaires de Saint Domingue, who fought for American independence during the Siege of Savannah in 1779."

With Savannah secure, the British moved on Charleston, which would become their southern headquarters. They held the city under siege from March 29, 1780, to May 12, 1780.

Georgia's revolutionaries, who had become known politically as Whigs, controlled the Upcountry, dividing the colony. War and division ruined the economy, and when independence was achieved the task of rebuilding was enormous. Savannah's merchants spoke of having "to begin the world again," a phrase used by Thomas Paine in *Common Sense* and, whether they knew it or not, by the Georgia Trustees in describing the founding of the province in 1733.[25]

Notable Dates in Savannah's Later Colonial Period

1752	Slavery formally introduced
1754	Georgia becomes a royal colony
1764	French and Indian War ends, with Britain expanding to the Mississippi
1775	Savannahians join the independence movement
1778	Savannah seized by the British military
1779	Siege of Savannah by American forces fails

The Post-Revolutionary and Antebellum Era

This period of the city's story arc was the era that began with the ratification of the U.S. Constitution in 1788 and ended with the Civil War in 1861, encompassing the Civil War antebellum era dating from the War of 1812. The Constitution acknowledged the existence of slavery in the South (then still an emerging regional concept) and provided for three-fifths of the enslaved population to be counted in each state for purposes of representation in the House of Representatives. In Britain, on the other hand, an abolition movement was gaining strength, reinforced in 1772 by *Somerset v. Stewart,* which ruled that slavery was not supported by English law. Early opposition to slavery by Oglethorpe, his close friend Granville Sharp, and a handful of others blossomed into a formal abolition movement in the late 1780s, which in turn gradually influenced public policy.

In America, the northern colonies began turning away from slavery during the Revolutionary period. Pennsylvania passed An Act for the Gradual Abolition of Slavery in 1780 and was followed in short order by similar acts in Massachusetts, New Hampshire, Connecticut, and Rhode Island. By 1799, the North was on the cusp of being slave-free.

To the plantation elite of the South, however, it was far better to be in a house divided, but with constitutional protections, than subject to British law. In 1788 the southern tier of states was virtually an equal partner with those north of the Chesapeake in steering the ship of state and no longer a small piece of an expanding British Empire. Although Charleston was the epicenter of pro-slavery rhetoric, Virginia was the new nation's largest and most powerful state, offering a shield of protection to the institution of slavery that was far more effective in the United States than it had been under British rule.

It was in this context that Savannah was poised to become a junior partner to Charleston in advocating the positions of the slaveholding elite. While Savannah would never assume a role as important as that of Charleston in guiding the South to secession, it added new authority to pro-slavery positions as one of the region's most economically powerful cities.

Rebuilding after the Revolution involved reaffirming and reconstructing slave society. Savannah planter Joseph Clay wrote, "The Negro business . . . is to the Trade of this Country . . . as the Soul to the Body." It was, he said, "the foundation for all other business." Maintaining such a system required a deep belief in White supremacy. As the historian Walter Fraser wrote in his history of Savannah, "racism provided a common bond for all whites."[26]

The more natural a slave society became to Savannahians, the more bizarre it appeared to outsiders. The widely traveled founder of the *Savannah Georgian* newspaper (published from 1819 to 1856), John Milton Harney, wrote a poem about the city when he finally abandoned it to establish a Dominican mission in Kentucky: "Farewell, oh, Savannah, forever farewell, / Thou hotbed of rogues, thou threshold of hell, / . . . Where the greatest freeholder is the holder of slaves, / And he that has most, about freedom most raves."[27]

Decades after Harney's departure, the *Savannah Georgian* editorialized that slavery was "a blessing to both races": "Our slaves are better treated, better clothed, better fed, [and] . . . happ[ier] than the laboring classes of any part of the world." Northern visitors formed a different impression. Emily Burke saw enslaved people who were "half-starved" and "emaciated." Abolitionist Philo Tower saw "mournfully dejected" women working the docks under the crack of the whip, forbidden to speak, and subjected to the "sneers of gaping men and boys."[28]

But to slaveholders, Savannah was booming because of slavery. Exports increased sixfold between 1800 and 1820. Rice exports were supplemented by high-quality sea island (long-staple) cotton. The port expanded as it moved additional commodities from expanding inland producers.

New affluence was reflected in architecture. English architect William Jay practiced in Savannah from 1817 to 1822, designing prominent houses for the city's elite slaveholders and merchants, including the Owens-Thomas House, the William Scarborough House, and the Telfair House (now the Telfair Academy). He also designed the Savannah Theatre, one of the oldest continually operating theaters in the United States.

Charles Augustus Lafayette Lamar, son of the cotton and shipping magnate Gazaway Bugg Lamar, was one of Savannah's most audacious Fire-Eaters. He was active in the Know-Nothing Party (American Party) before the election of 1856, and he later became an ardent supporter of the Southern Rights Party. However, he gained infamy on November 28, 1858, when the slave ship *Wanderer* in which he had invested discharged its illegal human cargo on Jekyll Island, seventy miles south of Savannah. It was the second-to-last slave ship to land in the United States, the *Clotilda* being the last. Even though the slave trade had been prohibited since 1808, Lamar was never prosecuted for his crime. Lamar's final step toward infamy would come seven days after General Robert E. Lee surrendered at Appomattox, when he became the last man to die in the Civil War during the Battle of Columbus.[29]

Savannah became an industrial city as well as a port serving an extensive agricultural hinterland. The Steam Boat Company of Georgia was founded in 1817 and reached full production in the 1820s, weathering a national recession in 1819 and a financial panic in 1826. Other marine industries followed, and the riverfront boomed with activity. The Savannah River was navigable for two hundred miles to Augusta by steamboat, a much greater distance than Charleston's Ashley and Cooper Rivers.

Although Savannah and Charleston are virtually identical in climate and coastal environment, rivers gave Savannah a competitive advantage. In 1831 the Port of Savannah was linked to the Ogeechee River by the 16.5-mile Savannah-Ogeechee Canal. The canal expanded the city's hinterland over two hundred miles northwest to Louisville, Georgia. Louisville, like Augusta, was located at the fall line, where the coastal plain meets the harder rock subsurface of the hilly inland region, an area of rapids where further inland navigation is impractical. Combined, the parallel Savannah and Ogeechee drainage basins encompass 11,250 square miles, approximately twenty times that of the Ashley and Cooper basins.[30]

Had Carolina been founded on the Savannah River instead of at the confluence of the shorter Ashley and Cooper Rivers, the evolution of the colony might have been quite different. Colonists could have defied Grand Model regulations and pushed upriver, as happened in Virginia. A more dispersed settlement pattern would have followed, and a less distinct economy and political culture would have emerged. The Lowcountry as a powerful influence shaping southern political culture might never have materialized. The defining geographic elements of *site* and *situation* are through lines in the entwined story of Charleston and Savannah.[31]

During the later colonial and Revolutionary period, Savannah went from being a satellite of Charleston to a modest competitor. During the antebellum period, it became a *formidable* competitor. Economic growth was so strong in the early 1800s that by 1820 Savannah climbed to the nation's eighteenth largest city, while Charleston dropped to the sixth position.

In 1820, as Savannah was poised to make new progress, a catastrophic fire devastated the city (as one had done just twenty-four years before). At the same time, wetland rice production close to the city had enlarged the habitat for the *Aedes aegypti* mosquito, the carrier of yellow fever and other diseases. The census of 1830 reflected the twin ravages, and Savannah declined in national ranking to the thirty-seventh largest city, while Charleston held on to its status as the nation's sixth-largest.

Despite the economic vicissitudes of the 1820s, the city began a tree-planting beautification effort in 1824. Savannahians believed their city to be inherently more beautiful than Charleston, as well as most other cities, in part because the layout of the Oglethorpe Plan created a unique sense of spaciousness and intimacy within its public spaces. The sense of being a beautiful city became a permanent aspect of Savannahian's self-image and another through line in its story.

While affluence generally increased through the antebellum period, Savannah and Charleston were both vulnerable to wide cyclical swings, a result of their parallel, marginally diversified, and largely agrarian economies. The economy remained unstable well into the 1830s, but industrial investment was setting the stage for future growth. The Central Rail Road and Canal Company formed in 1833, later became the Central of Georgia Railway, adding feeder lines throughout the 1840s. In 1838, the first iron-hulled vessel was assembled in Savannah from parts made in England, then fitted with a steam engine made in England. The *John Randolph* became the first such steamboat in the United States.

Real economic growth returned in the 1840s, led by the rapid expansion of railroads. (The rise of Savannah as an industrial city is the subject of chapter 8.) By 1860, on the eve of the Civil War, Savannah was again prosperous. The economy was more diversified, with exports of cotton, rice, lumber, and manufactured goods. Four shipyards built dozens of vessels in the decade before the war. Savannah was arguably the most industrialized city in the South, its population

Notable Dates in Savannah's Post-Revolutionary and Antebellum Era

1789	City of Savannah established by charter
1800	Savannah enters a boom period
1820	Fire sweeps the city; the economy struggles
1824	Trees planted in first beautification initiative
1833	Central Rail Road and Canal Company formed
1838	First iron-hulled vessel assembled
1840	Savannah economy in full rebound

was growing, and its emergence as a regional and national transportation hub was inevitable.[32]

Civil War & Reconstruction (handwritten)

Civil War and Reconstruction

The Civil War and Reconstruction comprise a period in the story arc that was short and deeply disruptive. The Civil War occurred between 1861 and 1865, overlapping with Reconstruction, which began during the war in 1863 with the Emancipation Proclamation and ended twelve years after the war in 1877. Georgia's military-enforced period of Reconstruction ended in 1871. Although it was a traumatic period for Savannah, the impact was less severe than for Charleston.

As war neared, the attitude of Savannahians toward the North was no less hostile than that of Charlestonians. The philanthropist Eleanor Baker wrote from Savannah, "Southerners look upon all northerners as their enemies in all that regards slavery." Savannah's early reticence over slavery was long gone. In 1861 White superiority and Black repression had reached a zenith. After Lincoln's election, Savannahians gathered in protest, unfurling the state flag of resistance, a coiled rattlesnake with the words: "Our Motto Southern Rights . . . Don't Tread on Me."[33]

Much of the actual war was fought upstate. By the time General Sherman launched his Atlanta-to-Savannah "March to the Sea" (November 15 to December 21, 1864), the outcome was clear: coastal forces could not prevail, and terrible destruction awaited Savannah if it resisted. Confederate army forces defending Savannah retreated to South Carolina on hastily built pontoon bridges during the night of December 20. The following morning, city leaders surrendered Savannah to Sherman's army.

Sherman famously telegraphed President Lincoln, offering him the city as a Christmas present: "I beg to present you as a Christmas gift the City of Savannah, with one hundred and fifty guns and plenty of ammunition, also about twenty-five thousand bales of cotton." The president formally thanked him for the present in a letter dated December 26.[34]

Although Savannah had deeper ties to Charleston than to Atlanta, Sherman and his soldiers spared it because (by the width of a river) it was not in the state they blamed for starting the war. The army's wrath was reserved for South Carolina, the principal instigator of the war, where it went on to burn everything in its path related to the war effort (while generally protecting other property). Still, the infamous burning of Columbia, the state capital and Sherman's destination after Savannah, had more to do with Confederate soldiers burning valuable cotton as they retreated than fires started by Sherman's army.[35]

Sherman's brief occupation of Savannah was reasonably civil. Charles Green, a wealthy English cotton broker, offered his architecturally attractive, well-appointed residence to the general. The Green-Meldrim House, as it is known, is now a national historic landmark. Sherman engaged socially with city residents. On one such occasion, he visited Eleanor Gordon, wife of a Confederate army officer. They chatted, and Sherman bounced her daughter Daisy on his knee. Daisy was later better known as Juliette Gordon Low, founder of the Girl Scouts.[36]

Sherman had to face the reality of tens of thousands of displaced African Americans from the Lowcountry to the Florida border. After consulting with his superiors, officers in the field, and Black leaders, Sherman issued Special Field Order No. 15, confiscating abandoned coastal lands and allocating them to freed people (the "forty acres and a mule" order). Sea Island and river plantations extending thirty miles inland were affected by the order. However, the redistribution was temporary. Most land was returned to the original owners, and those who had been assigned land were left in untenable situations.

For Georgia, military-enforced Reconstruction began in 1865 and ended in 1871 (many historians date the entire Reconstruction era from the Emancipation Proclamation in 1863 to the Compromise of 1877), when federal troops and administrators were withdrawn. Nevertheless, pressure to change the old order remained as long as federal forces controlled much of the South. In a period called "Presidential Reconstruction," instituted by President Andrew Johnson occurred in Georgia and elsewhere in 1865 and 1866, many rights were restored to ex-Confederates and to the southern states in exchange for repealing secession orders and adopting new constitutions. President Johnson appointed James Johnson, a Columbus Unionist who had sat out the war, as provisional governor. Governor Johnson led the effort to repeal the Ordinance of Secession and frame a new, postwar constitution.

The Georgia legislature met after the election of November 1866 and nearly unanimously rejected the Fourteenth Amendment. It was only after Georgia was placed under the authority of General John Pope, supervisor of the Third Military District, which included Alabama and Florida, that African Americans were able to register to vote.

scalawag

In 1868 Georgia adopted a new constitution, written with the support of African Americans and White "scalawags" (supporters of Reconstruction), reflecting that of the amended U.S. Constitution. Equality of races was made clear throughout. Section 2, for example, states, "All persons born or naturalized in the United States, and resident in this State, are hereby declared citizens of this State, and no laws shall be made or enforced which shall abridge the privileges or immunities of citizens of the United States, or of this State, or deny to any person within its jurisdiction the equal protection of its laws."[37]

Those who wanted to end Reconstruction and restore White authority were called Redeemers. In Georgia, Democratic Party Redeemers prevailed when James M. Smith became governor in January 1872. In 1877 they succeeded in replacing the 1868 constitution with

Capital Cities of Georgia

1733–1778	Savannah
1779–80	Augusta
1780–81	Heard's Fort
1781–82	Augusta
1782	Ebenezer
1782	Savannah
1783	Augusta
1784	Savannah
1784	Augusta
1785	Savannah
1786–96	Savannah and Augusta
1796–1806	Louisville
1807–64	Milledgeville
1864–65	Macon
1865–68	Milledgeville
1868–present	Atlanta

Redeemers

Population of Principal Cities in Georgia

	1800	1850	1900	1950	2000
Savannah	5,146	15,312	54,244	119,638	133,237
Augusta	—	9,448	39,441	71,508	199,775
Atlanta	—	2,572	89,872	331,334	416,474

Sources: U.S. Census, historic reports

one that would restore White supremacy. Conservative Democrats would control state politics for the next 131 years.

Savannah's influence in state politics had been ebbing for decades as other areas of Georgia grew. As shown in the list of state capitals, Savannah had not been the capital since 1796, and even then it shared that position with Augusta. The city only briefly enjoyed the level of statewide influence that Charleston has enjoyed throughout its history.

Despite its large African American population, Savannah was unable to send a Black person to federal office until the election of Raphael Warnock to the U.S. Senate in 2020. Warnock, born and raised in Savannah, was senior pastor of Ebenezer Baptist Church in Atlanta when he was elected. He became the first African American Democrat elected to the Senate from the South.[38]

The only Black member of Congress elected in Georgia during Reconstruction was Jefferson Franklin Long, a Macon tailor, who filled a vacant seat in 1871. Georgia would not elect another African American to the House of Representatives for more than a century, when Atlantan Andrew Young was elected in 1973.

It was during Reconstruction that Atlanta emerged as the center of state power. The young city, growing with the expansion of railroads, overtook Savannah as the state's largest city in the mid-1870s.

With the Redeemers in control of the state, and in the face of hostility from the White populace, Black Savannahians pressed forward in the new era of constitutional rights. One of the new institutions at their disposal was the press. In 1875 the *Colored Tribune*, later the *Savannah Tribune*, was founded as a weekly newspaper covering matters of concern to African Americans. The newspaper has filled an important niche in Savannah to the present day.

Notable Dates in Savannah's Civil War and Reconstruction Period

1861	Port blockaded by Union forces
1863	First baseball game played at Fort Pulaski
1864	Union forces take Savannah
1870	Democrats take control of the legislature
1872	Conservative Redeemers acquire full control
1877	Reconstruction ends across the South

The Post-Reconstruction and Jim Crow Era

The fifth period of the Savannah story is the era in which White privilege was restored and Black constitutional rights were denied. The period began with tactics to suppress Black participation in the electoral process. It culminated in the emergence of Jim Crow laws, the laws adopted by southern states that specifically targeted Blacks as a means of curtailing their civil rights. As noted, those laws were upheld by the U.S. Supreme Court in *Plessy v. Ferguson* in 1896 and stood unchallenged until reversed in 1954 by *Brown v. Board of Education.*

While segregation existed through custom and ad hoc laws before Jim Crow, it evolved into a regime of repression in the late nineteenth century. State legislators enacted laws segregating schools in 1872, public spaces were de facto off-limits areas to Blacks, and interracial marriage was prohibited by state law.

The new freedoms available to Blacks in the 1870s and 1880s were lost in the 1890s. A comprehensive system of racial segregation, spuriously based on "scientific" racism, legalized White supremacy.

Black Savannahians periodically protested Jim Crow with no success. In the period from 1900 to 1906 they mounted boycotts of local streetcars. Lacking political representation, there was little that could be accomplished.

During the Jim Crow era, Georgia omitted the official biographies of Black elected officials from state records. Whites could not accept that formerly enslaved people could govern, and, to the extent that they served, they were perceived to be incompetent. Even historians, such as University of Georgia professor E. Merton Coulter, perpetuated racism and Lost Cause mythology. Coulter claimed that most Black delegates to Georgia's constitutional convention could not read or write, and other scholars repeated the charge. But subsequent research has revealed that at least twenty-two of twenty-nine Reconstruction congressmen across the South were able to read and write. A database of Black elected officials serving during Reconstruction now reveals a wholly different picture from the racist views perpetuated during the Jim Crow era.[39]

It was during Jim Crow that Savannah began to change physically. First with the introduction of streetcars in the late 1800s, and then with the proliferation of the automobile in the 1920s, new suburbs sprang up farther and farther from the historic city center. Before those transformative innovations, people generally lived where they could walk to work, which meant that Oglethorpe's original one-square-mile town and common was increasingly densely populated. In other words, Savannah grew inward rather than outward until new forms of transportation offered its citizens greater mobility.

The era of the streetcar, beginning in the 1860s with horse-drawn streetcars and evolving to electric streetcars in the late 1880s, produced new neighborhoods south and east of the historic city core. The best known of those areas later became known as the Victorian District and the Thomas Square Streetcar Historic District, which taken together nearly tripled the size of the city.

A book published in 1900 on the historic towns of the United States contained chapters on both Savannah and Charleston. Even then, the author observed, Savannah had a "tint of antiquity": "It has the heaviest commerce of all the Atlantic ports south of Baltimore. It is the largest naval stores market in the world, and its cotton and lumber receipts are very considerable. But in spite of its commercial primacy Savannah preserves a distinct flavor of the olden time."

After World War I, inexpensive, mass-produced automobiles gave city residents vastly greater mobility than in the streetcar era. Savannah's Chatham Crescent and Ardsley Park historic districts were the first areas developed in response to the new mode of transportation. Between World War I and World War II, a period of only twenty-three years, Savannah's urban area doubled in size due to the automobile.

Following World War II, skyrocketing sales of higher-speed automobiles affordable to mass markets led to the creation of suburbs that were several times larger than those of the period between the wars. The population of new suburban areas became greater than that of the older, denser urban area, giving them significant political power. By the 1960s, in less

Notable Dates in Savannah's Post-Reconstruction and Jim Crow Era

1877	Atlanta becomes the state capital
1891	Jim Crow laws enacted
1896	Supreme Court upholds segregation in *Plessy v. Ferguson*
1912	Girl Scouts founded in Savannah
1915	Ku Klux Klan restarted at Stone Mountain
1916	Boll weevil reaches Atlantic Coast
1936	*Gone with the Wind* published

Oglethorpe plan

than twenty-five years, Savannah had expanded from its one-square-mile core to an area of fifty squares miles.

As Savannah expanded, it benefited from the Oglethorpe Plan. The original plan established a square-mile grid system with access rights of way, which became the modern street grid that serves the city today. The contrast with Charleston is remarkable. The mother city relied on river transportation and a more inherently limited road network. It never developed a regional grid, and the roads linking suburbs and exurbs to the city center are comparatively chaotic (for a comparison, see the city grids on page 149.

Savannah's Modern Era   *Modern Era*

The present period of Savannah's story arc can be called the modern era. It began with the sweeping changes of the 1960s. One such change was the restoration of the promise of civil rights that was bestowed in the Thirteenth, Fourteenth and Fifteenth Amendments to the U.S. Constitution, only to be taken away after Reconstruction. Setting the stage for the era, Savannah leaders such as Ralph Mark Gilbert, an African American who expanded NAACP presence in Savannah, the African American historian and desegregation leader W. W. Law, and John G. Kennedy, a progressive White mayor, successfully advocated for structural reforms, including the addition of Black officers to the city's police department.

Unfortunately, the continuation of postwar suburbanization erased many of the gains made by the civil rights movement. Suburbanization arguably had an even more deleterious effect on historic Savannah than it had on the Charleston Peninsula as White-owned businesses and White residents fled from the city's historic core. City centers were not only hollowed out in the 1950s as businesses and residents moved to the suburbs, they were also often bulldozed in preparation for redevelopment. In Savannah, as in Charleston, the looming loss of history provoked a strong response, and the destruction of historic structures and land use patterns was largely avoided.   *Historic Savannah Foundation*

The Historic Savannah Foundation, chartered in 1955, stepped in at a critical point in time to halt the loss of historic buildings, even as vibrant poorer neighborhoods were razed. The initiative paid dividends in the 1960s with the preservation of prominent historic properties, the establishment of the National Historic Landmark District in 1966, and the adoption of a formal review process for development in the new historic district. Those actions in turn paved the way for transformative capital investments in the 1970s, when the city redeveloped the riverfront and Savannah College of Art and Design began renovating historic properties for educational purposes. With a growing tourist industry and the attraction of thousands of students to the downtown area, historic Savannah came out of postwar economic freefall and entered a period of renewal.

Economic renewal did not benefit everyone. While the civil rights movement brought an end to Jim Crow laws and some of the Jim Crow era's most egregious practices, it did not bring prosperity to the historically African American neighborhoods ringing the Landmark District. Some older, vibrant neighborhoods, such as Frog Town on the western edge of the city's planned wards, were bought out and bulldozed with federal urban renewal funds. Older industrial areas were cleared for public housing, which only further concentrated poverty along the perimeter of the historic district.

In the 1980s African Americans made gains in the formerly White-controlled apparatus of city government. Since then, the majority-Black city has had a majority-Black representation on the city council. Increasingly, African Americans have benefited from a strong tourist economy but not to the extent that much of a dent has been made in the level of poverty. In 2003 Mayor Otis Johnson addressed this issue with a "Two Savannahs" paper that called for more to be done to mitigate gentrification and bring African American Savannahians into the dynamic downtown labor force.

Savannah now has over eight thousand historic and cultural resources preserved in the Landmark District and the city's eleven other historic districts. Each district preserves not only the structures and architecture of the period but also the land use patterns inherited or derived from the Oglethorpe Plan. In doing so, Savannah is rare among historic cities, preserving and reinforcing a sense of historic continuity through the generations.[40]

The Landmark District encompassing most of Oglethorpe's town and common contains significant buildings in Colonial, Federal, Gothic Revival, Greek Revival, Italianate, Second Empire, Neo-Classical, Beaux-Arts, International, Moderne, Art Deco, Queen Anne, and Folk Victorian styles. Yet all of the styles, which could clash in other contexts, are unified by the historic ward pattern established by Oglethorpe. That pattern encompasses nearly half of the entire district of 570 acres, or 0.9 square miles, while the other half generally respects the mass, scale, and spatial organization of the original design.[41]

Savannah is one of the nation's major destinations for historical and cultural tourism. With a major convention center, a new arena, thousands of historic structures, a vibrant urban environment, public green space virtually everywhere, and more than six thousand hotel rooms concentrated in and around the Landmark District, the city's redevelopment strategy combining historic preservation, landscape conservation, and urban planning has paid off. Proof of that is found in high year-round hotel occupancy rates and virtually full occupancy in the temperate spring and fall seasons.[42]

Savannah's partially successful reinvention of itself, like that of Charleston, faces a need for renewal in the 2020s and beyond. A third Reconstruction would bring with it a new vision of social equity, environmental justice, and sustainable progress, challenges that are likely to be every bit as difficult as those faced during the second Reconstruction. The city's long tradition of planning will be among the institutions challenged as reinvention strategies are explored. Challenges include mitigating industrial traffic traversing the city's historic downtown and early suburbs; mitigating the increasingly adverse impacts of tourism; and retaining and creating affordable workforce housing near jobs in the downtown area. The infamous and often intractable problem of gentrification has led to the displacement of low- and moderate-income residents as block-by-block redevelopment consumes their previously affordable neighborhoods. Another challenge that will take more than city planning to resolve is one that might be called *elitification.* The enormous success of the tourism industry has set it on a course toward more high-end, luxury-elite investment, which in turn has made its offerings less affordable and less accessible to all but the wealthiest residents of the city. The result of this trend may well be that downtown Savannah becomes more of a resort enclave and less of a traditional downtown.

In 2020 Charleston removed its Calhoun Monument, the city's most visible symbol of its racist past. In 2021 Savannahians began a broad discussion of other old symbols: the Talmadge Bridge, named for segregationist governor Eugene Talmadge (proposed to be renamed for the late U.S. representative John Lewis, an icon of the civil rights movement), the Confederate Monument in Forsyth Park; and Calhoun Square, named for pro-slavery leader John C. Calhoun. According to *Savannah Morning News* columnist Bill Dawers, past efforts were scattershot, and "the current generation of community leaders needs a clearer framework if they want to do justice to the new emphases on equity, inclusion and historical authenticity."[43]

While such discussions are necessary for renewal, they are not sufficient to bring about the structural change of a third Reconstruction. The largest symbol of all is the city's historic core, which represents not only a revered founding plan and the past sins of slavery but also hope for the future and a common denominator for civic pride among all Savannahians. The story of Savannah in the modern era, including its emerging challenges, is continued in chapter 12, where historic preservation, tourism, politics, and other topics are taken up in more detail.

Many of the threads in Savannah's story are entwined with those of Charleston laid out at the end of the preceding chapter. The physical characteristics of both cities—their compactness, streetscapes, and transportation networks—owe much to their original plans. Their founding plans also imparted social characteristics that endured over time, gothic authoritarianism in the case of Charleston and an arguably more egalitarian lean in the case of Savannah, associated with its founding during the Enlightenment. The geographically isolated, geopolitically hostile, climatically challenging physical context rendered each city acutely aware of its vulnerability in a formative period, influencing the character of both. Also associated with geography, both cities matured while they were participants in the system of Atlantic triangular trade, a long period of slave trading and enslavement of Africans that ultimately resulted in a uniquely blended society. Finally, site and situation have imparted to each city unique advantages and disadvantages as competitors, such as the navigational advantages of the wide waters of the Ashley and Cooper Rivers, and greater reach into the hinterland provided by the Savannah River.

One through line unique in Savannah's story is pride in its city plan, open spaces, and urban forest. A second is the egalitarian ethic in the original plan, which faded after the Trustee period but survived to live another day in the modern period. Many other through lines, taken up subsequently, are also tied to the heritage of the founding plan. Another that can be noted at this point is that through most of its story it was the second city: it strove at first to differentiate itself from Charleston, then to catch up to its neighbor city in prosperity, and later to forge ahead as an industrial city. Eventually Savannah, like Charleston, became aware of its story, conscious of its through lines, and able to reinvent itself by repudiating the worst of the past while preserving the best.

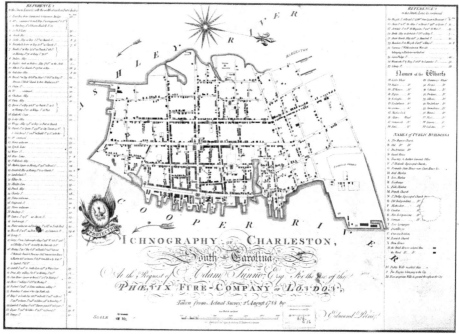

This early drawing reveals that the rectilinear grid began breaking up at an early stage of the city's development. *(Prints and Photographs Division, Library of Congress)*

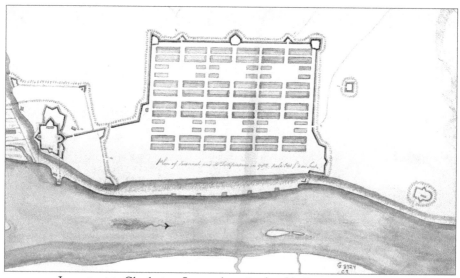

In contrast to Charleston, Savannah retained and built on its original city plan. *(Prints and Photographs Division, Library of Congress)*

PART III

Planning Legacy Cities

John Locke, as secretary to the Lords Proprietors, became the chief planner for the Carolina Colony, drafting its Grand Model. While serving in that capacity, he created the original city plan for Charleston.

Savannah was planned sixty years later by James Oglethorpe, who drew from his military and political experience, his classical studies at Oxford, and the Carolina Grand Model in conceiving the city's exceptional design.

In both cases some of the greatest scientific and philosophical minds of the time, many associated with the Royal Society, contributed to their designs.

CHAPTER FIVE

Charleston
England's First Comprehensively
Planned Colonial City

Anthony Ashley Cooper and the other seven Lords Propri-
etors began planning the Province of Carolina as a commercial venture in the
early 1660s, but the process of designing the capital city and its hinterlands
did not begin until 1666. The stimulus for thinking about urban design came
immediately after the Great Fire of 1666 that burned much of London. To
guide the recovery effort, Charles II launched a design competition aimed at
building a safer, more efficient, and more beautiful city. Among those who
submitted plans were the famous architect Christopher Wren, the scientist
Robert Hooke, the landscape designer and polymath John Evelyn, and the
surveyor Richard Newcourt. City planning was suddenly a topic of great interest among London's intelligentsia.[1]

In a historic coincidence, Anthony Ashley Cooper and John Locke met
and began discussing the Province of Carolina in the fall of 1666 as interest
in city planning peaked. Locke was a lecturer and medical student at Oxford
when Ashley Cooper sought treatment there for a liver ailment. The two men
were introduced, and they immediately liked each other. The political and
intellectual history of Western civilization was about to receive a jolt.[2]

In May 1668 Ashley Cooper suffered a health crisis when he vomited ex-
cessively and developed an enlarged hydatid cyst of the liver, now known to
be caused by a parasite transmitted from dogs and sheep. Locke and a medical doctor operated and implanted a silver drain in an experimental surgery
that saved Ashley Cooper's life (some antagonists called him "Tapski" as if he
had a beer tap installed). Locke's detailed notes on the procedure and recovery are an important record of the state of medicine at the time.[3]

According to K. H. D. Haley, Ashley Cooper's authoritative biographer,
Locke was not an employee so much as a friend invited to take up residence
at Exeter House, Ashley Cooper's home in London. Although their social
class placed them in very different tiers of English society, they became in-

tellectual equals and close collaborators. That is not to say that Locke did not give deference to his friend, giving due respect to him as a social superior, and there were almost certainly areas where he held back from challenging the senior man's opinions—an essential point to understand in assessing his subsequent career.[4]

In planning Carolina, Ashley Cooper was primarily concerned with land allocation, governance, and the best use of his plantation. He and Locke shared an interest in the emerging fields of modern science and no doubt discussed many details. But Locke's role as a collaborator on the project was to remain focused on vital details, including drafting the Fundamental Constitutions of Carolina and the initial "instructions" to colonists on how Carolina was to be settled. The two men named this comprehensive body of the work the Grand Model.

Locke was the principal drafter of the detailed instructions on how Charleston was to be laid out (a city plan) and how it was to be linked to the surrounding region (a regional plan). Locke thus became not only the chief planner for Carolina but also the first city planner (in the modern use of the term) in the history of English-speaking North America. That remarkable distinction is, of course, overshadowed by his later contributions to philosophy. As a philosopher concerned with knowledge and perception (epistemology) he became the founder of a school of philosophy known as British Empiricism. As a political philosopher, he challenged the entrenched belief that society is inherently paternalistic. In *Two Treatises of Government*, which he began writing while working with Ashley Cooper, he so thoroughly demolished the argument for patriarchal government that he earned an honored place in precipitating the Age of Enlightenment and western liberalism.

Most of the American Founders were strongly influenced by Locke. The Declaration of Independence draws its political philosophy from *Two Treatises*, and phrases such as "life, liberty, and the pursuit of happiness" were derived directly from Locke's work. Locke's argument that all humans are born equal in a state of nature profoundly changed perceptions of the nature of government and helped bring about modern democracy.[5]

Ashley Cooper and Locke on Slavery and Native Rights

Anthony Ashley Cooper, the first Earl of Shaftesbury, was steeped in a rigidly hierarchical "gothic" (or feudal) society, and so it comes as no surprise that he projected a class pyramid much like that described in Aristotle's *Politics* on

Carolinian society. Where he was progressive for his time was in framing a constitutional government that he believed would provide reciprocal benefits of all classes, and in codifying basic religious freedoms that could not be usurped by the government (as he believed had occurred in European states allied with the Catholic Church). While serfs and enslaved people would be subject to the absolute authority of their masters, they would remain free to practice their religion of choice, within an acceptable range, and they would enjoy security associated with stability. While Ashley Cooper's worldview would soon be made obsolete by the Enlightenment, particularly his protégé's contribution to it, exposure to that worldview undeniably accelerated Locke's progress toward an entirely new concept of government.

In the view of many scholars, Ashley Cooper bears a second burden of guilt on top of his explicit legalization of slavery. It has been widely accepted doctrine that he and Locke saw America as devoid of civilization and thus subject to the principle of *vacuum domicilium* (literally "empty dwelling"), a legal and moral rationale for conquest and taking possession of lands occupied by indigenous peoples. Other scholars question this, finding the Lords Proprietors clear in their desire to protect Native rights and nurture harmonious relationships with Indigenous nations. The political scientist Paul Corcoran has argued that Ashley Cooper and Locke were well aware of fifty years of history of negotiating legal contracts with Native Americans for land rights, considering them "neighbors," and had no intention of seizing Native lands. Even in the precolonial period, dating back more than a century, the interactions of Raleigh and other explorers were conducted within the bounds of established law, not overreach founded on cultural superiority. With regard to Locke, in particular, Corcoran finds that he was well-educated on the subject of exploration and settlement of America, having 195 volumes in his library on related subjects, and assertions that he provided the intellectual justification for conquest suffer from "evidentiary lacunae." A full reading of Locke's *Second Treatise of Government*, particularly the later chapters, makes it clear that he would never want to "extinguish native rights to property and possession."[6]

One of the great mysteries about Locke's role in planning Carolina is the extent to which he willingly designed a colony with slavery at the base of its social pyramid. *Two Treatises* begins with an explicit condemnation of slavery, written during or only shortly after Locke's association with Ashley Cooper. Historians take various positions in assessing Locke on this apparent contradiction, ranging from accusations of hypocrisy to assertions of the rapid evolution of political philosophy. Careful study of Locke's role in Carolina offers fertile prospects for understanding his ultimate intent.[7]

Locke's role as friend, colleague, and, to some extent, informal secretary to Ashley Cooper was transformed to formal status as secretary to the Lords Proprietors in 1668, a position he held until 1675. He maintained an interest in the colony after that and was frequently involved with the Proprietors on an advisory basis. Over the thirty years of his involvement, five versions of the Fundamental Constitutions were formally adopted by the Lords Proprietors.[8]

Locke's full-time engagement with Ashley Cooper and the Lords Proprietors ended in 1675, the same year Ashley Cooper fell out of favor with the government. Locke went to France that year, where he remained until 1679. In 1682 Ashley Cooper went into exile in Holland and died a short time later. Locke went into exile the next year. He returned to England with William and Mary in 1689 following the Glorious Revolution that sent James II (brother and successor of Charles II) into exile. Locke became an official of the new government, in which capacity he administered affairs related to colonial trade, thereby becoming engaged with Carolina again, at the very time its export economy became to show great promise. Recent evidence suggests that in his new capacity under the new regime he may have attempted to reverse the policies that enabled slavery in Carolina.[9]

Ashley Cooper and Locke as Proto-Scientists

The anthropologist Andrew Agha postulates that the founding of Carolina coincided with a new age of scientific inquiry. Ashley Cooper and Locke were both members of the Royal Society, founded in 1660, and they were disciples of the modern scientific method advanced by Francis Bacon. A month after rechartering Carolina in March 1663, Charles II rechartered The Royal Society of London as the Royal Society of London for the Improvement of Natural Knowledge. The new Royal Society charter aimed to advance the nation scientifically and expand its empire through a paradigm of "improvement" driven by experimental science. According to Agha, Carolina was reconceived in that light and designed by its planners as an experimental colony, the first such enterprise in the British Empire.[10]

Ashley Cooper's Carolina plantation, St. Giles Kussoe, became an experimental agrarian enterprise in two ways, first as an agricultural research center, then indirectly as a social science experiment that, Agha surmises, led to the development of Locke's labor theory of property. Hypotheses regarding crops, animal husbandry, organization, and labor were formulated and tested. As active members of the newly created Royal Society, Ashley Cooper and Locke viewed the colony as part of the larger laboratory of invention for imperial advancement.[11]

The intellectual challenges in planning the colony and implementing its settlement informed Locke's philosophical investigations and became part of the fulcrum of thought that launched the "long eighteenth century" (a period beginning in the 1660s) and the Enlightenment. It is, of course, deeply ironic that tenets of the Enlightenment and the creation of modern democracy would have any connection with Carolina, with its gothic (feudal) class structure and codification of slavery. On the one hand, we have Locke writing, "Every freeman of Carolina shall have absolute power and authority over his Negro slaves." On the other hand, only a few years later, we have him writing, "Slavery is so vile and miserable an estate of man, and so directly opposite to the generous temper and courage of our nation; that it is hardly to be conceived, that an Englishman, much less a gentleman, should plead for it."[12]

St. Giles Kussoe not only enforced slavery, it also sought to perfect through experimentation the system of slavery that would maximize property owner benefits. In this system of innovation, Agha reports, "the enslaved were coerced to become research technicians trapped within the prison of the plantation laboratory." From the earliest stages, enslaved Africans were selected to work on the plantation, based on their skill sets. Agha argues from convincing evidence that specific African labor skills were harnessed in conjunction with technological advancement sought for the colonies. As English "improvers" learned more about Africa and Africans, their demands for labor became more geographically refined, eventually focusing on the rice-growing coastal region of West Africa.[13]

Agha developed his thesis through extensive cross-disciplinary research, integrating findings in the colonial archives and recent archaeological research, diving deeply into the intellectual milieu of London and Oxford of the 1660s, and closely studying the relationship between Ashley Cooper and Locke. All this was done in collaboration with contemporary authorities on Locke and in cooperation with the Twelfth Earl of Shaftesbury and those he had assembled to study the record of Ashley Cooper's extended legacy.

Locke as City Planner

Locke was indisputably the administrative coordinator and chief planner for Carolina between 1666 and 1675, and again in 1682. Characterizing him as the colony's chief planner is based on his role in preparing drafts of the Fundamental Constitutions and his subsequent planning directives, or "instructions," which were in his handwriting. Additional notes on regional planning were found among his papers at Oxford.[14]

Locke's role as chief planner included drafting detailed design instructions for the layout of Charleston as a riverfront capital city. His urban design standards, as noted earlier, became the first comprehensive city plan in English-speaking America and a model for an emerging English empire (the term "British Empire" applies after the Acts of Union united England and Scotland under one king in 1707). The plan for Charleston became a notable influence on the plan for Savannah, founded sixty-three years later.

The first colonists were aware that city planning was an important part of the Grand Model being implemented by the Lords Proprietors. According to colonist Maurice Matthews, Charleston was laid out to "avoid the . . . irregularities" of other American settlements. Practical considerations, however, took a severe toll on Locke's detailed design specifications.[15]

The centerpiece of the Grand Model and its structuring document was the Fundamental Constitutions of Carolina. The Fundamental Constitutions, drafted by Locke under Ashley Cooper's supervision, was much more than a basic framework for government. It also provided frameworks for city and regional planning, the economy of the province, the practice of religion, and the gothic class structure of the colony. Detailed "instructions" on how to implement the Fundamental Constitutions made up the other elements that in totality comprised the Grand Model. All of the initial instructions were drafted by Locke, again acting under the supervision of Ashley Cooper.

The Fundamental Constitutions

Before discussing the details of Locke's city and regional plan, a brief discussion of the Fundamental Constitutions will provide context. The now archaic use of the word "constitutions" in the plural should be taken by today's reader to mean "articles." The document was one constitution, as the term is used today, that contained 120 articles, or "constitutions." It was probably the most detailed constitution ever written up to that time, and it contains more words (8,086) than the U.S. Constitution and all its amendments.[16]

The Fundamental Constitutions is an essential piece in understanding the political culture that formed in and around Charleston, one that eventually spread across the South. It appears on the surface that the document was largely ignored by the first generation of colonists and scrapped by those who came later. But a deeper investigation reveals that its feudal class structure, in particular, left a permanent imprint on the colony.[17]

The Fundamental Constitutions established a "palatinate," a domain governed by a nobleman, the palatine, who held special autonomy to control a frontier territory. The palatine model was originally used by William the Conqueror to create an administrative unit on the unstable Scottish frontier. The word "palatine" came from the Latin *palatium*, meaning "palace." The Fundamental Constitutions specified that the palatine presiding over Carolina was to be the eldest of the Lords Proprietors. The hereditary nobility of Carolina held the power to raise (promote) other aristocratic landowners to the nobility. The two classes of non-hereditary nobility specified in the Fundamental Constitutions were "landgrave" and "cacique."[18]

Although the palatine and the other seven Proprietors, along with landgraves and caciques, held a large share of governing authority, the province was envisioned by Ashley Cooper to be a model republic (but a gothic republic, since the idea of a modern democratic republic had not yet been conceived). Sixty percent of land was allocated to common landowners, "freemen" (presumably the yeoman stratum of the gothic social hierarchy), and those owning six hundred acres or more (the gentry). Collectively these social groups were qualified to hold forty-eight seats in the colony's parliament, whereas the hereditary and lower nobility would have forty-four.[19]

Land was to be allocated "amongst the people so that in setting out and planting the lands, the balance of the government may be preserved." The historian Thomas Leng concluded that the allocation of three-fifths of the land to freemen was intended to create a large class of farmers, thereby establishing "agrarian balance" and avoiding the sort of imbalance that had developed in Virginia where the landowning aristocracy was at cross purposes with a powerful merchant class. The concept of agrarian balance, or agrarian equality, was a central idea behind the constitution, one that was developed even further in Oglethorpe's master plan for Georgia.[20]

The Carolina republic, as one can readily discern, was not envisioned to be a democracy. The social fabric created by the Fundamental Constitutions explicitly sought to avoid "erecting a numerous democracy," which was in those days considered "mob rule." The Proprietors' concept of gothic class hierarchy was one of the elements retained by Carolinians long after most of it became obsolete elsewhere among Western societies.

Class structure included two forms of laboring classes, both of which had virtually no civil rights. The "leetmen," also known in gothic societies as vassals, serfs, or villeins, were peasant laborers serving the higher classes. They were to enter Carolina voluntarily and register as members of their class. They were tied to their superiors and required to obtain permission to travel outside of their place of registration. If married, their "masters" were required to allocate a ten-acre garden plot to the couple for which use the couple would be required to pay a share of the produce from the garden as rent.

Below the leetmen were enslaved people, a class that had no civil rights except to practice religion (a feature of the constitution included at Locke's instigation). Enslaved people were the property of landowners and could be bought or sold as a commodity. The constitution stated, "Every freeman of Carolina shall have absolute power and authority over his negro slaves, of what opinion or religion soever." Enslavement of people was legal in England at this time, although not common. In Europe, slavery was supported by the theological doctrine known as the Great Chain of Being. Mass enslavement in the form that later came to Charleston and the Carolina Lowcountry, was *not* envisioned under the Fundamental Constitutions. The colony began as a society with enslaved people (common throughout history) but not a *slave society* dependent on enslaved labor (far less common).[21]

Charlestonians today refer to "the Grand Modell" (preferring the archaic spelling with "ll") not in the sense used by the Proprietors but simply as the old planned area of the city (now an elite and touristy neighborhood) south of Broad Street. While the area south of Tradd Street between Meeting Street and Lenwood Boulevard, in particular, retains some of the elements of the original plan, the idea that there is a plan of historical significance is flimsy at best. The faint vestige of the original plan, although notable, does not rise to the level of significance that one finds in Savannah's Oglethorpe Plan. The comparison is expanded in the next chapter.

Locke's City and Regional Plan

Locke's initial instructions to the first colonists amounted to a fifteen-point list. Four points pertained to land planning. These directed colonists to 1) establish the capital city within a twelve-thousand-acre "square"; 2) lay out six adjoining squares for "colonies" where "the people" might farm, each one with a town where they would live; 3) provide additional twelve-thousand-acre "squares" for signories and baronies (that is, plantations for the nobility); and 4) allocate individual riverfront lots to freemen such that those lots were at least five times deeper than the width fronting the river. The intent of the last regulation was to maximize the number of freemen with riverfront lots and prevent control of river access from falling

Structure of the Carolina Colony	
Counties	750,000 square miles
Squares	40 per county
Colonies	24 squares per county
Signories	8 squares per county
Baronies	8 squares per county
Towns	1 per colony

Source: Wilson, *Ashley Cooper Plan*

into the hands of a few. Nothing was said in these initial instructions about the design of the town, except that it should be a fort.[22]

Instructions written in May 1671 offered additional detail for both city and regional planning. Procedures were provided for establishing county boundaries and preventing inefficient growth patterns. Baronies, for example, were required to have at least thirty settlers within seven years of the land being allocated to a member of the nobility, preventing land speculation. Such constraints would prevent the dispersal of settlement experienced in Virginia and elsewhere among the northern colonies. The comparatively systematic approach in Carolina would produce more efficient transportation networks, promote effective communication and governance, and facilitate the defense of the province.

The plan Locke was putting in place drew from the historical practice of "English husbandry." Under that model, family farms coexisted with larger estate farms, growing a mix of crops and raising a variety of domesticated animals. That vision would soon be undermined by settlers from Barbados who were more interested in quick profits than a balanced and sustainable economy. Instead of traditional husbandry, the Barbadians would vigorously pursue a large-scale rice monoculture similar to that of sugar production in the West Indies. The wisdom of the Grand Model in fostering a resilient complex economy as opposed to one reliant on a single crop is taken up in chapter 7.[23]

Locke's planning framework anticipated that most people would live in well-designed towns. Informal settlements that could spread far and wide across the province were not permitted. Each planned town was "to be laid out into large, straight and regular streets, and sufficient room left for a wharf if it be upon a navigable river." Smaller towns in the colonies (populated by yeoman farmers) were to be well planned, like the larger cities, with street grids that were "straight, broad and regular."[24]

The grid of twelve-thousand-acre "squares" (colonies, baronies, and signories), within which counties and towns were organized was to be oriented to the cardinal compass points or as close as possible to them. During the process of laying out all such boundaries, surveyors were advised to "reserve convenient high ways from the colony town to the plantations . . . beyond it, and from one colony town to another."[25]

In the instructions of May 1671, which provided a list of twenty design specifications, Locke referenced an attached "model" layout for Charleston and future towns. The attachment, presumably a detailed drawing, has never been found. However, the framework is clear from the written instructions. Once again he emphasized that streets should be "large, convenient and regular," forming a linear grid of mostly equal-sized blocks. Principal streets were to be eighty feet wide, and "back streets" or alleys associated with them were to be forty feet. Secondary street width was set at sixty feet, with back streets thirty feet wide. The street grid would form squares of six hundred feet on each side. Locke was presumably influenced in drafting these specifications by the effort to widen and standardize London's streets after the Great Fire of 1666.[26]

Lots associated with principal streets were standardized at 75 feet by 280 feet, while those for secondary streets were 60 feet by 285 feet. In a block of the larger lots, there would be a total of sixteen lots, or eight per block face (i.e., those facing the same street). In a block of the smaller lots, there would be a total of twenty lots, or ten per block face. The hereditary noblemen of Carolina would each have a five-acre town lot. That size of lot would not fit evenly within the standard street grid, so it seems likely that Locke's lost "model" showed how those lots would have been accommodated within the city grid.

The South of Broad historic enclave was laid out when these specifications were in force, and it originally bore some resemblance to Locke's plan. Today there is little resemblance to the original plan, despite the sense that the "Grand Modell" underlies that area of the city. Blocks are rectangular or irregular in shape rather than square, a consequence of overriding the plan in favor of immediate needs such as drainage ditches. They vary in length, with some blocks ranging from about 500 feet to considerably more than 600 feet, while others are in the 220 feet to 440 feet range.

Locke's regular grid thus devolved into irregular blocks, some of which were non-rectangular, bounded by oddly angled and curved streets. Street widths also vary greatly, ranging from sixty feet to twenty-five feet, with forty feet being common (including sidewalks). The many narrow streets can accommodate only a single lane of one-way traffic with parking and sidewalks.

Locke's Layout of Charleston	
Blocks	600 feet x 600 feet
Principal streets	80 feet wide
Principal lanes	40 feet wide
Secondary streets	60 feet wide
Secondary lanes	30 feet wide
Principal lots	75 feet x 280 feet
Secondary lots	60 feet x 285 feet
Source: Wilson, *Ashley Cooper Plan*	

Today the visual effect of the narrower streets, often lined with high walls, is in places more like that of an unplanned medieval city than the modern planned city foreseen in Locke's model. The effect, however, can be charming and intriguing. Curving and angular streets present little surprises to the visitor, adding to the sense of Charleston being a special city from another time.

Where there was river frontage, Locke wrote, "Nobody shall build a house within eighty feet of the low water mark, but it shall constantly be left for a wharf for the public use of the town." The intent was to prevent overdevelopment that would impede access and create health and safety issues. Once again, the precedent for this concern was set in the regulations that followed the Great Fire of 1666. The City of London established a forty-foot buffer along much of the Thames in which building was prohibited.[27]

Locke provided for a large common of two hundred acres. It would be used initially to plant family gardens. Once sufficient produce was available from outlying farms, the common would be used for raising cattle. Then, after a period of twenty-one years, residents of Charleston would be free to determine future uses of the common, such as "exercise of the people, enlargement, or any other conveniences of the said town as occasion shall require." Freeholders entitled to a home lot in Charleston were also entitled to an "out lot" for their family garden. The total acreage of the home lot and the out lot was limited to 5 percent of the total land grant to which the freeholder was entitled. So, if their land grant from the Lords Proprietors was one hundred acres, their house lot and out lot combined could not exceed five acres.[28]

To prevent land speculation, those owning and living in a house in Charleston were permitted to build additional houses but were required to build within twelve months of taking possession of a lot. Furthermore, any such additional houses had to be substantial structures of at least thirty feet in length, sixteen feet in width, and two stories in height ("besides garrets").[29]

No serious effort was made, apparently, to implement Locke's design at Charleston's (Charles Town's) original site on the south bank of the Ashley River. The Lords Proprietors and the colonial council recognized it as a less accessible, unhealthful, and potentially hazardous location. After a few years of scoping out prospects, they identified a permanent site for the town on Oyster Point at the confluence of the Ashley and Cooper Rivers. A layout for the town was drawn up in 1672 by the surveyor-general, John Culpepper, following Locke's specifications (and presumably the "model" layout sent by Locke the previous year). The first town lots, however, were not allocated until 1679, and relocation of the town was not completed until 1680. Even though the West Ashley site was outside city limits until recently, the founding date of Charleston has long been recognized as 1670 rather than 1680.[30]

Locke's Grand Model continues to be referenced today in describing Charleston's historic plan, particularly a large portion of the South of Broad neighborhood, as noted earlier. However, various later surveys, including major efforts in 1723 and 1746, resulted in wholesale alterations to the original design.[31]

The Palimpsest of the Grand Model

The Grand Model left a permanent mark, if only a palimpsest, on Carolina. Just as it was many things for many purposes—a constitution, a socioeconomic system, and a comprehensive plan for development—it also had many influences. It shaped southern political culture, it reinforced chattel slavery, and it created an American planning tradition. Many historians have dismissed the influence of Carolina in shaping the American South as secondary to that of Virginia, but many scholars who have closely examined early Carolina history argue otherwise.[32]

South Carolina, with Charleston as its nerve center, was muscular and assertive, whereas, in contrast, Virginia was cerebral and diplomatic. Together they forged the South, populating it with their descendants and perpetuating slave culture. But South Carolina's progeny were uniformly committed to the project of building an ever-growing empire of slavery, whereas many Virginians, including Abraham Lincoln's parents, sought to escape from a dark future they saw for that slave society.

So how did a plan that was largely scuttled influence future development in Carolina? Setting aside social and political influences for the present, and looking primarily at settlement and land development, it is clear that the Grand Model got off to a good start. Land was surveyed, allocated, and then developed largely as intended. A compact development pattern emerged in which Charleston held a prominent central position.

When the Thirteen Colonies declared their independence in 1776, Virginia had a population of well over half a million people, far more than any other colony. South Carolina, in comparison, had fewer than a quarter-million. The free population of Virginia was more than three times that of Carolina. Yet, from the Revolutionary era to the Civil War, Carolina exerted an influence far larger than its actual size. The magic behind its power was the wealth and vibrancy of its capital, Charleston, magic derived from the Grand Model.

Virginia was initially settled by investors who were required to form groups known as "hundreds," a hundred being an ancient unit capable of fielding one hundred soldiers. As practiced in the colony, hundreds were smaller groups merely capable of supporting and defending a plantation. Later, the colony was organized into "citties," shires, and eventually counties. While each of these reorganizations was aimed at improving governance and communication, the lack of an overall settlement plan, as asserted earlier, inhibited the growth of the capital city and other central places.

In Carolina, as in Virginia, plantation complexes competed with towns as centers of social and economic activity. Large plantations were in many ways like company towns, and so their existence slowed the natural formation of additional towns and cities. However, in Carolina, the principal city was by design highly accessible. By contrast, Virginia's earliest principal city, Jamestown, failed to mature since lack of planning led to scattered and disorganized development. Its second principal city and new capital as of 1699, Williamsburg, also lacked the regional connectivity of Charleston.

Settlement in Virginia was dispersed, fanned out over the 405-mile-long Potomac River, the northernmost of Virginia's principal rivers; the 195-mile-long Rappahannock River; the 35-mile long, estuarine York River; and the 100-mile-long James River. Virginia's plantations became even more scattered during the eighteenth century. Monticello was 125 miles as the crow flies from Williamsburg (the capital from 1699 to 1779) and seventy miles from the subsequent, more-central capital of Richmond. South Carolina plantations were clustered within thirty miles of Charleston, with secondary centers at Beaufort and Georgetown, each only fifty miles distant. Those secondary centers were on the coast and thus had both ocean access to the capital as well as overland routes.

climate

In addition to the influence exerted by the Grand Model, South Carolina's compactness and Charleston's centrality were also a product of its subtropical climate. The location of the city at the tip of a peninsula, facing the Atlantic, was often airier than the sultry plantations. But it was not only the heat that drove the plantation elite to the city. Malaria, yellow fever, and other diseases were prevalent in the rice-growing wetlands surrounding plantations. Many of the elite summered in healthier places such as Newport, Rhode Island, but Charleston was where they conducted their business affairs before leaving and upon return. The elite also enjoyed the city for its various cultural and leisure activities, including concerts, theatrical performances, balls, horse races, and cockfighting.[33]

Savannah followed the pattern established by Charleston. The Oglethorpe Plan, the model for Georgia town and regional planning, was influenced by Locke's plan for Carolina. But perhaps more importantly, Georgia became a social and economic satellite of South Carolina in the mid-1750s, adopting the pattern of compact development around Savannah. Some rice plantations were so close to the city that they became a threat to public health (as illustrated in the map on page 154. A cordon was established around the city in the early 1800s, and rice fields within it were drained.[34]

Charleston and Savannah were among the largest and most prosperous cities in the South during the late colonial period and the early decades of the United States. Many influences contributed to their success, but city planning was arguably chief among them. That planning legacy remains a key piece in their emergence as small but prosperous cities of the twenty-first century.

The sense of being a historic planned city has long contributed to Charleston's planning ethic. That sense has made the city supportive of advances in infrastructure and, in more recent times, zoning and historic preservation. Yet narrow streets and alleys and misalignments in the grid crept through the city, and, as it grew, the city became "notoriously crowded and dirty," prompting speculators to lay out several new suburbs in the 1780s.[35]

In the late 1850s, the city laid brick sidewalks with stone curb and gutter, greatly improving the lives of pedestrians. Much of the city was destroyed in the great fire of 1861, which covered 540 acres and burned down 575 homes and other structures. By the late 1870s, the city grid had over fifty-three miles of streets, one-third of which were paved with stones or shells (an all-purpose construction material in the Lowcountry). Sanitary infrastructure, although desperately needed, came later. Vast quantities of excreta produced daily were leaching into the soil, contaminating wells. In 1880, over 80 percent of city wells were contaminated, leading the mayor to call for a sewer system.[36]

The city's historic preservation movement began in 1920 when the city's elite met to discuss plans for the demolition of historic homes. They founded the Charleston Society for the Preservation of Old Dwellings, which became the Preservation Society of Charleston in 1957. Charleston adopted a zoning ordinance to protect the historic district in 1929 and amended it in 1931 to designate a twenty-three-square-block area as Old and Historic Charleston, the first such ordinance in the United States. At the same time, it established a Board of Architectural Review and became a national model for historic preservation.

Charleston remained a city of sharp contrasts from its founding to well into the twentieth century. At mid-century, the city was among the most blighted in the nation. Forty-nine percent of its houses had no indoor toilet, comparing unfavorably to the national average of 18 percent. Federal Housing Administration funding paid for the demolition of 350 structures and repair of more than 900 others. The mayor was able to announce that "slum areas are fast being erased."[37]

Earlier, in 1944, preservationists had published *This Is Charleston*, the nation's first citywide architectural survey. Surveys of architectural resources are routine in determining whether an area qualifies for recognition as a National Historic Landmark District or other protected status under state or federal statute. The convergence of protection of high-quality properties and improvement of low-income and moderate-income housing set Charleston on a course to its present status as one of America's premier historic cities.[38]

The Modern Vision for Charleston

The rise of Charleston from a struggling city mired in the Jim Crow era to the city it is today began with the election of Joe Riley as mayor in 1975. City planning was one of Mayor Riley's chief concerns. His overarching vision was one of an intensive commercial core, stable neighborhoods that nurtured unique characteristics, and a waterfront city perimeter with attractions for tourists and residents alike. Riley's transformation of Charleston began by securing a federal Urban Development Action Grant in 1978 for Charleston Center, a key piece in developing the urban core. Riley's biographer, Brian Hicks, a reporter with the *Charleston Post and Courier*, describes a relentless quest by the mayor to transform his city into what it is today through consensus-building, long-range planning, zoning amendments, partnerships, grants, and essential land acquisition.

In general, Riley's vision for the city bore little resemblance to that of Locke and the Lords Proprietors. However, some of the tenets of modern planning that fall under the headings "sustainable development" and "smart growth" were common denominators of Riley's vision and the Grand Model. Both emphasized developing a vibrant urban core, preserving waterfront access, and investing in regional connectivity for maximum synergy between the city center, its suburbs, and its hinterland.

The city adopted its first comprehensive plan, the "Charleston 2000 Plan," in 1991. A comprehensive plan is a policy document that places zoning within the larger context of a strategic vision for the future of a community. Zoning is the legal instrument through which local governments regulate the use of land and design of developments, theoretically in a manner consistent with the comprehensive plan. In 1994, near the middle of Riley's forty-year span as mayor, South Carolina enacted a law requiring cities and counties with zoning ordinances to adopt a comprehensive plan. In 2000, pursuant to the new state law, Charleston adopted the "Century V City Plan," which replaced the 1991 plan and complied with the 1994 law. The new plan provided an updated assessment of past growth and development, an analysis of current trends, and a set of goals and policies to guide future development for a period of ten years. In 2010 the city adopted a new Century V Plan consistent with the vision advocated by Mayor Riley and widely supported throughout the community.

Eight years after adopting the original Century V Plan in 2000, Charleston adopted a companion document specifically aimed at preserving the city's historic character. Titled *Vision | Community | Heritage: A Preservation Plan for Charleston*, the plan provided a detailed policy framework for preservation not only in the city's historic districts on the peninsula but also on James Island, John's Island, and the Cainhoy Peninsula. The new preservation plan replaced the preservation plan adopted in 1974, which had long been considered a national model.

The planning framework established by these two synergistic documents is remarkably similar to that of the Grand Model. The Grand Model consisted of a detailed policy document, the Fundamental Constitutions, and a set of "Agrarian Laws" and other "instructions" that collectively provided a strategic vision for growth and development as well as policies and strategies for achieving that vision. The core principles then were fundamentally those in effect today: to create vibrant central places that promote civility, ensure that outlying areas are well-connected to urban areas, and preserve areas beyond for orderly future growth.

If the Century V Plan and the preservation plan are to be criticized at all, it is in not invoking the Grand Model, in its broadest sense, as part of the city's heritage. It is understandable that city planners would not wish to shine a light on the Grand Model's deep flaws—provision for slavery and regulation of religion. However, many more of the principles codified by Ashley Cooper and Locke were visionary and laudable. For a city that is so closely tied to its past, this is its one glaring omission.

Charleston's unique blend of seemingly medieval streets, proto-Enlightenment design, and modern planning as fashioned by Mayor Riley makes it one of America's most exciting cities. If Charleston were to formally acknowledge the Grand Model as an inspiration for the future, the way Savannah recognizes the Oglethorpe Plan as a guiding light, its planning and design ethic would be complete.

CHAPTER SIX

Savannah
The Charleston Plan with Enlightenment Idealism

Charleston and Savannah are popular tourist destinations in part because they were planned cities. Charleston's impressive original plan was largely overwritten by later development, but its many narrow streets lined with a blend of architecturally significant buildings make it an irresistible destination. Savannah is fundamentally different. It retained nearly all the elements of the original plan, and, while it also possesses a unique architectural heritage, it is the *combination* of the city's public spaces and built environment that deeply impresses visitors to the city.

Where Charleston seems faintly like a medieval city when one walks its narrower, oddly aligned streets, Savannah seems like a product of Enlightenment rationality, one in which Isaac Newton would see mathematical order and harmony. In fact, such impressions are real: the planners of Charleston sought to transcend a gothic, medieval past, but the town lapsed back into it, whereas the designers of Savannah were firmly committed to the new, scientific era, the Age of Enlightenment, ushered in by Newton and Locke.

Residents of both cities are happily suspended in a state of perpetual admiration of their surroundings, and rightly so (although that could change if current threats presented herein are not addressed). Charleston residents were the first in the nation to create an effective architectural preservation program, and the city's architectural heritage remains proudly guarded. Savannah residents are also zealous about their architectural heritage, but it is the Oglethorpe Plan that is their greater source of pride. For Savannahians, the city's architecture and its plan are two different but interdependent aspects of its special charm. A third essential feature of the Savannah gestalt is its urban forest, which was made possible by the generous and orderly allocation of open space by the plan.

When Savannahians refer to the Oglethorpe Plan they often mean Oglethorpe's plan for the wards of downtown Savannah. The Oglethorpe Plan, however, was much greater in scale and ambition. Like Carolina's

Grand Model, it was a plan for an entire colony with comprehensive design guidelines for the layout of towns, regions, and villages (but without the plan of governance laid out by the Fundamental Constitutions). Oglethorpe built into the plan a form of social organization that provided both civil and defensive organization. To establish agrarian equality, he limited the amount of land allocated to any individual or family to prevent the amassing of property that would ultimately lead to inequities. Thus, the Oglethorpe Plan and the Grand Model were both much greater in scope than most Savannah and Charleston residents and visitors currently ascribe to them.

Oglethorpe's Milieu and the Origin of the Plan

James Edward Oglethorpe was the son of Eleanor and Theophilus Oglethorpe, senior employees of King Charles II and King James II. He was educated at Oxford, leaving early to take formal military training in Paris. He left Paris to serve as aide-de-camp to the brilliant military strategist Prince Eugene, who was fighting the Turks in the Balkans. Upon returning to England he was elected to Parliament, where he formed a circle of reform-minded associates and tackled the issues of the day.

While chair of a parliamentary committee investigating prison conditions, Oglethorpe became convinced that a colony in America would offer new hope to people who had been imprisoned for debt. That aim soon expanded, and his colonial vision became one more broadly directed toward relief of the "worthy poor" of England as well as persecuted Protestants throughout Europe. In addition, as explained earlier, several other goals were added to the project, including creating a buffer colony to protect affluent South Carolina, to increase trade, and to implement the theoretical concept of agrarian equality.

The breadth of Oglethorpe's knowledge and experience enabled him to conceive a unique, multifaceted plan. In formulating its details he was aided by talented and influential associates who shared his political and humanitarian views and brought wide-ranging expertise to the table. Among those who contributed materially or intellectually to the emerging plan were John Percival (later Earl of Egmont), an MP and close friend of Queen Caroline; George Berkeley, the famous philosopher for whom Berkeley, California is named; Sir Hans Sloane, president of the Royal Society succeeding Isaac Newton; Stephen Hales, scientist and inventor; John Burton, the lecturer at Oxford who introduced the study of Locke to the curriculum; and John Pine, the cartographer and engraver who likely laid out the original plan for the town of Savannah.

Some of those within Oglethorpe's circle would become members of the Trustees for the Establishment of the Colony of Georgia in America (the Georgia Trustees), while others would consult peripherally as advisors. It was essential for Oglethorpe to construct an organization of multilayered and overlapping groups to carry out his objectives. While some of those he recruited to the Georgia Trustees shared his values and political goals, he needed others who had leverage within government, technical knowledge of how to organize a colony, influence within the Church of England, and, among the wealthy, the ability to garner charitable contributions.

The new colony to the south of Carolina was approved by George II, for whom it was named in 1732. Oglethorpe's friend, John Percival, was appointed president. Funds were secured from Parliament to launch the venture. A significant bundle of private charitable funding was also garnered. With resources in hand to launch the project, Oglethorpe surprised the other Trustees by announcing that he would lead the first contingent of colonists to Georgia and depart England by the end of the year.

Oglethorpe had done considerable research necessary to create a settlement plan for the new colony. When the Georgia Trustees were formally created, he had already written *Some Account of the Design of the Trustees for establishing Colonys in America*, a detailed study of colonial planning practices, methods of recruiting and organizing colonists, and city planning. His next step was to create a detailed design for Savannah and its hinterland that would also serve as a model for other towns in Georgia. The original drawing, long sought by scholars, has never been located, but reproductions and revised versions were made later by colonial surveyors. The last, shown on page 148, is dated 1797, apparently after the great fire of late 1796 (the Library of Congress holds a contemporaneous map of blocks destroyed by fire). It appears (from the many alterations and palimpsests) to be the last version of the original layout before surveyors completely redrew the plan in the early 1800s.

Oglethorpe's sources for the design components of the Savannah plan remain a mystery. The Trustees specifically acknowledged a debt to Ashley Cooper and Locke in developing their own plan, but they did not specify which details they adapted for Georgia. Other influences may have come from Oglethorpe's military training (which included the study of Roman garrisons and city planning), knowledge among the Trustees of Renaissance designs for "ideal cities" by Da Vinci and others, and the layout of Hannover Square and other contemporary designs in London. Which of these and perhaps other influences was of greatest influence remains unknown.[1]

Some scholars have criticized Oglethorpe and the Georgia Trustees for not including a representative form of government for the colony in their design similar to the Fundamental Constitutions. Oglethorpe and his circle of associates appear to have thought through that possibility and rejected it out of concern that a potentially dangerous frontier would, at least initially, require a more top-down form of organization. Oglethorpe was the prime civil and defense authority in the colony. Appointed officials such as constables and magistrates maintained order. "Tythingmen" appointed for each ten households (constituting a tything) would represent the interests of that unit and also act as a unit leader in the colony's militia. The plan was thus drafted with integrated civil and military elements befitting a frontier colony. The town's spacious squares served as grounds for drilling militia units as well as places for markets and public gatherings.

Historical Context

When Savannah was founded in 1733, Charleston was a mature and flourishing city. Georgia's founders envisioned their capital as smaller and less mercantile than the southern coast's mother city. Savannah was similar in layout, however. Its plan drew inspiration from Charleston's original town grid and its compact and efficient regional plan. While Savannah would be Georgia's capital, it would primarily serve Georgia's yeoman farmers, consciously avoiding unchecked growth and accompanying social ills plaguing cities of the Old World. In that way, it was set on a very different course from that of Charleston.

Limiting the size of Savannah, and all other cities in Georgia, was especially important to Oglethorpe. Having chaired the parliamentary investigation into prison conditions, he saw London and the other great cities of Europe as places of moral decay, disease, and endemic poverty. Oglethorpe's friend and political ally Viscount John Percival, who became president of the Georgia Trustees, served with him on the prison committee and shared his social philosophy. Percival was close to the intellectual Queen Caroline (the brains behind the throne) and recorded a conversation with her in his famous diary in which he argued, "Populous towns have more roguery than little ones, for here men may hide it, but when men lived more in the country, as in former times, there was not the knowledge how to cheat, neither the temptation, nor the opportunity given."[2]

The view of cities as places of despair and moral decay was portrayed by the painter William Hogarth, who shared Oglethorpe's concern for social reform and painted a scene of the prison committee conducting an inquiry at the notorious Fleet Prison. Hogarth produced a series of works depicting urban social degradation, including *The Harlot's Progress* (1731), a series of six paintings, and *A Rake's Progress* (1733), a series of eight paintings. The paintings were contemporaneous with the conception of Georgia and the planning of Savannah. Oglethorpe, for his part, was painting on the canvas of the New World (as many were thinking of the Americas) in creating a city that would avoid the moral pitfalls of those in the "Old World," a city that would be small healthy, and tied to the land around it, not divorced from it.

By contrast, urban problems seemed less acute when Charleston was founded, and there was optimism about the future of London in particular. While the planning and rebuilding of the metropolis after the Great Fire of 1666 failed to achieve any of its grander visions, the city nevertheless was healthier, less congested, and more economically efficient as a result, at least for a time. Charleston, in contrast to Savannah, was designed and founded when there was a more positive outlook about the future of cities.

Another dramatic difference in historical context is that the Age of Enlightenment had not yet dawned when Charleston was conceived but was flourishing when Savannah was planned and founded. The new age began in 1688–89 with the publication of Locke's *Two Treatises on Government* and Newton's *Principia Mathematica*. Locke began writing *Two Treatises* while working for Ashley Cooper, who was in many ways his mentor but in some respects his opposite. The gothic document he created with Ashley Cooper ran counter to the humanistic principles he was soon to articulate in *Two Treatises*. But the occasion of Locke's engagement with Carolina was premature for asserting the emerging ideals of the Enlightenment, ideals would not gain wide acceptance until the eighteenth century.

The ideals of the Enlightenment are now ingrained in Western civilization, but they were revolutionary in Locke's time. The basic tenets of the age were that all humans are created fundamentally equal, that the universe is governed by laws (by God, perhaps, but not by a whimsical deity), and that reason has unlimited potential to elevate all of humankind. The Oglethorpe Plan was steeped in those principles. As such, it rejected the gross social inequalities assumed by Carolina's Grand Model, even as it drew on the plan's more forward-looking concepts.

Oglethorpe's Savannah Plan

Savannah's famous Oglethorpe Plan had four components: the Plan of Savannah, its best-known component; a regional plan for an area of more than sixty square miles surrounding the town of Savannah; the general plan for the settlement of the Georgia Colony, formally known as the Province of Georgia; and the quasi-martial governance plan discussed earlier, which was patterned on Roman frontier garrison towns.

The plan for Georgia and the design of Savannah were closely tied to political and philosophical principles of the early eighteenth century. The concept of agrarian equality as a means of maintaining a fair and level society through equal land allocation stood at the very heart of the plan. Land grants to nearly all colonists were made in equal fifty-acre allocations. An exception was made for those colonists who could pay their own way to Georgia, but even in those cases the grantees were limited to five hundred acres and required to bring one servant per fifty acres, thereby retaining equality in the allocation ratio. Servants would become yeoman farmers upon completion of service and would then be allocated the standard grant of fifty acres. The fifty-acre unit was thus common to everyone.

The system of agrarian equality thus prohibited amassing land through purchase or inheritance, thereby preventing the rise of a powerful landed class as well as formidable mercantilists. Each fifty-acre yeoman farmer grant consisted of three parts: a town lot of sixty feet by ninety feet, a garden

Oglethorpe's Layout of Savannah	
Ward (neighborhood)	675 ft. x 675 ft.
Tything lots (10 per ward)	60 ft. x 90 ft.
Trust lots (4 per ward)	60 ft. x 180 ft.
Square	270 ft. x 315 ft.
Bisecting streets	75 ft. wide
Lateral streets	37.5 ft. wide
Lanes	22.5 ft. wide

Source: Wilson, *Oglethorpe Plan*

lot of five acres, and a farm lot of forty-five acres (minus the area of the town lot to reach a total of an even fifty acres). In Carolina, by contrast, the basic unit of land allocation for a member of the hereditary nobility was fifteen thousand acres, and 40 percent of all land allocated for plantations was reserved for that upper tier of society. Additionally, thousands of acres were allocated to members of lower tiers of nobility.[3]

The town of Savannah was organized into wards of approximately ten acres. Each ward consisted of a central square surrounded by four civic lots and forty residential lots. The residential lots within each ward were organized into groups of ten and thus called tythings. Each *tything block* was allocated one square mile of farmland, which was divided into twelve farm lots, one for each family in the tithing who had been granted a *tything lot* and two reserved for the Trustees (a charitable trust) as a means of generating income to pay for the cost of governance.

Oglethorpe laid out six wards and allocated surrounding land for a town common, gardens, and farms. Savannah was thus designed as a city for 240 families. Immediately beyond the farms, all of which were allocated to town residents, there was an array of out-lying farm villages capable of supporting several hundred more settlers. The entire planned area fell within a grid of approximately sixty square miles. The fact that the town was encircled and contained by farms and gardens mirroring the ward-tything ownership pattern is a strong indication that the intent of the Georgia Trustees was to keep Savannah small and thereby free of the vice and corruption they associated with large cities.

Soon after the founding of Savannah in 1733, the Trustees formally prohibited slavery, which they viewed as a corrupting influence on the values they hoped to instill in the colony and contrary to the new ideals of their time, the Age of Enlightenment. The initial pragmatic prohibition of slavery evolved into a moral stand, with Oglethorpe, in particular, speaking out against it and eventually embracing abolition as a lifelong concern. Given that Carolina was by then a slave society, this difference became a fundamental source of tension between the colonies, as described earlier.

Plan Implementation

Savannah was founded in February 1733 when Oglethorpe retrieved the first colonists from Fort Frederick, thirty miles to the north, and brought them to the site he had selected for the town of Savannah. The work of laying out and building the town began immediately.

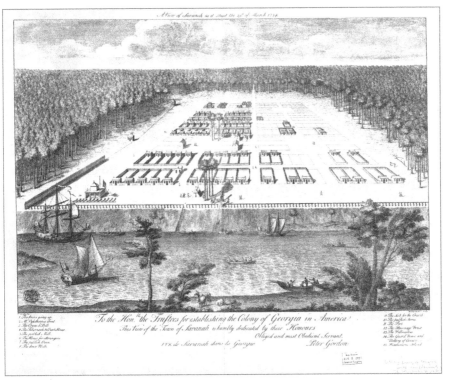

This 1734 drawing, known as the Peter Gordon map,
depicts the town of Savannah after a year of development.
(Prints and Photographs Division, Library of Congress)

The site Oglethorpe had selected for the town was ideally situated on a coastal ridge sixteen miles upriver. The ridge was nearly fifty feet above mean water and almost a mile wide, sufficient to lay out the town according to plan. Furthermore, the ten-mile-long ridge widened to eight miles in the middle, offering more than sufficient land for planned farms and out-lying villages.[4]

Charleston, by contrast, was initially sited in the floodplain of the Ashley River, and even after it was relocated to Oyster Point it remained vulnerable to flooding. While Charleston has flooded many times during hurricanes, Savannah has always remained safely above peak storm surge levels.

Connectivity was also a priority for Oglethorpe, and the high ridge provided ample room for an extensive network of wide public rights of way connecting the region with the town. Each square mile in the grid was bounded by a wide throughway (right of way), the original width of which is unknown but was likely more than 130 feet. Secondary throughways can be seen between farm lots, garden plots, and wards. This network was largely preserved

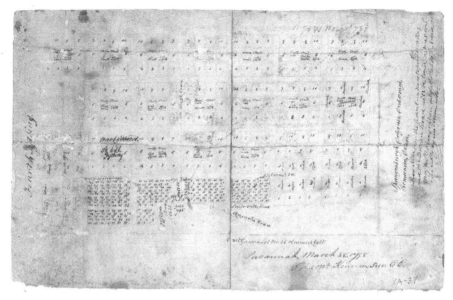

The original plan of Savannah, with surrounding farmlands
and rights-of-way. Although dated 1798, it is likely one of the
earliest plans, updated and overwritten many times.
(Courtesy City of Savannah Municipal Archives)

by future generations and became Savannah's modern street grid as it grew
beyond its historic wards.[5]

Charleston initially developed with fewer roads and greater dependence
on waterways. The Grand Model placed emphasis on locating towns on navigable rivers rather than creating an extensive network of roads. The presumption behind the Grand Model might have been that the very existence of a
planned grid, constructed as required to accommodate growth, would lend
itself to straight and regular roads. If so, there was little follow-through, and
many roads simply followed old trails, cow paths, and informal routes.

Present-day road networks for the two cities reflect the early planning
described above. Major roads ("arterials" to city planners) are linear in Savannah, while they are often curvilinear in Charleston. The grid pattern for secondary roads ("collectors" and "local roads") is generally linear in both cities,
although more regular in Savannah. Savannah developed with a well-defined
grid guiding its growth, whereas Charleston developed with a more ad hoc
network. The pattern reflects Enlightenment influences in the case of Savannah and pre-Enlightenment, gothic influences in the case of Charleston.

As the only person in the Georgia Colony with detailed knowledge of the

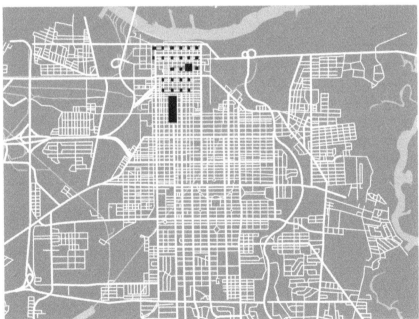

Comparison of the street grids of Charleston (*top*) and
Savannah (*bottom*), revealing the greater regularity of the
latter, attributable to the Oglethorpe Plan.
(Maps by Teri Norris)

plan and the training to carry it out, Oglethorpe's capabilities were spread thin. Initially he focused on implementing the Savannah plan and ensuring that colonists understood its intent and were capable of continuing the work. Soon, however, other demands required his attention, as detailed in chapter 4. He had to return to England to report on progress and secure additional funding from Parliament; when back in the colony, he needed to secure frontier settlement to the south for protection from Spanish invasion; and he needed to shore up the good relations he had initially established with Indigenous nations.

In addition to those critical demands, Oglethorpe had to finesse increasingly strained relations with South Carolina. His good relations with Native Americans put him at cross purposes with Carolina traders accustomed (from the Trustee perspective) to unethical practices. This source of friction added to that over slavery put him at odds with Charleston aristocrats and oligarchs. As if that were not enough, he also faced the ire of Carolina's land-hungry aristocracy over Georgia's restrictions on landownership.

Making matters even more difficult, the Carolinians forged a relationship with disgruntled Savannah colonists, the Malcontents mentioned earlier, for the purpose of increasing pressure to lift the Trustees' prohibitions. The group remained a thorn in Oglethorpe's side for most of the ten-year period he served in the colony. The debate over slavery, in particular, left a lifelong impression on him and shaped his later interest in abolition.

When Oglethorpe returned to England for the fourth and final time in July 1743, the colony was struggling. Arguably, many of its difficulties were orchestrated by Charleston oligarchs who wanted to re-create Georgia in Carolina's image. The Charlestonians ultimately prevailed, but Oglethorpe's legacy was indelible: the remarkably resilient plan for Savannah was set permanently in place, Enlightenment idealism was planted on America's shores, and the region was secured permanently for British America against threats from the Spanish and French.

The Benefits of Planning

Both Savannah and Charleston benefited from plans that emphasized the efficiencies of compactness. The pattern allowed for swift movement of goods to market, facilitated effective government, and created urban centers for vibrant economic coordination as well as intellectual exchanges. Virginia's sprawling development pattern, in contrast, inhibited communication, stifled innovation, and slowed industrialization.

Even though both Georgia and Carolina were essentially rural by design, their settlement patterns were not highly dispersed. Towns were well connected by roadways or waterways to farms and villages in their respective hinterlands. Leapfrog development whereby new towns or villages might form in distant areas was discouraged. Unplanned development was seen as lacking economic synergy and too costly to sustain, requiring a more extensive road network and a larger militia for protection.

The plans for Georgia and Carolina contained principles that are remarkably similar to those of modern "sustainable development." Those principles became ingrained in American city planning and were even found in the nation's early land ordinances promoted by Thomas Jefferson. Principles of sustainable development are sometimes attacked by the Far Right (e.g., by the John Birch Society, which supported Tea Party attacks on sustainable development beginning in 2008) for spurious political reasons, but such plans are in reality part of a long-standing American planning tradition.[6]

Planners today view a nation's cities as "engines of economic growth" and the homes of its "creative class" (think of Silicon Valley). In its present form, sustainable development attempts to reinforce efficiencies that promote or reinforce urban vitality and creativity—features such as a strong downtown and mass transit. To the planners of Carolina and Georgia, agriculture was still one of the strongest sectors of an economy and employed most of the population. Sustainable development and adaptive capacity, or "resilience," therefore, took the form of compact and efficient development patterns linking towns and their ports to agricultural production. The principles were the same as today but applied to the landscape of a less advanced economy.

Cities were newly emerging as engines of economic growth in the eighteenth century, first resulting from global trade then stimulated by the Industrial Revolution. The rapidly growing cities of that time were rife with destitution and depravity. Thomas Jefferson was appalled by cities in the later 1700s as much as Oglethorpe had been in the early-to-mid-1700s. While Jefferson was thoroughly American and of a newer generation, the two men's lives overlapped by forty-two years and they were witness to the same trends and formed similar social philosophies. Virginia like Georgia had the potential to become the yeoman republic of Jefferson's vision, but the literal chains of slavery placed a metaphorical yoke on society that slowed advancement. Georgia's yeoman society envisioned by Oglethorpe struggled under the weight of South Carolina's adjoining slave society; Virginia's yeoman republic could hardly arise from a White population that sought profit through slavery and enslaved more than 30 percent of its people.[7]

Once the Georgia Trustees relinquished their authority over the colony in 1752, wealthy Charleston aristocrats and oligarchs—its merchants and plantation elite—moved in unimpeded to acquire large landholdings to be worked by enslaved laborers. A noble experiment ended, but many features of the Oglethorpe Plan, the Enlightenment-inspired plan for agrarian equality, remained in the design of Savannah and the concepts behind it, paving the way for Savannah to become the exceptional place that it is today.

City Planning after American Independence

Generations of Savannah's leaders recognized the city's founding plan for its exceptional qualities and retained the basic layout for 120 years. A total of twenty-four wards, most anchored by a square, were laid out during that period, all of them fundamentally similar in specifications to Oglethorpe's original six. Today, twenty-two wards retain the design, the remaining two may be restored (entirely or in part), and new wards following the original pattern are envisioned for adjacent, formerly industrial areas.

During the period of expansion to twenty-four wards, Savannah grew from six wards clustered near the river to an area six wards wide and five wards deep. Anomalous wards not counted in that total include two on the east, which were laid out in a grid pattern, three other ward-sized areas on the west that were reconfigured for industrial uses, and one central area set aside for a cemetery during the colonial period. The two anomalous wards to the east (Bartow and Davis, comprising a neighborhood now anchored by the Beach Institute, a school established by the Freedman's Bureau) were among the first areas developed in a conventional rectilinear grid. They were laid out in the 1840s to accommodate African American railroad worker housing. Instead of a potential thirty wards having the original design, twenty-four were laid out in that manner.

By the time Savannah adopted a more conventional grid in the 1850s, the historic pattern had already filled most of the original town common, an area of exactly one square mile. This area represented a growth limit of sorts: most city residents walked just about everywhere they needed to go, whether it was to work or for shopping or visiting. Such a constraint meant that demand for housing and space for businesses was highest within the area of the original common. The city's population thus grew inward more than outward until mobility was increased by streetcars in the late 1800s. Higher density was achieved by splitting Oglethorpe's original sixty-foot lots into two thirty-foot lots or three twenty-foot lots. Multistory buildings constituted another means of accommodating population growth within the walkable city.

Horse-drawn streetcars appeared after the Civil War, spurring growth south of the original common. Electric streetcars appeared in the 1890s, accelerating expansion of the city boundaries. As Savannah grew, it continued using the ward as a unit for planning but without the organizing pattern of the central square. Instead, Forsyth Park was laid out as a larger center of civic space that was also used for militia training. The new park, which resembles a small version of New York's Central Park, was the width of one ward. In depth, it extended southward from the historic wards roughly the equivalent of three additional wards.

Forsyth Park in its initial phase was a botanical garden, and it remains so today. As the park grew, it provided the city with both open space and open fields for recreational uses. In doing so, the city retained its feel of "a city in a forest."

The ethic of cultivating elements of nature in the city became an ingrained trait that continues to the present day. It can be seen in the streetcar suburbs of the 1890s through the 1920s that advertised street gardens as a beautifying element. In the early suburbs of the automobile era of the 1920s and 1930s, large areas of green space emerged as marketing points. Squares, parks, and medians were featured in the popular Crescent and Ardsley Park neighborhoods in particular. The local ethic of blending green space with urbanism is directly traceable to the attractiveness of Oglethorpe's spacious wards.

The beauty of the city, springing from its public squares and wide streets, was periodically enhanced anew. In the 1820s more trees were planted for beautification. In the 1840s author Emily Burke wrote that the city's beautiful trees made it "look like a city built in a forest." The visiting humanist and philanthropist Eleanor Baker wrote of the "very handsome" effect of the city's forest. And around the same time, another writer described Savannah as having "a cool, airy, and rural appearance." Today, as a result of continuous planting and landscape maintenance, Savannah is still renowned for its urban forest.[8]

Savannah's openness as well as its elevation above surrounding wetlands,

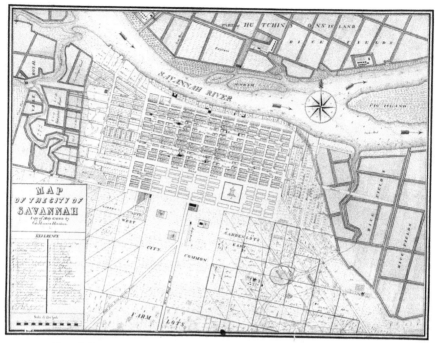

Rice fields surrounding Savannah became a breeding
area for mosquitoes and a public health hazard.
*(Courtesy of Hargrett Rare Book and Manuscript Library,
University of Georgia Libraries)*

both functions of the Oglethorpe Plan, enabled the city to promote itself as
a healthy alternative to the more congested, low-lying Charleston. Diseases
such as yellow fever, malaria, typhoid, and smallpox occurred in Savannah,
but the impression was that they were less frequent and less virulent. To further reduce the incidence of disease, in 1817 the city adopted a proposal of
Dr. William R. Waring to drain nearby rice fields and marshes to create a
cordon sanitaire around the city.[9]

Urban beautification remained tied to the Oglethorpe Plan through the
garden city movement, which took hold in England in the late 1800s and
spread to the United States in the early 1900s. The City Beautiful movement
of the same era was uniquely influential in America. In Savannah there was
renewed interest in the city's urban landscape. New parks were created, including Daffin Park, which was designed by the prolific and influential landscape architect John Nolen (1869–1937). The city's urban forest was sustained
for future generations with the planting of hundreds of live oaks, which now
shade city streets and squares.[10]

City Planning in the Era of Postwar Suburbanization

The Oglethorpe Plan absorbed occasional damage before the war, such as the extension of Montgomery Street through several squares, but the only serious threat to the posterity of the Oglethorpe Plan occurred after the passage of the federal Housing Acts of 1949 and 1954. The latter created Section 701, which awarded planning grants to cities and counties and established the now-infamous urban renewal program. More than a billion dollars flowed into urban areas for planning that ultimately led to the razing of older business districts and neighborhoods. Section 701 grants were intended to coordinate postwar growth through comprehensive planning, but the result was to create land use plans that depicted enlarged cities with vast suburbs while proposing to redevelop city centers to justify urban renewal funding.

Federal urban renewal funding was available to cities for the removal of "slums" and "blight." In the context of the emerging baby boom following World War II, suburbs were favored areas for urban growth. The federal government subsidized suburban growth by financing new roads, including freeways and interstate highways, and through mortgage insurance programs under the Veterans Administration and the Federal Housing Administration. As suburbs boomed, many older sections of cities were considered slums and targeted for demolition.

Many older downtowns and nearby neighborhoods were rebuilt in accordance with a new vision of "modernism" that emphasized high-rise office and apartment buildings surrounded by open space. Savannah was initially drawn to that vision, even though it meant largely repudiating the city's historic plan. In 1955, in order to secure federal funding and implement such sweeping change, the city and Chatham County jointly created the Metropolitan Planning Commission.

The city envisioned a revitalization initiative that would transform downtown Savannah and its urban neighborhoods into a model of modernism. In 1956, amid excitement over the emergence of suburbia and prospects of modernizing the downtown area, the *Savannah Morning News* editorialized that "bold new concepts" should be implemented, including a freeway to be built through downtown (over Bull Street) to shorten the commute time of workers from their suburban homes to their downtown workplaces.[11]

Such "bold new concepts" were proposed by the city's new planning agency in its Golden Heritage Plan, completed in 1958. The document proposed razing much of downtown Savannah, creating larger blocks and taller buildings, and running freeways into the middle of downtown as the newspaper had suggested. The use of the word "heritage" in the plan was something of a misnomer, if not an outright coverup, as its proposals would wipe out much of the Oglethorpe Plan and two hundred years of architecture built within that layout.

To be fair, the outline of Oglethorpe's ward layout was to be partially retained by the new plan, but the unique interior of those wards was going to change dramatically to accommodate large twentieth-century buildings. Selected historic structures would be retained, in deference to historic preservationists, but their original context would be lost.

For such proposals and plans to be carried out, they must be supported by local laws, or ordinances. The principal legal instrument for implementing plans is zoning. In 1960 Savannah adopted a zoning ordinance that codified into law many of the concepts in the Golden Heritage Plan, thereby securing eligibility for federal urban renewal funds. The 1960 ordinance would remain in effect for decades, coexisting with a preservation ordinance enacted to protect the city's planning and architectural heritage.[12]

City Planning in the Modern Period

Fortunately for Savannah, little of the new, modernist vision was ever implemented. The city did not completely escape the bulldozer, however. Some established African American neighborhoods were razed, unfortunately, but most of the original planned area remained intact and never again faced a threat of such a magnitude.

The bulldozer-oriented 1950s and early 1960s had the benefit of raising awareness of Savannah's architectural and urban design heritage. Initially, individual properties were saved from demolition. More recently, Savannah adopted a policy of restoring the original design of its wards when conditions allow. The first major example of such a restoration was Decker Ward, where Ellis Square was restored to civic space (with parking below grade).

Ellis Square was the site of the historic City Market complex until it was demolished in 1954 and replaced with an ill-adapted parking structure, the city's first urban renewal project. The redevelopment plan for Decker Ward was initiated in 2007 and completed in 2010. The plan for reintegrating the ward into the historic fabric of the city was based on a thorough analysis that took historical context and present-day land uses into account.

Even though Savannah emerged relatively unscathed from the urban renewal era, as noted above it retained the 1960 zoning ordinance adopted for the purpose of furthering urban renewal. For nearly sixty years, the city reviewed development proposals under an ordinance that was completely at odds with its planning policies and traditions. Zoning amendments were made on the fly, and variances to the ordinance were approved on an ad hoc basis. Some in city government defended the outmoded ordinance as one that was tailored by amendments as the need arose and thus always fit perfectly. Critics argued that a new zoning ordinance was needed to bring it into alignment with land use policies and historic design review standards.

In 2006 Savannah adopted a new comprehensive plan, the "Tricentennial Plan," so named because its planning horizon extended to 2033, the 300th anniversary of the founding of Savannah. The new plan reinforced long-standing planning policies and refined them for the modern city. It laid out the framework for a new zoning ordinance to replace the archaic 1960 one. The New Zoning Ordinance, as it ended up being named, was finally adopted in 2019.

It is also noteworthy that the Tricentennial Plan designated former industrial areas outside the Landmark District for redevelopment in a manner consistent with the city's planning heritage. Areas to the east and west of the historic district were designated to accommodate the growth of the city's central business district in a manner that would complement the historic town plan and architecture. New wards would be laid out as wards with a center square, thereby resuming the historic growth pattern where it left off in 1851.[13]

The Civic Master Plan adopted in 2006 was another effort to ensure the historical compatibility of future development. The plan was initially targeted to a former industrial area known as the East Riverfront. The plan ran into difficulties, not the least of which was the Great Recession. Nevertheless, the intent behind the plan reflects a positive movement toward compatibility and synergy between new development and existing historic assets.[14]

The city's Historic District Ordinance was amended in 2009 for similar reasons, increasing the compatibility of new development with historic patterns. Other initiatives are regularly considered to ensure that growth in the Landmark District, as well as adjacent areas, conforms with "guiding principles" of city policy documents. With many such pieces in place, the city is successfully melding an ingenious town plan from the eighteenth century and architecture from the nineteenth century with contemporary urban design practices. The ongoing work secures a place for Savannah among the world's best-planned cities.[15]

Urban planning and architectural preservation are separate but overlapping areas of local government. Planning is conducted through policy documents such as comprehensive plans and neighborhood plans ultimately given effect through zoning or, increasingly often, "form-based" codes that are less use-restrictive. Architectural preservation is typically administered by a city planning department but under a separate ordinance, with board members having backgrounds in architecture and historic preservation. In Savannah, both functions fall under the purview of the Metropolitan Planning Commission. The Historic District Board of Review administers the city's historic preservation ordinance. The subject of historic preservation vis-à-vis architecture and the built environment is sufficiently different to require a separate discussion in this book's conclusion.

Today Savannah benefits in several ways from being a planned city. The most obvious is that the city's historic downtown draws millions of visitors annually, creating a strong tourism sector in the economy. Somewhat less obvious but related is that downtown Savannah is an attractive business, educational, and cultural venue for those living in the metropolitan area. The tree canopy, compactness, friendliness to walkers, and vibrant mix of uses—all of which are built upon the city's planning heritage—together create an intriguing urban environment generally lacking in the American experience.

Savannah benefits from the Oglethorpe Plan on the metropolitan level. The city largely developed over the original plan, taking advantage of the efficiencies of compactness in the plan, orderliness of its grid, and the planned area's elevation above the flood plain. Commutes tend to be easier than in most cities, except where more conventional development patterns have taken root in exurban areas to the west. Business synergies are strong since clustering (or at least close proximity) of related activities is facilitated by compactness. And, finally, a sense of unity rather than disconnectedness is more pervasive in Savannah than in many other cities. The legacy of the Oglethorpe Plan is profound, and it is no wonder that most Savannahians understand that their city has thrived because of it.

What many Savannahians may not yet grasp is that threats loom on the horizon. While concerns such as heavy truck traffic through the historic districts can be solved (although solutions will be enormously expensive), threats to the *character* of the city will be more difficult to diagnose and address. Additionally, the local sense of ownership of the historic district may slip away as exclusionary luxury-elite markets increase their footprint. The city appointed a task force to study gentrification in the early 2000s, it has been proactive on the problem of homelessness, and it has developed concrete initiatives to improve established neighborhoods in the downtown area. Nevertheless, a slow-moving tide of increasingly upscale tourism can ultimately change the character and business dynamics of downtown Savannah and its adjacent historic neighborhoods from one that is enjoyed by all residents (and offers practical benefits to them) to one that primarily serves wealthy residents and affluent tourists. This looming prospect of *elitification* (a concept introduced earlier) will be taken up in more detail in the last two chapters.

PART IV

Rising Fortunes

Rice more than any other crop made Charleston a wealthy and influential city. Wealthy planters of the antebellum era believed their ancestors' ingenuity was responsible for that status, but to a great extent it was West Africans who supplied rice-growing expertise. Savannah also became wealthy in part from rice, but it had a more diversified economy and in the 1830s arguably became the South's most industrialized city.

CHAPTER SEVEN

Charleston
Once America's Wealthiest City

Charleston feudalism w/ a constitution

Charleston and Savannah were founded with antithetical visions. Charleston was conceived as a hierarchical, gothic society—feudalism with a constitution. Savannah was conceived as a more egalitarian society, reflecting the new ideals of the Enlightenment. The vision for Charleston ultimately prevailed, and both cities became metropolises of American slave society, an inescapable legacy.

Charleston was well-positioned from the beginning to become prosperous within a generation or two. In 1698 the king's customs collector for the colonies wrote, "Charles Towne is the safest port for all the vessels coming through the Gulf of Florida in distress, bound from the West Indies to the Northern Plantations." Missing Charleston, he said, could force ships to seek shelter as far away as Barbados, with winds being less favorable to reach more northern ports. At Charleston, he maintained, they would be secure and able to refit.[1]

By the time of the city's founding in 1670, England had developed lucrative sugar plantations on Barbados, and it had tapped into the existing Atlantic slave trade for its labor supply. Prevailing winds and ocean currents circulating around the Sargasso Sea made Carolina the next logical colony in an expanding, slave-based, economic empire.[2]

Settlers from Barbados, with fifty years of expertise in acquiring slaves and controlling an enslaved population, saw the new colony of Carolina as an opportunity for growth. Carolina had the added advantage of being near the mature colonies of the Mid-Atlantic and New England, and much closer to the motherland, thereby adding a new and strategic link in the Atlantic chain of trade.

It is implausible that the framers of the elaborate plan for Carolina envisioned creating a slave society modeled after Barbados. The Grand Model was a utopian political project, not merely a scheme to make the Proprietors wealthy (although in large part it *was* that). But the framers did envision a society with an enslaved class at the base of a social pyramid. Anthony Ashley Cooper and John Locke, the visionaries behind the plan, imagined a system of class reciprocity that benefited everyone, even (in their myopic view) a large class of enslaved people. It was a form of gothic idealism predating the revolutionary idea of democracy that arose with the Enlightenment and reflected Locke's own later thinking.[3]

Yet Carolina became a slave society within forty years of its founding, swaying to the will of the Barbadians who settled there and giving in to the compelling economics of the Atlantic triangular trade. Charleston was destined to become the economic hub and political capital of a slave empire, a course that must have mortified John Locke as his philosophical investigations led him in the opposite direction. Indeed, he was very likely shocked by what he saw occurring in Carolina even while still employed by the Proprietors, but certainly later, well before he died in 1704.[4]

England was late entering the Atlantic triangular trade. In the mid-1400s, before England was a sea power, Portugal dominated the Atlantic. Christopher Columbus sailed in the service of Portugal exploring the coast of West Africa before he sailed for Spain and "discovered" America (from the Eurocentric perspective). Portugal was a focal point for adventurers and experienced sailors like Columbus as it expanded its Atlantic empire.

Portugal began the slave trade two centuries earlier than England when it acquired enslaved Africans for its sugar plantations on the Atlantic island of Madeira. Portuguese sugar production shifted to Brazil in the 1500s and expanded dramatically. The slave trade expanded to meet the rising demand for labor in the New World.

The Portuguese succession crisis of 1580 was precipitated when there was no heir to the throne following the death in battle of King Sebastian I. Subsequently, King Philip II of Spain was able to unite the two nations for a period of sixty years under his reign. Portugal's dominance of the Atlantic declined as Spain ascended. Spain entered the slave trade when it brought enslaved Africans to its Canary Islands sugar plantations, following a pattern similar to that of Portugal in Madeira. As its empire expanded across the Atlantic, en-

The Atlantic Slave-Trading Nations

AFRICAN SLAVES TAKEN TO THE AMERICAS (MILLIONS OF PERSONS)

5.8	Portugal
3.3	Britain
1.4	France
1.1	Spain
0.6	Netherlands
0.3	United States

Source: Eltis and Richardson, *Atlas of the Atlantic Slave Trade*

slaved Africans were acquired to meet a wide range of labor demands in South America, Central America, and the Caribbean.

While Portugal and Spain controlled commerce and the slave trade in the Southern Hemisphere and the northern tropics, northern European countries perceived opportunities at the hemispheric edges and in North America. The Dutch West India Company (the most advanced trading concern in the world, developing modern institutions of finance, credit, and insurance) took over some of Portugal's Atlantic assets in the 1630s and 1640s. England, France, Denmark, and Sweden also entered the geopolitical fray.[5]

More than twelve million enslaved people were taken to the Americas, primarily by five European nations. Most nations in the Americas today have large populations that are the descendants of enslaved Africans. Portugal and England brought about the modern nations of Brazil and the United States, the countries with the largest populations of descendants of enslaved African in the world. Brazil's Black population in 2010 was 55.9 million, while that of the United States was 42.9 million. The third-largest African slave-descended population is that of Haiti, at fewer than 9 million. Outside of Africa, most people of African descent live in the Americas and are the descendants of enslaved people. Over 120 million people who can trace their ancestry to Africa live in the Americas. By comparison, fewer than 10 million people of African descent live in Europe.[6]

Situated at the confluence of Atlantic currents, the Caribbean, with about seven thousand islands, attracted nearly every seafaring European nation. Much of the region was sparsely populated, and thus there was little resistance to European colonization. Where the Carib and Arawak (Taíno) people had larger populations, in areas such as the Windward Islands and Hispaniola, they resisted colonization. Their populations, however, were devastated by the influx of diseases from Europe and Africa, making European conquest inevitable.

England gradually secured a hold on parts of the Caribbean and much of North America throughout the 1600s, entering the contest in the tropics by taking control of Barbados, the easternmost island in the region, which had been claimed earlier by Portugal and Spain.

As discussed earlier, it was in Barbados, a relatively small island of 169 square miles (smaller than present-day Charleston and North Charleston combined), that England began acquiring enslaved Africans to work its sugar plantations. The population of enslaved Africans became larger than that of free Whites in 1660, ten years before the founding of Charles Town.

Slavery in North America

The vastness of the slave trade left a permanent imprint on the Americas. In English colonial North America, it began in 1619 with the arrival of a slave ship in Virginia, and it began nearly a century earlier, in 1526, in Spanish-held territory. Although it was slave traders who took their human cargo to Virginia, colonists there had no experience with slavery and initially regarded the Africans as indentured servants. It would be several decades before a system of chattel slavery would emerge, with sharp distinctions between White indentured servants and enslaved Blacks. While Virginia remained the primary destination of slave traders for the remainder of the century, Charleston would emerge as the continent's principal slave port by 1700 and retain that status until the Civil War.[7]

Charleston's role as the primary port of entry of enslaved people in North America cannot be understated. Understanding the history, culture, and character of Charleston, the South, and even the United States today requires an understanding of the history of transatlantic slavery.

The primary ports of disembarkation in the present-day United States were Charleston, where 211,000 enslaved Africans disembarked, and the Chesapeake Bay area, where 129,000 disembarked. Secondary ports were in the Northeast, where there were 27,000 disembarkations and the Gulf Coast, including New Orleans, where there were 22,000 disembarkations. New Orleans's large slave market was both interregional, with an influx of enslaved people from the Upper South, and *intra*regional, with an influx of Caribbean slave traders. Charleston also acquired enslaved people from the Caribbean, rather than directly from Africa. Barbados, as previously discussed, imported 493,000 enslaved Africans to work its sugar plantations, and many thousands of those were eventually relocated to South Carolina.[8]

Charleston, having acquired a model for a slave society from Barbados, and later as the primary port of entry of enslaved Africans into North America, established the business model for the southern slave economy. It spread that model across the Deep South (as Virginia had spread its influence across the Upper South), beginning with Mississippi, where many of the Lowcountry elite resettled. The chief components of the model were 1) an enslaved majority labor force; 2) a land-and-slave-owning elite; 3) authoritarian control of society and the economy (often oligarchic); and 4) a focus on monoculture over agricultural and broader economic diversification.

With the rise of King Cotton in the Mississippi Valley, New Orleans became a busy slave market rivaling Charleston. Although it had many articulate advocates of slavery, New Orleans never surpassed Charleston as the intellectual center of slave society. Where it did perhaps exceed Charleston in its pro-slavocracy rhetoric was in building a conceptual "empire of slavery," not only to the west but also throughout the Caribbean and Central America. The Charleston aristocracy and oligarchy was more interested in developing a rationale for secession than one for territorial expansion.[9]

The Lowcountry model postulated slavery as a set of property rights, a culture, and a political system. More than in any other subregion of the South, its aristocrats were surrounded by enslaved African Americans who were intimately involved in every aspect of their lives on a daily basis, both in the city and on the plantation. With the North a fundamentally different society, it became necessary and essential by the 1830s for the oligarchy to equate survival with secession and to convince the rest of the South to go along with that daring plan.[10]

The 1860 census provides a detailed portrait of southern demographics on the eve of the Civil War. Four million people were enslaved throughout the South. The percentage of enslaved people in each state is shown in the table titled "Enslaved People in the Emerging Confederate States," and the distribution is shown in the historic map on page 168.

The enslaved population exceeded that of free people in South Carolina in 1708, only thirty-eight years after the founding of the colony. There was virtually no limit on the number of people Lowcountry aristocrats were willing to enslave to support their way of life. But for the vicissitudes of the global economy, the South Carolina Lowcountry and Midlands might have held more than 90 percent of its population in permanent bondage, as it had done in some of its coastal parishes. The aristocrats believed in their patriarchal moral authority to do so, and their merchant partners in the oligarchy fully supported that proposition.[11]

Enslaved People in the Emerging Confederate States, 1860 (percentage of total population)

57%	South Carolina
55%	Mississippi
47%	Louisiana
45%	Alabama
44%	Georgia
44%	Florida
33%	North Carolina
31%	Virginia
30%	Texas
26%	Arkansas
25%	Tennessee

Source: U.S. Census of 1860

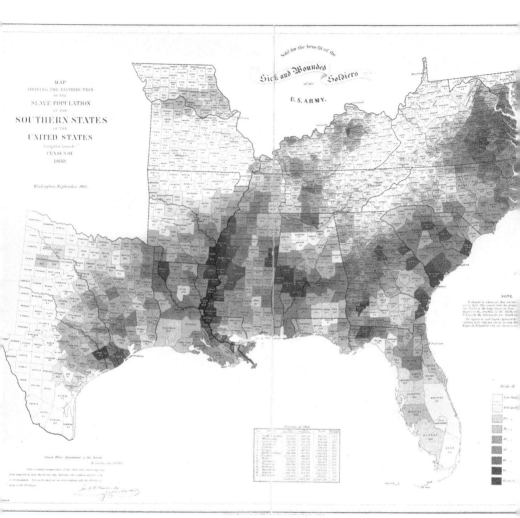

Geographic distribution of the enslaved population in 1860.
(Prints and Photographs Division, Library of Congress)

The Carolina frontier economy developed during the first British Empire initiated under Oliver Cromwell and the House of Stuart. It was the period when England and later Britain (after it was created in 1707) developed an imperial policy that focused on North America and the Caribbean. It was the period during which the nation learned how to establish and administer an empire. (The second British Empire, which began late in the eighteenth century, was the period in which Britain flourished as a global administrator of its territories, particularly in Africa and Asia.)

At the time of the founding of Carolina, English colonies were created on an ad hoc basis by individuals or small groups of people motivated by a quest for religious freedom or by the prospect of great wealth, such as that generated by Spanish and Portuguese colonies. There was as yet no model for founding colonies, building cities, and administering colonies like that of the Spanish Law of the Indies. The Fundamental Constitutions document was drafted in the absence of coherent national policy. Despite the efforts of the Proprietors, particularly Ashley Cooper and secretary Locke, to establish a model framework for Carolina, the lack of practical experience meant that the colony would struggle for several decades before finding a profitable place in the Atlantic triangular trade system.

The early decades in the Lowcountry were hardscrabble. Disease, weather disasters, violence, food shortages, grueling work, and sustained poverty prevailed in those early "grim years," as the historian John Navin describes that period. And while a hard life and grim prospects were faced by those who were free, for an increasing number of people held in servitude and, worse, slavery, life was even more dire.[12]

Initially, however, slavery was very different from what it would become in the next century. The hostile frontier forced people to work together to survive. Colonists, servants, and enslaved people were forced by circumstances to cooperate to eke out their existence. Radical class segregation was not yet rigidified into a political culture.

Colonial officials appealed to the Lords Proprietors for food, clothing, tools, cattle, and other necessities but received little of what they requested in those early years. The Lords Proprietors did, however, recruit more colonists in the hope that those with substantial means would invest their savings in the colony and stimulate economic growth. They worried about the rising influence of those who came from Barbados or adopted that mind-set, some of whom became known as the Goose Creek Men, and attempted to counter that by recruiting new colonists from other pools in England, Scotland, and

Europe. Recruitment included dissenters such as Baptists, Quakers, Presbyterians, Lutherans, and Huguenots. In time the strategy worked to stimulate the economy but failed to stem the power of the Goose Creek Men.

Land was free, but preparing it for cultivation was labor-intensive and costly. Experimentation with crops to find out what would grow was time-consuming. Colonists who did not engage in trade and relied entirely on farming had to draw from their savings or borrow money until they were able to grow profitable crops.

The quickest means of income was trade with Indigenous people. Deerskins and furs traded by Native Americans were the first profitable export, but revenues were modest. Naval stores (tar and pitch) for maritime purposes soon became another export. A third export in those early days was enslaved Indigenous people acquired in wars among Native Americans and sold to colonists, who, having the advantage of proximity, could sell them in Barbados at a lower price than Africans. While the Proprietors prohibited the enslavement of Indigenous people, traders circumvented the law by claiming they had the consent of the enslaved, who supposedly wanted to be free from their initial captors.

Rum, rifles, and other manufactured goods were traded for pelts and enslaved people. In the formative 1600s, England and its trading partners brought enslaved people from Africa to the English Caribbean, the nation's Caribbean colonies produced sugar and rum for export to North America and Europe, and England produced the manufactured goods in demand in Africa, the Caribbean, and North America. Prevailing winds and currents efficiently and increasingly carried English ships to Africa, from there to the Caribbean and North America, and then back to England in the English version of the Atlantic triangular trade.

Following the relocation of Charles Town to the peninsula in 1680, improvements in the built environment occurred but at a slow pace. New colonists arrived, the Proprietors invested in new infrastructure for the town, and trade picked up a bit. But letters from colonists largely reveal disappointment. The colony did not live up to the expectations built up by the Proprietors' promotional materials.

While a few of the colonists were prospering, largely due to building on wealth acquired in Barbados and elsewhere, the majority saw only modest improvement, if any, until the 1690s. It was in that final decade of the seventeenth century that the seeds of prosperity were planted, literally. That was the decade that rice became a profitable crop. And while prosperity never came to a majority of the population—the majority was enslaved, living in servitude, or scraping by—Charles Town was poised to become one of the wealthiest places in the empire.

Principally through Charleston's aggressive trading, the United States was destined to acquire one of the largest African diaspora populations in the world. It is second only to Brazil and larger than all other countries combined. Later chapters document how Charleston has faced down its past and, to its benefit, embraced the complex society it produced as a slave society.

Rice and Riches

Rice made Carolina rich. Rice may seem like a bland subject, and it may be tempting for the reader to skip over it. That would be an unfortunate decision. The story of rice is both rich and revealing—rich in the sense that it tells a fascinating story about Carolina, and revealing in that the story exposes a great deal more than was previously known about Africa and its influence on America.

According to a story promoted by the Rhett family, landgrave Thomas Smith, the family's patriarch, obtained a bag of rice in 1694 from a ship that had been to Madagascar, some of which he planted and the rest of which he distributed to friends. Experimentation with rice may have occurred even earlier, but it was in the 1690s that rice surfaced as a viable crop.

By the turn of the century, the technique for growing wetland rice was established. Records of exports were not kept until 1697, and some of those are lost, but it appears that Carolina began exporting rice in the first decade of the eighteenth century. Advances in thrashing and milling further increased production, so that rice exports more than doubled in the 1720s and tripled in the 1730s.

The story of Lowcountry prosperity and ultimately the broader cultural economy of the Deep South is inextricably linked with the story of rice in the Americas. Until recently it was believed that rice originated exclusively in Asia. Research has shown that one of two species of rice, *Oryza glaberrima*, originated in Africa, not Asia as previously thought. While both *Oryza glaberrima* and *Oryza sativa* (Asian rice) were important to the Atlantic triangular trade, the former has a unique relationship to Carolina.[13]

An understanding of that relationship requires looking back more than two thousand years into West African agricultural history. African rice was first grown in the Inland Niger Delta (IND), a "fertile crescent" similar to those in the Middle East and elsewhere that gave rise to the earliest civilizations. Desertification overcame the IND and ended the potential expansion of rice production in the region. The techniques for growing rice had spread southwestward, however, eventually reaching the coast of Africa.

Archaeologists have found evidence of rice cultivation in Jenne-Jeno (ancient Jenne Djenne), which was occupied from 250 BC to AD 900. Lying within the IND on the Niger River where cyclical inundation refreshed the soil, Jenne-Jeno was ideally suited to develop agriculture. The agricultural revolution that emerged there is considered a likely source of the later wealth of more famous Sahel cities such as Timbuktu.

Scholars differ over whether African rice cultivation originated at a specific location, such as Jenne-Jeno or another site within the IND, or emerged over a long period of diffuse experimentation throughout the broader region. In any case, sedentary cultivation practices developed over millennia, and West Africans eventually learned to cultivate varieties of rice that were adapted to a range of inland and coastal environments.[14]

By the time of the arrival of the Portuguese in West Africa in the late 1400s, coastal rice cultivation was an established practice, integral to the regional economy. Salt was another valuable commodity produced on the coast and the basis for trade with inland people. The Fulbe, or Fula, people from Guinea's central highlands (part of an ethnic nation of millions extending across the Sahel) traded cattle, cloth, dyes, gold, and iron for coastal salt and rice.[15]

Rice was grown in cleared mangrove forests as well as uplands along a six-hundred-mile swath of West Africa from present-day Guinea-Bissau to Liberia, an area that became known as the Rice Coast. Its monsoonal climate produces heavy summer and fall rains that inundate the region, creating an opportunity for agrarian people to harness natural flooding in a manner similar to that practices in the ancient fertile crescents, a cultivation system known as flood recession agriculture.

Coastal rice production in mangrove forests, vestiges of which can be found today in Guinea-Bissau, make use of a "landscape gradient" in adapting cultivation to coastal ecology. The indigenous system uses specialized implements for winnowing and milling; networks of canals, dikes, and causeways; reservoirs and sluice gates to regulate inundation; rice cultivation-cattle pasture rotation; and gender and age division of labor. The mangrove system captures rainfall for irrigation and impounds water to kill weeds. Fields are flushed at low tide to reduce salinity and desalinated for a period of two to three years to allow for cultivation. After cultivation, pasturing re-fertilizes the field with manure.[16]

A technique of this type developed by the Baga people of present-day Guinea was documented by Captain Samuel Gamble, whose slave ship was forced by weather conditions and "dangerously ill" crewmen to lay over in the Îles de Los in June 1793. Gamble's detailed description bears a remarkable similarity to rice cultivation in the Lowcountry. Baga rice was red-husked and less valuable than polished white rice grown in the uplands by other people.[17]

Whether African rice-growing technology and African rice were transferred to South Carolina (and, if so, to what extent) remains a matter of conjecture. Scholars have shown that Lowcountry rice cultivation largely mirrors that of the Rice Coast, and while it appears likely that there is a connection, more research is needed to confirm the precise channels through which transfer occurred. Did Lowcountry rice planters favor enslaved workers from the Rice Coast, as some scholars have hypothesized? The most recent evidence shows that 31 percent of the enslaved people taken to the Lowcountry were from the Rice Coast, as were 45 percent of those taken to Savannah and elsewhere on the Georgia coast, numbers that exceed those of other slave ports.[18]

Rice planters lost sight of the African connection over the course of generations. They came to believe that their achievements were the result of innate racial superiority. They wanted to believe that they were the sort of men "who worked with [their] brains on an extended scale" producing "an achievement no less skillful than that which excites . . . wonder in viewing the works of the ancient Egyptians." They saw their accomplishment as aided by "African savages fresh from the Guinea coast" who supplied only brute labor. The archaeologist Leland Ferguson estimated, "By [1800], rice banks on the . . . East Branch of Cooper River measured more than 55 miles long and contained more than 6.4 million cubic feet of earth. . . . [and] by 1850 Carolina slaves . . . had built a system of banks and canals . . . nearly three times the volume of Cheops, the world's largest pyramid."[19]

The reality of a century of wealth-generating rice production is that it was the result of distinctly different cultures meeting on the American frontier working together, creating an agricultural revolution. As the fog of America's racist past is cleared away by science and technology and diligent scholars, the past is more accurately understood, and the profound contributions of Africans in America become better delineated.

The Rise of the Lowcountry Economy

As the Lowcountry economy matured in the first half of the eighteenth century, two other export commodities supplemented rice as the driver of the thriving economy: naval stores (tar and pitch) and animal pelts (primarily deerskins). By mid-century, a fourth commodity, indigo, was introduced into the mix. The indigo plant was the main source of blue dye in Europe, and London merchants were the primary distributors.

Indigo was introduced to the Lowcountry by Antigua-born Eliza Pinckney (1722–93). The British-educated Pinckney (then Lucas) began experimenting with the crop when in her teens and made it a lifelong project carried out on her father's plantations. Pinckney became so well-known that George Washington served as a pallbearer at her funeral.

Rice, however, remained the principal export and source of wealth for most planters and merchants well into the 1800s. The innovator Jonathan Lucas (unrelated to Eliza Lucas Pinckney) introduced automated milling to Henry Laurens's plantation in 1794. The mills used tidal energy to raise industrial pestles and bring them down on the rice. Lucas continued to make advances in milling and was the first to use steam power for rice milling in 1817.[20]

The Rice Act of 1730 was enacted by Parliament in response to lobbying by South Carolina to remove restrictions on trade with other countries. The law enabled the colony to tap into the large markets in Spain and Portugal. Rice production continued expanding, and by the 1770s it was the third-largest export of the American colonies, behind tobacco and non-rice grains.[21]

London was the principal port for the rice trade, followed by Bristol and Liverpool. Merchants who were engaged in the trade on both sides of the Atlantic became rich and lived opulent lifestyles. Some who were based in London moved to South Carolina, while some Carolinians relocated to London. Samuel Wragg, a London trader, joined his brother Joseph in Charleston around 1710, forming Joseph Wragg & Co., which became Carolina's largest slave-trading enterprise. Others embedded in eighteenth-century Charleston history include Henry Laurens, a Charles Town slave trader and planter; William Middleton, who ultimately owned over fifteen thousand acres in the Lowcountry; and Robert Pringle, who became wealthy exporting rice and deerskins and importing consumer goods from Britain and Europe. Other important figures in the trading class were Charles Brailsford, James Crokatt, Ralph Izard, and John Nutt, two of whom were also planters.[22]

The Bull family was typical of the Lowcountry plantation elite. They were among the six families that dominated the Royal Council (the upper legislative house of the royal colony) from 1720 to 1763 as Charleston became the wealthiest city in the colonies. The six others were the Blakes and Izards, who also came directly from England, and the Draytons, Fenwicks, and Middletons who came from Barbados. Stephen Bull was the first to arrive in Carolina and was among those who founded Charleston in 1670. At first an Indian trader, he eventually began cultivating rice. The actual patriarch of the family was William Bull I (1683–1755), who had the frontier discipline of his father but also wealth and political influence. William, who had a plantation near the Savannah River, befriended Oglethorpe and assisted him in establishing the town of Savannah. He served as governor of South Carolina from 1737 to 1743.[23]

William Bull's son, William II (1710–91) became a "lynchpin of the governing class." He served as lieutenant governor and may have been among the first to develop a formal thesis of White superiority and Charleston's important destiny. A descendant, Kinloch Bull Jr., wrote that he "became an articulate and forceful spokesman . . . for the preeminence of South Carolina in the southeast [and advanced] the chauvinistic assertion by the volatile South Carolinians of their right to a role of leadership in the expanding areas of a slave-dominated economy." The Bull family intermarried with the Draytons, creating one of the largest landowning families in the Lowcountry. Their landholdings extended from near Charleston to the Savannah River, and from the Sea Islands inland more than fifty miles, and included Ashley Hall and Magnolia Plantation. The William Bull House, built by William Bull I in 1720, is located at 35 Meeting Street in Charleston.[24]

Even though the Lowcountry aristocrats and oligarchs had familial and well as business ties to London merchants, the latter eventually began taking advantage of their associates in Charleston. London merchants were able to manipulate the government bureaucracy and political processes to their advantage. Increasingly, Lowcountry producers received less than fair value for their exports. The indigo market was particularly difficult for those like Laurens who exported large amounts of the crop, a commodity tightly controlled by a group of London merchants.[25]

The Stamp Act of 1765 aggravated relations between the colonies and

Britain, and the homeland's trade practices only made matters worse. Mercantilism, the economic paradigm that prevailed before the liberalism of Adam Smith, postulated a zero-sum balance sheet in which one party's gains are another's loss. That outlook put Britain in a competitive posture toward its colonies as well as other nations. The prevailing environment was one in which the American colonies inevitably became increasingly aggrieved parties.

The Revolutionary War was an economic disaster for South Carolina and Georgia. Exports of rice, indigo, and other products came to a halt. The Paris peace talks of 1783 aimed to restore trade, but Britain resisted liberalization of its past practices. Moreover, it sought to block US trade with the Caribbean and other areas under its control to maintain its supremacy in Atlantic commercial and maritime theaters. Rice exports to Britain did not recover from the war until 1789, when they reached about 80 percent of prewar levels. The indigo trade recovered much quicker after the war, despite the loss of British government subsidies, but never attained previous levels. By the late 1880s, trade began normalizing to near prewar levels.[26]

After the war, Carolinians and Georgians took steps to avoid the manipulation and profiteering by British merchants and investors. They had seen their mistreatment as a form of "slavery" (i.e., oppression), and they wanted to ensure that it did not resume now that they were free of British domination. While they needed British trade expertise and investment to rebuild the economy, they also sought strict limits. Both states enacted laws that restricted absentee ownership with double taxation and forfeiture of land that remained uncultivated (laws that were somewhat less restrictive for American residents of other states. As a result, British merchants who had invested in South Carolina and Georgia suffered enormous losses. Henry Laurens was never able to sell off his assets, and John Nutt received only about 4 percent of the value of his assets in the colonies, estimated at over a quarter of a million pounds sterling. The Jay Treaty of 1794 attempted to normalize trade relations but had little effect on property disputes and limited American trade in the British Caribbean. Still, with all the difficulty adjusting to postwar conditions, the United States and Britain remained each other's leading trade partners.[27]

The Economic Tide Begins to Recede

After the turn of the century, Charleston and Savannah began losing their status as the most prosperous of southern cities. The Upper South was diversifying economically, and its towns were growing. Richmond surpassed Savannah in population and was growing faster than Charleston. To the southwest, New Orleans became part of the United States with the Louisiana Purchase in 1803 and soon rivaled Charleston in wealth. It also became another busy slave port, eclipsing a century and a half of Charleston's dominance of the trade in 1840.

The rise of New Orleans became inevitable after the invention of the cotton gin by Eli Whitney in 1794 and the invention of the steamboat by Robert Fulton in 1811. The former brought about mass processing of cotton fiber, while the latter revolutionized commerce by making it bidirectional on the Mississippi River and its major tributaries. Rising demand for cotton in the early 1800s and strong existing demand for Louisiana sugar put New Orleans in the right place at the right time. By 1820 it surpassed Charleston in population and became the South's largest city.

Wealthy South Carolinians, anxious to expand into emerging markets, invested in land in the Mississippi Valley and became cotton farmers. Their investments spurred the growth of cotton production from just over three thousand bales in 1790 to nearly four million bales in 1860. South Carolina Senator James Henry Hammond would famously boast in 1858, "No, you dare not to make war on cotton. No power on the earth dares to make war upon it. Cotton is king." The boast (with its typical Lowcountry flourish) gave rise to the name King Cotton.

Charleston and Savannah retained much of their status as influential southern cities through the antebellum period. While they steadily lost ground in population and economic importance, they remained centers of wealth and self-defined southern political culture. The Lowcountry aristocracy built up the idea of White racial superiority, which served the dual purposes of rationalizing their peculiar institution of slavery while also diminishing the likelihood of any Black-White alliance against the slaveholding elite. Jacksonian universal White male suffrage reinforced the sense of racial commonality.

Yet as racism grew and bonded the White population, other factors worked to deepen class divisions among Whites. The Specie Circular executive order of 1836, one of the last actions taken by President Jackson while in office, contributed to the Panic of 1837 and increased class divisions. Jackson's executive order required gold or silver (specie coinage) to purchase land, rather than paper money issued by state banks. The intent of the order was to reduce land speculation and price inflation following Native American removal. An unintended consequence was lowering the landowning prospects of poor Whites and increasing class divisions.

At the end of the Revolutionary War, the Deep South (or Lower South) was composed of South Carolina and Georgia, with populations of 249,073 and 82,548 respectively. The more populous Upper South (three and a half times larger than the Deep South) comprised Virginia and North Carolina, with populations of 747,550 and 395,005. The percentage of enslaved people was larger in the Deep South, at 41.1 percent, compared to 34.4 percent in the Upper South. Maryland and Delaware had substantial enslaved populations in 1790, at the time of the first census, but those populations were declining, and those states were realigning to the Mid-Atlantic region in political outlook.[28]

By 1860 the cultural economy of the Deep South had expanded to include Alabama, Florida, Louisiana, and Mississippi. The tobacco-growing Upper South added Tennessee and Kentucky. The two regions were nearly equal in population in 1860. The population of enslaved people, however, was quite different: 48.8 percent in the Lower South and 27.3 percent in the Upper South. The newer states of Texas, Arkansas, and Missouri were considered the Southwest during the nineteenth century; their combined population in 1860 was 2,221,677.[29]

The new states of the Deep South had followed the Carolina model in adopting labor-intensive monoculture. Where the South Carolina plantation elite perfected rice cultivation based on enslaved labor, the new states did the same with cotton. The less labor-intensive, more diversified crops of the Upper South, which had earlier been almost entirely dependent on tobacco, required fewer enslaved workers. The result was that enslaved people of the Upper South were "exported" to the Deep South, or "sold down the river" to the harsher conditions in that hardened slave society.

The tremendously profitable cotton monoculture in the newer states of the Deep South led South Carolina and Georgia to decrease rice production by the 1820s in favor of increased cotton production. The Industrial Revolution of the late eighteenth century increased demand for cotton worldwide, and the South had become the principal supplier.

The Lowcountry elite and their family members and associates in

Southern Population Realignment		
	1790	1860
Upper South	1,142,555	4,854,425
Deep South	331,621	4,364,926

Sources: U.S. Census, historical reports

the Savannah area retained their role as masters of political discourse, defending the institution of slavery on which their lucrative agricultural economy was built. The "Carolina way" was the southern way, and Charlestonians were resolute in keeping it that way. Secession fever, however, would prove their undoing.

The great wealth amassed in Charleston produced a small free Black class of artisans and skilled workers. By 1850 there were more than 250 free Blacks working as carpenters, brick masons, blacksmiths, tailors, and shoemakers, among other occupations. Their prosperity declined as the economy stalled and collapsed during the war. New opportunity would return briefly with Reconstruction, and some occupations dominated by Blacks, such as longshoremen, would become economically powerful. Ultimately they were doomed to suffer the constraints of a cultural economy centered on the premise of White superiority.[30]

The Fall of the Lowcountry Economy

The Civil War destroyed the southern economy and left Charleston and Savannah badly battered. Between 1860 and 1870, annual rice production decreased from 59,500 tons to 16,000 tons. Farm values stood at one-third of their former value at the end of that period, with the Lowcountry hit hardest in the state.[31]

Unchecked, the profit motive can drive humans to extremes. Charleston and Savannah had exemplified those extremes during the antebellum era. No other area in the United States enjoyed as much wealth, and no other area had as many enslaved people. Extreme wealth, and the quest for it, led directly to extreme racism as a rationalization for enslavement and racial tyranny.

Slavery in the Lowcountry did not begin with the premise of a White master race. It began with the premise that all societies have prisoners of war and miscreants who fall into enslavement. Racism in the early colonial era existed in the Lowcountry, but Whites for the most part then saw Africans as fellow American colonists, not as an inferior "race."

The English explorers and traders of the seventeenth and early eighteenth century generally accepted the Africans they encountered as equals. They did not see every African as a potential slave, only those who were prisoners of war in the ancient traditions of enslavement. Francis Moore, who took a post in West Africa before serving as Oglethorpe's aide in Georgia, wrote of his time on the Gambia River with no suggestion of racism. Mungo Park, who explored the interior of West Africa in the late 1700s wrote approvingly of African culture. The Lowcountry elite ignored all such accounts of Africa and constructed a narrative of savage Africans finding meaning and spiritual salvation on their plantations.

As the demand for slave labor grew, new justifications had to be formulated to justify enslaving more and more people. The Lowcountry elite masterfully led the South into a delusion of White superiority to justify an expanding, unending system of slavery.

Africa, in the American imagination, remains much like the continent portrayed by Lowcountry pro-slavery propagandists, and a persistent streak of racism and xenophobia in White America has a through line back to the antebellum rhetoric of the plantation elite. Charleston and Savannah today are in an ongoing process of recognizing and confronting those truths as part of their reinvention.

CHAPTER EIGHT

Savannah
A Southern Industrial City

Savannah was created in Charleston's image in the sense that the Georgia Trustees found inspiration in the Carolina Grand Model. While they rejected the archaic gothic social structure of the Grand Model, they found much to like in its planning and design elements, which prescribed exactly how Charleston and its hinterland would be physically situated and laid out. With modifications, Savannah was designed using the earlier plan as a template.[1]

In most respects, the city planning vision for Charleston failed, whereas in many ways that of Savannah succeeded. Charleston was founded on the flood-prone west bank of the Ashley River in 1670, then moved to its present site, which, at ten feet above sea level on average, proved to be only a marginal improvement. Savannah, in contrast, as has been noted, was sited farther inland on a coastal ridge fifty feet above sea level yet was still navigable for ocean-going vessels. Charleston's planned grid was only partially built out, whereas Savannah's was fully built out. Charleston intentionally relied on river transportation, unlike Savannah, which quickly built a road network above flood levels on its higher ridges. Central to Savannah's planning successes was that Oglethorpe was present to supervise the implementation of the plan and layout of a regional transportation network linking the town to its hinterland.

Savannah's successful city planning eventually paid dividends. Development patterns were established in advance of growth, thereby avoiding irregular land surveys and ad hoc siting decisions. Ample rights of way for roads were set out in the original plan, providing the city with much-needed road and rail corridors as it grew. Today's transportation network, consequently, is largely that envisioned by Oglethorpe and implemented in the 1730s.

Charleston's dependence on waterways was not a handicap during the early colonial period, but it became one when the city's hinterland grew beyond the reach of nearby rivers, requiring longer trips over land to outlying areas. By contrast, Savannah's location on high ground and ample provision of rights of way offered a big advantage as its hinterland grew, particularly after railroads became essential to industrial growth during the antebellum era. Early planning gave Savannah an adaptive capacity and resilience that Charleston, the mother city, has always lacked.

An advantage that both cities have long enjoyed, another product of early planning, is the planned development of strong urban centers to serve their agricultural hinterlands. Although Georgia ultimately adopted Carolina's plantation system of large estates worked by enslaved labor, both colonies had strong capital cities that were also major ports, a key feature of a growth model that stood in sharp contrast to Virginia's more dispersed settlement pattern, distant ports, and decentralized power structure.

Charleston remained the dominant city of the pair through the colonial period, but as the Revolution approached, Savannah reached near parity. A slaveholding elite had become wealthy from rice production, and by 1765 Savannah exported more lumber and other wood products than Charleston, much of it to the Caribbean. This expansion of trade meant that in the years before the war, numerous wharves and warehouses were built in the city along the Savannah River, strengthening the city's logistical infrastructure.[2]

Charleston Sabotage

Savannah, of course, started out the weaker of the two cities in terms of the wealth of its landowners. It began as a refuge for the "worthy poor" of England's cities and the persecuted Protestants of Europe. It was to be the capital of a level yeoman society based on "agrarian equality" and not at all a city like Charleston of wealthy planters and traders and masters and their enslaved workers. Oglethorpe and his closest associates among the Georgia Trustees believed that the accumulation of wealth through the amassing of large tracts of lands and the use of enslaved labor would destroy their objective of opportunity and upliftment for those in need.

Oglethorpe's opponents in Charleston were formidable, endowed as they were with wealth, political influence, and more than sixty years of accumulated knowledge of the region. His egalitarianism threatened the expansion of the slave society Charlestonians had built over three generations, as well as their amoral and sometimes immoral approach to trade with Native Americans. Colonists wrote to Oglethorpe during his first trip back to England, warning him of treachery orchestrated from Charleston. As one wrote, "There could be no description of any place (without the malice of hell itself) be made so dismal as the people of [Charles Town] endeavour to make of Georgia." Another wrote, "We raise the envy of the people of Charles Town, by whom we suffer many aspersions and false reports." And another informed Percival, "In Carolina, they will not name Col. Oglethorpe but with rage enough to set the very dogs a barking."[3]

On top of that, the Malcontents in Savannah found common cause with the Charleston elite. Their petitions for larger land grants and slave labor reached London and became a major distraction for the Trustees, who spent considerable effort marshaling opposing testimonials from local authorities and other colonists. The Salzburgers at Ebenezer, for example, wrote a letter discrediting claims that enslaved Blacks were necessary in the hot Georgia climate. They had been told upon arrival in Georgia, they wrote, that it was "impossible and dangerous for white people to plant and manufacture any rice, being a work only for Negroes, not for European people." But having experience, they added, "We laughed at such a tale, seeing that several people of us have had in the last harvest a greater crop of rice than they wanted for their consumption."[4]

The Trustees liberalized tenure and inheritance regulations in stages but held firm to the prohibition on slavery, even as Oglethorpe warned that if they went too far, they risked violating the "first principles" on which the Georgia Colony was founded. It was not until the late 1740s, after Oglethorpe left Georgia and ceased attending Trustee meetings, that they reluctantly lifted the prohibition on slavery.[5]

It was not inevitable that Georgia would fail to prosper if it remained egalitarian. Reports from colonists were at times encouraging. Many colonists wrote positive accounts and remained dedicated to the Trustees' system of agrarian equality. In the words of one, "Trading and planting goes on very fast, and the town of Savannah is so large, that from forty houses there are now almost four hundred, for the town is a mile long and as much wide and it is almost built." Another wrote, "Our town is in very good health and increases mightily."[6]

Had Oglethorpe not been sabotaged by the Charleston elite, he might have succeeded in establishing some version of the egalitarian colony he envisioned, one perhaps more like Pennsylvania than Carolina. However, with the opposition in Charleston, the internal resistance of the Malcontents, Indigenous American treaties to negotiate, and the Spanish threat in Florida nothing remotely utopian was likely to result. Oglethorpe's legacy would not be a society of opportunity for the "worthy poor" but a city plan that would prove efficient and resilient for future generations to build upon.[7]

The Economy of the Later Colonial and Revolutionary Period

After the Trustee period, Savannah became a satellite of Charleston. The Lowcountry elite moved in with their enslaved "property" and consolidated small farms into large plantations. Before long, however, Savannah would begin finding its own way. As described in chapter 4, it soon developed lucrative trade relations with the Caribbean that eclipsed those of more British-oriented Charleston.

By the early 1770s, Savannah was an emerging economic powerhouse in its own right and no longer a mere satellite of its powerful neighbor. Savannah's export economy—although it included a segment of large-scale rice cultivation—was diversified and less dependent on slave-intensive rice than the Charleston economy.[8]

In the next century, with impetus from the Industrial Revolution, Savannah would distinguish itself as an industrial city. Yet it would also follow Charleston in becoming more dependent on cotton. Rice cultivation continued through the antebellum period at declining levels and ceased with the Civil War and the unavailability of enslaved labor.

Both Savannah and Charleston would suffer economically from the war. The British controlled the Lowcountry, and the loss of trade devastated the economy. After the Revolution, planters would be forced to build the economy anew. Once they did, prosperity returned and Savannah once again grew rapidly. The devastating fire of 1796 was a major setback, but the federal census of 1800 revealed that Savannah had become the fourteenth-largest city in the new republic. It was still smaller than Charleston, then the nation's fifth-largest city, but it was on the rise.

The Industrial Economy and River Transportation

During the early 1800s, the wharves and logistical infrastructure necessary for trade were improved and expanded in Savannah and Augusta, while increasing numbers of landings, ferries, and access roads were built in between. The Trustee period had set the stage: landings had been built on the Georgia side of the river at Abercorn, Ebenezer (the Salzburger community), Mount Pleasant (near the present-day town of Clyo), Sister's Bluff, and Tuckasee

King Landing. Several of these sites played a role in later development. The Tuckasee King Landing, named for a Yuchi (Euchee) village, for example, later became the site of a stagecoach station on the Savannah–Augusta route.[9]

Savannah entered an exciting period of "creative destruction" in the nineteenth century as new forms of production and transportation rose and declined in rapid succession. The term "creative destruction," first used by Marxist economists, was adapted to free-market economics by the economist Joseph Schumpeter (1883–1950) to describe the constant destruction of existing capital as new capital is created. Today it is easy to understand the concept as applied to the technological revolution, which results in new products coming out in rapid succession, rendering the products they replace obsolete. At the turn of the nineteenth century, it was the Industrial Revolution that jolted the Lowcountry's frontier economy with creative destruction.

In Savannah and its hinterland, colonial-era roads, river crossings, landings, and wharves, and the products they carried, rapidly became obsolete in the new era of independence and industrialization. Canal and river transportation replaced horse-dependent transportation. Steamboats replaced pole boats, and within a generation railroads replaced steamboats. New crops replaced old crops as technologies changed. Prosperity was built on the destruction of one form of capital and the creation of another.

Savannah was a notable focal point for creative destruction in the South. Eli Whitney invented the cotton gin in Savannah in 1793. William Longstreet in Augusta conceived a steamboat design in the 1790s and launched a prototype in 1807, days after Robert Fulton, credited for the invention, launched his steamboat on the Hudson River. DeWitt Clinton Jr. laid out the Savannah-Ogeechee Canal in the late 1820s. Innovation abounded as these technically trained northerners financed their innovations with southern agricultural capital.

Many of the early roads, landings, and river crossings built in the eighteenth century fell into disuse during the nineteenth century as new infrastructure built for new products created new nodes of activity. Massive cargoes of cotton and lumber required greater emphasis on waterways, making the Savannah River the principal artery of commerce for the economically expanding region. With the invention of steamboats in the early nineteenth century, trade would no longer depend on ocean tides, which twice daily reverse the flow of the Savannah River past Savannah and inland another ten miles. With steamboats, the Savannah was navigable in both directions all the way to Augusta, two hundred miles inland. While the introduction of steamboats made the river economically preeminent for several decades, the growth of railroads through the mid-century period once again dramatically altered the spatial dynamics of the region. As a major hub for both modes of transportation, Savannah would begin passing Charleston as an industrial powerhouse in the 1830s.

Steamboats began operating in Savannah in 1817 and soon became the principal means of river transportation. Pole boats propelled by human labor had been essential to expanding the Savannah economy, moving rice and subsidiary commodities such as corn and tobacco to market, then moving ever-larger volumes of cotton as it replaced rice as the area's principal commodity. Pole boats continued to play a role in the transportation system after 1830, the heyday of steamboat transportation, and moved large quantities of rice as well as cotton well into the 1850s.[10]

The Steam Boat Company of Georgia was founded to manufacture vessels locally. Savannah became the first city to successfully send a steamship across the Atlantic in 1819 when the SS *Savannah* sailed to Liverpool and subsequently visited St. Petersburg, Stockholm, and other Baltic ports before returning home. The *Savannah* was a hybrid of a sailing vessel and a sidewheel steamship. National Maritime Day is observed in the United States on May 22, the date in 1819 that the SS *Savannah* set sail from her home port.

River steamboats were particularly well-suited to accommodate the large cargoes of cotton that had been made possible by the cotton gin. Its inventor, Eli Whitney of Massachusetts, was one of the northerners drawn to opportunities on the southern frontier. Whitney was invited to Mulberry Grove Plantation, a few miles upriver from Savannah, by the widow of Revolutionary War general Nathanael Green (who had been awarded the plantation for his service). During his stay at Mulberry Grove in 1793, Whitney invented the cotton gin, the machine that revolutionized cotton processing and brought postwar prosperity to the Deep South.

Cotton cultivation boomed after the invention, and the Savannah River was a principal artery for its conveyance. In 1807 William Longstreet, who moved to Georgia from New Jersey, partnered with Isaac Briggs in designing the river's first steamboat, a prototype for many more that would follow. The next year Longstreet invented both horse-powered and steam-engine-powered cotton gins, and from there he went on to build a steam-powered lumber mill.[11]

In 1814 Samuel Howard, another partner of Longstreet, who had recently died, was given exclusive rights by the Georgia Assembly to operate steamboats on the Savannah River for a period of twenty years. On January 17, 1816, the steamboat *Enterprise* was launched from the Savannah shipyard of John Watts. The steam engine powering the ninety-foot vessel was estimated to have "the united force of 32 horses." A primary purpose of the new vessel was to tow oceangoing sailing ships up and down the river while also carrying cargo and passengers. The *Augusta Chronicle* reported that she reached Augusta moving at three knots against the current.[12]

Another experiment in powering vessels on the river took place in 1820 when the *Genius of Georgia*, a "teamboat" built near Savannah, used actual teams of horses on a treadmill to turn the paddlewheel. The design was inspired by a prototype launched in New York in 1814. For several months the vessel operated successfully, except for a tendency to run aground, but there are no records of the teamboat operating on the river in subsequent years. By 1820 there were seven new steamships on the river in addition to the *Enterprise*—the *Georgia*, the *South Carolina*, the *Charleston*, the *Altamaha*, the *Samuel Howard*, and the *Columbia*. These seven were all built in Charleston, which for the time being maintained greater industrial capacity.[13]

By the end of the decade, there were as many as thirty steamboats on the river, most still built in Charleston, with others built in New York, Philadelphia, and the young city of Mobile, Alabama. Exports grew over 600 percent between 1800 and 1820. Savannah's rise as the major industrial city of the South would begin in earnest in the 1830s. During the decade more than fifty steamboats plied the river from Savannah to Augusta, giving the region the appearance of rising prosperity. A golden age for the steamboat on the Savannah River had begun.

After 1830 more steamboats were manufactured in Savannah than in Charleston, although most were still manufactured in the more industrial North. Records show that ninety-one steamboats were in service on the river during the nineteenth century, with eleven unknown as to their place of manufacture. Some of the boats operated for decades, while others were lost prematurely to fire, boiler explosion, or running aground.[14]

Iron-hulled steamboats, introduced in the 1830s, were lighter and less prone to running aground or being breached than wooden-hulled boats. The average life span of steamboats was about six years due to such hazards. A few iron-hulled vessels, by contrast, had life spans of over twenty-five years.

Savannah made history once again with the in July 1834 launch of the ss *John Randolph*, America's first commercially successful iron steamship. The "ss" designation preceding the name referred to an oceangoing "steamship" as distinct from a river-going steamboat (modern ships have the designation "MV" for "motor vessel"). The vessel was prefabricated in England for Savannahian Gazaway Bugg Lamar, a cotton and shipping magnate. The ship was assembled in Savannah. It was one hundred feet long, with a twenty-two-foot beam, similar in size to the ss *Savannah*. The *John Randolph* had immediate success in ocean and river trade, and according to its historical marker on the Savannah Riverwalk it was "the first of a great fleet of iron steam-powered vessels plying America's rivers and shores."[15]

Following the launch of the *Randolph*, Lamar arranged for the construction of another steamship, the *Pulaski*. The new ship was built in Baltimore for Lamar's Savannah and Charleston Steam Packet Company. The *Pulaski* went into service in 1837, but it sank thirty miles off the coast of North Carolina on its fourth voyage. The *Pulaski* was built as a packet steamer, meaning its mission was to provide scheduled mail and passenger service. Based in Savannah, its northern destination was Baltimore with intermediate service to Charleston. The wooden steamship was powered by double paddle wheels with twin copper boilers, as well as twin masts. One of the copper boilers exploded on June 14, 1838, sinking the ship and killing at least 128 of the more than 190 people on board. The survivors endured a harrowing two-day struggle before reaching land. Lamar's wife and four children died. The story of the *Pulaski* is told in gripping detail in *Surviving Savannah*, a novel by bestselling author Patti Callahan. While the characters in the novel are invented or embellished, Callahan accurately presents the facts surrounding the sinking of the *Pulaski* and the fates of her passengers.[16]

The city added four shipyards in the 1850s that built dozens of vessels. In addition to river steamboats, or "steamers," operating out of Savannah, sixty oceangoing vessels, or steamships, regularly served Boston, New York, Philadelphia, and New Orleans. Expanding transportation systems led to a boom in exports of cotton, rice, and lumber. Well before the Civil War, exports from Savannah exceeded those out of Boston. By then it was the most industrially developed city in the Deep South, finally surpassing Charleston a century after it became that city's satellite.[17]

The 16.5-mile Savannah–Ogeechee Canal, which opened in 1831, added another vast area, that of the Ogeechee River watershed, to Savannah's hinterland. The Ocmulgee River, a tributary of the Ogeechee, extended Savannah's market reach to Macon, which rapidly grew from a trading post to a major city once connected to the coast. The canal was designed by DeWitt

Clinton Jr., son of New York governor DeWitt Clinton who enabled the construction of the Erie Canal, completed in 1825 (the second longest canal in the world at the time). DeWitt Jr., an engineer who shared his father's scientific interests, had participated in canal developments in New York before taking on the Savannah project.[18]

The canal was an essential element of Savannah-area economic infrastructure from the 1830s to the 1860s. In the 1890s it ceased operating entirely as Savannah's industrial westside consumed its right of way for railroads and industrial land uses. Commodities transported through the canal during its heyday included cotton, rice, corn, naval stores, and lumber. The last was particularly notable as Georgia had become a major lumber exporter during this period.

The Industrial Economy and Railroads

Charleston saw an industrial competitor emerging in Savannah during the 1820s and sought to gain an advantage by initiating a new era of rail transportation. The South Carolina Canal and Railroad Company (SCC&RR) was chartered with private financing in 1827. The railroad began operating in 1831, and by 1833 it conducted scheduled service over a 136-mile route from Charleston to Hamburg (now North Augusta). At the time, it was the longest railroad in the world and the first scheduled steam-powered service in North America.

The pioneering railroad had met with stiff resistance from Charleston aristocrats, whose prime concern lay with land and slaves, not industry and infrastructure. Accordingly, they opposed the railroad and secured state opposition to any such projects "for the benefit of South Carolina or any of her citizens." A divide opened up between Charleston's outward-looking mercantile oligarchs and the politically dominant plantation aristocrats who cherished their agrarian way of life above all else.[19]

Georgia's trade oligarchs and their aristocratic allies were more pragmatic, supporting a wide range of developing industries and willing to invest in essential infrastructure. The Hamburg line thus prompted Georgians to obtain state charters to build competing lines. Carolinians in turn were forced to reexamine their inflexible ideological opposition to industry, and a race to build railroads began in the 1840s. Politically savvy aristocrats and pragmatic oligarchs realized that expansion into the Midwest through railroads was a way not only to strengthen the economy but also to project political influence into that rapidly growing region. To that end, the South Carolina legislature partnered in financing the Louisville, Cincinnati & Charleston Railroad. Progress in both cities slowed in 1836, however, as the national economy slumped. A full recession then followed the Panic of 1837, which persisted to the mid-1840s. Nevertheless, rail transportation caught on, and its ascendance became inevitable.[20]

Savannah entered the railroad age in 1833 when a group of Savannah businessmen concerned about competition from Charleston's new railroad to Hamburg formed the Central Rail Road & Canal Company. Construction of the railroad began in 1835. The company was renamed the Central Rail Road & Banking Company of Georgia (CRRG), reflecting the importance of capital investment in building railroad infrastructure. The first segment of the rail line was completed to Oliver on the Ogeechee River in 1839, and the line reached the outskirts of Macon in 1843, although it did not reach Macon's city center until a bridge was constructed in 1851. The line connected with the Macon & Western Railroad, which provided service from Chattanooga to Macon. Chattanooga was a commercial entrepôt on the Tennessee River that would also become an important rail city in the 1850s.

Steamboat operators began seeing the railroads as serious competitors in the 1850s. An advertisement in the Savannah newspaper on January 26, 1852, read, "Agents of the steamer David L. Adams [engage] to take freight for Augusta and Hamburg [North Augusta] at 20% less than railroad rates." As the decade progressed, Savannah River steamboat operators changed their business model to emphasize multimodal connectivity, where steamers would link steamship cargoes arriving in Savannah with railroads serving Augusta and other cities farther inland. An advertisement on February 14, 1859, announced that the "new, fast, and light draft steamer Excel" was connecting steamships arriving in Savannah from New York, Philadelphia, and Baltimore with the Georgia Railroad at Augusta. The advertisement asserted, "Merchants will find this the cheapest route by which they can receive their goods. Freight forwarded free of commissions."[21]

The steamboat era all but ended after the Civil War, as the new era of rail transportation reached maturity. From the 1870s to the end of the century, only two or three steamboats offered regular service between Savannah and Augusta. In 1900, only one, the *Ethel*, was in service. Although the river trip between the two cities was less than thirty hours, two or three times faster than the early steamers, travel by rail and highway was much faster, and these had become the preferred modes.[22]

The once-busy midsection of the Savannah River continued moving cargoes between Savannah and Augusta in the twentieth and twenty-first centuries, although at a greatly reduced pace. Most traffic in the modern era has been heavy bulk cargoes carried by barge. As recently as 2016, a 700,000-pound device used to produce anhydrous ammonia was transshipped from the Port of Savannah to Augusta, demonstrating the river's ability to carry super-sized cargo inland on a barge. But such activity is rare, and for the past century most cargo movement on the river has been concentrated in Port of Savannah facilities.[23]

The CRRG merged and reorganized a number of times over its history. It became the Central of Georgia Railway (CGRR) in 1895 after a reorganization. Subsequently it merged into the Illinois Central Railroad, the Frisco line, and Southern Railway. The line, in its various forms, maintained passenger service between Atlanta and Savannah by way of Macon until 1971, when Amtrak took over most of the nation's passenger train service.

The CGRR invested heavily in facilities in Savannah over the years. The large complex that began emerging in the 1850s included a depot, train shed, roundhouse, machine shop, blacksmith shop, carpentry shop, boiler house, and various other facilities. The extensive complex was closed by Southern Railway and transferred to the City of Savannah in the 1960s. It is now preserved as the Central of Georgia Railroad: Savannah Shops and Terminal Facilities National Historic Landmark District.

In the 1840s, Savannah was the largest city in Georgia and arguably on the way to briefly becoming the most industrialized city in the South. Atlanta was a rail junction known as Terminus until 1842, having built up around mile marker zero of the new rail line authorized by the state. The city became incorporated as Atlanta in 1847 and reached a population of 2,572 in 1850. Macon's population in 1850 was 5,720, while that of Savannah was 15,312.[24]

The development of river, canal, and rail transportation over the nineteenth century led to extensive port expansion in Savannah. The commercial and industrial waterfront grew to a mile and a half in length, and other facilities were built on Hutchinson Island opposite the city riverfront. Today's historic Factor's Row in downtown Savannah preserves most of the nineteenth-century warehouses and commercial buildings occupied by the factors (brokers and ship agents) of that era.

By 1860 Georgia had 1,420 miles of track, nearly 50 percent more than South Carolina's 973-mile system, second only to Virginia in the South and seventh among the nation's thirty-one states. Savannah was at that point the section's largest railroad hub. With rail transportation, cotton, rice, and lumber exports boomed. In the 1850s exports were greater than those of Boston: 4.1 million bales of cotton, 300,000 million casks of rice, and 353 million feet of timber and lumber were exported in that decade. Savannah's smartly chosen location on a coastal ridge gave it an advantage over Charleston for railroad accessibility, enabling it in many respects to become the more industrialized of the two rival cities.[25]

A Joint Venture: The Charleston & Savannah Railroad

Although Savannah and Charleston were competing for inland trade, especially cotton, a new railroad line connecting the two cities was conceived in the early 1850s as a means of linking both cities to northern and western commerce. The project's backers believed northern railroad lines from New York would expand through Wilmington, North Carolina, link with the proposed Charleston & Savannah line, and then reach Pensacola, which was considered the best harbor on the Gulf of Mexico. The Pensacola terminus would tie in with packet steamers serving Latin American and Caribbean markets. Promoters envisioned a "great thoroughfare" from New York to the Gulf in which Charleston and Savannah would be centrally positioned.[26]

The proposed line was chartered on December 20, 1853, and stocks were issued the following year. The 102-mile line swung inland nearly fifty miles to avoid the extensive estuaries between the two cities. To keep costs low, the new railroad required all work to be done "exclusively with slave labor." The railroad began operating on April 21, 1860, during the week the fateful Democratic National Convention was being held in Charleston. The railroad immediately became the long-anticipated "iron link" between the two cities. At a celebratory dinner was held in Savannah on November 2, 1860, one of the celebrants declared the two states now "united in heart, feeling, hopes, [and] institution, by blood." It was a rare moment of complete unity and camaraderie between the two cities.[27]

The following month South Carolina seceded from the Union, pulling the rug out from under investors' grand plans for the new railroad. For the next four years, the line was an essential part of the war effort, draining its resources. In 1865 as Sherman advanced through the Lowcountry, thirty-eight miles of track were mangled into "Sherman's neckties," its stations were burned, and its bridges destroyed. The railroad's rolling stock of passenger and freight cars had been scattered far and wide across several other lines, but fortunately all twelve of its locomotives survived intact and soon became a desperately needed source of revenue servicing other lines.[28]

On December 21, 1866, the company was reorganized as the Savannah & Charleston Railroad. The company was able to rebuild some of its destroyed infrastructure and resume operations in February 1867. It was not until March 1870, however, that the line was fully operational and able once again to provide service between the two cities. The still-faltering line was purchased by railroad magnate Henry B. Plant in 1880 and renamed the Charleston & Savannah Railway. Plant integrated the railroad into a network of other lines he had acquired, creating a viable system out of small, dying lines. During the 1890s the Charleston and Savannah line reported operating 22 locomotives, 23 passenger cars, and 725 freight and other non-passenger cars. The line was later absorbed by larger railroads, and the original right of way is currently in the CSX system, which has extensive freight operations throughout the eastern United States. The founding vision behind the Charleston & Savannah Railroad, that of a great thoroughfare connecting the East Coast and Gulf Coast, was finally realized.[29]

Savannah's Prewar Economic Profile

The Lowcountry led the calls for secession, and on the eve of the Civil War its principal cities, Charleston and Savannah, still saw themselves as the leading cities of the South, defending their aristocratic heritage and driving its westward expansion to the Mississippi and beyond. Savannahians were particularly proud of their ascension in economic prowess and independence from Charleston. Savannah in the 1840s and 1850s had arguably become the most industrial city in the South, not yet realizing that newer cities like St. Louis (which quadrupled in size between 1840 and 1850) were about to leave it in the dust.

The 1860 U.S. Census provides a snapshot of the southern states and their urban fabric (such as it was) across the South on the eve of the Civil War. Georgia's population, at 1.1 million, was 50 percent larger than that of South Carolina, which had dispersed some of its population across the Cotton Belt. Charleston remained the larger city, however, with a population of 40,522 compared to Savannah's 22,292. Charleston was the fourth-largest city in the South, but its *national* rank had dropped from fifth to twenty-second since the first census was taken in 1790. Savannah was the sixth-largest city in the South and ranked forty-first in the nation. The Mississippi River cities of New Orleans and St. Louis ranked first and second, respectively, in the South.[30]

Savannah's labor force had become more diversified with the addition of European immigrants. Irish had come in large numbers to work on the railroad, and they stayed in the city (which today has one of the largest St. Patrick's Day parades in the nation). Germans also arrived in significant numbers. The Jewish population, first established in Savannah in 1733, also increased (after many fled Georgia in fear of a Spanish invasion during the 1740s).[31]

Free Blacks were also a significant component of the labor force in Savannah, although less so than in Charleston. Black people usually acquired freedom in one of three ways: they were born free (i.e., no one "owned" them), through manumission, or by purchasing their own freedom. In 1860 Charleston had 3,237 free Blacks, compared to only about 700 in Savannah, and of those proportionately fewer in Savannah were in semiskilled or skilled trades such as carpentry or masonry. In 1850s Charleston, Black carpenters outnumbered Irish and German carpenters by three to one, a far greater ratio than in Savannah. At the end of the Civil War, Savannah had only nineteen carpenters, eighteen brick masons, and eleven coopers.[32]

In addition to experiencing population and economic growth, Savannah was gaining a sense of identity. It billed itself as a healthier city than Charleston, and it prided itself on its beauty. Savannah's architectural form, preserved today in its historic districts, began to take shape in the 1820s as many of the older wooden buildings were replaced with relatively fireproof structures, addressing the long-standing problem of disastrous fires that plagued both Savannah and Charleston. Much of the city's character is derived from its historic riverfront, where the offices of shipping agents and freight forwarders are carefully preserved shells now filled with condominiums and cafes.[33]

The National Historic Landmark District established in 1966 recognizes both architectural heritage, much of it from the antebellum period, and the underlying city plan laid out by Oglethorpe. Savannah is among only a few famous historic districts in the nation that owes a large share of its recognition to the melding of a city plan with the built environment, the other most notable examples being Washington, D.C., and Philadelphia.

Savannah and Charleston were devastated by the war of secession that had been so fervently desired by Lowcountry Fire-Eaters like Robert Barnwell Rhett. It would be more than a century before either city would fully recover and regain its status as a leading American city in both commerce and culture. Their recovery and reinvention had much to do, once again, with their Sargasso Sea geography. But even more important to their present-day success is an acknowledgment of the many positive attributes of their shared multicultural heritage.

Sargasso Sea

PART V

Projecting Influence

The rise of Charleston and Savannah was not limited in its impact to the Lowcountry and coastal Georgia. Their cultural influence extended across the Lower South, while their political influence reached the entire South—and beyond.

The story of the two Lowcountry cities is inextricably tied to the politics of enslaved labor. Would "the South" exist without the political economy of slavery and the political culture that evolved with it? The two cities were the hives of activity that rhetorically created "the South," binding together states that had little else in common. Without the intensely political discourse emanating from the Lowcountry, Americans today might understand the nation's regional geography in quite different terms.

CHAPTER NINE

Charleston
Prototype for the Deep South Cultural Economy

In their beginnings, Charleston and Savannah were laboratories of innovation in the Americas, planned cities founded first and foremost on philosophical principles formulated by members of England's political class. Neither city fulfilled the destiny imagined by its founders, although both have carried strains of their founding DNA, so to speak, through the generations to the present.

The inherent differences between the two cities, coupled with their proximity, have made them competitors at various stages in their respective histories. Savannah, for example, as detailed in the preceding chapter, gained an upper hand in its competition with Charleston when the Industrial Revolution offered it an opportunity to become a center of innovation, a near-equivalent of one of today's high-tech magnets. But the dominant city was always Charleston, a city so driven by an elite with intense passions about its way of life that it spread its influence far and wide.

The Incipient South

In his book *The Indian Slave Trade*, historian Alan Gallay undertook an extensive study of the forces that shaped the emergence of the South as a culture region. He identified South Carolina, and the aristocrats and oligarchs of Charleston in particular, as one of four major influences. The other three were the Native American nations, Spanish Florida, and French Louisiana. Contrary to accepted theory, and as argued herein, Gallay maintains that Virginia was not a primary influence.[1]

Once the Spanish and French were eliminated from the region, and Native Americans were no longer threats to the British colonies, Charleston stood alone as a force shaping the culture, economy, and geopolitics of an incipient (or proto-) South. The word "incipient" is used because no one yet thought of the southeastern region as a distinct culture region. People did not yet call themselves "southerners" or refer to themselves as being from the "South." Their geographic identity lay with the colony in which they lived.

The Emergence of Southern Culture

Students learn in elementary school that the United States is a "melting pot," a blend of many cultures (although some today prefer to call it a "salad," recognizing that immigrant identities do not entirely melt away). In the book *Albion's Seed*, historian David Hackett Fischer lays out the ingredients that went into the colonial melting pot, the formative cultures that combined to make one nation. Fischer identifies four regions of the British Isles that transferred their "folkways" to Anglo-America through immigration. The Scots-Irish from North Britain were a formative influence on the Deep South and West. Quakers left a permanent imprint on the Mid-Atlantic and Midwest. Cavaliers (royalty associated with the House of Stuart) and their servants shaped the Upper South. And Puritans were an indelible influence on New England.

Other scholars have similarly reduced present-day national culture to formative elements. The late political scientist Daniel Elazar came to the same broad conclusion as Fischer and others, including one of the first formal theorists of American culture, Alexis de Tocqueville, that the Puritans were a primary formative influence, having established democracy and social and economic equality in their communities. Elazar also agreed that the Scots-Irish shaped the character of much of the South. But Elazar also found that the Dutch were a formative influence on the Mid-Atlantic region, where their pragmatic commercial culture took root. Elazar argued that three primary *political* cultures grew from those original influences.[2]

Authorities generally agree that the South developed a unique culture associated with its rural, plantation-oriented, slave-based economy (hence "cultural economy"), one that was quite distinct from other regions of the United States. Only one out of eight urban places in the United States in 1860—defined as towns with populations of twenty-five hundred or more—was in the South. The region's protracted history as a rural society with an agrarian economy, which persisted to the mid-twentieth century, locked its cultural economy in place until external forces once again tore it apart.[3]

One of the first students of American culture was François Jean de Beauvoir, Marquis de Chastellux, the liaison between French forces and George

Washington's army during the Revolutionary War. He became a lifelong friend of Washington and made a point of visiting many American leaders and luminaries of the Revolutionary era. Chastellux traveled widely through the former colonies and later published his observations.

In one of the first assessments of American political culture and mores, Chastellux wrote that the thirteen states were all committed to the same fundamental purpose but that each was decidedly different in its "manners and opinions." His most detailed analysis was of the political culture of Virginia, which he found to have inherited from the aristocrats who first settled the colony. He concluded that "the spirit of the government itself will be always aristocratic," reinforced by the "peculiar privilege to possess negroes," which inculcates the vices of "vanity and sloth" in White society. More than forty years before Tocqueville's work on American democracy, Chastellux found a sharp contrast in the origin and evolution of political culture in New England, which was built on principles of "equality and industry."[4]

Chastellux's observation that slavery divided the United States into at least two distinct political cultures was reinforced by the French magistrate Gustave de Beaumont, who toured the country with Tocqueville on a fact-finding mission for the French government. Beaumont and Tocqueville were sent to America to study its prisons, which were launching a new concept of criminal rehabilitation. While studying prisons, they also studied American society as a whole, dividing up their research into a study of institutions, conducted by Tocqueville, and a study of cultural mores, conducted by Beaumont. Their findings were published separately as *Democracy in America*, which made Tocqueville famous, and *Marie, or Slavery in the United States*, which was initially well-received but soon afterward was all but forgotten. The latter, which was part novel and part notes, made the case that slavery was the nation's original sin (as some now like to say), inculcating unsustainable prejudice into the population and dooming it to an eventual reckoning.[5]

Beaumont did not divide the United States into separate political cultures based on geography. The principal division was between free and enslaved people, with the consequences of that division affecting the entire nation. He found that to a great extent prejudice was a stronger force than laws in creating irreparable damage to American society, an observation that he sought to bring to light in *Marie*. It was a gloomy prediction, which he and Tocqueville shared, mirroring Jefferson's assessment that "deep-rooted prejudices entertained by the whites [and] ten thousand recollections, by the Blacks, or the injuries they have sustained . . . will probably never end but in the extermination of the one or the other race."[6]

Their depressing prognosis was influenced by the Haitian Revolution that ended in 1804 when formerly enslaved people overthrew French rule. It was an abject lesson for the French and a nightmare of what might lie in store for White Americans. Yet implicit in the work conducted by Beaumont and Tocqueville on the American experiment in democracy was a hint at how the nation might survive: the egalitarian Puritan culture that took root in New England was the bedrock of society. It would guide the arc of history toward equality, with staggering mortality but without one side exterminating the other.

Charleston did its utmost to bend the arc of history toward a very different trajectory from that feared by Beaumont, Tocqueville, and Jefferson. Charlestonians believed that a paternalistic state was biblically ordained and would not only survive but also attain unprecedented greatness—if only the egalitarians in the North would permit history to play out as it should. They constructed a worldview that had a place for everyone, a hierarchy with God at the top, angelic beings forming a second-tier, higher White human society below the angels, and lower non-White human society forming the next tier, followed by animals, plants, and minerals. Further, human society was neatly organized by the plantation elite into an Aristotelian class pyramid in which they occupied a position at the top while enslaved people were at the bottom.[7]

Many authorities today, such as Fischer, maintain that southern culture had its origins not in Carolina but in Virginia. Fischer admits that some influence was projected from Carolina, but he maintained that it "never developed into a major cultural hearth." Alan Gallay, as noted above, and others have argued that the character of the Deep South, and perhaps the South more generally, was influenced more by Lowcountry slave society than by anything else.[8]

Virginia was a leader in shaping Anglo-American thought, and it became a powerful player in the early politics of the United States. It had the largest population among the colonies, it was centrally located, and it produced the leading statesmen. South Carolina was relatively small and isolated, but it cultivated a more powerful and regionally persuasive political ideology. By the mid-1700s, enslaved people accounted for 60 percent of South Carolina's population, twice that of Virginia. With a majority of its population enslaved, South Carolina developed a disciplined, authoritarian system of rule that evolved into a formidable political culture, and it defended its social and economic system with well-practiced rhetoric.

Increasingly, those studying southern culture are recognizing the potent influence of Lowcountry slave society. As the aristocracy grew dependent on an enslaved labor force it developed a culture of resistance to outside authority, which evolved into a defining characteristic of regional political culture. The direct effect was the formation of a distinct "Carolina way," as the early Georgians called it. Virginia, by contrast, was torn between its Enlightenment values and its dependency on the institution of slavery. It questioned both the morality and sustainability of slavery. Chastellux notes the "courage" shown by James Madison to propose abolition as early as 1781. But ending dependence on slavery proved too difficult to implement. Virginia had a wolf by the ear and could neither hold on to it nor let it loose, in Jefferson's often-cited metaphor.[9]

Carolina's governing class of planters and traders never worried about the morality of slavery and became far more committed to the institution of slavery than other southern colonies. Its commitment continued beyond the Revolution and firmed up rhetorically through the antebellum period. The source of South Carolina's near-total dependence on slavery arose from its dependence on an African labor force to labor in its rice monoculture. Free labor would have been virtually impossible to secure for the exhausting and often deadly work that went into coastal rice cultivation.

The profitable rice crop led plantation owners to bring more and more land under cultivation, which in turn required more and more slave labor. By 1708 the population of enslaved exceeded that of free people, and South Carolina's population remained a Black majority for over two centuries. For a free minority to repress an enslaved majority and prevent revolt, harsh measures had to be inured into the culture and enacted into law, accompanied by extreme rhetoric to rationalize such a regime.

Members of the Charleston governing class gradually cultivated explicit racism as a pillar of their rationale for a safe society. In doing so, they built a racial alliance in which many Whites could (however unrealistically) aspire to be wealthy slaveholders. Bacon's Rebellion in Virginia had taught the elite that such an alliance was essential to their survival. In 1676 Black and White Virginians—enslaved people, indentured servants, and freemen—joined in armed rebellion against the administration of Governor William Berkeley, who was also one of the Lords Proprietors of Carolina. While the government's initial reaction was to execute the principal instigators, the long-term effect on the elite was the realization that solidarity between races had to be discouraged at all costs.

Charleston was a rich city, and its power elite, more than in any other southern city, used inflammatory language, constructed from self-delusion, to rationalize and propagate its model of a slave society beyond its boundaries. The culture that took root in Charleston over four generations, and was transferred to Savannah in the mid-eighteenth century, became that of the Deep South by the late eighteenth century. At the time of the Civil War, rigidly hierarchical society and the institution of slavery that accompanied it had become entrenched over eight generations. That cultural paradigm in subtle ways, with a history of rhetorical underpinning, arguably continues to guide southern perceptions, even as the region and newly progressive cities like Charleston and Savannah seek pathways to a more egalitarian future.

The Multicultural South

Country music today is considered both southern and White in its origin and orientation. That notion is a misconception, however, as Ken Burns illustrated in the 2019 documentary series *Country Music.* The origin of the genre is multicultural, a blend of both musical forms and musical instruments (the banjo is African in origin). More and more, southern culture is being recognized as an amalgam of European, African, and Indigenous American influences.

The ethnocentric idea that a single British culture, the Scots-Irish, was the primary influence in forming southern culture is giving way to the broader understanding of multiple influences. Until the 1970s the prevailing view about southern culture was distorted by presumptions of White superiority. Such presumptions were common among scholars, not just the general public. It was presumed that Africans and their descendants contributed little to the mainstream culture. Entire histories of the South were written with barely a mention of Indigenous or African contributions, even though the latter constituted a majority of the population of South Carolina and nearly 40 percent of the population of the South upon independence from Britain.

Until recently, prompted by the 1960s civil rights movement, scholars have underappreciated African American influence in particular on the broader culture, and, to the extent that they recognized such influence, it was with condescension. It was a widely held view that enslavement stripped virtually every vestige of African culture from the poor souls taken from their homeland. They were stripped not only of their freedoms but also of their ability to practice their traditions. Thrown in with other enslaved people who spoke unfamiliar languages, and prohibited from forming normal families and friendships, they were made blank slates for the plantation elite to train for the single purpose of providing free labor eternally.

It is now known that this understanding of African American history is distorted by racism. While slaveowners used every method at their disposal to reduce their "property" to compliant laborers, the indomitable human spirit found ways to prevail under the worst of conditions. Cultural traits from Africa blended in the African American diaspora took root and influenced the larger culture.

Since the 1970s, scholars have been able to document African contributions to southern culture. The historian Walter Edgar, author of *A History of South Carolina*, has synthesized and generally made available much of that scholarly material in his long-running "Walter Edgar's Journal" on South Carolina public radio and television. South Carolinians and Americans in general are inching past old prejudices and coming to accept the fact that Africa played a large part in forming North America's unique culture.

The idea that American culture is fundamentally a blend of Puritan, Quaker, Scots-Irish, and other British influences is inaccurate and passé. It is now generally accepted that African influences are high up on any list of formative ingredients in America's blended culture. And within the broad category of African influences, a number of distinct and descendant cultures arising in the diaspora left their mark.

blended culture

Africa in the American Imagination

Africa in the American imagination is a hapless place with a bleak future. Sub-Saharan African, many believe, has none of the glorious history of other continents. This belief, however, reflects a general ignorance of African history abetted by entrenched racial attitudes that create a presumption that the current state of Africa is only a continuation of a supposed inglorious past. The reality of Africa is quite different. The failure to understand that reality is a failure to appreciate the blended culture of the Lowcountry and America beyond that, one that Charleston and Savannah are gradually rectifying.

The tale of Charleston and Savannah is a tale that, if told in full, is as much about Africa as it is about Europe. Earlier, it was shown that the mantle of greatness assumed by White rice planters was a false claim. Lowcountry rice plantations were an illicitly contrived joint venture between English planters and enslaved Africans in which the latter contributed a large portion, if not the bulk, of the technological expertise. Lowcountry rice plantations mirrored centuries-old practices found on the Rice Coast of West Africa.

Many of the enslaved people taken from Africa and deposited in Charleston came from West Africa and brought that region's traditions with them. Some were from the Rice Coast, the Grain Coast, the Gold Coast, and other subregions. Their histories are interconnected and linked to ancient civilizations that arose along the interface between the Niger River and the Sahara, the region of the Inland Niger Delta (IND) discussed earlier. Long covered by the encroaching Sahara, little has been known about such early societies until recent decades. But it was likely in this area that rice was first cultivated in Africa.

The IND and downstream regions oriented to the Niger produced a succession of trans-Saharan trading nations and empires over a period of more than a thousand years, including Timbuktu. The Ghana Empire, established about AD 700, was the first to rise from trans-Saharan trade. The Mali Empire founded in AD 1230 extended from the coast over one thousand miles inland past Timbuktu, the ancient city known for its wealth and scholarship during Europe's medieval period.

Mansa Musa (ca. 1280–1337), the tenth *mansa*, or emperor of Mali, famously began the hajj to Mecca in 1324 with sixty thousand men, each carrying several pounds of gold. His spending and generous monetary gifts in Egypt and elsewhere had the consequence of depressing the economy in those areas by reducing the value of gold. The largest dynasty in West Africa was founded with the Songhay Empire, which held territory that included the former Mali Empire.

The famous empires of the Sahel waned as oceanic trade eclipsed trans-Saharan trade. Power and wealth throughout much of West Africa flipped from inland to coastal regions with the growth of transatlantic trade. The well-documented Ashanti Empire, established in 1670, was one of the products of that realignment. West Africa's coastal nations faltered, however, when the slave trade came to dominate the trade relationships between Africa and Europe. By the late eighteenth century, Africa reached a tipping point where the slave trade resulted in "demographic exhaustion" and economic collapse.

Scholars are uncertain whether rice growing expertise reached the Rice Coast through diffusion from the IND and the civilizations it spawned or primarily developed over generations of experimentation by coastal people. If the former, then South Carolina's rice production has truly ancient roots in the Sahel. In either case, rice cultivation in the colony had ties of some form to Africa and Africans and was not the exclusive invention of Europeans but rather a collaborative effort.[10]

By denying the specific influences of Africans in rice cultivation and the more general influences of Africans in forming a new American culture, Charlestonians and Savannahians were able to construct a rationalization to defend their peculiar institution in the face of increasing scrutiny by northern states and the world beyond.

Southern Political Discourse

Language was the primary mechanism through which the plantation elite rationalized their behavior, altered conceptions of reality, and fought back against their critics. In the colonial era, language was class-oriented. Later it became racialized. Before the American Revolution, slavery was an accepted condition that befell some people, primarily prisoners of war and others who had done something to warrant the loss of freedom. Enslaved Africans up to a point fell into that category, having been purchased from other Africans who had captured them in the course of war. Later, of course, European demand for enslaved labor was so great that it created war among Africans for the very purpose of taking slaves, upending traditional economies in West and Central Africa.

Before the Revolution, however, little thought was given to the morality of slavery. Oglethorpe was one of the first to question the morality of the institution, writing in 1737, "If we allow slaves we act against the very principles by which we associated together, which was to relieve the distressed." But it was not until the 1770s that Oglethorpe became an active abolitionist, joining forces with Granville Sharp, who had been challenging the legality of slavery in Britain. It was in the 1780s, after the American Revolution, that his social circle began discussing abolition, and it was after his death in 1785 that the abolition movement was formally launched with the founding of the Clapham Sect, founded by William Wilberforce, Granville Sharp, Hannah More, and other notable pioneers of the movement. (Their early meetings were held in the Clapham district of South London.)[11]

With very few people before the Revolution questioning the morality or the long-term sustainability of slavery, there was no need to defend it as an institution. In the thinking of the time, slavery was not unlike feudal vassalage.

That is, it was a type of social class, although a class situated at the very bottom of the social pyramid. Although slavery was accepted as an institution, it was also considered a human condition that was the opposite of liberty. The very first sentence of Locke's *First Treatise of Government* condemned slavery. But in that opening sentence, Locke was writing about an unwarranted taking of liberty, especially by an authoritarian figure, resulting in a form of slavery. He still made an exception for the enslavement of prisoners of war, among others who through just defensive action lost their freedom and were thus seen as legitimately placed in the bottom tier of society.[12]

Locke's liberty-slavery polarity reflected the historical English disdain for absolute power. The popular sentiment as well as the formal argument for liberty transferred in whole from England to the colonies. Unfair taxes were attacked as a form of enslavement by government. Restrictions on worship were attacked as a form of enslavement by the Anglican Church. At the time of the Revolution, the soon-to-be states were a patchwork not only of thirteen political divisions but also of religious and ethnic divisions (English, Scots-Irish, Scots, Irish, European Protestants, and others). Each group professed love of liberty and a deep suspicion of the powers that might enslave them.

The Language of Liberty

Liberty was a concept the Lowcountry plantation elite and the business oligarchs from Charleston to Savannah took to heart and implanted indelibly in southern political culture. For an outsider or a detached cultural insider, the southern attachment to liberty looks like sheer hypocrisy. As the eighteenth-century writer and lexicographer Samuel Johnson wrote just before the American Revolution, "How is it that we hear the loudest yelps for liberty among the drivers of negroes?" According to Johnson's dictionary, the only comprehensive dictionary of the late eighteenth century and early nineteenth century, "liberty" was defined as "freedom, as opposed to slavery," while "slavery" was defined as "servitude" and "slave" was defined as "not a freeman."[13]

To understand the apparent contradiction seemingly inherent in the persistent southern use of the word "liberty" coupled with its relentless embrace of slavery (followed by the repressive Jim Crow regime and modern opposition to civil rights legislation), one has to figure out what liberty meant to the thought leaders of the antebellum South. They were, without question, paternalistic and hierarchical. They believed White superiority justified dominance over non-White "savage" races. Further, they believed in the superiority of some Whites over other Whites. In the view of the plantation elite, liberty was a condition for naturally superior people who warranted it by virtue of their higher intelligence and moral authority. Those who were lower in the hierarchy were no more deserving of liberty than children. Enslaved Blacks, they believed, were even less deserving than White children, requiring absolute control for their own good.[14]

The paternalistic and hierarchical worldview held by the plantation elite and many other southern Whites ran against the tide of thinking nearly worldwide. All of the nations formerly engaged in the Atlantic slave trade outlawed the practice by the early 1800s, as the South was becoming ever more committed to it. A belief that "all men are created equal" was taking root and expanding, in part due to John Locke's effective demolition of natural paternalistic and hierarchical authority articulated in *Two Treatises of Government*. Since all humans are created equal in the state of nature, Locke concluded, authority was derived from the consent of the people led or governed. People conferred authority on their leaders through a compact, and they had the right to change leaders if that compact was violated.

Locke's reasoning was foundational to the Enlightenment and a powerful influence on the Founders. Jefferson, Madison, Monroe, and Washington, all Virginians, questioned the morality of slavery and the long-term viability of a slave society within a democratic republic, even though Virginia's enslaved population was proportionately smaller than that of Carolina, where no such concerns found traction. Virginia formally debated the future of slavery. But where Virginia was a moderating influence on the Upper South and arguably might have negotiated an end to slavery, the Lowcountry plantation elite, sitting atop a Black majority, took a more rigid position on their peculiar institution. They believed that slavery was a "positive good," as John C. Calhoun strenuously argued in the Senate.

The Lower South, led by South Carolina, had a larger percentage of enslaved people than the Upper South and a profound commitment to the institution of slavery. As that commitment grew over the eighteenth century and into the nineteenth century, the region's leaders forged a rhetorical sword-and-shield armamentarium to fight their opponents. The sword was the aggressive defense of "liberty." The shield was a biblical interpretation of history in defense of paternalistic authoritarianism.

The English historian J. C. D. Clark has argued that "traditions of political thought and action were carried within and articulated by the mosaic of religious denominations" in America, reaching a crescendo during the Revolution. In *The Language of Liberty*, he maintained that the Revolution was "a war of religion" of "ancient divisions and hatreds" more than a war over pure political ideology. Subtexts of base prejudice are seldom articulated, and thus it was that the South learned from Revolutionary rhetoric, acquiring a self-serving, post-Revolutionary articulation of higher ideals, the ideals of liberty and constitutional first principles.[15]

CHAPTER TEN

The Lowcountry Cultural Economy Moves West

James Oglethorpe's early success in establishing a slavery-free colony and maintaining good relations with Native Americans became increasingly irritating to the Lowcountry elite by thwarting their plans to expand rice cultivation and inland trade. Acting in concert with the Malcontents in Savannah, who aspired to be slaveholders, Charlestonians began attacking Oglethorpe and belittling his colony of yeoman farmers. "There is hardly a man in the universe," Oglethorpe wrote from Frederica, "that has had more lies raised of him." He added that the commercial class in London and Bristol, having close ties with Charleston, added fuel to the fire to protect their burgeoning trade with Carolina.[1]

With all the disapproving chatter in Charleston, visitors from that city and its surrounding farms and villages were sometimes surprised at Georgia's progress. One such group, while touring Savannah with local officials in 1739, was impressed with the state of the young colony, admitting that production exceeded their expectations. Nevertheless, they expressed skepticism that Georgia would advance any further without slavery, which they saw as essential to lowering production costs.[2]

One visitor observed that Georgia was much better off than when he had previously visited, and he spoke of the "vanity" of South Carolinians and their "inveterate ill-will" toward their neighbor. Carolinians, he said, were apprehensive that the new colony would overtake them in "trade and manufactures" in a matter of a few years principally because Carolina was invested almost exclusively in rice. The visitor added that the attorney general in South Carolina was planning to assert a claim to land in Georgia, implying that Carolinians were coveting neighboring properties in anticipation of overturning the Trustee administration and claiming large tracts of land south of the Savannah River.[3]

Unable to outmaneuver Oglethorpe and the Trustees, slaveholders began surreptitiously crossing the river and cultivating land in the 1740s, at times with the acquiescence of local landowners. In 1749, six years after Oglethorpe had returned to England, officials at Savannah reported the problem to the Trustees. The officials noted that abuse was widespread and would be impractical to enforce, and thus the Trustees should consider lifting the prohibition against slavery and instituting a humane and strictly limited form of slavery. As reported earlier, the Trustees were indignant and ordered local officials to crack down on offenders. By then, however, the battle was lost, and the Trustees eventually conceded defeat and enacted regulations that they viewed as humanitarian for the treatment of enslaved people. Two years later, in June 1752, the Georgia experiment was over.

In a victory gesture, Charlestonian slaveholder Jonathan Bryan marched sixty-six enslaved workers to Savannah, leading a "parade" of Carolina planters into the Georgia Colony. Regulations enacted by the Trustees for humanitarian treatment of enslaved people were soon replaced by the repressive South Carolina slave code. Charleston was now poised for a new era of westward expansion. The belief of the Lowcountry elite, articulated by men such as William Bull II, that it was their exclusive destiny to lead a new era of expansion of their empire of slavery was becoming a reality.[4]

Taking Indigenous American Territories

The westward expansion of the "Carolina way" from the Lowcountry to the Mississippi Valley was initially impeded by the presence of numerous Indigenous nations. However, war, disease, treaty violations, displacement, and relocation cleared the way for yeoman farmers and slaveholders alike to encroach on and cultivate Indigenous American lands.[5]

The posture of Carolinians toward Native Americans after the Proprietary and Trustee periods continued to be one of exploitation. By 1730 Charleston authorities saw their colony as the heart of the British Empire in the Southeast. Respect for Native Americans prescribed earlier by the Lords Proprietors quickly dissipated, and many English settlers dismissed their Indigenous neighbors as savages. As one put it, they had "nothing but the shape of Men to distinguish them from Wolves & Tigers." Indians were merely part of the American wilderness, a new world to be subdued and Christianized.[6]

Four large Indigenous nations and various smaller communities populated the southeastern region of North America west of Carolina and Georgia. The largest of those was the Creek, or Muskogee, Confederacy, which encom-

passed much of present-day South Carolina, Georgia, Alabama, and Tennessee. The confederacy consisted of a large number of small, town-centered nations that formed the alliance in the face of European encroachment in the region in the seventeenth century. The Cherokee Nation was concentrated in the southern Appalachians but maintained a strong trading presence in the coastal lowlands. The Chickasaw and Choctaw populations were concentrated farther west in present-day Alabama and Mississippi.

Numerous settlements of indigenous people resided in the Lowcountry and nearby. The Kussoe lived between Charleston and the future site of Savannah and were among those who never welcomed the English. Accusations of murder made against Kussoe people led to a brief war and their eventual suppression by Charleston forces. The Stono indigenous people lived near the Kussoe in the Lowcountry and were also unwelcoming. They too eventually had to seek peace under disadvantageous terms. The Yamasee were a third group that had periodic hostile relations with the English that eventually led to war.[7]

The Westo people, who lived along the Savannah River, had initially hostile relations with the English, but after a short war they arranged peace through Henry Woodward (ca. 1646–ca. 1690), the Proprietors' agent, who had become skilled in negotiating with Indigenous people. The Westo then began supplying Carolina with enslaved workers.[8]

The Savannah Indigenous people, after whom the river was named, lived upriver from the Westo. The Savannah, more generally known as Shawnee, were from the Ohio River Valley and had migrated to various places east of the Mississippi. Throughout their diaspora, numerous towns they established retained contact with each other. Their language was a lingua franca in many areas, allowing them to establish a pan-Indian movement. They initially allied with the Westo but later reversed course and allied with the English against the Westo, destroying their settlements and driving survivors out of the Lowcountry.[9]

The Yuchi (Euchee), a linguistically distinct nation with a dispersed urban culture, formed a town on the Savannah River near Augusta and engaged in trade with the English. They joined the Creek Confederacy and maintained generally good relations with their neighbors.

Ignoring the Lords Proprietors' instructions, Carolina traders were infamous for their duplicity and aggressive marketing of rum to young Indigenous men despite the protests of elders. Such practices, together with encroachments into Native lands, precipitated the Yamasee War of 1715, which temporarily destabilized the Carolina frontier. William Bull I, a friend of Oglethorpe, was among the few who advocated fair and honest relations with Native Americans. However, such men were in the minority and were out-maneuvered by those seeking quick profits.[10]

The Southeast was unique in that it was the only region where three European powers competed and where their machinations were at the same time reflected in European geopolitics. European nations often entered into alliances with Indigenous nations to defend their interests. English and Creek forces, for example, fought the Spanish and their Indigenous allies over disputed territory between Georgia and Florida. The English also entered into a treaty with the Creek Nation, among others, to defend their territory from the French and their allies who posed a threat in the west. South Carolina eventually became sufficiently strong to become the dominant force in the region, ultimately prevailing in the Yamasee War and winning later wars with the Cherokee Nation between the late 1750s and early 1780s.[11]

Colonial officials and subsequent U.S. authorities and the settlers they represented frequently violated treaties when it was convenient to do so. Alexander McGillivray (1750–1793), born Hoboi-Hili-Miko, who represented multiple nations in negotiating treaties to preserve sovereignty, attempted to prevent British expansion onto Creek territory. In 1785 he wrote, "We have received friendly talks and replies, it is true, but while they are addressing us by the flattering appellations of Friends and Brothers, they are stripping us of our natural rights by depriving us of that inheritance which belonged to our ancestors and hath descended from them to us since the beginning of time."[12]

President George Washington, Vice President Thomas Jefferson, and Secretary of War Henry Knox, envoy to the Native American nations, advocated formal recognition of Indigenous nations as sovereign states. As such, the federal government would have sole authority to negotiate treaties with them. They believed that such a policy was consistent with the principles of the Revolution.[13]

Having established a conceptual foundation for sovereignty, the United States and the Creek Nation signed the Treaty of New York in 1790. Alexander McGillivray led the multination Native American presence at the treaty conference. The purpose of the treaty was to establish permanent borders and future stability. Federal enforcement was weak, however, and Carolina and Georgia were able to ignore it and permit White settlers to take Native American lands. Whites poured across federally recognized borders by the thousands. Knox wrote that "a lawless set of unprincipled wretches" were violating the treaty "without receiving the punishment they so richly deserve[d]." Washington also expressed concern, writing, "Scarcely anything short of a Chinese wall will restrain . . . the encroachment of settlers upon the Indian Country."[14]

Andrew Jackson, who became president in 1829, ended the principle of sovereignty of Indigenous nations and enforced the Indian Removal Act of 1830, overseeing the forced removal of approximately sixty thousand Native Americans from their homelands in the Southeast to the present-day state of Oklahoma. The forced relocation of the Cherokee, Creek, Seminole, Chickasaw, and Choctaw Nations known now as the Trail of Tears began in 1832 and continued to 1839. Distances of the relocation ranged from approximately five hundred miles to over one thousand miles. The torturous march caused thousands of deaths of Native Americans as well as Whites and Blacks who endured the march with them. The mass deportation made possible a White takeover of the entire region, which then was dominated culturally and politically by the Lowcountry elite.[15]

Empire of Slavery

By the mid-1700s three European slave societies were well established in the Southeast: Virginia, South Carolina, and Louisiana. Virginia dominated the Tidewater region (which included most of Maryland) as well as North Carolina. South Carolina by then had just brought Georgia under its influence. Louisiana encompassed a substantial portion of the Lower Mississippi watershed. It was a province of France until the Louisiana Purchase of 1803, except from 1763 to 1800 when it was ceded to Spain. Those three slave societies would expand, each penetrating into the other and in the process creating the larger region, or "section," that became the South.

Spanish Florida was a fourth geopolitical factor in the region. Florida was not a slave society and sought to destabilize Carolina by offering freedom to enslaved runaways. Carolina and Georgia had encroached on territory that Spain had long claimed, coastline that paralleled the Gulf Stream, the essential current that carried Spanish ships back to the homeland. In 1742, as discussed in chapter 4, Oglethorpe secured the southern flank of the Thirteen Colonies for Britain by turning back a Spanish incursion at the Battle of Bloody Marsh.

After its de facto annexation of Georgia as a slaveholding, satellite colony in 1752, South Carolina pushed westward across the region, eventually meeting and joining the established slave culture of Louisiana, where the plantation elite had become rich from sugar. At the same time it percolated northward, mixing its culture with that of Virginia, Tennessee, and Kentucky, creating the larger region, or section, known as the South—a geographic term that entered the lexicon in the late 1780s as the slaveholding states south of the Mason-Dixon Line maneuvered to draft a constitution that would protect their economic system (as observed earlier, southern colonies did not yet self-identify as the "South" in the colonial era).

On the surface, Virginia and South Carolina appear to have always had a uniquely southern political culture. They were agrarian and rigidly hierarchical, controlled by aristocrats and oligarchs, and economically dependent on monoculture and enslaved labor. In the antebellum South, as the historian Eugene Genovese observed, their shared "source of pride was not the Union, not the nonexistent Southern nation; it was the plantation, which they raised to a political principle."[16]

A closer examination, however, reveals significant differences between the two slave societies. Jefferson wrote in 1820 of the need to confront the sustainability of slavery and the difficulty of doing so: "Justice is in one scale, and self-preservation in the other." In 1830 the Virginia House of Delegates formally entertained gradual abolition, but the proposal was narrowly defeated. In 1790, when Congress considered the gradual abolition of slavery, Virginia was again poised to consider it. South Carolina, by contrast, never considered a future without slavery. Instead, its aristocracy and oligarchy perfected a language of liberty while tightening the noose of tyranny, and it never wavered in its opposition to abolition.[17]

The "Carolina way" spread westward more slowly at first than the Virginia model, but ultimately it spread farther and produced the legacy of repression associated with the Deep South. The two political cultures met west of the Appalachians and united to preserve the system of slavery and single-crop dominance on which they both depended. The rice and tobacco plantation models of each became the cotton plantation models of the Lower South.[18]

The consolidation of the South as a slave society began in 1767 when Georgia, by then modeled on the Carolina way, claimed most of the present states of Alabama and Mississippi. After the Revolution, the area was settled through fraudulent land grants awarded by successive Georgia governments. In the infamous Yazoo land scandal (named for Native Americans who once lived in the Yazoo River basin), a political contrivance awarded large land grants to the political and aristocratic elite, thus perpetuating the gothic (or feudalistic) social pyramid engrained in South Carolina.

During the Revolution thousands of loyalists from South Carolina and Georgia settled in Natchez, bringing about a "plantation revolution" along that segment of the Mississippi River. In the 1780s, settlers migrating from Kentucky and Tennessee to the Lower Mississippi entered that milieu and reinforced its slave society. Sugar plantations expanded rapidly around New Orleans in the late 1790s, creating an unbroken chain of plantations that extended upriver for 250 miles. Virginians encouraged the westward expansion of slavery, believing it to be an opportunity to disperse enslaved populations across a larger region, thereby reducing the threat of rebellion. However, such a strategy required cutting off the importation of enslaved people to be effective, a measure strenuously opposed by the Deep South.[19]

The Lowcountry elite were the dominant influence across the Lower South for a century and a half until rising inland wealth and congressional reapportionment shifted power westward. In the assessment of geographer Donald Meinig, "South Carolina was in an excellent position to exert a very marked influence upon the newer Gulf States." Large numbers of Carolina planters, such as the prominent planter-politician Wade Hampton, invested heavily in Mississippi Valley plantations, relocating much of their enslaved labor force as they did so. The South Carolina slaveholder-politician James Henry Hammond said of the trend, "to the West [went] . . . nearly every one of the young men with whom I was brought up." They concentrated their power in county seats where they were able to shape the evolution of the new territories. South Carolina thus exerted its influence across the Deep South, injecting, in Meinig's words, "many prominent persons—governors, judges, lesser officials, and local leaders—who had received training in South Carolina" into the region in its formative period. On the eve of the Civil War, South Carolinians outnumbered Mississippians at the Mississippi secession convention. In contemplating secession, many in the Upper South wondered if it would not be preferable to be the South of the northern states rather than the North of a southern confederacy.[20]

The Upper South had the potential to become a distinct third section with features of northern and southern political culture. With its dominating votes in Congress, the slave trade could have been ended, slavery in the territories banned, and slavery phased out in terms considered by the Virginians. An "empire of liberty" was theoretically within reach. But incessant pressure from the Deep South, led by South Carolina, undermined any prospect of that happening. The Deep South thus took on the character of South Carolina as it grew dramatically after the Revolution, and the Upper South let the tail wag the dog. The "Carolina way" meant that there was no concern over the number of enslaved people in the population, no limit to the cruelty in maintaining the system, and no end to the rhetoric defending slavery as fundamental to a great civilization. James Henry Hammond encapsulated the prevailing attitude: "I repudiate, as ridiculously absurd, that much-lauded but nowhere accredited dogma of Mr. Jefferson, 'that all men are born equal.'"[21]

In 1860 a book compiling the writings of various pro-slavery southern intellectual leaders was published under the title *Cotton Is King*. The rise of King Cotton in the early 1800s made the plantation elite of the Deep South wealthy and powerful actors on a global stage. A million enslaved people were relocated to the Mississippi Valley, one-third through plantation relocations and two-thirds through the domestic slave trade (primarily with the Upper South selling enslaved workers to the Deep South). Cotton wealth came from the British capital, an enslaved labor force, the invention of the cotton gin, and the introduction of steamboats on the Mississippi. By the 1850s, the region was producing as much as 80 percent of the world's cotton, with most of it going to Great Britain.[22]

King Cotton, which dominated the Deep South from South Carolina to East Texas, came with fatal flaws. A "radical simplification" of the landscape for a cotton monoculture left the region overly dependent on a single crop, dependent on outside capital, and overinvested in land and enslaved labor while lacking a manufacturing sector, with limited food production for local consumption, and with poorly developed road networks.[23]

Over the forty years from 1810 to 1850, eight new southern states were admitted to the union. Growth in the core Cotton Belt states of Georgia, Alabama, Mississippi, and Louisiana was dramatic, and the population increased from 368,315 to 3,520,794 free and enslaved people during that period. About one million enslaved people from the Upper South were "sold down the river" or marched down to Georgia and then westward into the harsher conditions of the Deep South. Slaveholders made up about a quarter of the population in the South and held 93 percent of the region's agricultural wealth. Many non-slave-owning Whites aspired to become slaveholders. Slavery was not dying out as Lost Cause mythology later claimed; it was in a state of dynamic growth.[24]

While the Virginia, Carolina, and Louisiana primary slave cultures were blending and influencing the character of the Southeast, newer territories were opened up by the Louisiana Purchase and the annexation of the Republic of Texas. East Texas and the Delta region of Arkansas joined the other states of the Deep South in adopting the South Carolina practices of unrestrained slavery, harsh treatment of enslaved people, and the anti-federal, pro-slavery rhetoric of aristocratic destiny promoted by the Lowcountry elite.[25]

The struggle between a northern "empire of liberty" and a southern "empire of slavery" reached a peak with the fight over Missouri statehood. Fear of breaking up the Union, brought on by Deep South agitation, led instead to the Missouri Compromise, which divided the lands acquired in the Louisiana Purchase into free and slave territories. Missouri was admitted to the Union in 1821 as a slave state, absorbing the militant grand vision of the future of slavery of the Deep South along with its contempt for the federal government.[26]

The plantation elite had grander ambitions than the annexation of the western territories. Expansion was an essential feature of a slaveholding society. As a Georgian declared before the state legislature in 1856: "Whenever slavery is confined within certain specified limits, its future existence is doomed." Acting on that principle, slavery advocate William Walker led several military ventures into Latin America, becoming president of Nicaragua after an insurrection in 1855. The secretive Knights of the Golden Circle supported various actions to bring about a Central American–Caribbean southern empire. As long as the South had room to grow, it was content to let the North's "hireling civilization" grow as well—toward the Arctic.[27]

The southern aristocracy promoted the belief that through their enlightened, paternalistic leadership, coupled with the obedience of enslaved people and lower classes, the South would reach a pinnacle of civilization. In their view, aristocracy and inequality were essential elements of an advanced society. South Carolinian James Henry Hammond wrote: "Slavery does indeed create an aristocracy—an aristocracy of talents, of virtue, of generosity and courage. In a slave country, every freeman is an aristocrat." At the same time, Hammond stated, "Inequality is the fundamental law of nature, and hence alone the harmony of the universe." Another South Carolinian, William Harper, insisted, "The institution of slavery is the principal cause of civilization," and he was among the many political theorists who asserted this. If inequality led to a "state of tyranny," according to the southern political theorist Albert Taylor Bledsoe, it was because that was the natural abode of Blacks.[28]

South Carolinian Leonidas Spratt spoke of two civilizations, one modeled on the White male as a husband, father, and slave master, the other intent on pursuing a "delirium of liberty" for all, which would only create a "carnival" of social disorder. The "culture wars" decried by some today echo the rhetoric of the debate over slavery. A commentator in *DeBow's Review*, a southern business magazine launched in 1846, described the divide between the slaveholding states and "the wage states" as a divide between home, family, and the Bible on one hand, and pluralism, democracy, and anarchy on the other.[29]

A result of the South's plantation-centric socioeconomic model was that in its zeal to reach external markets it failed to develop intraregional rural and urban markets of sufficient size to sustain diversified agriculture or industry. In 1860 the urban population of the Deep South stood at only 7 percent of the region's total population, and there were only three cities with more than fifteen thousand people—New Orleans, Charleston, and Savannah. The South Carolina state geologist warned farmers not to grow more corn than they could consume since there was no infrastructure to connect surpluses with markets. Kentuckian Cassius Clay observed, "A home market cannot exist in a slave state."[30]

States' Rights Platform

One can say that the South had talked itself into a bind. The region's elite romanticized the plantation as the paternalistic nucleus of southern life. It characterized its success with monocultures—rice, tobacco, and ultimately King Cotton—as grand achievements. The elite convinced themselves that they were a superior race of Anglo-Saxon Cavaliers. From such constant rhetoric, many White southerners came to believe the South was superior and invincible. A disproportionate share of that myopic and overconfident rhetoric emanated from Charleston.

Cries of "liberty" and "states' rights" permeated paternalistic southern political culture as it struggled to find a footing against the moralistic antislavery stance of the North and much of the world beyond. By the 1830s, rhetoric that would carry the South to secession was firmly entrenched in the culture and arguably persists to this day.

"States' rights" is perhaps second only to "liberty" in the lexicon of southern political culture. The antebellum states' rights movement found its strongest voice in the Lowcountry, growing out of the "nullification" thesis advanced by the plantation elite. Under that thesis, states have the right to nullify federal laws that they determine to be unconstitutional. The opposing position is that federal law is supreme, as the Constitution makes clear in Article VI, Clause 2 (known as the Supremacy Clause), and it is not the states but the federal courts and ultimately the Supreme Court that are empowered to interpret the constitutionality of federal laws.

Advocates of nullification found sufficient ambivalence in the opinions of Thomas Jefferson, James Madison, and Andrew Hamilton to build a case for state-initiated nullification. Thus, if a state determined that a federal law was unconstitutional it had the right to nullify that law within its boundaries without having to seek that remedy through the federal courts. Madison ultimately believed that, if carried to an extreme, nullification would lead to anarchy. Nevertheless, during the early 1800s several states took the nullification route in objecting to what they saw as federal overreach. In each case, the Supreme Court ruled that the authority for interpretation rested with the federal courts.

The Nullification Crisis arose in 1828 when Charlestonian John C. Calhoun argued that the Tariff of 1828, which favored northern manufacturing, could be vetoed by South Carolina. The state acted on that opinion in 1832 when it vetoed both the Tariff of 1828 and the Tariff of 1832. President Andrew Jackson rejected the state's claim to a right to veto federal legislation. The tariff issue was of intense interest in South Carolina because it was tied to the issue of slavery through the state's desire to protect its economic institutions, which were built upon slavery.

Charlestonian Robert Barnwell Rhett added his voice to Calhoun's arguments for states' rights, calling them "a great principle of self-government." Rhett's intentions were transparently pro-slavery as detailed in chapter 4. He spoke of states' rights and slavery as virtually unified concepts, and when South Carolina seceded from the union he declared that slavery was the "proximate or immediate cause," while simultaneously asserting with a sense of moral authority that the principle of states' rights had caused a sectional divide.[31]

Ironically, the South viscerally opposed states' rights when it came to the Fugitive Slave Law, which compelled northern states to return runaway slaves to their southern "owners." Enslaved people were "property," and property rights were sacrosanct. In this case, it was the northern states that pursued a states' rights position, losing that argument in the Supreme Court, which estopped them from aiding escapees in their quest for freedom.

The rise of states' rights politics in the antebellum period was mirrored in the rise of the States' Rights Democratic Party, or Dixiecrats, before the election of 1948. South Carolina governor (later senator) Strom Thurmond and other governors from the Deep South reacted to civil rights initiatives put in place by President Harry Truman (integrating the military and forming a civil rights commission) by organizing a convention to create a new party that would embrace Jim Crow laws and the belief in White superiority. The convention, held in Birmingham, Alabama, on July 17, 1948, just days after the Democratic National Convention, nominated Thurmond and Mississippi governor Fielding Wright for president and vice president. The States' Rights Democratic Party carried Louisiana, Mississippi, Alabama, and South Carolina. At a second convention, held in Oklahoma City, on August 14, 1948, the party formally endorsed racial segregation and characterized the Truman administration as an enemy of liberty who was leading the nation into totalitarianism.

Outsized Influence

Charleston, and more broadly the Lowcountry, including Savannah, exerted an outsized influence on antebellum politics and southern political culture. Although South Carolina remained much less populous than Virginia through the colonial and antebellum periods, its influence expanded, first through its wealth from rice exports, then through its aggressive political culture, a survival trait acquired in the face of an enslaved Black majority.

Although a certain level of tyranny is necessary for any slave society to survive, the reign of tyranny in the Lowcountry and its growing hinterland went to excesses seldom seen in the Tidewater region. Slave revolt was feared throughout the South but more intensely in the Deep South where the "Carolina way," as the early Georgians called it, prevailed. Often driven by wild rumors, persistent fears of revolt continued right up to the Civil War. To protect its interests, South Carolina invented a regimented society with laws designed by the plantation elite to preserve the status quo, militias to enforce transgressions, and Christianity molded by the slave society to justify its existence and to pacify those it enslaved. It was a society that indoctrinated White children "to tyrannize over, to beat and abuse out of sport," as missionary Charles Wesley wrote.[32]

While a select few among an enslaved population enjoyed limited freedoms working as servants on plantations or as tradesmen in Charleston and Savannah, the vast majority toiled long days under "masters of violence," as the historian Tristan Stubbs characterized plantation overseers. A layer (sometimes layers) of such men operating between the elite and those they enslaved enabled the elite to sublimate their role in preserving the system, glorify their position atop slave society, and see their paternalism as benevolent and built on a biblical model. Spending much of their time living in opulence in Charleston and Savannah, and retiring to temperate northern cities such as Newport, Rhode Island, during the long, hot summers, the elite indulged in self-glorification and promoted a political class and an industry of writing and publishing to rationalize their "peculiar institution."

Several of those South Carolina rhetoricians formed the core of the "sacred circle" of southern writers and politicians who justified slavery. South Carolinian William Harper wrote that "the institution of slavery is the principal cause of civilization." Another South Carolinian, James Henry Hammond, wrote, "I firmly believe that American slavery is not only not a sin, but especially commanded by God through Moses, and approved by Christ through his apostles." Charlestonian William Gilmore Simms wrote the novel *The Sword and the Distaff* in reaction to Harriet Beecher Stowe's *Uncle Tom's Cabin*. Simms's novel became part of a southern apologist genre known as Anti-Tom literature.[33]

Slave Society Through Lines

Southern political culture and intense regional divisions did not end with the Civil War. Reconstruction met with intractable southern resistance and northern fatigue and failed to initiate a new order of racial equality. The nation returned to a new acceptance of racial inequality and the rationalizations for it that would set in for a century.

Gradually, following the civil rights revolution of the 1960s, the regional character of the nation started slowly dissipating and reaggregating into finer-grained patterns at metropolitan and county levels. Old regional beliefs and attitudes that had formed during the colonial and antebellum eras largely remain, reorganized into a new geographical pattern. Like its predecessor political models, New England and New Amsterdam, the South has proven to be one of the more enduring influences on American political culture, still owing largely to South Carolina's unwavering adherence to traditional social hierarchy, exurban development, property rights, religion, and intense anti-federalism.

Although the United States is acquiring a new political geography, the Solid South (a historic term, but one that remains applicable) retains those attitudes. While southern states are uniformly red (Republican) at the state level, they are turning blue (Democrat) at the urban level. Nearly every city in the South shows up as blue on maps of county and voter precinct election results. The South has changed political parties, but, except in its cities, it has not changed its fundamental White political culture of authoritarian one-party dominance and opposition to all new civil rights initiatives in more than three centuries.

With its transition from overtly racial rhetoric to the subtle rhetoric of the Republican Southern Strategy, White southern political culture unwittingly injected colonial ideals into contemporary politics. The gothic republicanism of Ashley Cooper never completely faded from southern political rhetoric, but federal neglect of the South after Reconstruction and during the Jim Crow era left the region free to ignore once again the immorality and un-sustainability of racial repression while exercising only the more newly acceptable and expedient rhetoric of White supremacy. With the latest rise of the South as a force in national politics, the nation's three primary political cultures once again took on competing positions in a war of ideas dating to the colonial era. And once again the South leads the way in framing that war as one of race (dog-whistle politics), class (the "elite" versus the rest), and external threats (immigrant invasions).

PART VI

Decline and Reinvention

After the Civil War, Charleston and Savannah entered into a long period of stagnation and decline. While their fortunes waxed and waned
with the national economy, the overall trend was to fall behind other
cities across the nation in population and economic vitality.

The post–World War II era of growth and the soon-to-follow civil
rights movement era presented both cities with an opportunity for
self-examination and reinvention. Their economic successes in recent
decades come from confronting the past and charting a new, more inclusive course.

CHAPTER ELEVEN

Stagnation and Decline

Charleston and Savannah grew steadily in population for more than two centuries, with ever-larger numbers of enslaved Blacks and poor Whites producing greater and greater wealth for the small minority of aristocrats and oligarchs. Population and economic growth leveled off before the Civil War as investment moved west toward the cotton plantations and newer cities of the Lower Mississippi Valley. A reversal of fortunes set in after the Civil War, and the two cities entered a century-long period of decline. The civil rights movement of the 1960s gave both cities renewed opportunity. They recognized their past as deeply flawed and rebuilt by becoming more inclusive and featuring their rich history in a more enlightened manner.

The Fall of the Old Cultural Economy

Scholars in various disciplines use the terms "cultural economy," "political culture," and "political economy" to label the intersections among various facets of a society and the complex relationships that exist within those intersections. The cultural economy of the South emerged in Virginia and Carolina as they became slave societies—that is, societies built on the institution of slavery. Cultural attributes that came to define the South—the likes of paternalism, oligarchy, White superiority, honor, and agrarianism—developed together with slavery as it became entrenched in the economy.

While the region's cultural economy was forced into two sudden and unwanted structural realignments, first by the abolition of slavery and then by the abolition of Jim Crow laws, its political culture and political economy (as already discussed) have to this day retained some features that have persisted since colonial times. Although the South's cultural economy has become antiquated, it has not entirely disappeared. Instead of disappearing altogether, it has retreated into the conservative domain of rural areas even as southern cities have adopted more inclusive, egalitarian, and cosmopolitan postures.

The cultural economy of the South first emerged in Virginia and then in Carolina with the adoption of monoculture—tobacco in Virginia, rice in Carolina—and the enslavement of a labor force to cultivate those crops. A wealthy aristocracy and oligarchy—slaveholders, slave merchants, and exporters—took form, gained control of government, and influenced social institutions. A formula for the southern cultural economy was set:

COLONIAL ERA CULTURAL ECONOMY
plutocracy + large-scale monoculture + specialized slave labor

The formula was reinforced and enhanced through the creation of a legal framework enforcing the institution of slavery. In this area of development, Carolina had a head start with a constitution written in 1668 that established and protected slavery. Slave codes adopted by the colonies were increasingly specific and detailed with regard to crimes and punishment. Initial codes, modeled after the Barbados Slave Code of 1661, were adopted in Carolina in 1691, and in 1705 in Virginia.

The term "plutocracy" may be applied to this early era because the colonies were generally controlled by a singular wealthy elite. Later, during the antebellum era, a more dynamic form of rule emerged, better described by the words "aristocracy," "patriarchy," and "oligarchy," the three together forming a complex of associations controlling the economy and government. "Aristocracy" and "patriarchy" may also be used to describe an upper class without necessarily directly linking either to the reins of economic or governmental power.

The evolution of a southern slave-based cultural economy, which historians refer to as a slave society, became *consciously directed* by its economic beneficiaries in its later stages. In the colonial era, this took the form of eliminating enslavement of Indigenous Americans, creating tensions between Native Americans and Blacks, encouraging a narrower form of racism among poor Whites, and ceding some political power to lower-income Whites, particularly after Bacon's Rebellion in 1676. During the Revolutionary period and later, other tactics developed to strengthen the cultural economy. These included heightening racist rhetoric, creating elaborate mythology of White superiority, and warning Whites that abolition would result in Blacks taking their jobs.[1]

When the leaders of Virginia imagined independence from Britain, they imagined creating a democratic republic based on principles of the Enlightenment articulated by John Locke and an entire network of thinkers, known as the Republic of Letters, that spanned Europe and the Atlantic. Slavery was a thorny issue, one that they knew could not be resolved immediately but that would have to be addressed methodically for the safety of the White population, if not for the greater good. The intention, over the long run, was to create a better society than the one they had inherited.[2]

When the leaders of Carolina imagined independence from Britain, they imagined the very kind of society that Locke argued against in *Two Treatises of Government*. Locke began the "First Treatise" with an attack on patriarchy and used the "Second Treatise" to frame the first principles for a society based on natural human rights and a theory of government by the people through a contract or compact (he used both words) with their leaders. South Carolina's governing elite envisioned an extreme form of patriarchy that was antithetical to the central ideals of the Enlightenment that inspired the leaders of Virginia and other colonies.

The fundamental differences between Carolina and Virginia, described in previous chapters, boil down to the fact that there was a higher percentage of enslaved people in the Lowcountry than in the Tidewater, and the Lowcountry elite were wealthier and could afford to replace enslaved workers, who died at a higher rate on rice plantations than in the tobacco farms of Virginia. The life of a slave mattered less in Carolina, pretentions of paternalism notwithstanding.[3]

The preceding discussion should not be construed as arguing that Carolina and Virginia were at opposite ends of a spectrum. They were both slave societies. Jefferson, Mason, Washington, Madison, and Monroe saw tyranny in their society, yet they were all members of that society. Those who were immersed in slavery were often, in fact, the most ardent republicans. The cultural economy, political culture, and political economy of Carolina and Virginia had more common features than differences. And Carolinians would work to advance common themes so that when discussion of secession began, all southern states would recognize their regional family resemblance.[4]

When the Declaration of Independence was ratified, there was no region known as "the South," as observed earlier. Each colony, as it became a state, saw itself as quasi-independent, a member nation of a federation. State citizens did not yet call themselves southerners, and they had no sense of regional identity. It was only during the Constitutional Convention that a sense of identity began to emerge: the southern states had slavery in common, and to protect that institution they needed to pull together. The U.S. Constitution emerged with provisions necessary to protect slavery, including the three-fifths provision that gave White voters in slaveholding states the right to use 60 percent of the Black population to determine their representation.

The plantation-centric southern tier of colonies became the South during the late eighteenth century to protect a cultural economy and its system of slavery that would later be called "the peculiar institution." But regional, or sectional, unification of the southern mind was only the first step in forming a unified South. The unified South had to discover that it had a unified cultural economy, the existence of which it could rationalize across state borders. The Lowcountry took the lead in establishing such a unification.

The term "peculiar institution" and variants such as "peculiar labor" used to describe the core element of the region's cultural economy began with South Carolinians John C. Calhoun and Robert Barnwell Rhett, becoming part of pro-slavery rhetoric from the early 1830s and remaining in use until the Civil War. Georgian Alexander Stephens, the future Confederate vice president, used the term in his Cornerstone Speech delivered in Savannah on March 21, 1861.[5]

Once the idea of "peculiar institution" was well established, its various facets could be portrayed as part of a grand system. Rhett would proclaim in the 1830s, "The institution is sanctioned by Christianity and best for the race over whom it prevails." Calhoun would assert, "There never has yet existed a wealthy and civilized society in which one portion of the did not, in point of fact, live on the labor of the other." Alexander Stephens asserted that the "cornerstone" of southern society rested on "the great truth that the negro is not equal to the White man." The seceding state of Mississippi, dominated by South Carolinians, declared, "Our position is thoroughly identified with the institution of slavery—the greatest material interest of the world. Its labor supplies the product which constitutes by far the largest and most important portions of commerce of the earth."[6]

Rhett and others warned that free labor would seize control of the government and bring mob rule such as occurred in the French Revolution. They portrayed the South as an advanced society constructed of an agrarian oligarchy and slavery, producing liberty and stability, resulting in a civilization the likes of which had never before been seen in human history.[7]

ANTEBELLUM ERA CULTURAL ECONOMY
oligarchy + large-scale monoculture + specialized slave labor

Agrarianism was deeply embedded in the South's peculiar institution. The plantation-centered slave society that emerged from that basic formula structured the larger cultural economy. Political power emanated from the plantation, while wealthy traders in Charleston and Savannah felt their lives were incomplete without rural property and slave ownership. The entire cultural economy was built on slavery. Virginians purchased enslaved people to cultivate tobacco, and Carolinians purchased enslaved people to cultivate rice. These two crops created most of the wealth in the South until King Cotton spread across the Deep South, following the model for its cultural economy established in the Lowcountry.

The plantation elite—the aristocrats and oligarchs, their extended families, and their business associates—molded the economic, social, and political world around them. But, of course, they and their mostly enslaved labor force were not the only two classes of people to populate the South. Poor and semiskilled Whites arrived in increasingly large numbers throughout the colonial and antebellum periods. Most notably, Scots-Irish migrated south along the Appalachians to Virginia, the Carolinas, and Georgia as well as across the mountains to Kentucky and Tennessee. Others arrived from Ireland, Britain, and continental Europe at Charleston, Savannah, and other port cities, pulled to America seeking a better life (or pushed there by misfortunes or misdeeds).

Whereas the Scots-Irish were mostly farmers, other White immigrants sought specialized jobs in the cities. These two groups became two additional social classes in southern society, and none particularly liked any other. While there is some truth to the thesis that a racial bond developed among Whites and that poorer Whites aspired to be wealthy slaveholders, resentments among classes of Whites crossed many lines.

In the classic work *The Mind of the South*, W. J. Cash asserted that slavery conferred superiority to all White men, thus making the common southerner with no enslaved workers committed to the institution, even if it was contrary to their interest. Ordinary Whites acquired "notions of aristocracy," a sense that they could attain the sort of life enjoyed by wealthy slaveholders.[8]

Cash published *The Mind of the South* in 1941 when Lost Cause mythology was widely accepted and difficult to refute. The strength of Cash's rhetoric blew holes in many common beliefs while reasserting others. There were scholars who also challenged orthodoxy, but Cash, as a journalist, reached a wider audience and began a discussion about the real South versus the mythological South.

A half-century later, the digital revolution produced the internet and placed previously hard-to-find data at every computer user's fingertips. Between 1990 and 2010, information storage capacity shifted dramatically from analog to digital format. Archived records were scanned and made publicly available. Suddenly, by historical standards, it became possible to access wide-ranging firsthand accounts in digital format from across the South on one's computer, or at least from almost any public library. While Cash's observations about southern character were prescient and continue to serve a rhetorical purpose, they are in many instances inaccurate at a detailed empirical level. In other words, facts do not support all his arguments.

Recent scholarship reveals a more detailed picture of the antebellum South than W. J. Cash and other students of the region were able to construct before the digital revolution. The historian Keri Leigh Merritt compiled and analyzed new findings in *Masterless Men: Poor Whites and Slavery in the Antebellum South*. Merritt's work draws on newly available records and challenges the theory that poor Whites admired the elite and aspired to be slaveowners.

Poor Whites with no land and no enslaved workers made up about one-third of the southern White population. As discussed earlier, class divisions had deepened with the Specie Circular order of 1836, which required gold or silver to purchase land, and the Panic of 1837. Poor Whites lost land and did not have the purchasing power to get it back. Poor Whites who held on to their land could not afford enslaved laborers. Merritt estimates that the average cost of purchasing an enslaved person in 1860 was far in excess of what most small farmers could afford—$130,000 in present dollars. In the antebellum slavocracy, the rich got richer and the poor got poorer. By 1860, just over one thousand families held nearly half of the wealth of the Deep South.[9]

Many poor Whites living in southern towns and cities had skilled and semiskilled occupations, but they struggled as well. The slaveholding elite often trained-up their enslaved workers for positions poor Whites believed were rightfully theirs. The elite tapped into the resulting tensions by warning Whites that abolition would put them in direct competition with Blacks for free-labor jobs in the trades and similar occupations. According to Merritt, White "mechanics" (as they were called) holding such jobs were manipulated into supporting secession, if necessary to preserve the existing social order.[10]

Championing a Fictional World

On the eve of the Civil War, White Charlestonians and Savannahians were living in an altered reality of their own construction, and they were aggressively championing their fictional world across the South. They believed in an expanding empire of slavery, one that would expand westward and, if their collaborators in New Orleans could carry it off, into Central America and the

Caribbean as well. They believed in a master race of Anglo-Saxon Cavaliers who were equipped and destined to rule. They believed that the master race had conceived and built a great cultural economy rivaling that of ancient Egypt. They believed that enslaved Africans were saved from a life of savagery in Africa. They believed that their enslaved people were happy in their condition of enslavement. They believed that slave society was consistent with Christian principles and God's hierarchy, the Great Chain of Being. They believed that liberty was the sacred right of those patriarchs who stood atop society and irrelevant to others. They believed that questioning their belief system, as abolitionists dared to do, was an insult to their honor. And those who did not entirely believe the foregoing mythology were nevertheless instilling it in others as a means to an end.

Whereas the colonial era adopted the English first principles of liberty, patriarchy, and class, the antebellum belief system with its accompanying misty mythology expanded on those principles. The expanded belief system had been refined in Charleston over two centuries, eight generations of increasing commitment to building and maintaining a slave society. The overarching themes driving secession were "liberty" for the elite, superiority of the White race, honor among aristocrats, greatness through patriarchy, confirmation in religion, preservation through states' rights, and strength through unity in the face of the enemy within (the threat of slave rebellion) and enemies without (abolitionists and Republicans).

Rhetorical justification of slavery created an elaborate template for southern political economy, political culture, and cultural economy. The Civil War stopped the cultural economy dead in its tracks, at least until the South outlasted Reconstruction and reinstated some of the old features of that economy. The political culture, on the other hand, remained solidly fixed in the mind of the South, persisting through the Jim Crow era, through the national agony of desegregation, and even, arguably, to the present day.

On the surface, the economy of the pre–Civil War South seemed powerful. Agricultural production was fourth in the world economy in 1860. The region was the world's greatest cotton producer, and mills in the North and in Britain relied on the South's cotton production. But economic growth was quantitative, not qualitative or sustainable. There was little capital reinvestment in infrastructure or education; there was no serious effort at diversification; the region lacked urban markets and middle-class merchants. The South was thus poorer on average than the North. Per capita income in 1860 was $141 in the North but only $103 in the South. The White literacy level was lower in the South, and there was no significant public education. The aristocracy regularly sent their children elsewhere for an education.[11]

One-quarter of southern Whites owned enslaved people during the antebellum period, and that slaveholding segment held 93 percent of the region's wealth. The three-quarters who did not own enslaved people tacitly supported the institution out of racism, fear of what would happen to them if Blacks were emancipated, a growing sense of regional patriotism, and, in some cases, an aspiration to own enslaved people themselves (even if, for most, slave ownership was financially unattainable).[12]

New Prospects Yield to Old Ways

After the Civil War, thousands of formerly enslaved people streamed into Charleston to celebrate victory and freedom. By 1870 there were more Blacks than Whites in the city, a development that angered and alarmed Whites. While the city's Black middle class remained respectful and courteous toward the White elite, Blacks from rural areas were unencumbered by that tradition. The city's Whites held the reins of power and put their weight behind reestablishing a rigid social hierarchy. After Reconstruction, they regained control of state government and restored, as best they could, the reign of White supremacy.[13]

The postwar economy slowly rebounded, thanks in large part to the federal government. After the war, the port was in ruins, sunken ships littered the channel and harbor, and landside infrastructure was destroyed by bombing. The federal government undertook the rehabilitation of the Charleston Navy Yard from 1869 to around 1900, first clearing the channels of sunken ships and then constructing jetties designed to harness the ebb tide to maintain channel depth. By the turn of the century, Charleston was once again competitive as a major port city.[14]

Steamship service resumed as the channels were cleared and docks repaired, railroad service also resumed as tracks were repaired, streets were paved, and cotton exports grew once again. Phosphates for fertilizer were mined near Charleston and shipped out of the city, and the fisheries industry boomed, leading to a more diversified economy. A large police force, with more officers per capita than New York City, maintained order. A global economic slump slowed growth for a while in the 1870s, but Charleston's economic health gradually improved over the decades following the war. Yet the city was no longer the economic powerhouse it had been before in the antebellum years.[15]

Enjoying an economic rebound, a large, affluent segment of the White population was unable to grasp the fact that a return to the old ways was unsustainable. A regime based on White superiority and an inflexible social hierarchy was archaic and would eventually fall, and fall hard. Yet for another couple of generations, Whites would enjoy their advantages, and the elite, in particular, would resume their lifestyle of aristocratic pretensions and cultivated leisure, very much in the style of their Charleston ancestors.

Jim Crow became firmly established across the South in the early twentieth century, and it became deeply rooted in Charleston. When Theodore Roosevelt appointed Dr. William Demosthenes Crum (1859–1912), a Black physician, as customs collector, the city's elite rose in indignation. The son of a White father and a free Black mother, Crum received his medical degree in the North, where he married Ellen Craft, who wrote *Running a Thousand Miles for Freedom* based on her parents' experience as fugitive slaves. Senate opposition to the appointment forced Roosevelt to make a rare recess appointment, thwarting local efforts to sabotage Crum. Thirty-five years later, when President Truman commended Judge Julius Waties Waring (1880–1968), the White federal judge in Charleston, for decisions in favor of equitable treatment of Blacks, Waring was ostracized from White society. These two high-profile events in Charleston's Jim Crow Era history were among the few that were highly publicized. Acts of discrimination, horrendous by today's standards, were commonplace.[16]

JIM CROW ERA CULTURAL ECONOMY
oppressor class + low-wage industries + Black underclass

Truman commended Waring, saying that more judges like him were needed. Waring and his wife Elizabeth became the first White couple to invite Black people to their home for social events, breaking the traditional social code. But Charleston's old guard was not yet ready to advance into the modern world of social diversity. When Martin Luther King Jr. visited the city in 1962, speaking at the historic Emanuel AME Church, a movement for change took form. It became known as the Charleston Movement, and it chipped away at inequality by boycotting segregated facilities and protesting low wages and lack of employment opportunities.[17]

Charleston might have suffered the consequences of its antiquated social order sooner but for the presence of the navy. During World War I, the Charleston Navy Yard became headquarters for the Southeast region, employing about five thousand civilians. The military payroll offset the loss of revenue from Sea Island cotton crops destroyed by the boll weevil, and it continued to keep the city out of destitution through the Great Depression, World War II, and into the 1950s.

The city's turnaround began in 1959 with the election of Mayor J. Palmer Gaillard Jr., who began addressing dysfunctions within the cultural economy, including the racial divide. The city more than tripled in area and population under Gaillard, and a modern tourist industry was born. Between 1970 and 1976, visitors increased by 60 percent, and during his term in office the city hosted 3.4 million tourists.[18]

Progress accelerated when Joseph P. Riley Jr. entered the Charleston political scene, first representing the city in the legislature and then serving as mayor for forty years. Riley faced down Charleston's conservative elite and old guard politicians in state government. One of his first achievements was negotiating a satisfactory end to a hundred-day hospital strike in the spring of 1969, improving conditions for long-underpaid Black Charlestonians. When Governor Olin Johnson was rebuking the civil rights movement, asserting "God didn't see fit to mix them and I am tired of people agitating social equity of races in our state," Riley was supporting the Charleston Political Action Committee in advocating progressive, transformative policies. Mayor Riley quoted the Declaration of Independence founding principle that "All men are created equal" at his first inauguration in 1975, emphasizing equality, unity, and "racial harmony."[19]

MODERN CULTURAL ECONOMY
diversified economy + wage equality + dynamic workforce

Charleston needed the new vision offered by Mayor Riley to find its way into a new, more diverse and egalitarian era. The navy would reduce its presence during Riley's tenure, and textile mills that once dotted the state and shipped through the Port of Charleston were closing. Single crop dominance and limited industry had once again left the region vulnerable to shifts in national and global markets. The mills had brought a measure of prosperity in times of high demand but were doomed by the dramatic increase in Asian textile production beginning in the 1960s. The city needs to leave the old economy behind and reinvent itself for modern times, but many obstacles remained, not the least of which was entrenched sentiment about the Old South.

The 1960s comprised a clear turning point in the city's history, but this was not apparent at the time. The old system of White superiority and Black oppression maintained its grip, in part because the White conservative political machine was a formidable force resisting change. In a 1962 gesture of Lost Cause defiance, the conservative state legislature hoisted the Confederate flag atop the statehouse dome, where it flew with the U.S. and South Carolina flags. Men such as Senator Strom Thurmond from upstate and Congressman Arthur Ravenel Jr. of Charleston switched political parties before the 1964 election when it became clear that Democrats and Republicans were reversing polarity with regard to civil rights. The Confederate flag flying over the statehouse in Columbia became emblematic of the division, with many Democrats calling for its removal and most Republicans hailing it as an enduring symbol of White heritage. It was not until the 1990s, however, that the case of the Confederate flag plaintiffs gained a broad swath of support. In 1996 Republican governor David Beasley switched sides and supported removal. After the legislature rejected Beasley's recommendation, the NAACP launched a tourism boycott in 1999, and on April 2, 2000, Mayor Riley led a five-day march from Charleston to Columbia to demand action.[20]

While Riley, the NAACP, and others were gaining support for removing the flag, Ravenel and other conservative stalwarts held fast. State senator Glenn McConnell adamantly resisted their efforts, calling the Riley-led march a publicity stunt. In the disparaging manner in which Whites were accustomed to speaking to Blacks, Ravenel referred to the NAACP as the "National Association of Retarded People," and when that was met with outrage he apologized to mentally handicapped people. The conservatives prevailed until McConnell finally relented and began negotiating removal with Democratic legislators. In 2000 the flag finally came down from the statehouse dome, but, in the compromise worked out by Charleston state senators McConnell and Robert Ford, an African American, the symbol of the Confederacy remained flying on capitol grounds. It would take the mass shooting of worshippers by a White racist at Mother Emmanuel AME Church in 2015 to finally move the flag off the grounds and into a museum. Several prominent Republican state senators declared it was time. Governor Nikki Haley, normally one to tack to the right, led from behind once she sensed she had sufficient cover to support removal without damaging her Tea Party credentials. Ravenel and McConnell remained insinuated in Charleston civic life despite their resistance to change. Ravenel had the Cooper River Bridge named for him in 1999, and McConnell became president of the College of Charleston in 2014.[21]

Transformations in the Cultural Economy

The southern cultural economy persisted largely unreconstructed after the Civil War and Reconstruction, despite being severely disrupted. A new partially modified cultural economy that retained White supremacy and other basic tenets of the Old South was named the New South. The business leaders who repackaged the old system promoted a shift from agrarianism to urban industrialism. But while the means of economic output changed somewhat, the cultural approaches to sustaining the economy remained much the same. Low-wage labor and opposition to unions prevailed. Investment in general education lagged behind the rest of the nation. The oligarchy framed political discourse through single-party messaging. The belief in White superiority continued, modified only by a claim of adopting a more humane form of paternalism.[22]

As the nation entered an advanced industrial era of mass production in the twentieth century, the New South not only lagged in industrial development but also began exporting its labor force to other regions. A Great Migration of African Americans left the South for industrial jobs in the North, beginning in the 1920s and continuing through the 1950s. White southerners also migrated out of the region, first during the Great Depression, then during the post–World War II period.

From the late 1930s to the late 1960s more than six million southerners migrated to industrial cities of the North and to Southern California. By 1970, 11 million southerners lived outside the South, 7.5 million of whom were White. By the 1960s, California had the largest share of southerners in the nation outside the South, with most in Southern California. Some of the westward-bound southerners were driven there by the Dust Bowl tragedy dramatized in John Steinbeck's *Grapes of Wrath*. But many others, particularly during the postwar boom, were attracted by perceived opportunities on the West Coast as much as being driven from the South by lack of opportunity.[23]

Southerners took their conservative political and religious views with them, and southern ministers moved as well, reinforcing entrenched beliefs. J. Frank Norris, a Baptist fundamentalist minister from Texas by way of Alabama, saw the South as leading a great awakening of conservatism and religion. He and others endorsed Landmarkism, a fundamentalist Baptist tradition rejecting the validity of other faiths, particularly more liberal religious institutions like the Federal Council of Churches, which sought to build Christian unity during the New Deal.

John Birch, who trained at Norris's Fundamental Baptist Bible Institute in Texas, became the great hero of southern conservatism and American nationalism. The John Birch Society later emerged as an advocacy arm of fundamentalism and conservatism, opposing federal action on civil rights and labor practices as well as public education. The Urban League leader Floyd Covington observed that California was southernizing: "On all sides can be sensed a general change of attitude toward the Negro, due to the impress of this southern influence."[24]

Those migrations, coupled with federal government policies, profoundly altered urban form across the United States. Southern Blacks moved into older urban neighborhoods while Whites took advantage of Federal Housing Administration and Veterans Administration mortgage insurance to secure affordable financing in new suburbs. (The standards generally precluded mortgage insurance for older urban homes.) The process was speeded along by federal investment in highway infrastructure that made the suburbs more accessible. The nation's inner cities, suburbs, exurbs, and rural areas became political units, with regional political culture and racial undertones influencing elections.

Unfortunately, government actions designed to ameliorate inequity and racial segregation had the perverse effect of intensifying racial politics. Such actions include dismantling the Jim Crow laws and the 1954 U.S. Supreme Court landmark case, *Brown v. Board of Education of Topeka*, which found racial segregation in public schools unconstitutional. Another was passage of the Voting Rights Act of 1965, designed to enforce the Fourteenth and Fifteenth Amendments to the Constitution. Such actions led to the exploitation of racial divisions by political parties. Democrats gained African American voters, while Republicans gained southern White voters and those influenced by the southern White diaspora. Much has been written about the latter, which came to be called the Southern Strategy after the publication of *The Emerging Republican Majority* by Kevin Phillips, advisor to President Richard Nixon.[25]

Political maps of U.S. elections since the civil rights era have continued to show the old regional patterns at the state level and to some extent at the metropolitan level. However, recent mapping of voting precincts reveal an obvious new pattern. Cities are Democratic strongholds, rural areas are Republican strongholds, and the rest is up for grabs. The new political geography is part of the more general urban-rural divide discussed by political scientists and commentators today.[26]

Urban areas contribute disproportionately to the nation's wealth, innovation, and global competitiveness. While many exurban and rural areas are a net positive in those economic areas, most are far less productive than urban areas. And many urban areas are less productive than others due to factors like sprawl, which reduces cluster formation (in which related enterprises develop synergistic relationships) and other productive linkages. But, in general, urban areas are a nation's engine of wealth and innovation.[27]

This digression from the story of Charleston and Savannah is offered for one purpose: to assert that both cities are now part of a truly new southern cultural economy, one that is most often urban and promotes intense interaction among diverse groups of actors. The new cultural economy is integral to the modern South, the successor to the earlier New South conceived after Reconstruction with built-in patriarchy and racism. The new cultural economy has replaced the obsolete version that existed throughout the South from colonial times to the 1960s. While the older cultural economy still exists in rural areas, its light is dimming. Virtually every city in the South is progressive at its core, having adopted basic tenets of liberal democracy and equality.

Charleston and Savannah are regional centers of higher education, creative professions, diverse ideas, and strong service economies. While both support major seaports and notable industries, they do so within a larger context of a vibrant mixed economy.

CHAPTER TWELVE

Reinvention and Sustainability

The story of Charleston and Savannah now reaches the present. Before proceeding, the challenge of terminology again needs to be addressed. The two cities have changed in fundamental ways. Their metropolitan areas are vastly larger, and the majority of their citizens only infrequently venture into the historic core. So what are the cities now?

Throughout most of their history, both Charleston and Savannah were small in area, growing from less than one square mile at their founding to only five square miles in the early twentieth century. Both cities are now well over one hundred square miles in area, of which more than half is suburban and exurban in character (and a great deal is water). Therefore, in speaking of "Charleston" and "Savannah," one might be referring to the core area imbued with unique historic character or the entire city, much of which is like all other American cities, or even the county or the multi-county metropolitan area, which the two cities anchor. The tables on the following page illustrate the population differential.[1]

Each of the four geographic designations cited above (historic core, city, county, and metro area) is an important manifestation of both cities, and their story cannot be completed without keeping that fact in mind. However, the historic core of both cities, although diminishing in relative size, remains the principal actor in the story. The core, remarkably, remains largely intact as the central business district for each city, the primary destination for visitors, a regional center of government and culture, and, unlike the cores of most cities, a place where many people still reside year-round. The character of the core is also more than the sum of its parts, which distinguishes it from the relative monotony of the surrounding suburbs and exurbs.

Before assessing the core areas in greater detail, a look at the population of each metropolitan area provides necessary perspective. The Charleston Metropolitan Statistical Area (MSA) encompasses Charleston, Berkeley, and Dorchester Counties. The Savannah MSA encompasses Chatham, Bryan, and Effingham Counties. Although rapidly growing Beaufort and Jasper Coun-

Urban Composition
AREA IN SQUARE MILES

	Charleston	Savannah
Core	4	5
City	128	109
County	1,358	632
Metro	3,163	1,569

City, county, and metro areas include wetlands and open
water within their boundaries.
Source: U.S. Census, 2010

Urban Composition
POPULATION IN 2020 AND 1920

	Charleston		Savannah	
	2020	1920	2020	1920
Core	40,707	67,957	38,056	83,252
City	150,227	67,957	147,780	83,252
County	408,235	108,450	295,291	100,032
Metro	799,636	150,467	404,741	116,360

Sources: U.S. Census, 2020 redistricting data; core estimates by author; 1920 census

Core Population Density and Share of City and County

	Density PERSONS/ SQUARE MILE	Core/City SHARE OF POPULATION	Core/County SHARE OF POPULATION
Charleston	10,076	0.31	0.10
Savannah	7,246	0.26	0.13
Chattanooga	3,987	0.06	0.03
Mobile	4,404	0.09	0.05
Asheville	4,691	0.06	0.02

Source: 2017 ACS census tract data

ties in South Carolina are economically linked to the Savannah metropolitan are, they are not counted in the MSA population. The area of the five counties around Savannah including the South Carolina counties is 3,256 square miles, virtually the same as the 3,161 square mile area of the Charleston MSA. The population of the five-county area is 620,706, about a quarter less than the Charleston MSA.[2]

Savannah and Beaufort County have become complementary destinations, with the former having rich historical and cultural offerings, and the latter having more outdoor offerings such as golf and boating. Beaufort County's original premier destination, Hilton Head Island, is now only part of a much larger subregion with dozens of destination resorts. When visitors fly into Savannah, they are welcomed to the Savannah/Hilton Head International Airport.

The historic core of Charleston is an area of about four square miles occupying most of the peninsula formed by the Ashley and Cooper Rivers. Over forty thousand people live in that area. The historic core of Savannah occupies an area of a little over five square miles, supporting a population of nearly thirty-eight thousand. On any given day, even in the "off season," if one counts visitors, employees who commute into the core, and temporary residents such as students who are not counted by the census, the total number of people in the core of either city easily exceeds fifty thousand.[3]

In comparing these figures to those of other similarly sized cities with notably vibrant cores, Charleston and Savannah stand out. Chattanooga, Mobile, and Asheville are comparably sized tourism destinations with vibrant, livable downtowns.[4]

Suburban population density typically ranges from two thousand to four thousand persons per square mile, far less than the range of seven thousand to ten thousand or more found in the Charleston and Savannah core areas. Exurban densities, where lot sizes are most often a half-acre and larger, are less than one thousand persons per square mile.[5]

Many city core areas in the United States, even those with established historic districts, are virtually devoid of residential population. They are filled with downtown work commuters during the day and empty at night and on weekends. Charleston and Savannah are 24/7 cities with vibrant cores that define the character of an entire metropolitan area, in defiance of the proliferation of automobile-oriented suburbs, shopping centers, and industrial parks.

Even as the core of each city declines in population and area relative to the metropolitan area, it remains the most essential part of each city. Although parts of the economy are physically outside the core, they interact synergistically with the core. The suburbs send more of their residents to the core than to other areas, and they constitute a large market for core businesses. The large retirement communities spread through the Lowcountry draw people attracted not just to golf and boating but also to the cultural amenities in the historic cores of both cities. Industries outside the city limits attract high-wage employees through the lure of amenities associated with the core.

A challenge faced by both cities, as yet poorly met, is the extent to which they take the assets of their historic cores (e.g., aesthetics, neighborhood character, public spaces, walkways, diversity, and fine-grained mixed-use development) and project them outward. To date, the distinction between the core and outlying areas developed since World War II could not be sharper.

Historical and Modern Economies

Seaports comprise the industrial anchor that has always been essential to both cities. The dynamics of global trade are, of course, very different today than during the time when Charleston and Savannah became players in the Atlantic triangular trade. The triangular trade system was dependent on the winds and currents swirling around the Sargasso Sea. Collection and distribution of trade products were similarly dependent on nature, making use of river and tidal currents until the advent of railroads. The early nexus between compact development and river-oriented transportation ensured the economic success of both cities.

Modern maritime trade connects producers and consumers through direct trade routes with little regard for natural elements. Port cities that minimize shipping distance and maximize market reach are growing, and the ports of Charleston and Savannah once again are among those that are positioned to prosper from today's global trade environment. Extensive railroad and trucking facilities enhance each port's ability to handle a high volume of container traffic, transporting it to local and inland manufacturing and distribution centers, and in doing so multiplying the ports' economic impact. In the case of Charleston, the South Carolina Ports Authority has developed Inland Port Greer, located in the industrialized upstate Greenville-Spartanburg corridor. And just ninety miles to the south, the Port of Savannah serves as Atlanta's most vital link to global maritime trade.[6]

The focus of this chapter is that part of the contemporary economy that is most rooted in history, namely tourism. Since the successes and challenges

Employment Percentage in Largest Sectors

NAICS	Charleston MSA	Savannah MSA
Trade, transportation, and utilities	23	28
Leisure and hospitality	17	17
Professional and business services	18	13
Education and health services	14	16
Manufacturing	10	12

Source: U.S. Bureau of Labor Statistics, Quarterly Census of Employment and Wages, Fourth Quarter, 2018, by Metropolitan Statistical Area (MSA)

of tourism are closely tied to historic preservation, cultural preservation, and city planning, those subjects are also examined in this chapter. To a notable extent, new residents and businesses are attracted to Charleston and Savannah for the quality of life they offer, and since this includes historical attributes, that subject is introduced here.[7]

Historicity, Preservation, and Tourism

Charleston and Savannah have become desirable places to live and visit largely because historic and cultural preservationists found common ground with social equity and civil rights activists. By working in concert, these inclusive movements projected a new image to the world: they were southern cities that had reinvented themselves for the modern age and had a lot more to offer than Old South nostalgia and elitism. Inclusivity and democracy are messy projects, of course, and keeping everyone at the table is a never-ending challenge, but the old ways of making decisions by and for the elite are in retreat.

The preservation movement in both cities began as an elitist White heritage movement. During the 1960s and 1970s, many within the movement recognized that times were changing rapidly and a new age was dawning. Preservation would have to become more inclusive by focusing on entire neighborhoods rather than individual structures, and entire communities rather than the upper strata of society.

The so-called New South that coexisted with Jim Crow for a century began yielding to a modern South that grew out of the trauma of the civil rights movement. The transition from the New South paradigm, which retained features of the antebellum era, to a modern South that embraces diversity and democracy, if only at times for business reasons, began with urbanization. Urban population size in the South began approaching that of cities in the North and Midwest during the 1960s. All regions, including the West, reached near parity in the 1980s, with urban dwellers making up 50 percent of the total population. Almost all of the shift in the South came from internal migration, thus it was southerners who urbanized, accepted the second Reconstruction, and liberated themselves at last from the old ways.

The rigidity of the past has given way to a fluidity that can be uncertain and uncomfortable: issues like wage equity, fair housing, voting rights, and gentrification are never fully resolved to everyone's satisfaction and thus require continuous renegotiation. Wealthy investors and business operators retain a grip on the levers of power that ordinary people know little about. Nevertheless, elected officials and community advocates in cities like Charleston and Savannah have had a notable degree of success in bringing diverse voices to the table and improving the lives of their constituents.

In June 2019 the Charleston *Post and Courier* convened a panel to discuss preservation and tourism. Mayor John Tecklenburg and three industry representatives were asked to address the impact of tourism on the city's quality of life. Workforce needs, particularly affordable housing and transportation, were identified as the greatest concern. There was concern that the city had reached a tipping point where tourism would overwhelm traditional residents and destroy the character and affordability of their neighborhoods. The quality of life of Charlestonians was at stake, and tourism somehow had to be harnessed for the betterment of all people, not just the few with a financial interest in the industry.[8]

It has been clear in the minds of Charleston's "thought leaders" since the 1960s that an essential nexus exists between the city's economy and its diverse communities. Historic preservation and tourism, in particular, depend on the health of both communities (people sharing common interests) and neighborhoods (places that people consider home). In the past, "community" and "neighborhood" were nearly synonymous, but now they can be quite different. Employees of the hospitality industry, for example, are often young and mobile and connected by social media and shifting social gathering places. They may form a community without occupying a neighborhood. Communities are now often communities of choice rather than communities of geography.

On the other hand, neighborhoods are sometimes not communities at all. Areas of Charleston referred to as "drive-by neighborhoods" may have little social vitality because of a high proportion of second homeowners or other absentee owners. Yet such neighborhoods are a reality of life in a city with a successful historic preservation movement. The task of city leaders is to find the common interests of all communities and neighborhoods and build, to whatever extent possible, a common bond in the shared experience of being Charlestonians. The task is ongoing and never-ending. It requires continual recalibration to work. Such is the complexity of the modern historic city.[9]

Since the 1960s, Savannah, unlike Charleston, zigzagged between mayors who strove to protect the White establishment and others who sought to address the concerns of a broader spectrum of city residents. Savannah mayor Julius Curtis Lewis, Jr. (1926–2005), elected to office in 1966, served one term. Lewis was a Republican who came into office on a wave of White backlash to the civil rights movement, ousting Mayor Malcolm R. Maclean, a Democrat, who had started a dialogue with civil rights advocates. While Lewis was a philanthropist who helped many in the city, he represented the traditional, White-controlled establishment.

John Paul Rousakis (1929–2000), a Democrat, served five four-year terms as mayor from 1970 to 1990. Rousakis modernized city government and ramped up revitalization of River Street, creating a substantial tourism attraction. Although Rousakis maintained dialogue with civil rights advocates, he did not stand out as a leader in that area.

Susan S. Weiner, a Republican, defeated Rousakis in the election of 1989, taking office in 1990. Weiner, the city's first female mayor, went about implementing an agenda highlighting "law-and-order" and privatization of public services. She served only one term before being defeated by Floyd Adams Jr. (1945–2014), the city's first African American mayor. The majority-Black city acquired a majority-Black city council while Adams was mayor, and it began addressing long-standing concerns of African American residents.

However, it was under the city's subsequent African American mayor, Otis S. Johnson (born 1942), that the City of Savannah adopted formal policies to address pressing wage, social equity, civil rights, and gentrification issues. Mayor Johnson directed the Metropolitan Planning Commission to begin community planning in the city's less affluent neighborhoods, an initiative that resulted in major redevelopment initiatives in the Cuyler-Brownsville and West Savannah neighborhoods. He established a Gentrification Task Force, while also challenging Black communities to increase efforts to combat crime. Johnson emphasized the importance of bringing together "two Savannahs"—one that traditionally benefited from the city's prosperous tourism economy, and one that largely remained stuck at the bottom of the economic ladder.

In 2011 Edna Jackson, a long-serving member of the city council, was elected the city's first African American female mayor. Jackson sought to balance a social justice and cultural diversity agenda with a pro-business stance. Her policies failed to secure the support of the White business establishment, and she was defeated in 2015 by Eddie DeLoach, who ran on a law-and-order and spending-reduction platform.

The tables turned again in 2019 when Van Johnson, an African American city alderman, defeated DeLoach in a runoff election. The election produced a clean sweep for progressive candidates who questioned the Savannah's past pro-growth policies. The new council is elevating environmental justice to a high priority and implicitly renewing Otis Johnson's "Two Savannahs" thesis as a policy priority.

Although mayoral leadership since the era of the civil rights movement has gone back and forth between Democrat and Republican, progressive and conservative, blue-collar and white-collar, and Black and White, there has been a general convergence in key areas that support an innovative and creative city. Political agendas are less overtly divided along racial lines, inclusion is a new political fact of life, and diversity is considered fuel for the economy. Although divisions still exist, common ground is slowly and inevitably increasing. Nevertheless, the class and race divides often produce a sense of dysfunction, a sense that the venerable city has "good hardware but bad software," in the words of a respondent to the survey conducted for this study..

Historicity and Urban Complexity

Most people in modern society seek a mix of simplicity and complexity in their lives. Stress drives them toward simplicity: the home in the suburbs as an everyday retreat from the stress of the city, or the beach vacation with drinks at the cabana to forget about the pressures of work. On the other hand, when feeling recharged, many people seek complexity: fine wines and fusion cuisine, adventures instead of chill-out vacations, "lifestyle" shopping centers that offer rich mixes of retail shops and entertainment rather than practical big box stores.

Charleston and Savannah have achieved (and must learn to protect) something extraordinary, a form of multidimensional *super-complexity*. The temporal dimension is the most obvious component of super-complexity. The past resides side by side with the present through architectural preservation, vibrant urban activity is superimposed on historic streetscapes, and urban design respects rather than erases the past.

A second dimension of super-complexity is that of culture. Many residents (though few visitors) fully appreciate the depth of character both cities derive from earlier periods of clashing and fusing of cultures. They appreciate cuisine unique to the region, the forging of etiquette among social classes fundamentally at odds with one another, the persistence of mythologies essential to belief in self-worth, and the music, crafts, and other cultural manifestations of a multifaceted society. While most people have not consciously studied those historical complexities, they sense and appreciate their existence.

A third dimension of super-complexity is that of creativity. Historic places are magnets for people seeking creative outlets. Such people are not particularly common in society at large. They think out of the box, take chances, launch creative enterprises, make connections that most people do not see, and add value to the more mundane facets of the city. They are artists, artisans, designers, builders, and entrepreneurs. They are transformative actors in the places where they choose to live, and they are present in extraordinary numbers in Charleston and Savannah. Their presence is felt through the hundreds of initiatives they pursue daily, imparting a sense of creative energy to the historic places they occupy.

A fourth, far less obvious dimension of super-complexity is that of interaction and inevitable *collision*. As urban complexity produces more interaction, some of it takes the form of ideas, values, aesthetics, norms, and aspirations colliding. A single city block of historic buildings may house people with radically different outlooks. One building may be a historic home occupied by an elderly person who has lived there most of their life, another may be a condo conversion occupied by creative professionals, a third may be an apartment conversion rented primarily to students, a fourth could be a bed-and-breakfast, and a fifth might be a restaurant. While collisions will occur in such an environment, the overall effect is that of a twenty-four-hour, multigenerational social complex. For those seeking complexity and adventure, they will have found it in such a neighborhood.

The Harbor Entrepreneur Center is a nonprofit agency in Charleston established for the purpose of promoting entrepreneurship. Its website site states that its mission is to "CREATE COLLISION" among entrepreneurs. Savannah's nonprofit initiative The Creative Coast states on its website that it is a place "where creatives, technologists and entrepreneurs create, code, & collide." Both are agencies that accept as a given that cities are places where differences are valued (in contrast to suburbs and exurbs where uniformity is valued). Cities are creative, innovative, inspirational, aspirational, dynamic, connected, diverse, and transformational—and that is how they succeed. Once, in the past, the southern city was a very different sort of place, one of conformity to the will of authoritarian oligarchs and aristocrats.[10]

Charleston and Savannah bequeathed a complex urban template to the modern world, one that can support a modern city while preserving visual evidence of a culturally rich past coded into its architecture. The Charleston double house displays the city's past prosperity, preserving (in several cases as a museum) the link to slave traders, rice and cotton merchants, and the plantation elite. The unique Charleston single (or side-yard) house, its dominant style, ranges widely in size from palatial to humble.

The single house nearly always has a false front door facing the street that leads to an elevated, colonnade porch, or piazza. Alternatively, the main entry door might open into a garden. It can be difficult to discern which is the case, as the entire street-facing façade might include a high stucco or brick wall. The functional front door to the house, located on the piazza, faces the garden. The historian William Freehling portrayed life in one of the more substantial single houses in *The Road to Disunion*.[11]

The master often greeted his guests not down below but up above, where second-floor reception rooms looked down on urban tumult. The street walls blockaded not only Whites' hidden entrance but also slaves' concealed yard. This little backyard village contained slave dwellings, kitchens, laundry facilities, and other centers of domestic service. The concealment, both of masters and enslaved people, made single houses' aesthetic neither English nor southeastern. Charleston's long piazzas, begging for a wisp of breeze, recalled not coolish England but the boiling West Indies and the homes of haughty West Indian slaveholders, from whence the first Lowcountry planters came.[12]

The historian Peter Coclanis has shown that while some authorities maintain that the single-house design is a local environmental adaptation, others have identified European and Caribbean influences. The single house, like the double house, appeared once Charleston became a wealthy city. Earlier housing was much more gothic or medieval in style.[13]

The sense of peering into history as one walks past such houses is magnified by the city's narrow streets and surprising turns. There is just enough

Charleston single house with
side yard and piazza.
(Photo by author)

Savannah row house.
(Photo by author)

order to create an impression of formality and just enough disorder to give a visitor the sense of being in an otherwise anachronistic medieval setting.

One also gets a sense of peering into history on a walk through Savannah, yet the experience on some level is quite different. The civic realm in Savannah is far more orderly. In any of Savannah's twenty-two preserved squares, one can take a 360-degree look at the surrounding buildings and ascertain a sense of neighborhood. Architectural styles are more variable than in Charleston, but they seem unified even where the assortment varies greatly, drawn together by Oglethorpe's ward layout. One also feels a greater sense of formality and classical design in Savannah. A mile-long walk from the riverfront southward along Bull Street to Forsyth Park offers an incomparable mix of architectural styles, urban design, public space, and historical monuments.

Notably, one can continue through Forsyth Park, then resume a southward walk along Bull Street through an additional three historic districts associated with later eras of development—a three-mile walk through time—before reaching newer, post–World War II suburbs, the earliest neighborhoods of which now have a modernist historical character.

A close inspection of Charleston and Savannah reveals two very different cities in their architectural heritage, their urban plan, and their streetscapes. Yet in both cases there is a remarkable underlying historical authenticity, or historicity. Both cities are being revitalized lot by lot as individuals focus their creativity on small projects with cumulative impacts far greater than the sum of individual contributions. The larger developments, mostly hotels, are most often located on the periphery of their historic districts in former industrial areas, or on commercial corridors where each city attempts to regulate mass and scale to conform to historical standards.

The Tourism Industry

Tourism in Charleston and Savannah has existed since antebellum times, when relatively small numbers of people visited both cities to take in their reputed charm. In the early-to-mid 1900s, both cities increased their efforts to draw visitors by hosting events (such as Charleston's Annual Azalea Festival, launched in 1933) and trade and professional conferences (some of which attracted thousands of participants). By 1939 tourism had become Charleston's second-largest industry.[14]

Tourism in both cities grew substantially as historic preservation expanded in the 1960s, and it grew in scope as history, architecture, and culture melded into a richer palette of offerings for visitors. The industry further expanded with heritage tourism and ecotourism beginning in the 1990s. Outdoor-oriented recreational tourism, including golfing, boating, and beach activities, is not essential to either city, but it is prevalent nearby throughout the Lowcountry region. Business tourism also has become an important component of the tourism sector as accommodations and other facilities expand to accommodate larger conferences and business events of various kinds.

The synergies created among these various forms of tourism have made the industry the fastest-growing sector of the economy in both cities since the 1980s. The tourism industry is second only to government, which includes large military populations in both SMAs.

The tourism industry in both cities has recently focused attention on increasing the share of the elite "upscale" and "luxury" market segments. Savannah tourism officials concede that Charleston has set a high bar in the competition for well-to-do visitors, but they maintain that their city's share has dramatically risen to where it is nearly comparable as an elite destination. When projected growth is taken into consideration, Savannah may surpass Charleston in revenues within five years. Savannah officials project that there will be sixty-six hundred rooms in the historic core by 2025.

The magnitude of the industry brings with it quantitative and qualitative impacts. Quantitative impacts include local government budget impacts, em-

Tourism Industry Profile, 2020

	Charleston	Savannah
Hotel/motel room nights	4.8 million	4.1 million
Hospitality employees	48,325	25,763
Rooms (core/metro)	4,500/17,400	5,000+/16,000

Figures are for metropolitan areas unless otherwise indicated; accommodations figures ("nights") exclude private short-term rentals, which number in the thousands.

Sources: J. Perrin Lawson III, Explore Charleston (Charleston Area Convention and Visitors Bureau); Savannah Area Chamber of Commerce 2021 annual report; Savannah Area Tourism Leadership Council

ployment and wage pressures, and costs associated with congestion. Quantitative impacts include factors affecting the quality of life of residents, such as traffic congestion, lack of parking, inappropriate behavior, noise, gentrification, elitification, concerns about the mass and scale of new development, disruptions in the overall rhythm of the built environment, adverse changes to neighborhood character, loss of residential rental housing to short-term vacation rentals, and higher costs of housing in the historic core. Both cities have attempted to mitigate those impacts through such programs as residential parking permits. However, the impacts are massive, and mitigation measures offer only marginal relief.

A 2017 study commissioned by the City of Savannah found that residents benefit from tourism by a ratio of thirty-eight to one: that is, for every dollar residents spend in taxes and other costs, they get thirty-eight dollars back from the industry. The study found a positive benefit-to-cost ratio for the city government of nearly two to one. A survey of residents found that 75 percent of respondents agree that the benefits of tourism outweigh the costs.[15]

While the quantitative benefits of tourism laid out in such reports are impressive, qualitative concerns will inevitably grow as impacts increase. When the quality of life of residents (whether those who live in the historic core, work there, or go there for business or pleasure) is eroded to the point that the negatives outweigh the positives, the reinvention of Charleston and Savannah will falter. Under the direst scenario, the richly textured character of the historic core will disintegrate, centrifugal forces will push residents out, and the core will become an exclusive domain for luxury-elite housing and tourism.

CHARLESTON'S TOURISM INDUSTRY

Charleston's modern-era tourism industry has taken decades to mature. The initial impetus came with an acceleration of interest in historic preservation during the 1960s. The stage was then set for an entire industry built around historical tourism. Large-scale public investment in tourism infrastructure followed in the 1970s. Then, in the 1980s, the vital link between historic and cultural tourism began forming, providing visitors with a richer experience.

At the South Carolina Governor's Conference on Tourism in February 1987, state representative Harriet Keyserling of Beaufort (one of the first women in the legislature and one of the first Jewish legislators) pointed out the success of Spoleto as a cultural attraction. Tourism ought to be about more than beaches and golf courses, she argued; it ought to also be about cultural resources. "We who are arts advocates have finally learned that we can sell the arts by demonstrating the arts are not only good for your soul, but they are good for your pocketbook. . . . Most humans have a need to expand their minds and their souls by participating in new and interesting activities. In cultural tourism, tourists are seeking new environments and new activities."[16]

Before Spoleto, for which Keyserling had engineered a crucial loan, cultural tourism barely existed as a concept. The aristocratic elite in Charleston and Savannah knew that historical architecture was an attraction. And, in the case of Savannah, the beauty of its public realm had long been a source of pride. Those physical resources, however, remained unlinked to their cultural interface until Spoleto led to new ways of thinking about tourism.

A paradigm shift took place in the 1990s in which architectural and cultural resources became a unified foundation for historical and cultural tourism. Now art, architecture, music, historic preservation, museums, historic sites, culinary experiences, ancestry travel, and traditional crafting enrich each other as components of a historic city's tapestry of offerings. Ecotourism is tied in as well, enabling visitors to explore the natural and cultural landscape holistically.

The success of the industry has come with quantitative and qualitative costs, as noted above. Those concerns have been intense topics of discussion in recent years. Following Charleston mayor Joe Riley's retirement, growth management came to the fore. Riley's successor, John Tecklenburg, ran on a pledge to enact a temporary moratorium on new hotel construction. Facing reelection in 2019, he issued a statement saying that market forces were creating an imbalance in favor of hotels: "Tourism has been a blessing, but it has reached a point where it is impacting our quality of life."[17]

The preservationist Kristopher King supports the mayor's efforts and wants to keep Charleston a "working city," rather than one that caters more to visitors than residents. King cites a tourism model known as Doxey's "cultural irritation index," or "irridex," that describes the process whereby residents become increasingly frustrated with the impacts of tourism. The model postulates four stages of residents' attitudes toward tourism: 1) euphoria, 2) apathy, 3) irritation, and 4) antagonism. The progression to "antagonism" is not inevitable, but its avoidance requires the affected community to achieve a broad consensus before the industry becomes an unstoppable juggernaut.[18]

Early in the antebellum era, Savannah promoted itself as a healthier city to visit than Charleston, but rampant disease during the "sickly season" initially undermined that claim. When the city started draining nearby rice fields, this obstacle was removed, and beautification measures such as street tree planting were initiated to attract more visitors. The Oglethorpe Plan provided a tableau on which such measures found early success. Savannah's boosters even hyped the city as the "New York of the South." The regularity of the plan created a more urban feel than that found in other southern cities.[19]

The city was further beautified from 1837 onward when multipurpose squares gave way to aesthetically enhanced civic spaces. Bull Street became an arterial of monuments, with obelisks memorializing Casimir Pulaski in Monterey Square and General Nathanial Greene in Johnson Square; a sculpture of Oglethorpe in Chippewa Square; a monument to Sergeant William Jasper in Madison Square; and a massive stone with a dedication to Yamacraw chief Tomochichi, and a monument to William Gordon, a founder of the Central Railroad, in Wright Square. An English travel writer, James Silk Buckingham, wrote in 1839, "There are no less than eighteen squares, with green plants and trees, in the very heart of the city, disposed at equal distances from each other in the greatest order."[20]

It wasn't until the 1960s, however, that historic preservationists were able to articulate an economic future based on the city's three principal assets: historical architecture, the historic city plan, and public spaces shrouded in urban forest. In other words, as in Charleston, it was during the 1960s and then into the 1970s that preservationists convinced elected officials and the business community that historic resources could be monetized, thus warranting significant public investment.

The emphasis on making Savannah more like Jacksonville or Atlanta, which peaked in the mid- to late-1950s, largely ended in the 1970s. Mayor John Rousakis, in office from 1970 to 1991, led a reprioritization in city investment from modern infrastructure (such as road widening to accommodate vehicles) to historic infrastructure. The historic riverfront was improved to accommodate more pedestrians and to create a river-oriented string of plazas where tourists could gather to enjoy the ambiance of the city. At the same time, tourist-oriented business activity increased along River Street, illustrating the value of coordinated public-private planning and investment.

While the development of a riverfront nucleus for tourism was widely supported, not all investment was welcomed. The primary case in point is the Hyatt Regency, which many saw as out of scale and out of character. To the city's long-term benefit, however, reaction to the hotel produced support for effective design review in the city's new National Historic Landmark District.

As hotel construction proliferated in the decades following the 1970s, its scale and character were tamed, though not always to everyone's satisfaction, and made to fit within design guidelines for the historic district. The city's obsolete 1960 zoning ordinance, evaluated in chapter 6, remained in place, often working at odds with the design review process. The new zoning ordinance adopted in 2019 is now finally aligned with historic district design standards.

Cities like Charleston and Savannah that build synergy between historic and cultural preservation on the one hand, and tourism development on the other, can do so incrementally, at modest cost to local budgets, often supplemented by grants. Unlike high-tech corridors, office and industrial parks, or transportation hubs, preservation and tourism can begin with low-cost streetscaping, improved maintenance protocols, and grants or loans to improve façades of small businesses. Tax increment financing, authorized in both states, can be used to redirect property taxes directly into such improvements. Later, as tourism tax revenues flow more swiftly into city coffers, larger investments into civic auditoriums, arenas, and convention centers can follow.

The benefits that accrue from the synergies between preservation and tourism can reach the tipping point described above, the point where residents become antagonistic toward tourism and believe its costs exceed benefits. Concern about negative impacts is rising in Savannah as it is in Charleston, as reflected by the 2019 local elections. The preservationist Beth Lattimore Reiter has heard a mounting range of complaints about "the surge of tourism and the attending over commercialism, too many vehicles, too many visitors, too many trinket shops." She says, "The commercialism downtown is sucking the livability out of the historic district—million-dollar houses with no permanent residents or used as second homes [where] the owners don't in many cases vote or take part in local issues. Permanent residents have to live next door to vacation rentals or across the street from mega-hotels whose construction damages historic homes." These issues are not as acute as in Charleston, but it will not be long before they reach that point.[21]

Historic Preservation

The historic preservation movement in Charleston began in 1920 when concerned citizens founded the Charleston Society for the Preservation of Old Dwellings, which later became the Preservation Society of Charleston. In 1929 the city adopted a zoning ordinance as a means of protecting its historic resources. Then in 1931 it designated twenty-three square blocks within the old walled city as Old and Historic Charleston and established the Board of Architectural Review to maintain aesthetic compatibility within the district. The initiative made Charleston a national model.

Historic Charleston Foundation (HCF) was founded in 1947 to foster historic preservation advocacy and build educational programs. The following year HCF launched a Festival of Houses, one of the nation's oldest architectural heritage tours. In the mid-1950s, HCF began purchasing architecturally significant buildings, stabilizing the properties, and then reselling them to preservation-minded buyers. Some of the more substantial properties were converted to museums. HCF was instrumental in drafting the Historic Preservation Plan of 1974, which inventoried and evaluated 2,288 historic structures. The plan became the basis for later refinements to the city's preservation program, such as building height restrictions. HCF owns and operates two museums, the Nathaniel Russell House, built in 1808 by merchant Nathaniel Russell, and the Aiken-Rhett House, built in 1820 by merchant John Robinson and expanded in the 1830s by Governor William Aiken Jr.[22]

The City of Charleston created the Charleston Old and Historic District in 1960, and in the same year most of the area was designated a National Historic Landmark District. In 1966 the area bounded by Broad, Bay, South

City of Charleston National Register Districts, 2020

District	Acreage	Year
Charleston Historic District	1,194	1960
The French Quarter	1.8	1973
Hampton Park Terrace Historic District	31	1997

"Year" represents first designation (date initially included); subsequent boundary increases are included in acreage figures.
The vast, 23,826-acre Ashley River Historic District abuts the city on the northwest.
Source: National Register of Historic Districts

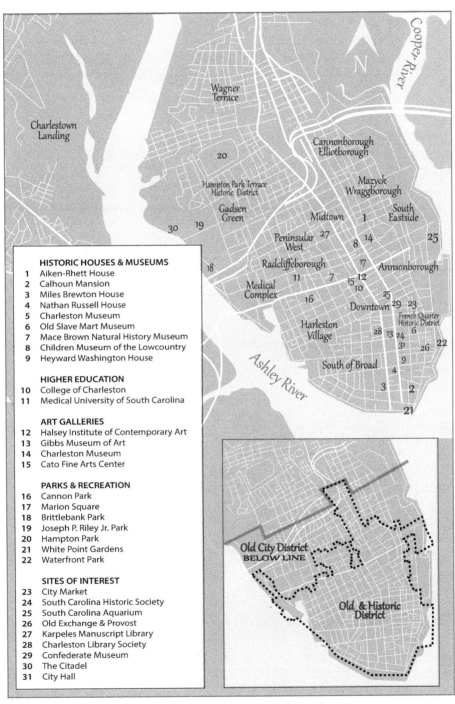

HISTORIC HOUSES & MUSEUMS
1. Aiken-Rhett House
2. Calhoun Mansion
3. Miles Brewton House
4. Nathan Russell House
5. Charleston Museum
6. Old Slave Mart Museum
7. Mace Brown Natural History Museum
8. Children Museum of the Lowcountry
9. Heyward Washington House

HIGHER EDUCATION
10. College of Charleston
11. Medical University of South Carolina

ART GALLERIES
12. Halsey Institute of Contemporary Art
13. Gibbs Museum of Art
14. Charleston Museum
15. Cato Fine Arts Center

PARKS & RECREATION
16. Cannon Park
17. Marion Square
18. Brittlebank Park
19. Joseph P. Riley Jr. Park
20. Hampton Park
21. White Point Gardens
22. Waterfront Park

SITES OF INTEREST
23. City Market
24. South Carolina Historic Society
25. South Carolina Aquarium
26. Old Exchange & Provost
27. Karpeles Manuscript Library
28. Charleston Library Society
29. Confederate Museum
30. The Citadel
31. City Hall

Historic districts, houses, and sites in Charleston. *(Map by Teri Norris)*

Battery, and Ashley, and an additional area of Church Street bounded by Cumberland and Chalmers, was listed in the National Register of Historic Places. The boundaries have been enlarged several times since then.[23]

Savannah has a long tradition of preserving and honoring its city plan, the Oglethorpe Plan, which guided city development from 1733 to the 1850s. Organized efforts to preserve architecture and landmarks arose much later, following the Historic American Buildings Survey in 1934. The survey's findings became the basis for creating a city agency the following year, the Savannah Commission for the Preservation of Landmarks. A private initiative, the Society for the Preservation of Savannah Landmarks, was established soon afterward. Such efforts, however, were minor compared to the bolder steps taken by Charleston. It would not be until the 1950s that Savannah's preservation movement began catching up.[24]

The Historic Savannah Foundation (HSF), which remains active today, was established in 1955 by seven women determined to begin a preservation movement in Savannah and to counter efforts to model the city's downtown on those of the "modern" cities of Jacksonville and Atlanta. Their efforts began in reaction to the demolition of Savannah's City Market building in Ellis Square in 1954 and then crystallized with the proposed demolition of the Isaiah Davenport House in early

City of Savannah National Register Districts, 2020

District	Acreage	Year
Ardsley Park–Chatham Crescent Historic District	394	1985
Central of Georgia	41	1978
Cuyler-Brownville Historic District	194	1998
Daffin Park–Parkside Place Historic District	162	1999
Eastside Historic District	157	2002
Fairway Oaks–Greenview Historic District	96	2009
Gordonston Historic District	86	2001
Isle of Hope Historic District	92	1984
Juliette Gordon Low (also national historic landmark)	1	1966
Savannah Historic District	534	1966
Savannah Victorian Historic District	168	1974
Thomas Square Historic District	310	1997

"Year" represents first designation (date initially included); subsequent boundary increases are included in acreage figures.

Sources: National Register of Historic Districts; Savannah Tricentennial Plan

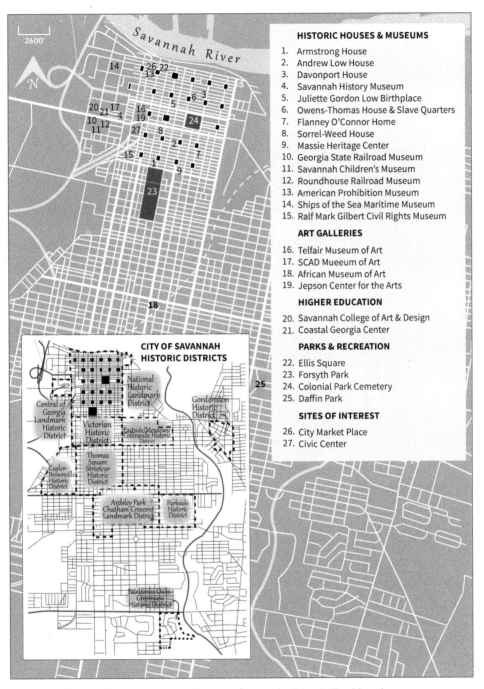

HISTORIC HOUSES & MUSEUMS

1. Armstrong House
2. Andrew Low House
3. Davonport House
4. Savannah History Museum
5. Juliette Gordon Low Birthplace
6. Owens-Thomas House & Slave Quarters
7. Flanney O'Connor Home
8. Sorrel-Weed House
9. Massie Heritage Center
10. Georgia State Railroad Museum
11. Savannah Children's Museum
12. Roundhouse Railroad Museum
13. American Prohibition Museum
14. Ships of the Sea Maritime Museum
15. Ralf Mark Gilbert Civil Rights Museum

ART GALLERIES

16. Telfair Museum of Art
17. SCAD Mueeum of Art
18. African Museum of Art
19. Jepson Center for the Arts

HIGHER EDUCATION

20. Savannah College of Art & Design
21. Coastal Georgia Center

PARKS & RECREATION

22. Ellis Square
23. Forsyth Park
24. Colonial Park Cemetery
25. Daffin Park

SITES OF INTEREST

26. City Market Place
27. Civic Center

Historic districts, houses, and sites in Savannah. *(Map by Teri Norris)*

1955. The Davenport House was saved by the HSF and preserved as a museum. The HSF later developed a revolving loan fund to purchase historically significant structures and resell them to buyers who agree to ensure their preservation.[25]

The city's architectural resources were surveyed by the HSF in 1962 in collaboration with University of Virginia preservation authorities. This original survey encompasses a period of significance of 1733 to circa 1880. The Savannah Historic District was designated a National Historic Landmark in November 1966 for its significance in town planning as well as architecture. In 1977 and again in 1985 the National Register district boundaries were expanded, and the period of significance was extended to the mid-1900s. In 1992 the historic preservation department of the Savannah College of Art and Design worked with the National Register Program of the National Park Service and resurveyed every building in the National Historic Landmark District. Further revisions were made in 2005.[26]

City Planning as the Arbiter of Quantity and Quality

City planning has two primary responsibilities: long-range comprehensive planning and regulation of development. The former is much like organizational strategic planning but writ large for an entire city. It sets long-range goals, objectives, and strategies for growth. The latter is theoretically the regulatory regime that enforces the former, primarily through legal mechanisms such as zoning and design standards (e.g., architectural, historical, and cultural compatibility) for which specialized boards are often established to review proposed development projects. An overarching role of city planning is to balance the expectations of investors with those of residents, and the need to effectively carry out that mission has become acute in both cities.

Comprehensive planning updates are frequently conducted in five- or ten-year cycles to ensure that the goals of a city are current and meaningful. Regulatory updates are far less frequent and often done on a piecemeal basis to meet specific needs with pragmatic action. For that reason, development regulations gradually become misaligned with long-range goals. As a result, development in historic districts can run afoul of citizen expectations for authenticity in those districts. For this reason, some cities establish offices of sustainability tasked with ensuring that goals are sustainable and appropriately supported by the regulatory regime.

In the 1950s, comprehensive planning was emergent but often ineffective, and the idea of sustainability did not yet exist. Preservationists and city planners were often working at cross purposes. Postwar suburbanization driven by federal housing and transportation policies rapidly transformed America's urban landscape. Federal Housing Administration and Veterans Administration mortgage insurance expedited suburban homeownership, while the Federal Highway Administration funded highway and freeway construction to enhance suburban mobility. The programs, in their early phases, were racially discriminatory and left African Americans without the full range of options available to Whites.

City centers began to decay as many of those who could afford to do so moved to the suburbs. The federal response was urban renewal, a program of grants to cities put into effect by the Housing Act of 1954. The program funded "slum clearance" and remediation of "blight." The concept of environmental justice, which calls for an assessment of the impacts of major development projects on vulnerable communities, did not exist. In practice, lower-income neighborhoods were often sliced apart or demolished to accommodate freeways and large-scale developments. For that reason, the novelist James Baldwin famously equated urban renewal to "Negro removal."[27]

Lower-income city residents were left to founder as higher-income residents moved out of the historic core of the city and the remaining neighborhoods were demolished or sliced apart by new, high-capacity roadways. As downtowns and urban neighborhoods decayed, the process accelerated. Investors joined the exodus to the suburbs.

For elected officials and city planners, the chief means of responding to the threat posed by suburbanization to core areas was wholesale redevelopment. New city plans had to attract investment in large-scale and modernist (and out-of-character) office buildings and retail development that would supply jobs for suburbanites. Bringing those employees to the city would require freeways and road widening to increase mobility. Such plans threatened to destroy the historic character of traditional downtowns.

Charleston and Savannah escaped the worst ravages of urban renewal, as observed earlier, but the program took a toll. In addition to the loss of some neighborhoods, interstate construction intruded into both cities, with I-26 bisecting the Upper and Mid-Peninsula areas in Charleston, and I-16 slicing through historic neighborhoods on downtown Savannah's lower-income western edge.

For the most part, suburbanization and urban renewal enjoyed wide support among those who were able to move out of the city. Shopping centers, malls, and fast food arrived, and backyards became big enough for family activities and garden parties. New freeways could speed suburbanites to and from the city for work or as needed for other purposes.

The paradigm shift that occurred in the 1960s brought preservation and city planning into closer alignment. By working together, preservationists and planners managed to bring both cities back from the brink of the kind of disaster that had befallen so many other cities. Over subsequent decades, preservationists and planners worked together to establish limits on demolition, historic district development review standards, identification of historic neighborhoods (which became National Register districts), and development of community plans to address issues such as gentrification and affordable housing. More recently, preservationists and planners have worked together to address systemic concerns such as environmental justice. Whether they can join to address the looming challenge of elitification remains to be seen.

Savannah's core is now expanding into areas on the east and west that were originally wetlands, later rice plantations, and then industrial areas. The scale of such changes to each side of the historic district, coupled with changes within the district, led the National Park Service in 2018 to downgrade the landmark district to "threatened" status from its previous "satisfactory" condition. Although the city has had a rigorous review process in place for decades, the downgrade has forced it to take even greater care to avoid approving new plans that undermine the character of the core area.

On Savannah's west side, a mixed-use riverfront hotel will anchor an entertainment district built over a 107-year-old coal-fueled power plant. Nearby, in the recently designated Canal District, the city is building a new arena where its waterworks once stood. Apartments, retail space, and walking and biking trails are also planned. The planning process for the area has taken years to unfold to meet the requirements of preservationists, developers, urban designers, traffic engineers, neighborhood advocates, and many other stakeholders.

A similar expansion is occurring on the east side, anchored by the large Eastern Wharf project. The project was first conceived in 2005 but ran into regulatory difficulty and then was hit by the recession of 2008. It was reconceived ten years later by new developers and is moving forward. The former industrial area will have a new hotel, retail stores, a residential tower, and townhouses.

A *New York Times* business article quoted David McDonald, president of the Downtown Neighborhood Association, as supportive of the development: "It's a good development," he said. "We encouraged them to have more green space and maintain the squares and integrity of the Oglethorpe Plan." The additional scrutiny brought on by the landmark district's threatened status has paid off in the form of wider consensus on the compatibility of new construction adjacent to the historic district.[28]

The abundance of high-quality historic architecture and urban design in Charleston and Savannah has influenced modern development in the Lowcountry. Beginning around 1990, developers began experimenting with neo-traditional development, now known as New Urbanism. Within a decade, New Urbanism became a viable alternative to conventional, sprawling suburban development. The new paradigm draws from development patterns of the late 1800s and early 1900s for single-family housing and digs even deeper in history for higher-density development in its town centers. Communities are internally connected by sidewalks, trails, and nodes of civic space. Houses are built up close to the sidewalk to engage with the public realm, rather than withdraw from it as in conventional suburban development.

The Lowcountry has a greater concentration of New Urbanism than other parts of the nation. Two of the first developments were I'On in Mount Pleasant, three miles from the Cooper River, and Newpoint, near Beaufort. Visionary developer Vincent G. Graham worked with the pioneering New Urbanist design firms Duany Plater-Zyberk (DPZ) and Dover Kohl on community design. Graham later partnered with Robert Turner and Billy Keyserling in creating the Old Village of Port Royal, an infill development project in the hollowed-out center of the town of Port Royal.

While New Urbanism became widely accepted from Charleston to Beaufort, it came later to Savannah. The city's housing department led the way with an affordable infill project in the Cuyler-Brownsville neighborhood in 2004. Since then, other subsidized and market-rate developments with elements of New Urbanism have been built in the city.

The reflection of historic Charleston and Savannah in newer development reinforces the value of traditional design patterns, which in turn add value to the Lowcountry at large by establishing its prominence as a livable place and a character destination. Nevertheless, preserving and enhancing traditional character remains a continuing struggle. As I'On builder Vincent Graham wrote in a Charleston op-ed, there is still "a sprawl-building industrial complex of massive proportions" that prioritizes the movement of motor vehicles over the civil interactions of people. This threat to the future of Charleston and Savannah is evaluated in the concluding chapter.[29]

CONCLUSION

The goals of the conclusion are to 1) draw together the threads running through chapters 1 through 12; 2) draw conclusions regarding those threads, including identifying trends suggesting current and future challenges facing both cities; 3) identify and compare specific features of the built environment of each city; and 4) place both cities in the context of the greater Lowcountry and then to speculate two generations into the future on the prospect of a united Charleston-Savannah metropolitan region.

Numerous threads, or through lines, of the entwined story of Charleston and Savannah have been highlighted in the preceding chapters. The first of those reveals that both cities were comprehensively planned prior to settlement, and the plan of each indelibly influenced its future physical characteristics. Differences between the cities today, in their streetscapes and transportation networks, for example, can be traced to the plans that were in place at their founding.

A second thread in the story reveals that the founding plans imparted a set of enduring character traits to each city. The most important of those traits can be described as a spirit or ethos. Charleston's ethos is that of seventeenth-century gothic society (described by some as "medieval"); Savannah's ethos is that of the eighteenth-century Enlightenment. The presence of an ethos, however different, reveals each to be steeped in history and different in that regard from most other American cities.

A third thread reveals that Charleston has repeatedly magnified and projected its political culture across the South and throughout the nation. Even now, Charleston projects an aura of character, enjoys notoriety, and has political leverage through the South Carolina early primary that far exceeds what might be expected from its size. With influence comes responsibility, and if Charleston is to genuinely exorcise the specter of White supremacy it must tell the world that tolerance is more than equal opportunity employment, diversity is more than blended cuisine, and social equity means more than minority business loans. Charleston and Savannah must both reinvent themselves again and find a way to make the historic city core a place for all people to live in, to enjoy, and to prosper in. Both cities made a down payment on reinvention by overcoming overt practices of segregation and discrimination, and by celebrating cultural diversity, yet a far greater challenge lies ahead in looming decisions (or lack thereof) on the future of the historic heart of the city. Reinvention is a process, one that requires periodic renewal, and both cities must confront the issues of equity and racism that boiled over in 2020. Charleston and the Lowcountry should adopt this third Reconstruction as not only a local project but also one to project nationwide in making amends for its past.

A fourth thread reveals that the rise, fall, and reinvention of both cities is closely associated with geography. Both cities rose to become major players in transatlantic trade and then fell as cotton exports favored Gulf ports, particularly New Orleans. Then they rose again as conditions once more favored their position on the Atlantic coast, first with the U.S. Navy command in Charleston, then as feeder ports for the rising New South cities of Atlanta and Charlotte. Ultimately they reinvented themselves as modern cities, shedding institutionalized patriarchy and inequality, and embracing diversity. With broader economic freedom, the trade-related economy boomed, feeding the 250-mile Interstate 85 industrial and distribution corridor running through Greenville.

Another aspect of geography is geopolitics. Both cities were exposed to multiple external threats: the Spanish to the south, the French to the west, and Native American allies and the nearby Indigenous nations that chafed at their expansion. Added to the resulting sense of vulnerability was a constant threat of slave rebellion. A sense of siege became a cultural trait that may have added to the Lowcountry's willingness to lead the South to secession.

Geography also meant vulnerability to hurricanes, and disastrous flooding in the case of Charleston. The exposure to existential threats made both cities more resilient and more willing to confront adversity with the knowledge that a city's spirit will prevail even if its buildings are in ruins.

A fifth thread reveals that the Lowcountry environment contributes significantly to the character of the two cities. In addition to being vulnerable to the more destructive elements of nature, they share an estuarine setting that became part of the character of both cities. Vast marsh vistas, tides that bring the ocean almost to everyone's doorstep, and the sultry climate are aspects of the Lowcountry that have melded with the character of its residents.

A sixth thread reveals that their reinvention was associated with urbanizization. As rural influences began diminishing across the South in the 1960s, reaching near parity with cities in the 1980s, the creative potential of cities like Charleston and Savannah was awakened. They embraced a new, more diverse cultural economy, which led to the rapid expansion of tourism.

A seventh thread reveals the odd and evolving relationship between the two cities. They began working in concert, then they quickly became estranged over deep differences concerning slavery, Native American trade relations, and land tenure. Then, for a time, Savannah became a satellite of Charleston, but then it quickly found its own way, establishing trade relations with the Caribbean that overshadowed Charleston's influence in that region. After that, the Industrial Age brought intense competition, then cooperation when a new railroad tied the two together. Later they found common cause in Jim Crow, sister cities in the South that rejected the new constitutional principles of the nation's "Second Founding" as Reconstruction has been called. Finally the two cities drifted apart, and for more than a century, despite their close proximity, they have had little to do with each other.

An eighth thread reveals that although Charleston and Savannah have found a viable path to reinvention, it is not necessarily a sustainable path. The principal threats to sustained progress are a lack of meaningful social equity in public policy and inadequate urban planning strategies to implement equitable policies. Without inclusive and meaningful comprehensive planning, strong growth management, design-oriented zoning, and effective development review processes, the influx of investment (whether for tourism or other industries) can turn a livable city into a despoiled nightmare. The interrelated problems of urban sprawl, congestion, and flooding are topics of intense debate today in Charleston. The problem of increasing industrial traffic through the historic urban core remains unresolved after decades of study in Savannah. And in both cities, gentrification, elitification, short-term vacation rentals, and absentee homeownership pose threats to long-term residents and established neighborhoods. Perhaps most importantly, planning for rising sea level and other impacts of climate change is only now beginning to get the emphasis it deserves by either city.[1]

The final thread is the central subject of this concluding chapter. Both cities have consciously embraced a *past as present* philosophy, acknowledging the wrongs of Native American relations, chattel slavery, racism, aristocracy and oligarchy, and class stratification, while also acknowledging that a complicated past created the rich, blended culture existing in the present. Whereas in the past, before their reinventions, each city's varied component cultures acted in the charade of elitism and white supremacy, now even most descendants of white supremacists accept the premise that people of widely different origins shaped their city's unique character and continue the project of its enrichment.

Past-Present Tension

The United States as a whole, and the South in particular, perpetuated White supremacist myths that were shaken to the core by the civil rights movement—the "second Reconstruction"—and the related social upheaval of the 1960s. Lingering supremacist myths were later exploded by the arrival of the internet and ready access to digitized historical primary documents such as speeches and formal declarations. Proof of aggressive racism and intense advocacy of slavery is now available at everyone's fingertips. Lost Cause mythology, riddled with white supremacist fictions, has finally been debunked.

Greater self-awareness led Americans to begin reinventing themselves. In cities, where new ideas spread fast, profound change came rapidly. In southern cities, the legacy of racism became a two-way street linking the present to the past. Thought leaders took aim at the worst of the past and renounced it, while also reaching to the best of the past, elevating it to revered status. Architecture thus became a way to tell the story of past sins while simultaneously building pride in the present. Neighborhoods with a legacy of segregation became neighborhoods with character. The visual arts, culinary arts, and music similarly became features of southern cities that showcased a rich, diverse, blended past.

Charleston and Savannah are among the leaders in the process of reinvention. Both are now economic success stories built on pluralism. But new challenges come with success, and one of those is wealth disparity. The great disparities that arose with slavery should serve as a warning: without mechanisms to share prosperity, profits will rise to the top income brackets, and along with increasing money comes increasing power. Oglethorpe's Georgia set out to create a level society by limiting the amount of land one could own. Oglethorpe and the Trustees recognized that without some form of checks and balances, a plantation elite would take form and seize the levers of power. The process of reinvention in Charleston and Savannah has yet to formally recognize the need to equitably share the fruits of prosperity and put in place mechanisms to achieve it. Failure to do so may result in permanent structural inequity.

Another lesson of history is clear. Lowcountry plantation prosperity was a result of not only social inequity but also the increasing reliance on an unsustainable, single-crop economic model, initially rice monoculture and later cotton monoculture. Today tourism is becoming a monolithic, arguably un- ~~Tourism~~ sustainable industry. While the tourism industry has driven the reinvention ✗ of Charleston and Savannah, it has the potential to become an all-powerful industry largely in the grip of a few powerful people, the oligarchs of the new economy.

Such a future for Charleston and Savannah could be an ominous one and should be contemplated in policy discussions. It could mean that traditional neighborhoods in the historic core are destroyed more surely than by the bulldozers of urban renewal. It could mean that traditional employers flee the city. It could mean that service-sector workers will face long and expensive commutes, reducing net income. It could mean that middle-income residents would be pushed out next, completing an economic and demographic hollowing of the historic city as an elite domain. It could end the honorable period in which both cities were *working* cities first and tourist destinations second. It could end the larger metropolitan dynamic in which everyone takes pride in the historic core and enjoys going there for traditional events. Ultimately it could result in civic functions moving out to accommodate upscale and luxury development. The policy questions that must be asked are: To what end are we as a city promoting unrestrained growth of tourism? Who will be the principal beneficiaries of such growth? What sort of character and soul will the city have if present trends continue?

During the antebellum era, southern and northern White elites became rich through a system that Massachusetts senator Charles Sumner called an "unhallowed alliance between the lords of the lash and the lords of the loom." Large cotton plantations joined the Industrial Revolution and created the nation's first big industry. By 1810, five million cotton spindles were producing textiles for the world.[2]

Historians have long associated the development of modern business models with the nineteenth-century railroad industry, overlooking plantation slavery and the textile industry as a foundational model. The old theory allowed historians to brush off an uncomfortable relationship, but in recent decades they have been more willing to confront it. The business practices of the plantation elite became infused in nineteenth-century American industry. The cotton plantation was big business, and it made cold calculations that ignored the many for the benefit of the few.[3]

Today elected officials in Charleston and Savannah are expected to make cold calculations to benefit the tourism industry on the assumption that it will continue to benefit everyone. In local elections in both cities in 2019, the electorate sent a message that there needs to be a pause for reflection. That election and the next few may be the chance for either city to formulate a strategic growth plan taking into account the needs of the populous first before its future course is dictated by a powerful elite. History repeats, and it would be a wise leader who revisits the economic model of the Lowcountry plantation elite in view of current trends.

Charleston and Savannah are prime examples of southern cities that have changed course, reinventing themselves to overcome the original sin of slavery and creating a better place for all of their citizens. Neither is a perfect place, to be sure, but they both diversified their labor force, enlarged electoral participation, and professionalized government by attracting experienced personnel. Both cities effectively marketed their historical and cultural resources, attracted a new generation of creative talent, and built a complex and diversified economy.

Charleston and Savannah transformed themselves from static urban environments with stagnant economies to dynamic, modern cities built on a rich and complicated past. Being dynamic means constantly changing. Friction and collisions occur, adjustments are made, and a cycle of change incrementally produces a more inclusive and democratic city.

Dynamic cities tacitly invite the social and economic participation of anyone with an idea they wish to explore. Instead of being orchestrated by an elite and governed by authoritarians, they are directed by the individual choices of thousands. As the Enlightenment economist Adam Smith wrote, "It is the great multiplication of the productions of all the different arts, in consequence of the division of labour, which occasions, in a well-governed society, that universal opulence which extends itself to the lowest ranks of the people."[4]

The architect Witold Rybczynski captures a sense of how individual actors become transformative in *Charleston Fancy: Little Houses and Big Dreams in the Holy City*. Rybczynski takes his reader through the creative process of several builders, concluding that it is they who collectively impart character.[5]

> Charleston's peculiar character is above all a matter of scale. Historically, the peninsula grew in small increments—one house at a time—and the

patchwork-quilt result is a major part of its appeal. Building in a manner that is sensitive to local tradition requires local experience and expertise, not likely to be found among national developers and international construction firms. Small local builders are not only more knowledgeable, they are also more flexible, and what they build is more likely to respond to changing needs and conditions, especially over time. It is also more likely to achieve that elusive but recognizable quality: authenticity.

Historic cities like Charleston and Savannah have always absorbed substantial contributions from many individuals. Vernacular architecture, shotgun houses, and adaptive versions of single houses add to the overall texture of both cities. But now the constraints are off, more people are able to contribute to the advancement of their city, and creativity and entrepreneurship seem almost boundless. People with wealth and a grip on levers of power will always attempt to assert their will, but political, social, and economic power is currently decentralized to the extent that oligarchs seem to be a dying breed and aristocrats but a lingering anomaly.

Oligarchic impulses never completely go away, of course. Power brokers are always prepared to enrich themselves and reassert authority. Democracy, by contrast, must always play defense. As wealth has poured into Charleston and Savannah, new, elite markets have emerged, particularly in the tourism sector. If left to their own devices, investors in those markets would seek ever-higher profit margins by attracting an increasingly larger share of high-end tourism (the "upscale" and "luxury" markets, as they are known in the industry). The risk of this trend is elitification, the process of reorienting an area to appeal primarily to the elite resident or visitor. When elitification occurs, the oligarchs return to protect their consolidated and highly profitable investments in the elite market.

Charleston and Savannah can guard against elitification through strategic planning that balances the interests of all sectors of the existing community. While strategic plans addressing all sectors of the economy are typically developed within the framework of local comprehensive plans, they are often shelved and forgotten once the process is completed. Some cities have created ongoing sustainability and resilience initiatives in conjunction with strategic planning, and both Charleston and Savannah will almost certainly have to do the same. And at this point in their story arc, they will need to enlist the creative class within to participate in charting a course of renewal.

Reinvention

Lowcountry slave society persisted for nearly two centuries, and its successor, the New South–Jim Crow era persisted for another century. The modern South coming out of the civil rights movement (the second Reconstruction) is a more tenuous regime. Charleston and Savannah had to reinvent themselves by renouncing the evils and inequities of the past and embracing the virtues of a plural and democratic society going forward, but in addition they had to sort out and highlight the good from the bad and foster the rich and complex amalgamated cultures that draw visitors by the millions. Unlike the authoritarian regimes of the past, which sustained themselves through terror and tyranny, new, reinvented cities such as Charleston and Savannah require strategies for resilience and sustainability to endure.

Resilience is the adaptive capacity to withstand shocks. For Charleston and Savannah, resilience requires surviving environmental shocks such as those brought on by climate change and pandemics and also economic shocks such as recessions, banking-related fiscal crises. Political crises may also arise, causing alienation like those of past eras. Sustainability is the long-term durability of a system. A sustainable city requires environmental stewardship, democratic processes capable of ironing out inequities as they inevitably arise, strong institutions that have broad support, and strategic planning to identify and manage strengths, weaknesses, opportunities, and threats on a recurring basis. Resilience and sustainability require metacognition—that is, critical self-awareness, observation, learning, and self-correction.[6]

Neither city as of 2020 has instituted sophisticated resilience and sustainability initiatives, nor have they acquired a capacity for metacognition within their social, economic, and political institutions. Some of their leaders recognize this and are striving to push their cities to the next level of reinvention, one with a commitment to long-term viability.

In order to assess the current state of self-aware reinvention in Charleston and Savannah, questions about growth dynamics were added to interviews conducted by the author with local officials and development professionals in both cities. The narrative that follows is a distillation of their observations on the character of their city, its uniqueness, and the challenges that lie ahead.[7]

Attributes of Character

Character is difficult to define. It is a blend of attributes that produces surprising or intriguing results. Several attributes were highlighted in the preceding chapters that collectively paint a picture of the contrasting character of Charleston and Savannah. Those attributes include historicity, urban authenticity, "Europeanness" of urban form melded with African cultural attributes, physical formality, social formality, wealth, and race and class. Each of these seven attributes is briefly introduced here.[8] The discussion of attributes is followed by an assessment of the challenges that lie ahead in maintaining the character that made each city famous.

1. *Historicity.* Many respondents interviewed in both cities expressed alarm about new hotel construction and other forms of development that are altering the more fine-grained historic character of their city. For many decades, preservation and tourism enjoyed a symbiotic relationship, but now that relationship appears to be deteriorating.

2. *Urban authenticity.* The authenticity of a city is the extent to which its normal urban functions are maintained. Many respondents in both cities expressed concern that traditional, working residents are being displaced by the transient population of tourists, absentee homeowners, and a non-resident (commuter) workforce more vested in the suburbs and exurbs than the historic core. In addition to a traditional workforce, both urban cores have large creative populations that add value to the urban environment that is difficult to quantify. One Savannah respondent said of the loss of such populations: "There is a danger of [the city] losing its soul and the uniqueness that makes it special." By the time authorities figure this out, some fear, it will be too late to change course.[9]

3. *Europeanness and Africanness.* Several respondents noted a "Europeanness" about Savannah that they believed to be unique in the United States. It was compared to Quebec City in Canada, which also has a uniquely European flavor. Some of the common attributes cited were a slower-paced, easier lifestyle, walkable mixed environment, landscaped boulevards, and numerous public spaces. An official in Charleston took the opposite position, arguing that European cities historically begin with a core and grow organically, which has been the case with his city. Savannah, on the other hand, by virtue of being planned has less of a European feel. Charleston, he added, is aged and weathered. It is on softer earth that moves, and there have been earthquakes. It has had hurricanes and fires, and it floods. It is more exposed to the elements and more aged as a result. While Charleston's detached homes place it in the Americas almost by definition, everything else about it seems European and

African in character. The Africanness of Charleston is everywhere. It is engrained in the city's character, embedded in its historic structures, and deeply structured in its way of life.

4. *Physical formality.* There are aspects of physical formality and informality that are part of the character of each city, about which respondents from both cities were in agreement. Charleston has a less formal, "ancient," medieval feel engendered by its narrower and sometimes oddly angled streets and the patina of age. In some ways, in some neighborhoods, it is richer in detail than Savannah. Its streets, public spaces, and architecture are, on the whole, less formal. Were it not for consistency in architectural styles, particularly the single house, Charleston might have a haphazard appearance. As Christina Rae Butler shows in *Lowcountry at High Tide*, much of the peninsula's built environment was developed on an ad hoc basis.[10]

5. *Social formality.* Charleston is the more socially formal of the two cities. Some Savannahians have choice words for the elitism they have encountered among their Carolina neighbors. Charleston can seem snobbier and ruder, and its politeness is often contrived, they say. For their part, younger Charlestonians recognize that elitism persists, but most see it as declining. Many are more concerned with building the next generation of egalitarian and socially progressive residents. Savannah is more sociable, more easy-going, according to respondents from both cities. The urban forest and public spaces make it easier to meet and interact in informal ways. There is a culture of civility associated with the city's civic space. Alfresco dining is more prevalent in Savannah. You can walk down the street with a drink in your hand, and in that way Savannah is more like New Orleans and Key West. Savannah is a pedestrian paradise.

6. *Wealth.* Charleston's relative wealth, maintained throughout most of its history, is another source of differences according to respondents. Charleston is the richer, older sister, but she can be "jealous," in the words of one respondent. She does not appreciate competitors and pretenders. Savannah has mostly been less wealthy, although there were times, such as the heyday of the steamboat era, when it rivaled its older sister.

7. *Race and class.* The rise, fall, and reinvention of Charleston and Savannah are phases of their history tied closely to race and class. Any meaningful comparison of the two cities must account for that connection. Although

Charleston has reinvented itself in modern times, projecting an image of a diverse and inclusive society, race and class remain strong undercurrents in local society. Elitism can be seen in the mayor's office, which has been held by well-connected members of the city's upper class. While the forty-year tenure of Mayor Riley harnessed elitism for enlightened purposes, the city's next phase of social advancement will require a new generation of leadership.

In Savannah, race more than class is the primary undercurrent in society. A Black-majority city (unlike Charleston, with a 74 percent White majority), Savannah has had four mayors from that demographic in recent times. Investment interests, however, have targeted the mayor's office as a means of countering rising African American political power. The mayoral election of 2015 was particularly fraught with racial messaging, ushering a White candidate into office. The mayoral election of 2019 was less fraught with racial messaging and may signal a step forward in the city's reinvention.

The top challenges ("weaknesses" and "threats" in strategic planning terminology) identified by the informed respondent interviews can be distilled from the preceding assessment. The top three facing Charleston, surmised from the informed respondent interviews (conducted prior to the COVID-19 pandemic), are 1) climate change, 2) transportation funding, and 3) historic core sustainability.

Charlestonians are acutely aware of their environmental vulnerabilities, so it is not difficult to see the threat posed by climate change, particularly rising sea level but also the potential increase in hurricane frequency and intensity. Transportation funding is a top concern because the city has a serious congestion problem and little control over funding; transportation has no funding stream and must go through political and bureaucratic hurdles to fund priority projects. Historic core sustainability is a challenge because the city has been losing traditional working residents and gaining part-time residents and vacationers competing in the residential real estate market, a trend that increases traffic, potentially worsens crime, and erodes working-city character.

Other major challenges cited in interviews include the scale of recently approved hotels; sprawl overwhelming the historic core and surrounding it with congestion and characterless development; neighborhood stability and tourism, which may be reaching a point at which their interests are at cross purposes; short-term vacation rentals (although a new model ordinance is addressing this issue); and the loss of a sense of ownership of historic core by all Charlestonians, including those in the suburbs and exurbs, creating a potentially a serious future problem in which urban leaders lose control of its destiny.

In Savannah, the top three challenges overlap with those in Charleston, although the city (which has less direct exposure to storm surge than Charleston) has not yet come to terms with the seriousness of the threat posed by climate change. City planners are attempting to change that by fostering a discussion of sustainability and resilience. The top three challenges seen facing Savannah: 1) funding to mitigate east-west traffic through the historic core, 2) historic core sustainability, and 3) political leadership.

The Savannah historic core extends four miles from the Savannah River to Derenne Avenue, the dividing line between historic Savannah and its suburbs. Heavy traffic traverses the central business district and older neighborhoods at levels that have been unacceptable since the 1990s. Solutions have been prioritized, but their costs and impacts have thus far been deemed unacceptable. The sustainability of the historic core is a major concern because the city, as with Charleston, has been losing traditional working residents while gaining part-time residents and vacationers competing for residential accommodations, a trend associated with numerous long-term problems, as cited above. Consistent political leadership has been lacking in Savannah, primarily due to a lingering racial divide, which has resulted in a flip-flopping of mayors and other elected officials.

Other serious challenges include excessive commercialization, which is overshadowing the neighborhood atmosphere; gentrification, which is displacing traditional residents; elitification, which is reorienting the historic core to serve upscale tourists and affluent part-time residents rather than city residents; and the flow of investment capital into the city from Atlanta and even more distant financial centers such as New York and Boston, which comes with little concern for local priorities.

Character and Urban Form

American cities that were well established by the mid-nineteenth century were compact, and most residents lived within an area of about one square mile. Residents of those cities walked nearly everywhere they needed to go. Transportation innovations beginning with streetcars led to the formation of suburbs. The widespread adoption of automobiles beginning in the 1920s led to further suburban growth, and through annexation cities typically expanded to a size of more than a hundred square miles. The inner suburbs of the streetcar era and the early automobile era produced today's Victorian and Arts and Crafts neighborhoods. Those neighborhoods aged along with the original downtown core area and eventually became today's historic districts.

While older cities often have outlying historic districts, their historic cores, comprising a downtown business district, adjoining neighborhoods, and early suburbs, occupy only a few contiguous square miles. Charleston's historic core on the peninsula occupies an area of four square miles, and Savannah's historic core is five square miles. Those core areas were locked in place by the Great Depression and World War II, a period lasting sixteen years during which there was little urban growth and after which there was profoundly rapid growth and the formation of far-flung suburbs, very different in character from the more compact pre-Depression era core.

Cities that preserved their pre–Depression era neighborhoods and business districts have discovered that those early places broadly define their character. Those core areas became assets that could be promoted to attract investment, particularly where there was an effective historic preservation movement coupled with public investment. First, cities promoted their core areas to build a tourism industry, and later they discovered that many other industries were attracted by the quality of life available in quaint and walkable neighborhoods and revitalized historic business districts full of entrepreneurs mingling in close proximity with fresh ideas, exhibiting a vitality that stood in sharp contrast to the chain store sameness of the suburbs.

This section looks specifically at the attributes of urban form that contribute to the quality of life in the historic cores of Charleston and Savannah, making them desirable places to live and work. Seven physical characteristics discussed earlier in greater detail are important to mention in this closing chapter: public space, environmental quality, an urban forest, block size, street width, building envelope, and architectural themes.

The foregoing characteristics relate to four conditions for a vibrant city famously identified by Jane Jacobs in *The Death and Life of Great American Cities*. Jacobs, an urban sociologist, observed that cities flourish when they support diversity in the built environment. She found that diversity arises when certain conditions are met: blocks are small, land uses are finely mixed, population density is high, and buildings are sufficiently varied to be able to house a diverse population. Jacobs's observations have withstood recent empirical testing by Marco De Nadai and associates at the University of Trento in Italy. The De Nadai team studied six cities and found that those that best met Jacobs's four conditions attained higher degrees of urban vitality. The remainder of this section examines Charleston and Savannah through the lens of Jacobs's four principles.[11]

1. While Charleston's founding plan allocated public space for various purposes, much of it was lost as the city developed. Lack of public space and rights of way prevents the city from establishing an urban forest. Absent ocean breezes, the streets and public spaces of Charleston can be "blistering hot," diminishing the outdoor activity that Jacobs describes as an intricate, improvisational "ballet." Savannah's planned open space, by contrast, has allowed the city to cultivate an urban forest and mitigate the effects of urban heat islands. Savannah's conviviality is in part attributed to its famous squares, parks, and wide sidewalks.

2. Charleston benefits from its many nearby historic plantations. Those offer a blend of cultural history and environmental quality in serene settings that not only draw tourists but also create an attractive landscape—in some cases hundreds of acres in size—that is appealing to residents. To some extent, this enveloping landscape offsets the lack of an urban forest in the historic core by providing alternative venues for public activities and special events. Savannah is somewhat the reverse. It offers a meticulously maintained urban forest but lacks vast areas of historic plantations with their pristine landscapes. Nevertheless, it has other contextual assets that add environmental quality to its overall character: former plantation wetlands, now nature preserves; the Savannah River National Wildlife Refuge; natural areas around Fort Jackson and Fort Pulaski; Bonaventure Cemetery; vast expanses of marsh similar to those around Charleston; and extensive maritime forests of palmettos, oaks, and pines that create the distinctive look of the Lowcountry.

3. Jacobs maintained that small blocks are an essential element of city character. Charleston's original, planned block size was a large six hundred feet by six hundred feet. While the original plan was largely abandoned, large block sizes persisted. Large blocks necessitate the interior subdivision of lots, with driveways and narrow lanes to service them. These alterations add visual interest, but they do little to encourage Jacobs's street ballet. The Charleston pattern stands in contrast to that of Savannah, where one finds a more fine-grained pattern of smaller blocks. Savannah's block pat-

Maps of Charleston and Savannah, 1855.
*(Courtesy of Hargrett Rare Book and Manuscript
Library, University of Georgia Libraries)*

tern was well established by 1855. The building block of the Savannah plan
is the ward, which at 675 feet by 675 feet is only slightly larger than the
original Charleston block. Unlike the large Charleston block, the ward is
open, with a civic square at its center. The ward, in a sense, is an inverted
Charleston block.

4. Street width is another simple but essential element of city character. The
Grand Model specified a hierarchy of streets with ample rights of way.
However, that set of standards was not preserved, and Charleston developed with an ad hoc network that has created a medieval-like pattern
of streets. Whether one is a resident or a visitor, walking (or wandering)
those streets is an experience unlike any other in terms of visual interest
and a sense of historical authenticity. The Oglethorpe Plan, in contrast,
specified an urban and regional network of rights of way that has largely
been respected throughout the city's history. Seven of its streets, each

nearly a mile long, allow for wide vehicular travel lanes, ample sidewalks, and street trees, creating a Parisian appearance on a less grand scale.

5. *Building envelope* is the width, height, depth, and shape of buildings. Collectively, building envelopes contribute character to an area of a city. The wharves in Charleston and Savannah, for example, have a peculiarly long and tall façade, and relatively short depth. The buildings of neighborhoods and commercial streets are narrow by comparison, creating a different sort of character. Charleston faces a challenge in that its only area of consistently large-envelope buildings is on its waterfront. Large-envelope buildings sited elsewhere are likely to be out of character with their surroundings. Marion Square is an exception and could become a functioning central business district if planned as such. Large-envelope buildings such as new hotels can disrupt the rhythm of city districts. Savannah, by contrast, has a well-established pattern of larger-envelope buildings extending two to three blocks south from its nearly mile-long riverfront. Hotels and other larger-envelope buildings can be accommodated within that band without disrupting the established character of the area, subject to effective design review. (See the discussion of "height gradient" below.)

6. Architectural themes are the leitmotifs of the built environment. Charleston has significant architectural resources dating back to the colonial period, despite ravaging hurricanes, fires, wars, and earthquakes. The city's architectural character is a unique fusion of styles covered by a provocative patina of age created by a sometimes-harsh environment. The mix of architectural periods represented in the city, coupled with the unifying themes of the single and double houses, creates a fascinating palette for restoration and new construction to meet modern demands. Commercial architectural heritage is primarily corridor- and waterfront-oriented, and the city lacks a defining central business district.

Savannah has virtually none of the colonial and federal-era architecture of Charleston, although its historic plan dates to 1733. The city's architectural character is a fusion of nineteenth- and early twentieth-century styles amalgamated with its urban plan and shrouded in its urban forest. Historic resources in the National Historic Landmark District are primarily of the nineteenth century. Early twentieth-century high-rise office buildings create a well-defined central business district with an aesthetically pleasing height gradient (with few anomalies). Updated zoning standards to maintain that gradient were adopted in 2003 and strengthened by the new zoning ordinance of 2019. The city manifested a tiered growth pattern in which successive eras of development (antebellum, postbellum, Victorian, and streetcar) established areas that are now well-defined neighborhoods that have been designated National Register districts.

Creative Enterprises and Monolithic Industry

The term "creative class" was popularized by the urbanist Richard Florida in *The Rise of the Creative Class*, published in 2002. Cities like Charleston and Savannah already saw themselves as creative cities, places valuing the arts and humanities, architecture and design, and creative entrepreneurship (particularly as directed to historical and cultural resources). However, the sudden popularity of the idea of a creative class put additional focus on attracting and retaining investors and entrepreneurs in that sector of the economy.

Florida's thesis is built on the work of others in the United Kingdom, Canada, and the United States pointing out the growing importance of "cultural and creative spaces" and "creative ecologies." Some scholars are now claiming that an entire "creative economy" is emerging that cuts across both manufacturing and service sectors. The new creative economy is driven by a web of imagination, creativity, and innovation rather than the top-down dictates of corporate executives.[12]

Cities across the United States began experimenting with initiatives aimed at strengthening the creative sectors of their local economies. A study of such initiatives funded by the National Endowment for the Arts was published in 2013. The study found an "enormous diversity in opinions and approaches" to promoting a creative economy. In particular, the definition of "creative industries" based on North American Industry Classification System (NAICS) codes varied greatly. Of 264 codes evaluated in the study's sample, 70 were common to over half. The finding suggests that a paradigm shift is well underway but far from complete.[13]

Urban economic development officials are fond of saying that cities are "engines of prosperity." The one hundred most populous U.S. cities produce 90 percent of the nation's innovation. Their productivity adds disproportionately to the national gross domestic product. Smaller cities, however, are no longer necessarily at a disadvantage. According to Bob Steel, New York City's deputy mayor for economic development from 2010 to 2014, his city was competing with smaller cities in attracting talent, forcing it to "up its game."

Charleston and Savannah have been attracting and retaining creative talent by emphasizing quality of life and by maintaining strong educational systems. Maintaining affordability and livability in each city's creative historic core will be essential to sustaining this strategy.[14]

The creative "collision" of ideas in Charleston and Savannah is encouraged by initiatives such as the Charleston Digital Corridor, The Harbor, and the Creative Coast. Their approach is a new paradigm for building the creative sector within the economy, thereby adding higher-wage jobs. It requires featuring quality of life and work-life balance to recruit and retain talent, which in turn depend on a dynamic historic core. Cities like Charleston and Savannah attract creative people because they offer a culturally diverse and stimulating urban environment with a high concentration of other innovators like them. Both cities are much like a big city in overall profile, but in their historic cores they are comparatively undiluted by a massive middle class. Creatives can easily move about on foot or bicycle and interact with others like themselves.

The Charleston Digital Corridor (CDC) initiative was established to promote the city's tech economy through a range of activities, leveraging Charleston's reputation for livability. The CDC facilitates synergies between the business, education, and social environments that are collectively attractive to tech innovators and tech-related companies. The organization maintains that the technology sector it promotes is vital to the future of the city because of its high-income levels (averaging over $93,000 in 2019) and the benefits it offers for economic diversification.

Chris Miller moved to Savannah from Atlanta at age forty-two, leaving behind a rising career with internet start-ups. Miller was looking for early retirement that offered "larger living in a smaller place." Before long, Miller and several other technology-minded collaborators teamed up and got involved in economic development, specifically to promote the creative sector and grow higher-wage jobs in sustainable industries. The result was the Creative Coast initiative, launched in 2003 with local government funding to foster creative business investment and entrepreneurship. Miller attributes to the initiative a reversal of a long history of wage decline in Savannah.

The Creative Coast initiative was data-driven from the beginning. By overlaying U.S. Occupational Index data with data from the Bureau of Labor Statistics and then filtering by regional MSA NAICS code data, they were able to define and detect even small movements of wage and labor numbers, which they then used for "competitive tracking" of other cities and return-on-investment indexing.

The dial began moving in a positive direction, as Miller put it, but Savannah had more inertia to overcome than Charleston. It lacked cohesive leadership, it still had vestiges of racial politics that inhibited concerted action, the booming tourism industry masked the need to grow other industries, and entrenched mind-sets were wedded to older approaches to economic development. Charleston, by contrast, according to Miller, had more money to promote itself, more cohesive leadership (including a strong mayor), a higher national profile, and a head start in promoting tech industries. Nevertheless, he believes Savannah possesses inherent advantages: more students per capita and with a high proportion of them in creative fields, the largest art and design school in the nation, better technology and infrastructure (e.g., thirty thousand miles of fiber optic cable), less "stodginess" than Charleston (a through line found in the interviews), and its location in a state with a better business reputation.

According to urbanist Dan Doctoroff, a former New York City deputy mayor for economic development, one of the most important productive interactions that must be cultivated to attract technological investment and a creative labor force is between urbanists (e.g., city planners, urban designers, and architects) and technologists (e.g., hardware and software developers). In most cities there is a divide between those professions; they speak different languages. One reason the "smart city" movement advocated by Doctoroff has thus far not met with great success is its failure to bridge that divide. Creative partnerships among planners, designers, and innovators will be essential to the success of "smart cities."[15]

Geographer Waldo R. Tobler has postulated a "first law of geography," stating, "All things are related, but near things are more related than far things." Dense urban populations have more relationships and more interactions than rural areas. Cities create a sort of *idea field* (analogous to a magnetic field or a gravity field) in which high-intensity interactions occur in high-density areas where intensity drops in an s-curve manner, declining rapidly as density decreases. Geographers call this a distance decay model, and some use the formula for gravitational attraction to describe this relationship (calling it a gravity model).[16]

The internet has fostered nonspatial communities of choice, defying the distance decay model. The Enlightenment produced a phenomenon called the Republic of Letters in which thinkers, scientists, and innovators across Europe maintained regular contact through the mail (which had become highly efficient in the eighteenth century). Yet the French *philosophes* spent time in London's coffeehouses, British thinkers spent time in the Netherlands, and Berliners during the relatively enlightened reign of Frederick II were often in Paris. The Republic of Letters sustained creativity between periods of physical contact and collaboration, but it did not replace the city as a hub of creativity.

Decentralization—and a futuristic Republic of Letters—is perhaps inevitable, reversing the effects of thousands of years of urbanization. One can imagine technologies that would allow that to happen. Physical and virtual cities could pop up like conventions as needed or desired. But, for several more decades, unless there is pandemic-related acceleration, cities will continue to be hubs of creativity and engines of prosperity. Quality of life (e.g., amenities, ease in walking, creative environments, work-life balance) will continue to be essential to the attraction and retention of talent. And "networks of opportunity" associated with diversity, innovation, and educational institutions will be central to the post-industrial economy.

Charleston and Savannah possess many of the fundamental attributes necessary to build sustainable post-industrial economies. They require vision and stewardship—effective political, business, and educational leadership—to succeed. But they face a significant challenge in bringing the benefits of the post-industrial economy to a broader spectrum of the population. Many service-sector occupations with the fastest-growing demand do not pay a living wage, presenting perhaps the greatest urban challenge of the foreseeable future.

The Political Divide

Following the 1920 U.S. census, Congress was unable to carry out its constitutional responsibility for the reapportionment of congressional districts. The population had shifted toward cities, and for the first time the nation was evenly divided, half urban and half rural. Congress was thus deadlocked as its rural members refused to cede power to urban areas.

The "urban-rural divide" has remained a political fact of life for a century, even as newer, related divides have opened throughout the nation. Another major divide, the "sectional divide" that formed over slavery during the Constitutional Convention of 1787, has persisted throughout the nation's history, driven through time by competing political cultures. Since World War II and the subsequent expansion of automobile-oriented suburbs, urban-suburban-exurban divides have created an even more complex political map.

Nearly all cities in the United States, whether they are in blue or red states, are blue at the core. Charleston and Savannah follow that pattern. On the Charleston peninsula, nearly all voter precincts swing heavily for more left-leaning candidates. In the 2016 presidential election, most of those precincts voted at a 90 percent level for the Democratic candidate. The exceptions were two precincts in the historically affluent and conservative South of Broad neighborhood, which voted at a combined 54 percent for the Republican candidate.[17]

Charleston County is internally divided into red and blue precincts, with more affluent suburbs leaning Republican, but those internal divisions are not as sharp as the surrounding urban-exurban and urban-rural divides. Charleston County as a whole voted 51 percent for Democratic candidate Hillary Clinton in 2016, whereas exurban Berkeley and Dorchester Counties voted at 39 and 38 percent levels for Clinton.[18]

Within the city, all historic neighborhoods voted heavily Democratic in 2016, with half voting at over a 90 percent rate for the Democrat. The more affluent suburbs voted at a 70 percent rate for the Republican. South Carolina's First Congressional District, which spans most of the Lowcountry and was once held by libertarian Republican Mark Sanford, went for Democrat Joe Cunningham in 2018 in a close election swung by Peninsula voters (although suburban women also showed a shift to the Democratic Party). Cunningham narrowly lost the seat to Republican Nancy Mace in 2020.[19]

Charleston is decidedly liberal for the same reasons that most other cities are liberal. It is an amalgam of creatives, students, young service-sector workers, people with higher education, and minorities, all of whom tend to vote for liberal or progressive candidates. Those groups have a higher tolerance for diversity of opinion, lifestyle, ethnicity, and religious opinion in their social environment.

Savannah is similarly divided. Chatham County voted 55 percent for the Democrat in the 2016 presidential election, in contrast to exurban Effingham County, which voted at a 21 percent rate for the Democrat. The sharper divide may have a racial component. Chatham County has a 40 percent African American population, and Savannah is a Black-majority city. Charleston County, by contrast, has a 30 percent African American population, and Charleston is a White-majority city. White flight from Savannah appears to

Charleston Urban-Exurban Political Divide

REFLECTED IN THE 2020 PRESIDENTIAL VOTE (%)

	Biden	Trump
Urban Area		
Charleston core	76	24
Charleston County	57	43
Exurban Area		
Berkeley County	44	56
Dorchester County	45	55

Source: "Extremely Detailed Map of the 2020 Election," *New York Times*; the interactive map contains election results at the precinct level

Savannah Urban-Exurban Political Divide

REFLECTED IN THE 2020 PRESIDENTIAL VOTE (%)

	Biden	Trump
Urban Area		
Savannah core	88	12
Chatham County	60	40
Exurban Area		
Bryan County	32	68
Effingham County	25	75

Source: "Extremely Detailed Map of the 2020 Election," *New York Times*; the interactive map contains election results at the precinct level

have transformed the political landscape more than in the Charleston area, and politics is insinuated into the process.[20] The tables showing the results of the 2020 election reveal the same pattern of urban-exurban political division found in the 2016 election.

In recent years popular books on political culture such as *The Big Sort* have maintained that Americans are increasingly sorting themselves into enclaves of like-minded people. In 1976 less than a quarter of the national population lived in a presidential landslide county (defined as one where a party's candidate won by 20 percent or more). By 2004 almost half lived in a landslide county, and the exurban counties around cities such as Charleston and Savannah are increasingly exhibiting that level of division. Existing social divisions are reinforced by political divisiveness, and politics in turn is reinforced by social division.[21]

Increasingly Charleston and Savannah are acquiring similar features as modern cities. Higher education has expanded in the historic core of both cities, increasing the number of students and faculty living in those areas. Once-obsolete buildings are being converted to condominiums to accommodate those populations as well as the growing ranks of service-sector employees and the expanding vacation home (and status home) market. Creative pursuits are also increasing in both cities as writers, designers, artists, artisans, and musicians locate in or near the historic urban core. As city residents, they are attracted to and thrive on diversity and variety. On the other hand, those who seek greater uniformity and predictability have been leaving the city for the suburbs and, increasingly, the exurbs. The urban-rural divide is no less defining than it was a century ago when it brought Congress to a standstill in its duty to reapportion congressional districts.

The Future of the Lowcountry

Charleston and Savannah grew inward from colonial times to the early twentieth century. They became denser, more populous, and more vibrant. During those times, people walked almost everywhere, so they needed to be close to family and friends and goods and services. To the extent that Charleston grew, it did so primarily by filling wetlands and river banks to increase the size of the peninsula rather than expanding across either river.

Even during the streetcar era of the late nineteenth century, the historic core of both cities continued to grow, mature, and evolve. That pattern began changing when waves of mass-produced automobiles reached urban markets in the 1920s. City structure was even more dramatically altered across America following World War II. Suburbs and exurbs rose, and cities declined. Charleston and Savannah fell into decay.

In the modern era, that dynamic has once again changed. Cities that preserved their historic assets are popular again. Downtowns are being rebuilt, historic neighborhoods are thriving, and first-ring streetcar suburbs are being revitalized. Cities are growing inward again, especially those whose historic cores retained substantial legacy resources.

Charleston and Savannah are both capable of absorbing more development in their urban cores (which include older industrial areas as well as historic districts). Inefficiently used buildings are being subdivided into more efficient uses of space such as condominiums. Vacant or underused lots are being targeted for new infill development. Obsolete industrial buildings are being converted to mixed-use projects. The trend will continue.

The trend will also change. Higher property values accompanied by higher property taxes will force lower-income residents and marginally capitalized businesses and investors to look elsewhere. Higher rents will force individual entrepreneurs to start businesses outside the city. Lack of workspace will force innovators to search for new creative environments. The result will be gentrification and elitification, which, without intervention, will change the character of the historic core from eclectic and electric to predictable and sedate.

The gentrification-elitification process following successful historic preservation initiatives and associated public investment can be one in which creative people, poor neighborhoods, and local businesses subsidize their own displacement by luxury-elite markets. Decades of dedicated effort to rebuild a decaying city may have only been paving the way for wealthy residents to move in and capital to move out.

To be clear, gentrification need not be a zero-sum process. In *Charleston Fancy*, Rybczynski provides a specific example of dynamic neighborhood change in Elliotborough, in which old residents and new residents and buyers and sellers appear to gain from the process of change. The example is anecdotal, and more research is needed to draw firm conclusions, but it appears at least possible to gentrify a historic neighborhood in a manner that does not harm displaced residents.[22]

Gentrification may also be offset by recognizing that many African American city residents have extended families with valuable property outside the city limits that lacks immediate liquidity. Such properties, called "heirs' property," lack clear title and are difficult to sell or use as collateral. Pro bono legal services have addressed this issue in recent decades, but more work needs to be done to free locked-up equity in the property of African American families.

Interviews conducted for this book, taken as a whole, lead to a conclusion that gentrification and elitification can kill off the vibrant city that emerged from tireless efforts of preservationists, neighborhood activists, local builders, city planners and architects, and many others. Such efforts also had the support of local taxpayers, who had a vested interest in seeing their traditional downtown become an exciting place once again, a source of civic pride. There is a growing sense of ominous change altering their reinvented city for the worse. Their city is becoming a museum for the few who can afford the price of entry, but it is losing its soul in the process. Authenticity and character are giving way to elite contrivances. For those who work in the city but can no longer afford to live there, their former pleasant walk to work has become an expensive and unpleasant commute in mounting traffic, all for the purpose of creating an enclave for wealthy visitors and drive-by residents. Meanwhile, the profits from the transition largely flow to investors in Atlanta and other capitals of capital.

If gentrification and elitification go unchecked, traditional residents, local entrepreneurs, and creative, innovative people will look elsewhere. As they turn away from the historic cores of Charleston and Savannah, they will look for alternative locations that have many of the same qualities: nearby small

Diversity Curve
The Authentic City Has the Highest Level of Complexity and Diversity

AUTHENTICITY

	REINVENTION	Modernity and historicity thrive together; a complex and creative urban ecology is reinvented; diversity is maximized.	DEINVENTION	
RECOGNITION	Tourism and historic preservation develop a productive alliance; reinvention begins.		Luxury and upscale markets begin to displace other socio-economic segments.	CONTRIVANCE
Historic resources recognized for potential to revive the historic core.				Historic core becomes economically resegregated from the whole city.

ECONOMIC SEGREGATION	→	DE-SEGREGATION	→	COMPLEXITY DIVERSITY	→	RE-SEGREGATION	→	ECONOMIC SEGREGATION

towns with historic assets and walkable streets; planned towns with similar attributes; and industrial sites with conversion potential.

As the search for new frontiers takes place, Charleston and Savannah will for a time remain anchors for creativity and innovation throughout the region. They will provide the civic resources for social interaction by individuals and through events. They will house cultural assets such as larger galleries and museums. Their educational institutions will interact with and support a wide range of intellectual, creative, and business endeavors. But those roles will diminish, and the future of the historic core of Charleston and Savannah will once again become dangerously dependent on a single industry.

The centrifugal forces driving many out of the historic core are already apparent, especially around Charleston. Summerville, Daniel Island, Sullivan's Island, and Mount Pleasant increasingly resemble Charleston in their creative character. I'On, the New Urbanist town adjacent to Mount Pleasant, reflects some of Charleston's traditional architectural attributes as well as its dense urban form.

Growth in rural areas from centrifugal forces and residential sprawl threatens the stability of established African American communities as well as others whose wealth is in their land and not held in cash assets. As property values rise, their taxes increase, eventually to the point of driving them from their homes. Local planning agencies have made efforts to address this, but state tax laws will need to be addressed as well. And the issue of heirs' property, as noted earlier, will need to be an ongoing project.[23]

As one projects centrifugal trends farther into the future, a radically new picture emerges. A cluster of four towns lying between Charleston and Savannah may absorb much of the creative and entrepreneurial out-flow from the region's two principal cities. Beaufort, Port Royal, Bluffton, and Hilton Head (all in Beaufort County) will be drawn closer and closer to the historic magnet cities.

Bluffton and Hilton Head are home to upscale resorts and retirement communities. Their affluent residents will increasingly provide the financial incentives to draw investors. However, they lack the urban qualities that draw many of those who feel at home in a city like Charleston or Savannah. Their role will be significant in financial terms but not in character terms.

Beaufort and Port Royal, on the other hand, are historically linked to Charleston and Savannah, and they possess many of the same intrinsic qualities—architectural heritage, historic districts, pleasant walkways, a planned urban grid, urban civic space, and waterfront access. Critically important, planning and zoning since the late 1990s have encouraged historical growth patterns such as New Urbanism and discouraged urban sprawl.

It appears inevitable that the contiguous towns of Beaufort and Port Royal will continue on course and become a third major urban center of innovation and creativity in the Lowcountry. Given that Beaufort and Port Royal are forty miles from Savannah and for the most part connected by four-lane highways, the two towns will likely return to the close relationship they had

Lowcountry Highway Distances
CITY HALL TO CITY HALL

	Charleston	Savannah	Beaufort	Georgetown
Charleston	—	107	69	62
Savannah	—	—	51	172
Beaufort	—	—	—	134
Georgetown	—	—	—	—

Source: Google Maps

historically with that city. Similarly, given that U.S. 17, a high-speed highway, connects the two towns with Charleston with an hour-and-a-half commute, more linkages will predictably develop.

The scenarios described above will become all the more likely with anticipated transportation innovations. The advent of autonomous vehicles and automated highway systems will bring about profound changes in the way people view distance. Cars will become workstations and play stations. A trip from Charleston to Beaufort, or Savannah to Port Royal, will not be substantially different from sitting at one's desk or in one's living room. The "friction of distance" will be minimal.

Beaufort County has grown from a rural backwater in the 1980s to a rapidly urbanizing area, increasing in size from less than seventy thousand in 1980 to nearly two hundred thousand in 2020. The Charleston Metropolitan Statistical Area (MSA) had an estimated population of 775,831 in 2017, while the Savannah combined metropolitan area had an estimated population of 527,106. The total population of the nine-county, 120-mile coastal region is well over 1.5 million, sufficient to drive urbanization and creativity in new locations as the historic cores of Charleston and Savannah shed population. A more significant population statistic in analyzing the future of urbanism in the Charleston-Savannah Lowcountry region is the population of the three urban counties. The combined population of Charleston, Berkeley, and Chatham Counties is now over 800,000 and will reach one million at current growth rates between 2025 and 2030.[24]

Based on its urban population, accessibility, historical resources, and environmental attributes, a new Lowcountry is emerging, one that will ultimately tie Charleston and Savannah back together into a place with a unique identity. It will be a place of entrepreneurship, innovation, and creativity. It will be diverse, it will be progressive, and it will be a desirable place to live, work, and invest. Many, however, will lament the loss of character in the urban core of the mother cities if current trends continue.

Much of the story of Charleston and Savannah told here has been about the character of the two cities. In that regard, the story is not unlike that of the virtues and vices of the South told by W. J. Cash in *The Mind of the South*, published in 1941. But when Cash told that story, the South had not yet turned a corner in a conscious effort to shake off its most infamous vices. Cash's South was proud, brave, honorable, courteous, and generous, he wrote, but it was also beset with a "narrow concept of social responsibility, attachment to fictions and false values, above all too great attachment to racial values and a tendency to justify cruelty and injustice in the name of those values."[25]

Charleston and Savannah, like nearly all other cities of the South, have publicly rejected racial obsessions described by Cash, the exclusionary policies of the elites, and the long-held Lost Cause fictions held by the White majority. Those vices linger privately, but they are receding from public discourse and observable business practices. Charleston, in the words of many who have been interviewed for this story, is said to have retained some of its old aristocratic elitism and formality. It can still be difficult for newcomers to gain acceptance, ancestry-bragging is common, and the city's business environment can be predatory. But its new values of diversity, equality, and creativity are inexorably surpassing the old ways. The economic and creative vitality associated with those new values reflects a remarkable transformation.

Savannah is said to be "two Savannahs"—a place of the successful and of the left-behinds who have seen little benefit from its economic successes, a city that zigzags politically, leaving it without long-term solutions to chronic problems such as crime. But a new Savannah is immeasurably more diverse, equitable, and creative than the old. It is an African American–majority city with African American leadership, it has a deeply ingrained culture of civility, and it continues to find inspiration in its founding vision.

For the two cities to sustain their success story, they will need to better address the higher-level planning paradigms of sustainability and resilience or they will be overtaken by congestion, storm-related flooding, sea level rise, increased hurricane impacts, gentrification, elitification, loss of identity, loss of character and authenticity, and even a betrayal of preservationists, visionary leaders, and taxpayers who made reinvention possible. The story of these two cities does not end with reinvention but with a dawning recognition that reinvention is an unending challenge in a continuing process of reflection and reassessment, much like democracy itself.

AFTERWORD

If there is a single compelling message among the many through lines in the preceding chapters, it is that reinvention is not an achievement so much as it is a heightened form of awareness. The dawning of awareness coupled with the willingness to act on it and reinvent a society is rare. In founding Georgia, the Trustees believed it was a time "to begin the world again," to reinvent society. Forty-four years later, on the eve of the founding of the United States, Thomas Paine also wrote that it was time "to begin the world over again." It was clear to the Trustees and to the Founders whose interests they were serving in remaking the world—those of ordinary citizens, not the elites. Local leaders today must also be clear-eyed about whose interests they are serving and who benefits from their decisions in the long run. Above all else, they must set aside clichés served up by industry advocates and ask basic questions about whose interests are ultimately served by the decisions they are asked to make.[1]

In Charleston, the mass shooting at the Emanuel African Methodist Episcopal Church on June 17, 2015, wiped away all pretense that racism had receded into the past. Then the killing of George Floyd in Minneapolis on May 25, 2020, made it clear that more than the Confederate flag and Lost Cause monuments had to come down—institutional changes were necessary as well. Three weeks after the Floyd killing, following an initial night of rioting and subsequent peaceful protests, Mayor Tecklenburg announced that the towering, 115-foot monument to John C. Calhoun in Marion Square would be removed. The announcement was made on the fifth anniversary of the Emanuel AME Church shooting.

During that five-year period, new questions emerged about gentrification and the nature and quality of life in the city. The luxury-elite tourism and home-buying markets were seen as pushing out not only lower-income residents but also virtually all working residents at an accelerating rate. A new era of segregation is emerging in which the financially elite are displacing all others in the historic core. Asking the right questions is essential to the recognition of such structural problems and reinvention to overcome them. One of the most basic questions is how individual decisions we make about our historic core, taken as a whole, affect the citizens who call it home.

In Savannah, the election of November 2019 presaged the major events of 2020. The Black-majority city elected a progressive Black-majority city council and mayor with a social justice agenda. Following the George Floyd killing, the city experienced robust nonviolent protests. City officials responded swiftly, launching a hundred-day review of police department policies and procedures. After the urgency of the moment was addressed, elected officials returned their attention to the broader spectrum of social equity issues they were elected to tackle.

As in Charleston, a tidal wave of luxury-elite tourism and affluent out-of-town home buyers is permanently altering the historic core, and not in a way that is to the obvious benefit of many long-standing residents. The new awakening has brought the onrush of gentrification and elitification into sharper focus. Prosperity in the historic core and its emergence as an exclusive enclave are increasingly unlikely to be acceptable to the larger population and readily ceded to the wealthy. The historic core is now seen as belonging broadly to the people, and they increasingly sense that they should not be driven out of their vibrant city and forced into a life of commuting from less stimulating outlying communities.

The awakening in 2020 and the transformative changes being brought about by that new awareness were also influenced by a succession of anniversaries: the 150th anniversary in 2011 of the start of the Civil War (and the reading of the Emancipation Proclamation in Port Royal in 2013), the anniversary of the beginning of the Reconstruction era, and the 400th anniversary in 2019 of the introduction of slavery in the English colonies. Suddenly slavery, lynching, Black codes, Jim Crow, segregation, assassinations, relentless persecution, redlining, mass incarceration (the "new Jim Crow"), gentrification, and other forms of oppression came into clearer focus, jolting the entire nation into a new consciousness. At the same time, a reactionary, authoritarian movement gained momentum, as evident in the sacking of the U.S. Capitol and attempted coup d'état.[2]

The reinvention of Charleston and Savannah begun in the 1960s, which had lost some of its energy in the early 2000s, is under way again, and its proponents are set to remake the world. The big issues are democracy and voter participation, public safety and policing, incarceration, and environmental justice. Together these concerns comprise the aspiration of social equity. For both cities, these issues in many ways revolve around the future of the historic core.

Social Equity and the Historic Core

The historic core of both cities is only about one-tenth of 1 percent of its metropolitan area, an area that will further decrease as new suburban areas sprout up. Yet the core is immeasurably important to the image the entire area projects to the world, to its ability to retain and attract talented people, to the vitality of its cultural life, to the cohesion of its otherwise bland and disparate parts, and to a sense of pride and place it engenders in its residents. The transformation in the core areas since the 1960s was initially made possible by local investment, supplemented by state and federal funds. Private capital mostly stayed away until local investment paid dividends. Current arguments that private capital should now dictate local policy to expand the tax base ignore earlier positive trends in the local economy.

Preservation of the historic core is now a social equity issue. As the core increasingly becomes an exclusive enclave for wealthy visitors and home buyers (who often reside in the city only part-time), it becomes not only less affordable for traditional residents but also less dynamic as a nucleus of urban life. Residents are reduced to commuting to the core for employment and little else of value in their lives.

Sustainable and Resilient Historic Core Preservation

In the 1950s and 1960s, residents and businesses fled historic downtowns and neighborhoods for the suburbs. Those areas fell on hard times. It took an alliance of preservationists, visionary leaders, and investors to reverse the trend and rebuild the urban economy. Tourism was essential to the rebuilding effort, but local investment was equally needed. Eventually higher education added another essential piece. The effort produced a complex, creative, and vibrant urban environment.

The problems facing the historic core were met with democratic solutions. Nearly everyone participated in recovery and reinvention. The people took pride in their cities, supported initiatives to rebuild infrastructure with their votes and their dollars, began going downtown again, started businesses, and renovated houses. The core once again shined. Civic pride returned, and the entire region benefited.

Since 2000 both cities have tacitly permitted the broad-based, democratic solution to be replaced with an exclusionary 1 percent solution. Luxury-elite hotels are attracting more and more of the wealthy, the 1 percent. Houses once occupied by local residents are becoming expensive short-term vacation rentals or homes for wealthy part-time residents. Local businesses and creative enterprises are leaving and being replaced by high-end retail and services for visitors.

The initial democratic solution involved everyone and benefited everyone by creating a spectrum of opportunities for local businesses and entrepreneurs. Small investments in housing renovation, infill development, the arts, and locally owned shops and restaurants enriched the life of the city and created a collision of ideas that led to still more creative entrepreneurship.

The emerging 1 percent solution has narrowed the band of opportunity to well-heeled investors and chain stores. The attraction of the 1 percent solution is that that it generates higher property tax and sales tax revenue. Its proponents argue that it also generates more employment. But it is resulting in a less-vibrant, less-entrepreneurial, less-creative city, and replacing it with a zone of exclusion occupied primarily by the luxury-elite class.

As a result, both cities are sacrificing their character. Some even say, without intending hyperbole, that they are losing their soul. The long-term consequences of this trend are likely to be disastrous. The historic core that was once a source of regional pride will be seen with indifference or even disdain. Indifference and disdain will lead to loss of support for urban infrastructure projects that require raising tax revenue. Businesses looking at relocation opportunities in creative, high-amenity urban environments will no longer see Charleston or Savannah as a prospect. The dominance of a single industry will lead to vulnerability when that industry experiences a downturn. And the reputation of each city will suffer as it becomes widely perceived as more contrived than authentic.

The 100 Percent Option

The reference to a "1 percent solution" is derived from popular usage of the term "the 1 percent," meaning the wealthy elites with disproportionate influence in society. The term also appears in a book of that title, *The One Percent Solution*, by political scientist Gordon Lafer. The book describes how the elite achieve their aims by influencing government laws and policies, as in the 2010 *Citizens United* Supreme Court decision.[3]

The "1 percent solution" accepts the premise that wealthy people and luxury-elite markets create prosperity by driving large projects and creating more employment than local investors would create in building for more modest markets, including housing for local residents. Local investment is displaced by out-of-town investment, and local builders are displaced by national builders. Thus, it is not only low-to-medium-income residents who are displaced by gentrification and elitification but businesses and investors as well.

A sustainable and resilient solution to the challenge of generating revenue and producing meaningful jobs is a 100 percent alternative, an option that engages the whole community, including the wealthiest. It is entirely possible to have democratic participation by the 99 percent coupled with 1 percent. To do so, each city needs to be mindful of the playing field it creates through development regulations and the many invisible incentives and disincentives it creates for residents and investors.

Currently the playing field favors out-of-town investors who can afford to assemble a team of local and national consultants to navigate the development approval process. Just as residents are being pushed out of the core area housing market, local entrepreneurs are being pushed out by the high cost of doing business. This means that fewer small-scale developments are built, and, to the extent that they are built, the cost of regulatory approval pushes the cost of housing above locally affordable levels.

Bringing local entrepreneurs back into the historic core is essential to preserving character with fine-grained development patterns. Drawing diverse, full-time residents back into the core is also essential to preserve the character of the city. Charleston and Savannah reinvented themselves by recognizing the value of diversity and turning away from the wrongs of the past while recognizing the value of the blended culture that took root centuries ago. To deconstruct that legacy by making the historic core an enclave of wealthy, mostly White people living in a luxury-elite environment, is to turn away from the achievements of the civil rights era. The benefits of diversity and complexity in the urban environment may be summarized as:

- Authenticity
- Resilience
- Creativity
- Civic pride and meaningful lives
- Public safety

- Work-life balance
- Congestion reduction
- Workforce stability

A city is a human ecosystem. Complexity in ecosystems is essential to stability. Cities that are diverse and vibrant are more resilient and sustainable than those that depend on a single industry and support only a narrow socioeconomic spectrum.

The Pandemic

The story of Charleston and Savannah would be incomplete without noting the impact of the COVID-19 pandemic. While both cities responded quickly and effectively, the pandemic introduced a number of uncertainties into the future of the historic core areas of both cities. Is it wise to have a heavy reliance on tourism, an industry sensitive to public health crises? Will global mobility spread more deadly variant viruses in successive waves? Is the local economy sufficiently diverse to remain resilient in the face of such shocks? Both cities will need to evaluate alternative scenarios, reflect on the threats they face and their consequences, and prepare new policies to guide future development.

Historic Core Housing for a Diverse Population

The greatest social equity challenge in preserving the historic core is maintaining a range of housing choices affordable to area residents. Providing affordable housing in historic districts in the face of gentrification and elitification is difficult but not impossible. The most obvious obstacle is the escalating cost of land and existing market-rate housing. All but wealthy buyers and renters are priced out of the market as hotels, high-end condominiums, and luxury apartments push aside all other forms of new construction. Conversions of existing properties focus on the lucrative short-term rental market, thereby reducing the availability of housing for people working in the historic core. Housing costs are also driven up by the strict regulations found in most historic districts. The review process is often time-consuming and costly. Height limits mean that the cost per square foot for units is above the range of affordability. Architectural requirements further add to the final per-unit cost. Additionally, the high cost of navigating the regulatory process eliminates small, local developers from enriching the built environment with myriad forms of infill housing—the very kind of housing that historically added character to the district and made it attractive in the first place.[4]

Without affordable housing in the historic core, the reinvention of Charleston and Savannah will not be sustained and its potential for a third Reconstruction will not be attained. The future is clear: either the historic core will be an inclusive, vibrant, and creative nucleus for the region in which all residents take pride, or it will be an exclusive playground for wealthy visitors and occasional residents with whom those who live there feel little connection.

Additional details and discussion relevant to the material covered in this book is available at https://ugapress.manifoldapp.org/projects /charleston-and-savannah/.

NOTES

PREFACE

1. Dickens, *Tale of Two Cities*, 450. The definition of social equity is from IGI Global, an international academic publisher of scientific research, https://www .igi-global.com/dictionary/support-for-and-behavioral-responses-to-tolls/27342 (accessed November 30, 2020).

2. The term "deep map" is from William Least Heat-Moon, whose book, *PrairyErth: A Deep Map* (1991), introduced the concept. A deep map is a multidimensional exploration of the character of a place.

3. See chapter 8 for more on the city's technological advancements in such areas as shipbuilding, logistics and intermodal transportation, inventions, and refinements to new technology.

4. The story was provided to the author by Charleston architect Christopher Liberatos, who found it in *The Federalist Architect*, October 1937, page 13. The story, as originally printed, used the common racist trope of an educated White man encountering an obsequious Black man.

INTRODUCTION

1. The historian Walter Fraser must be acknowledged for his separate comprehensive works on Charleston and Savannah, grounded in part on his firsthand experience in both cities. To see the vast array of more specialized books on these two cities, one need only drop into any of several independent bookstores in their historic districts.

2. For greater detail on planned cities, see Wilson, *Ashley Cooper Plan*, 12–13, and chap. 1, "Carolina: The First Planned Colony."

3. "June 29, 1789," in *Journals of the Continental Congress, 1774–1789*. Library of Congress. https://memory.loc.gov/.

4. Jones, *Dreadful Deceit*, location 129. See also Wood, *Black Majority*, and Navin, *Grim Years*, both of which trace the arc of changing attitudes. The author's research on Trustee-era Georgia supports the finding that power and greed, rather than notions of White superiority, motivated the enslavement in perpetuity of Africans and their descendants. Where rationalizations were provided they came down to the rights of Englishmen not extending to Africans, and Africans being well-suited to work in a subtropical climate.

CHAPTER ONE

Historic City Character Study

1. The tactile experience of reaching out and touching the built environment, sensing its past while feeling it in present time, engenders a special connection between person and place. Charleston and Savannah are among the few places in the United States where this mingling of past and present are a part of everyday life. The author is indebted to Amy Sottile of Sottile & Sottile in Savannah for an articulation of this idea.

2. A recent example of the new approach is John J. Navin's *The Grim Years*, which looks at Carolina's early colonial period through the eyes of ordinary people. Another example is Keri Leigh Merritt's *Masterless Men*, a broader look at poor Whites in the antebellum South but with considerable attention given to South Carolina. A third example is Noeleen McIlvenna's *The Short History of Free Georgia*, which delivers a more socially balanced analysis of the Lowcountry's early colonial period as well as a feminist perspective.

3. "Model, Grand," index entry, Ashley Cooper, *Shaftesbury Papers*, 506, notes various references and differentiates where the term refers to the broader plan for Carolina or specifically to the town plan.

4. For remarks on the long-term influence of the Grand Model, see Sirmans, *Colonial South Carolina*, 10; Weir, *Colonial South Carolina*, 72; Rogers and Taylor, *South Carolina Chronology*, 7; and Edgar, *South Carolina*, 42.

5. One of the best accounts of weather and climate conditions confronted by colonists can be found in Stephens, *Journal of the Proceedings in Georgia*, vol. 1, 37, January 4, 1739.

6. Butler, *Lowcountry at High Tide*, 13–14, 118.

7. Ibid., 48, 227.

8. Fraser, *Lowcountry Hurricanes*, 21–22.

9. Fraser, *Charleston! Charleston!*, 131.

10. Debbie Dalhouse, "World-Renowned Artists to Gather in Charleston," *Spartanburg Herald*, March 26, 1976.

11. See online supplement for updated enrollment figures: https://ugapress.manifoldapp.org/projects/charleston-and-savannah/.

12. Quote from *Gone with the Wind* in Berendt, *Midnight in the Garden*, 26.

13. Lee and Emma Adler invoke the comparison to a European city in *Savannah Renaissance*, 2. Schneider, "Charm, and Challenge, of Savannah," quotes William W. Hubbard, president of the Savannah Area Chamber of Commerce Savannah, as calling it "a European-style city" with continental charm. The Haussmann plan of Paris devised for Emperor Napoleon III established formal ratios of street widths and building heights, proportions that have been matched in recent decades in Savannah through increased height of infill development.

14. Berendt, *Midnight in the Garden*, 29.

15. Ibid., 31.

CHAPTER TWO

Transatlantic Culture in the Lowcountry Landscape

1. Conroy, *Lords of Discipline*, 21.

2. See Thornton, *Africa and Africans in the Making*, 46–52, for a discussion of the type and quality of African exports. Had slavery not come to dominate African-European commerce, a very different trade relationship likely would have emerged and stimulated African manufacturing.

3. There are more than fifty major sea islands that are inhabited or designated for preservation in the Lowcountry, including those in the Savannah area.

4. The *Oxford English Dictionary* and Oxford's online dictionary, Lexico (accessed June 10, 2017), offers the Spanish-Taino etymology; however, it is unclear whether the Savannah Indians inhabiting the region similarly acquired their name from that source or lent their name to the river. See Gallay, *Indian Slave Trade*, for more on the Savannah Indians.

5. The full title of *Bartram's Travels* is *Travels through North and South Carolina, East and West Florida, the Cherokee Country, the Extensive Territories of the Muscogulges, or Creek Confederacy, and the Country of the Chactaws, Containing an Account of the Soil and Natural Productions of Those Regions, Together with Observations on the Manners of the Indians*. For more on Michaux, see André Michaux (a website of the Daniel Stowe Botanical Garden, Belmont, North Carolina): http://www.michaux.org/michaux.htm.

6. Tibbetts and Mooney, "Sea Level Rise Is Eroding"; Fausset and Flavelle, "In Charleston, S.C., Saving Historic Homes."

7. The ancient cycles of climate change have occurred over a period of more than two billion years. Those cycles have produced at least five glacial epochs when global ice formation lowered sea level and associated interglacial periods when global ice melted and sea levels rose. The most recent glacial period, the Würm glaciation, ended about ten thousand years ago. Over the past twenty thousand years, sea level has risen over four hundred feet.

8. Brockwell, "Before 1619, There Was 1526."

9. The history of European settlement in the region between Charleston and Savannah, specifically in Port Royal Sound, has been extensively documented in recent years by the Santa Elena History Center, located in Beaufort, South Carolina. The center was the source of the settlement chronology in chapter 1.

10. U.S. Census Bureau "Population in Colonial and Continental Periods."

11. The U.S. census adopted the twenty-five hundred population threshold for a city at the first census in 1790. The Oxford English Dictionary more generally defines a city as "a municipal center incorporated by the state or province."

12. Data Center (Greater New Orleans), "Historical Population by Race over 300 Years."

13. For more on usage of the word "gothic," see Pocock, *Politics, Language and Time*, 94, 120, 122.

14. See online supplement for extensive discussion of ports of Charleston and Savannah: https://ugapress.manifoldapp.org/projects/charleston-and-savannah/.

CHAPTER THREE

A Brief Biography of Charleston

1. While the Proprietary period formally ended in 1721 when South Carolina became a royal colony, the Proprietors maintained large financial interests until 1729, when they were bought out by the Crown.

2. For a brief bio of Ashley Cooper in connection to Carolina, see Wilson, *Ashley Cooper Plan*, 35–43. For a definitive biography, see Haley, *First Earl of Shaftesbury*.

3. Another complaint against Ashley Cooper was that he was anti-Catholic. However, while he was opposed to the bond between the Catholic Church and monarchs of Europe, he was probably not a bigot, nor did he dispute Catholic doctrine—he appears to have been agnostic toward religion. Ashley Cooper's life was reassessed following 1968 publication of the thoroughly researched biography by the Oxford historian K. H. D. Haley.

4. See Navin, *Grim Years*.

5. Agha summarizes Ashley Cooper's investment in Barbados in "Shaftesbury's Atlantis," 70–71.

6. Dunn, *Sugar and Slaves*, 112–16.

7. See, for example, Carrington, Fraser, Gilmore, and Forde, *A–Z of Barbados Heritage*. For early settlement by the Scots and others, see Smith, "Beaufort." Huguenot settlers and their descendants have retained an ethnic identity to the present time, and their history is preserved by the Huguenot Society of South Carolina. The story of Jews in Charleston can be found in Hagy, *This Happy Land* (see p. 6 for Jewish emigration by way of Barbados).

8. Historians and other scholars fell into a form of political correctness in telling the American story in ways that would be respectful of and inoffensive to White audiences. This approach served the purpose of reuniting North and South in a common understanding of history, but it postponed the eventual reckoning over race that led to the Civil War. After the civil rights movement of the 1960s, scholars reevaluated their approach and scrubbed much of the "Lost Cause" mythology that their predecessors had perpetuated for a century. An example of the earlier approach is found in Hennig Cohen's *The South Carolina Gazette*, a book about Charleston's first newspaper. Cohen's book highlights the high culture of white society while leaving out any reference to the majority Black population and their enslavement. While the omission may appear bizarre to today's reader, it was the accepted and politically correct practice at the time.

9. Gallay, *Indian Slave Trade*, 7, 29.

10. See the online supplement (https://ugapress.manifoldapp.org/projects /charleston-and-savannah/) for statistical tables and references.

11. See Bull, *Oligarchs in Colonial and Revolutionary Charleston*, for a profile of life on the plantation, in the city, and on retreat.

12. John Carteret, 2nd Earl of Granville, was the only Proprietor who refused to sell his property. Instead, he negotiated with the Crown to be granted a large tract of land in North Carolina.

13. Fraser, *Charleston! Charleston!*, 42.

14. Wilson, *Ashley Cooper Plan*, 115–21.

15. *South Carolina Gazette*, January 29, 1736, available on microfilm at UCSB Library, University of South Carolina Beaufort Library.

16. Coclanis, *Shadow of a Dream*, 64, 74.

17. Fraser, *Charleston! Charleston!*, 107–13. See Wilson, "The Grand Model and the Genesis of Southern Political Culture," chap. 4 in *Ashley Cooper Plan*, for more on the evolution of the concept of "liberty."

18. *Slavery and Justice*; quote by historian Adam Domby, College of Charleston, *If These Walls Could Talk*, Vimeo, https://vimeo.com/511619775/0b028ec374 (accessed April 17, 2022).

19. The finding is based on a review of Charleston County property records conducted by the author in the fall of 2016.

20. Cohen, *South-Carolina Gazette*, 17–29.

21. Davis, *Rhett*, 352–53.

22. In *The Road to Disunion*, vol. 2, 10, historian William Freehling referred to the "domestic charade" as part of a "long-running play."

23. In North Carolina, the Regulator Movement was concerned with a concentration of wealth in the hands of a few. In South Carolina, government corruption was the greater concern. In modern times, state senator Tom Davis (Beaufort) has maintained that Charleston has disproportionate influence in obtaining state infrastructure funding.

24. Fraser, *Charleston! Charleston!*, 144–50.

25. Ibid., 150–52.

26. South Carolina Encyclopedia, "African Americans in the Revolutionary War, 1775–1782," https://www.scencyclopedia.org/sce/entries/african-americans-in-the -revolutionary-war/ (accessed March 8, 2021).

27. Fraser, *Charleston! Charleston!*, 175.

28. "A Brief History of the College," College of Charleston, https://www.cofc.edu /about/historyandtraditions/briefhistory.php (accessed January 25, 2021).

29. Davis, *Rhett*, 100; Mitchell, *Gone with the Wind*, 141.

30. Davis, *Rhett*, 20, 66, 47.

31. This social philosophy arguably remains engrained in the South to the present. Core ideas of this belief system were reinforced in the early twentieth century by the Southern Agrarians, an alliance of writers who published a southern manifesto: Twelve Southerners, *I'll Take My Stand*.

32. Davis, *Rhett*, 53–54.

33. Robertson, *Denmark Vesey*, 112–13.

34. Ibid., 114–15.

35. National Park Service, "South Carolina: Mother Emanuel AME Church."

36. Sinha, *Counterrevolution*, 34–35.

37. Ibid., 35, 39–40.

38. Freehling, *Road to Disunion*, 42, 55. For more on the modern take on race, see

Rutherford, *Brief History of Everyone*; and Reich, *Who We Are and How We Got Here*. According to Rutherford (p. 18), a geneticist and science writer, "There are no essential genetic elements for any particular group of people who might be identified as a 'race.' As far as genetics is concerned, race does not exist."

39. Freehling, *Road to Disunion*, vol. 2, 22–23.

40. Marrs, introduction to *Railroads in the Old South*.

41. Ibid., 91, 100.

42. Ibid., 23.

43. Ibid., 137.

44. See James M. McPherson, *Battle Cry of Freedom*, for the view that the Fire-Eaters sought to provoke secession by splitting the party.

45. Fraser, *Charleston! Charleston!*, 240, 271–72. For a spatial understanding of the Jewish imprint on Charleston, see College of Charleston, Pearlstine/Lipov Center for Southern Jewish Culture, "Mapping Jewish Charleston."

46. Davis, *Rhett*, 16–18.

47. Doyle, *New Men, New Cities, New South*, 52–56, 60.

48. Foner, *Freedom's Lawmakers*, xv.

49. Ibid., xxiii, xxviii.

50. U.S. Bureau of the Census, "Census of Population and Housing," https://web.archive.org/web/20200224035043/https://www.census.gov/prod/www/decennial.html.

51. *History of the South Carolina State Ports Authority*, vi–vii.

52. Rogers and Taylor, *South Carolina Chronology*, 95, 103, 110, 117.

53. Shuler and Bailey, *History of the Phosphate Mining Industry*.

54. Fraser, *Charleston! Charleston!*, 308–10.

55. *History of the South Carolina State Ports Authority*, 12–15.

56. Ibid., 18–20.

57. Ibid., 23–29.

58. Ibid., 57–59.

59. Ibid., 58–59.

60. Ibid., 74–81.

61. Ibid., 145–47.

62. U.S. Bureau of the Census, "Census of Population and Housing," https://web.archive.org/web/20200224035043/https://www.census.gov/prod/www/decennial.html.

63. Estimated hurricane intensities are published by the National Weather Service. For Charleston history, see https://www.weather.gov/chs/TChistory.

64. Fraser, *Charleston! Charleston!*, 359–61.

65. Ibid., 381–87.

66. Rogers and Taylor, *South Carolina Chronology*, 133–34.

67. Fraser, *Charleston! Charleston!*, 402.

68. Ibid., 408–17.

69. Ibid., 420–25.

70. Ibid., 366, 372, 377.

71. Hicks, *Mayor*, 114.

72. Ibid., 21–22.

73. Ibid., 65, 80.

74. *History of the South Carolina State Ports Authority*, 154, 172–75.

75. Ibid., 187–89.

76. Charleston, *Post and Courier*: Byrd, "Charleston Forum on Reparations"; Charleston, *Post and Courier*: Behre, "Despite Pushback, Charleston Historic Sites Expand."

77. Charleston, *Post and Courier*: Hobbs, et al., "John C. Calhoun Statue Taken Down."

CHAPTER FOUR

A Brief Biography of Savannah

1. Oglethorpe letter dated February 10, 1733, in Lane, *General Oglethorpe's Georgia*, vol. 1, 4–5.

2. "Peter Gordon's Journal," in Cashin, ed., *Setting Out to Begin a New World*, 34–35.

3. Ibid., 35.

4. Lane, *Colonial Letters*, vol. 1, 19, August 12, 1733.

5. Ibid., 27, December 1733.

6. Percival, *Manuscripts of the Earl of Egmont, Diary of Viscount Percival (hereafter DVP)*, vol. 2, 111, June 19, 1734.

7. Sweet, *Negotiating for Georgia*, 58.

8. Lane, *Colonial Letters*, vol. 1, 44, July 17, 1734.

9. *DVP*, vol. 2, 256, March 31, 1736; *DVP*, vol. 2, 281–83, June 16, 1736.

10. Wilson, *Oglethorpe Plan*, 105–6.

11. Lane, *Colonial Letters*, vol. 1, 280, November 3, 1736; *DVP*, vol. 2, 274, May 19, 1736.

12. Stephens, *Journal of the Proceedings in Georgia*, vol. 1, 11–12, 40–46.

13. *DVP*, vol. 2, 325–26, January 8, 1737.

14. *DVP*, vol. 2, 376, March 23, 1737; Candler, *Colonial Records of the State of Georgia*, vol. 1, 282, April 18, 1737.

15. *DVP*, vol. 2, 460, January 11, 1738.

16. Ettinger, *James Edward Oglethorpe*, 200–201; 33°50′N falls near Myrtle Beach, South Carolina, at the time a remote area; Stephens, *Journal of the Proceedings in Georgia*, vol. 1, 255, August 4, 1738.

17. Mellon, "Christian Priber's Cherokee 'Kingdom of Paradise,'" 319–23.

18. Bowne and Bowne, "Natives, Women, Debtors, and Slaves," 56–80.

19. Candler, *Colonial Records of the State of Georgia*, vol. 2, 504, April 11, 1750.

20. Fraser, *Savannah in the Old South*, 41.

21. Ibid., 36–43.

22. Pressly, *On the Rim of the Caribbean*, Kindle locations 513, 1028, 1039, 1404.

23. Ibid., Kindle locations 1460, 1509, 4216.

24. *Atlanta Constitution*, April 9, 2019.

25. Fraser, *Savannah in the Old South*, 139; Wilson, *Oglethorpe Plan*, 59.

26. Fraser, *Savannah in the Old South*, 140, 160.

27. Ibid., 191–92.

28. Ibid., 285.

29. Jordan, "Charles Augustus Lafayette Lamar," 247–90. See also Callahan, *Surviving Savannah,* for a fictionalized but accurate depiction of Lamar and his family.

30. U.S. Army Corps of Engineers, "Drainage Basins: Savannah River Basin Fact Sheet, U.S. Army Corps of Engineers, Savannah District, https://www.sas.usace.army .mil/Portals/61/docs/lakes/hartwell/PlanaVisit/LakeLevelMngt/drainagebasins.pdf.

31. As defined by geographers, the term "site" refers to the land on which something is placed, while "situation" refers to its broader physical context.

32. Fraser, *Savannah in the Old South*, 240–55.

33. Ibid., 311–12, 313, 317.

34. "Telegram from General William T. Sherman to President Abraham Lincoln Announcing the Surrender of Savannah, Georgia, as a Christmas Present to the President, 12/22/1864," U.S. National Archives, https://www.archives.gov /historical-docs/todays-doc/index.html?dod-date=1222 (accessed October 12, 2021).

35. Davis, *Sherman's March*, 161–67.

36. Ibid., 118, 120, 124.

37. GALILEO historical database, https://web.archive.org/web/20180619065509/, http://georgiainfo.galileo.usg.edu/topics/government/related_article/constitutions /georgia-constitution-of-1868.

38. Herndon, "Raphael Warnock's Win Is One for the History Books."

39. Foner, *Freedom's Lawmakers*, xii.

40. Savannah, City of, "Chatham County-Savannah Tricentennial Plan," Community Assessment, 8-3; Community Agenda, 5-5.

41. Ibid., Community Assessment, 8-3-5.

42. In 2009 there were 4,135 hotel rooms. Personal communication through email with Joseph Marinelli, president, Savannah Area Convention and Visitors Bureau, December 14, 2009.

43. Bill Dawers, "Inaction on City's Ugly Past to Haunt Future," *Savannah Morning News*, March 2, 2021.

CHAPTER FIVE

Charleston: England's First Comprehensively Planned Colonial City

1. Cooper, Michael, *More Beautiful City*, 105–9, for the king's proclamation of intent. See ibid., 129, for Rebuilding Act of 1667, which sought "to build a city more regulated, uniform and graceful."

2. Haley, *First Earl of Shaftesbury*, 202–3.

3. Ibid., 203–5.

4. Ibid., 206–7.

5. Locke became an intellectual influence on the U.S. Right and the Left, the

former because of his concern for property rights, the latter for his concern with labor and equality. He is arguably the one person most historically aware Americans would agree is the nation's philosophical mentor. See Louis Hartz, *Liberal Tradition in America*, for an interesting perspective.

6. Corcoran, "John Locke on the Possession of Land."

7. See Glausser, "Three Approaches to Locke," for a comparison of views on Locke. Use of the word "slavery" by Locke and others in that era was often rhetorical and did not refer specifically to chattel slavery; nevertheless, he likely would have considered Carolina slavery an evil, as characterized in *Two Treatises*.

8. Farr, "Absolute Power and Authority," 4, 28, 35–36.

9. Wilson, *Ashley Cooper Plan*, 46–47.

10. Agha, *Shaftesbury's Atlantis*, 7–10.

11. Ibid., 9–10.

12. Locke, *Two Treatises*, 1; Shaftesbury, "Fundamental Constitutions of Carolina," in *Shaftesbury Papers*, article 107.

13. Agha, *Shaftesbury's Atlantis*, 9–10, 19, 54, 73.

14. The historian David Armitage found city planning notes among Locke's papers and conveyed its contents to the author.

15. Fraser, *Charleston! Charleston!*, 7.

16. Wilson, *Ashley Cooper Plan*, 70.

17. See Wilson, "The Grand Model and the Genesis of Southern Political Cultures," chap. 4 in ibid., for more on this topic.

18. Ibid., 70–71.

19. The term "landgrave" was borrowed from the German feudal tradition; "cacique" was a Native American term for chieftain.

20. Leng, "Shaftesbury's Aristocratic Empire," 106–7.

21. The issue of slavery was first addressed in the context of religion in article 107 of the Fundamental Constitutions: "Since charity obliges us to wish well to the souls of all men, and religion ought to alter nothing in any man's civil estate or right, it shall be lawful for slaves, as well as others, to enter themselves, and be of what church or profession any of them shall think best, and, therefore, be as fully members as any freeman. But yet no slave shall hereby be exempted from that civil dominion his master hath over him, but be in all things in the same state and condition he was in before."

22. Ashley Cooper, *Shaftesbury Papers*, 120.

23. Wood, *Black Majority*, 27.

24. Rivers, *Sketch of the History of South Carolina*, 358, 365–67.

25. Ashley Cooper, *Shaftesbury Papers*, 322–23; Rivers, *Sketch of the History of South Carolina*, 366. Rivers includes detail left out of the Shaftesbury volume.

26. Ashley Cooper, *Shaftesbury Papers*, 323–34; Cooper, *More Beautiful City*, 131. See also Wilson, *Ashley Cooper Plan*, 112, for a summary table of design specifications.

27. Rivers, *Sketch of the History of South Carolina*, 367; Cooper, *More Beautiful City*, 131.

28. Rivers, *Sketch of the History of South Carolina*, 367.

29. Ibid., 393–94.

30. Smith, *Historical Writings of Henry A. M. Smith*, vol. 2, 42.

31. Ibid., 42–43.

32. Wilson, *Ashley Cooper Plan*, 134–35.

33. Cohen, *South Carolina Gazette*, 71–121.

34. Fraser, *Savannah in the Old South*, 186.

35. Fraser, *Charleston! Charleston!*, 175.

36. Ibid., 239–40, 253–54.

37. Ibid., 381, 399.

38. Ibid., 392.

CHAPTER SIX

Savannah: The Charleston Plan with Enlightenment Idealism

1. Thomas D. Wilson, "Implementation of the Plan," chap. 3 in *Oglethorpe Plan*. For the link to Locke and Shaftesbury, see Oglethorpe, *Publications of James Edward Oglethorpe*, 211–12.

2. Percival, *Manuscripts of the Earl of Egmont*, vol. 1, 264, April 29, 1732.

3. A letter from Oglethorpe to the Trustees dated July 4, 1739, described "agrarian equality" as "one of the first principles" in founding the colony.

4. Much of the military training Oglethorpe and other officers of his time received can be traced back to Vitruvius, the Greco-Roman designer who set out the earliest principles for siting towns and forts.

5. Wilson, *Oglethorpe Plan*, 83, table 4.

6. Wilson, *Ashley Cooper Plan*, 205.

7. Wilson, *Oglethorpe Plan*, 159.

8. Fraser, *Savannah*, 209, 258.

9. Fraser, *Savannah*, 158, 165–67, 185–86.

10. The garden city movement was inspired in part by Ebenezer Howard's book *To-morrow: A Peaceful Path to Real Reform* published in 1898 (republished in 1902 as *Garden Cities of To-morrow*). The concept envisioned a small central city connected to satellite towns with populations of about twenty-six thousand set in a landscape of farms, parks, and nature preserves. The movement led to the development of numerous greenbelt towns in the United States, while also raising consciousness of urban beautification through landscape planning. John Nolen's Daffin Park in Savannah was built during this period. In North America, the City Beautiful movement was influenced by garden cities but also grew out of the World's Columbian Exposition of 1893 in Chicago.

11. Editorial, *Savannah Morning News*, February 6, 1956.

12. Savannah, City of, "Golden Heritage Plan."

13. Savannah, City of, "Chatham County-Savannah Tricentennial Plan," Community Agenda, sec. 2-2 (par. F).

14. Savannah, City of, "Civic Master Plan."

15. Savannah, City of, "Historic District Ordinance" (amendments).

Charleston: Once America's Wealthiest City

1. *History of the South Carolina State Ports Authority*, 1.

2. See the online supplement (https://ugapress.manifoldapp.org/projects /charleston-and-savannah/) for statistics on the transatlantic slave trade.

3. See Thomas D. Wilson, "Carolina: The First Planned Colony," chap. 1 in *Ashley Cooper Plan*, for an elaboration.

4. Wilson, Ashley Cooper Plan, 46–47.

5. The global impacts of the transatlantic slave trade can be seen in tables in the online supplement, (https://ugapress.manifoldapp.org/projects/charleston-and-savannah/).

6. See the online supplement (https://ugapress.manifoldapp.org/projects/charleston -and-savannah/) for detail and sources.

7. Brockwell, "Before 1619, There Was 1526."

8. See Eltis and Richardson, *Atlas of the Transatlantic Slave Trade*, for maps and detailed statistics. The database associated with the atlas can be found online at SlaveVoyages, https://www.slavevoyages.org/# .

9. Freehling, *Road to Disunion*, vol. 2, 155–59.

10. See Wright, *Slavery and American Economic Development*, 2–13.

11. For relative populations, see "Enslaved People in the Emerging Confederate States, 1860," table in the online supplement (https://ugapress.manifoldapp.org /projects/charleston-and-savannah/).

12. Navin, *Grim Years*.

13. Carney, *Black Rice*, 33–38.

14. Fields-Black, *Deep Roots*, 30.

15. Fields-Black, *Deep Roots*, 36–47; Thornton, *Africa and Africans*, 135.

16. Carney, *Black Rice*, 19–29, 64.

17. Mauser, *Slaving Voyage to Africa*, 75–76, 86n282.

18. Fields-Black, *Deep Roots*, 49–50, 159, 174–77.

19. Carney, *Black Rice*, 97–98; Ferguson quote from Carney, *Black Rice*, 93–94.

20. Tuten, *Lowcountry Time and Tide*, 20–21.

21. David, *Trade, Politics, and Revolution*, 1–6

22. Ibid., xix–xxv.

23. Bull, *The Oligarchs in Colonial and Revolutionary Charleston*, xi, 9, 15.

24. Ibid., xi, 16–17, 224; Poston, *Buildings of Charleston*, 258–59.

25. David, *Trade, Politics, and Revolution*, 115–19.

26. Ibid., 150–57.

27. Ibid., 176–84.

28. University of Virginia Library, Historical Census Browser, http://mapserver .lib.virginia.edu/, site discontinued, researchers are referred to National Historical Geographic Information System, https://www.nhgis.org/.

29. Ibid. See also the regional population comparison table in the online supplement (https://ugapress.manifoldapp.org/projects/charleston-and-savannah/).

30. Powers, *Black Charlestonians*, 42–46, 126–32.

31. Tuten, *Low Country Time and Tide*, 24, table 1.2.

CHAPTER EIGHT

Savannah: A Southern Industrial City

1. See Oglethorpe, *Publications of Oglethorpe*, 211–12; and Martyn, *Some Account of the Trustees Design*, 37.

2. Fraser, *Savannah in the Old South*, 61–63.

3. Lane, *General Oglethorpe's Georgia*, vol. 1, 47–48, September 3, 1734; Lane, *General Oglethorpe's Georgia*, vol. 1, 67, December 14, 1734; Percival, *Manuscripts of the Earl of Egmont*, vol. 3, 218, April 20, 1741.

4. Percival, *Manuscripts of the Earl of Egmont*, vol. 3, 53–56, April 29, 1739; Lane, *Colonial Letters*, 2:397–99, March 13, 1739.

5. Lane, *General Oglethorpe's Georgia*, vol. 2, 389–90, 414, January 17 and July 4, 1739.

6. Lane, *General Oglethorpe's Georgia*, vol. 1, 180, June 1, 1735; ibid., vol. 1, 89, January 16, 1735.

7. For additional speculation about Georgia following an alternative course such as that of Pennsylvania rather than Carolina, see McIlvenna, *Short Life of Free Georgia*, 89, 106, 110–11, 113.

8. Rahn, *River Highway for Trade*, 13. See the online supplement (https://ugapress .manifoldapp.org/projects/charleston-and-savannah/) for a profile of exports from Georgia.

9. Ibid., 9–10.

10. Rahn, *River Highway for Trade*; online supplement (https://ugapress .manifoldapp.org/projects/charleston-and-savannah/).

11. Rahn, *River Highway for Trade*, 17.

12. Ibid., 19–21.

13. Ibid., 21–22.

14. Ibid.; online supplement (https://ugapress.manifoldapp.org/projects /charleston-and-savannah/).

15. The Georgia Historical Society and the historical marker on the Savannah River refer to the *John Randolph* as a steamship (see "SS Savannah and SS John Randolph," Georgia Historical Society, https://georgiahistory.com/ghmi_marker_updated /savannah-and-john-randolph). Ruby A. Rahn, in her extensive study *River Highway for Trade*, classifies the *John Randolph* as a steamboat that was not built as an ocean-going vessel (see pp. 37, 46).

16. Callahan, *Surviving Savannah*. For facts surrounding the construction and sinking of the *Pulaski*, see the author's research notes that follow the novel.

17. Fraser, *Savannah in the Old South*, 246–53.

18. For more information on the canal, see Savannah Ogeechee Canal Museum and Nature Center, http://www.savannahogeecheecanal.org/. For more on DeWitt Clinton Jr., see Jones and Angell, "Birthplace of DeWitt Clinton," 115. For more on the Erie Canal, see "Clinton's Big Ditch," http://www.eriecanal.org/.

19. Stone, *Vital Rails*, 1–2.

20. Ibid., 3–4.

21. Rahn, *River Highway for Trade*, 45.

22. Ibid., 51–52.

23. Mayle, "Barge Delivers First Cargo up Savannah River in 40 Years."

24. For a quick check of historical populations, see the privately maintained website, population.us ("Population of Savannah, GA," https://population.us/ga/savannah).

25. Marrs, *Railroads in the Old South*, 5; Fraser, *Savannah in the Old South*, 244–48.

26. Stone, *Vital Rails*, 7, 12.

27. Stone, *Vital Rails*, 24–41.

28. Ibid., 274.

29. Ibid., 300–313.

30. University of Virginia Library, Historical Census Browser, http://mapserver .lib.virginia.edu/, site discontinued. Researchers are referred to National Historical Geographic Information System, https://www.nhgis.org/, for historical census records.

31. For a brief account of Jewish history in Savannah, see the website of the Savannah synagogue Mickve Israel, https://mickveisrael.org/history.

32. Johnson, *Black Savannah*, 108, 187; Powers, *Black Charlestonians*, 42–46.

33. Fraser, *Savannah in the Old South*, 165–67, 186.

CHAPTER NINE

Charleston: Prototype for the Deep South Cultural Economy

1. Galley, *Indian Slave Trade*, 31–32.

2. Elazar, *American Mosaic*, 130–37.

3. U.S. Bureau of the Census, "Population in the Colonial and Continental Periods."

4. Chastellux, "Return to Williamsburgh—Conclusion," in *Travels in North America*, 286–87.

5. Schaub, "Perspectives on Slavery," 608–26.

6. Ibid., 617.

7. Wilson, *Ashley Cooper Plan*, 57–61.

8. Fischer, *Albion's Seed*, 817–18; Gallay, *Indian Slave Trade*, 31–32; Thomas D. Wilson, "The Grand Model and the Genesis of Southern Political Culture," *Ashley Cooper Plan*, chapter 4. For other typologies of American political culture, see Donald Meinig, *Shaping of America*; Woodard, *American Nations*; Chinni and Gimpel, *Our Patchwork Nation*; and Garreau, *Nine Nations of North America*. In more recent work and in a new book, *How Enslaved People Expanded American Ideals* (2022), Fischer identifies Carolina and Georgia as a distinct cultural hearth.

9. Chastellux, *Travels in North America*, 293–96, 369.

10. Fields-Black, *Deep Roots*, 188.

11. Lane, *General Oglethorpe's Georgia*, vol. 2, 389, January 17, 1739. See Wilson, *Oglethorpe Plan*, 201–6, for a discussion of antislavery sentiments.

12. Locke, *Two Treatises of Government*, 1.

13. Johnson, "Taxation No Tyranny." Definitions of "liberty" and "slavery" from Which English?, http://www.whichenglish.com/Johnsons-Dictionary/1755-Letter-A .html.

14. Under the Lost Cause mythology cultivated throughout the South after the Civil War and somewhat successfully exported to the country at large, the liberty enjoyed by slaveholders was integral to maintaining a cohesive and productive society, which benefited all, included those who were enslaved. Since the 1960s, however, historians and other scholars have increasingly documented a very different reality from that imagined in southern mythology. One of the earliest works was Winthrop Jordan's *White over Black*, which documents the evolution of racial attitudes. Another early work specific to the Lowcountry that influenced the direction of many younger historians was Peter Wood's *Black Majority*. Philip Morgan's *Slave Counterpoint* is an example of the many books that followed, with detailed primary research on Lowcountry racial attitudes and conditions of enslavement. Since the 1990s, with primary data sources (contemporary letters, official records, newspaper accounts, etc.) increasingly uploaded to the internet, the cloud of Lost Cause mythology is being cleared away by well-documented research.

15. Clark, *Language of Liberty*, 45.

CHAPTER TEN
The Lowcountry Cultural Economy Moves West

1. Lane, *General Oglethorpe's Georgia*, vol. 2, 542, 1742.

2. Stephens, *Journal of the Proceedings in Georgia*, vol. 1, 403–4, February 12, 1739.

3. Stephens, *Journal of the Proceedings in Georgia*, vol. 2, 416–17, June 24, 1740.

4. Wilson, *Oglethorpe Plan*, 116; Rowland, Moore, and Rogers, *History of Beaufort County*, 178; Bull, *Oligarchs in Colonial and Revolutionary Charleston*, 245.

5. Diamond, *Guns, Germs, and Steel*, 211. See also Crosby, *Columbian Exchange*, which contains a comprehensive assessment of the effects of European contact on Native Americans.

6. Oatis, *Colonial Complex*, 41, 74–76, 105, 143.

7. Gallay, *Indian Slave Trade*, 51–52.

8. Ibid., 53–56.

9. Ibid., 56–57.

10. Sirmans, *Colonial South Carolina*, 30, 77–78, 81; Rowland, Moore, and Rogers, *History of Beaufort County*, 80; Morgan, *Slave Counterpoint*, 481.

11. Oatis, *Colonial Complex*, 1, 41–44.

12. Quoted in Ellis, *American Creation*, 145.

13. Ellis, *American Creation*, 162–63.

14. Ibid., 158–59.

15. Wilson, *Ashley Cooper Plan*, 163–64.

16. Genovese, *Political Economy of Slavery*, 31.

17. Ibid. J. C. Hammond, *Slavery, Freedom, and Expansion*, 1–3, 74; Oakes, *Ruling Race*, 236–37; Kolchin, *American Slavery*, 86, 89.

18. For a comparison of South Carolina and Virginia, see Morgan, *Slave Counterpoint*.

19. J. C. Hammond, *Slavery, Freedom, and Expansion*, 17–18, 34–36.

20. Meinig, *Shaping of America*, 291–92, 476, 494. See also Wyatt-Brown, *Southern Honor*, 262; and Oakes, *Ruling Race*, 236–37. Hammond quote from Wright, *Old South, New South*, 25–26. See also Wilson, *Ashley Cooper Plan*, 167–60.

21. J. C. Hammond, *Slavery, Freedom, and Expansion*, 1–3; Kolchin, *American Slavery*, 188; population statistics from online supplement (https://ugapress.manifoldapp.org /projects/charleston-and-savannah/). For a more detailed discussion, see Wilson, *Ashley Cooper Plan*, 172–77.

22. Johnson, *River of Dark Dreams*, 40–41, 73–78, 86–87, 170–76, 408.

23. Ibid., 159, 176–181, 283.

24. Kolchin, *American Slavery*, 178–81; Johnson, *River of Dark Dreams*, 5, 41, 72.

25. Johnson, *River of Dark Dreams*, 282; Lind, *Made in Texas*, 24, 45, 162.

26. J. C. Hammond, *Slavery, Freedom, and Expansion*, 8, 66–70, 76–80.

27. Quote from Genovese, *Political Economy of Slavery*, 266–67; Johnson, *River of Dark Dreams*, 366–71, 418; Genovese, *Consuming Fire*, 89.

28. Kolchin, *American Slavery*, 195; Genovese, *Slaveholders' Dilemma*, 18, 47, 89; Johnson, *River of Dark Dreams*, 203, 414–15; Oakes, *Slavery and Freedom*, 73.

29. Johnson, *River of Dark Dreams*, 414–15.

30. Genovese, *Political Economy of Slavery*, 34, 171–73.

31. Davis, *Rhett*, 532.

32. Fraser, *Charleston*, 53–54.

33. Johnson, *River of Dark Dreams*, 203; J. H. Hammond, *Selections from the Letters and Speeches*, 124.

CHAPTER ELEVEN
Stagnation and Decline

1. Gallay, *Indian Slave Trade*, 96, 345; Merritt, *Masterless Men*, 6, 291–92.

2. Sinha, *Counterrevolution of Slavery*, 1, 11; Kolkin, *American Slavery*, 86, 89.

3. Manisha Sinha additionally notes in *Counterrevolution of Slavery*, 11–12, that South Carolina was the first state with a white slaveholding majority (from 1850) and had the largest average farm size.

4. E. Morgan, *American Slavery, American Freedom*, 375–76.

5. Davis, *Rhett*, 64–66.

6. Ibid., 113; John C. Calhoun, "Slavery a Positive Good," speech on the Senate Floor, February 6, 1737, http://en.wikisource.org/wiki/Slavery_a_Positive_Good (accessed February 22, 2013); Andrew H. Stephens, "Cornerstone Speech," Teaching American History, https://teachingamericanhistory.org/document/cornerstone-speech (accessed April 14, 2022); "Mississippi" in "Declaration of Causes of Seceding States."

7. Davis, *Rhett*, 123–24.

8. Cash, *Mind of the South*, 66, 154.

9. Merritt, *Masterless Men*, 3–10, 45.

10. Ibid., 3–6.

11. Kolkin, *American Slavery*, 74–77.

12. Merritt, *Masterless Men*, 291–92.

13. Fraser, *Charleston! Charleston!*, 71–74.

14. *History of the South Carolina Ports Authority*, vi–vii.

15. Fraser, *Charleston! Charleston!*, 306–10.

16. "Crum, William Demosthenes," in *South Carolina Encyclopedia*; Fraser, *Charleston! Charleston!*, 342, 397–99.

17. Fraser, *Charleston! Charleston!*, 415–17.

18. Ibid., 425.

19. Hicks, *Mayor*, 40–41, 65–67, 114.

20. For an account of the flag issue, see Steve Estes, "From *Charleston in Black and White*," in Williams, Williams, and Blain, *Charleston Syllabus*, 310–14. The recounting of events here is also informed by the author's experience living in South Carolina during that period.

21. Ibid.

22. See Doyle, *New Men*, xi–xiii, for a review of how historians have characterized the New South.

23. Dochuk, *From Bible Belt to Sun Belt*, xv–xvi.

24. Ibid., 27–77.

25. Phillips, *Emerging Republican Majority*. The book presaged the emergence of the Republican Southern Strategy.

26. Bloch, Buchanan, Katz, and Quealy, "Extremely Detailed Map of the 2016 Election."

27. Badger, "Scientific Proof that Cities Are Like Nothing Else."

CHAPTER TWELVE
Reinvention and Sustainability

1. Additional tables of contemporary demographic data can be found in the online supplement (https://ugapress.manifoldapp.org/projects/charleston-and-savannah/).

2. The Office of Management and Budget (OMB) term for an enlarged metropolitan area that combines adjacent MSAs is "Combined Statistical Area" (CSD). For Savannah's CSA, the OMB includes two additional Georgia counties rather than the two more economically integrated South Carolina counties.

3. Estimates are the author's, based on employment data (see the online supplement, (https://ugapress.manifoldapp.org/projects/charleston-and-savannah/)). Charleston and Savannah are "24/7" cities with respect to the leisure and hospitality industry, active at all hours and throughout the year, making it difficult to estimate the number of employees in the historic districts, where the industry is concentrated. During peak times, the author estimates that a quarter of the workforce commutes into those areas. Add to that government and other industries, and it would appear fifty thousand is a conservative estimate.

4. Census tract population data from the U.S. Census American Community Survey of 2017 was used as the basis for calculations. Tract area was adjusted to eliminate open water, marsh, and large nonresidential areas such as cemeteries. The following tracts

were used in the analysis: Charleston: 1, 2, 4, 5, 6, 7, 9, 10, 11, 15, 16, 43, 44, 51, 52, 53, 54; Savannah: 1, 3, 6.01, 9, 11, 15, 20, 21, 23, 26, 27, 28, 29, 30, 112, 113, 114; Chattanooga: 11, 14, 16, 26, 31, 124; Mobile: 2, 9.01, 9.02, 9.03, 10.1, 10.2, 11; Asheville: 1, 2, 6.

5. Figures cited here are drawn from the author's firsthand experience as a city planner.

6. A detailed profile of the Port of Charleston and the Port of Savannah as well as other major employers can be found in the online supplement (https://ugapress .manifoldapp.org/projects/charleston-and-savannah/).

7. Historical attributes are supported with data in the online supplement (https:// ugapress.manifoldapp.org/projects/charleston-and-savannah/). More detailed profiles of other sectors of the modern economy can also be found in the supplement.

8. Charleston, *Post and Courier*: Williams, "Has Tourism in Charleston Reached a Tipping Point?"

9. The author's associate Teri Norris, who worked for the City of Charleston, at times directly for Mayor Riley, provided the following list of initiatives started by the mayor that required recalibration: early implementation of the Historic Preservation Plan, forming a true planning department, Central Business District revitalization, tourism impact and management plan, housing and neighborhood plans, height ordinances, waterfront master planning, scattered-site public housing, park improvements, tourism management planning, signage ordinances, growth management, architectural surveys, Lowcountry Open Land Trust, accommodations district ordinance, the downtown Charleston Place, Spoleto/Piccolo, the downtown farmer's market, the Tree Preservation Ordinance, and annexations that extended many ordinances to James and Johns Islands. According to Norris, "The focus had to keep changing as awareness dictated. I used to think the mayor just started things, put someone in charge, then moved on, starting something new."

10. Harbor Entrepreneur Center, harborec.com (accessed July 19, 2019); Creative Coast, thecreativecoast.org (accessed on July 19, 2019).

11. Freehling, *Road to Disunion*, 358.

12. Ibid.

13. Coclanis, *Shadow of a Dream*, 8–9.

14. See National Park Service documentation, https://npgallery.nps.gov/NRHP /GetAsset/NRHP/78002497_text (accessed April 6, 2022).

15. See *Cost-Benefit Analysis of Savannah's Tourism Sector* (Wayne, Pa.: Tourism Economics, 2017), https://www.savannahga.gov/DocumentCenter/View/15329 /TOURISM-ECONOMICS-STUDY_2017?bidId=. (accessed July 22, 2019).

16. "State Should Tout Culture to Visitors, Panel Told," *Greenville News*, February 6, 1987.

17. Sasso, "Overrun by Tourists, American Cities Are Taking Aim."

18. Ibid.

19. Fraser, *Savannah in the Old South*, 205.

20. Martin, *Classic Savannah*, 20–21.

21. See "Resources" section preceding bibliography for notes on informed respondent interviews.

22. Historic Charleston Foundation, https://www.historiccharleston.org/ (accessed February 6, 2018).

23. For greater detail, see National Park Service documentation, https://npgallery .nps.gov/NRHP/GetAsset/NRHP/78002497_text (accessed April 6, 2022).

24. Adler and Adler, *Savannah Renaissance*, 5–6.

25. For more on the founding of the Historic Savannah Foundation, see Davenport House Museum, https://davenporthousemuseum.org/about-davenport-house.

26. To plumb the extraordinary depth of historic resources in both Charleston and Savannah requires more attention than is practical in this chapter. A fuller discussion of historic resources and a more complete listing of historic neighborhoods, monuments, sites, and forts can be found in the online supplement (https://ugapress .manifoldapp.org/projects/charleston-and-savannah/).

27. An instance of Baldwin's use of the term "Negro removal" can be found in "Urban Renewal . . . Means Negro Removal," from 1963 Baldwin interview by Kenneth Clark, https://www.youtube.com/watch?v=T8Abhj17kYU.

28. McDonald quoted in Schneider, "Charm, and Challenge, of Savannah."

29. Vincent G. Graham, "Charleston Needs Common-Sense Transportation Policy, Not Wider Roads," *Post and Courier* (Charleston, S.C.), August 12, 2019.

CONCLUSION

1. Charleston has taken a bold step in allowing some homes to be elevated to prevent flood damage. See Fausset and Flavelle, "In Charleston, S.C., Saving Historic Homes."

2. Matthew Desmond, "In Order to Understand the Brutality of American Capitalism, You Have to Start on the Plantation," *New York Times Magazine*, August 14, 2019.

3. Ibid. Desmond cites the 1977 publication of Alfred Chandler's classic study *The Visible Hand: The Managerial Revolution in American Business* as promoting the theory that railroads created the framework for the nation's modern economy.

4. Adam Smith Institute, https://www.adamsmith.org/adam-smith-quotes.

5. Rybczynski, *Charleston Fancy*, location 3295.

6. See Folke et al., "Resilience and Sustainable Development."

7. See the "Resources" section preceding bibliography for a list of those who contributed observations and insights to this study.

8. Discussed in more detail in the online supplement (https://ugapress.manifoldapp .org/projects/charleston-and-savannah/).

9. See "References" section for notes on informed respondent interviews.

10. Butler, *Lowcountry at High Tide*, 13–14, 118.

11. "Data Mining Reveals the Four Urban Conditions That Create Vibrant City Life," *MIT Technology Review*, March 24, 2016, https://www.technologyreview.com/s/601107 /data-mining-reveals-the-four-urban-conditions-that-create-vibrant-city-life.

12. For pioneering work on these concepts, see Coy, "Creative Economy"; and John Howkins, www.johnhowkins.com. See also the National Creativity Network, https://nationalcreativitynetwork.org/.

13. Harris, Collins, and Cheek, "America's Creative Economy," 7, 13, 26.

14. CityLab 2013 urban initiatives conference: "Engines of Prosperity: Urban Success Stories of Economic Development," Aspen Institute, October 22, 2013, https://www.aspeninstitute.org/videos/engines-prosperity-urban-success-stories -economic-development (accessed April 6, 2022).

15. The Aspen Institute. https://www.aspeninstitute.org/videos/a-city-the -ultimate-startup/.

16. For Tobler's law, see Caitlin Dempsey, "Tobler's First Law of Geography," Geography Realm, https://www.geographyrealm.com/toblers-first-law-geography.

17. See Bloch, Buchanan, Katz, and Quealy, "Extremely Detailed Map of the 2016 Election."

18. Ibid.

19. See "2020 United States House of Representatives Elections in South Carolina," Wikipedia, https://en.wikipedia.org/wiki/ 2020_United_States_House _of_Representatives_elections_in_South_Carolina.

20. See Bloch, Buchanan, Katz, and Quealy, "Extremely Detailed Map of the 2016 Election."

21. Bishop, *Big Sort*, 6, 9.

22. Rybczynski, *Charleston Fancy*, 31.

23. Beaufort County in particular has made progress with its community protection zoning overlays and other initiatives. Nonprofit organizations have also partnered to address the challenges. See, for example, Beaufort Island Open Land Trust, https://openlandtrust.org/2020/11/st-helena-island-protecting-a-cultural-and -historic-treasure.

24. Author estimate based on growth rates since 2010, using U.S. Census figures.

25. Cash, *Mind of the South*, 428–29.

AFTERWORD

1. John Burton, "The Duty and Reward of Propagating Principles of Religion and Virtue exemplified in the History of Abraham: A Sermon Preach'd before the Trustees for Establishing the Colony of Georgia in America," sermon delivered at the first anniversary meeting of the Trustees, March 15, 1732, Gale Digital Collections: Eighteenth Century Collections Online, accessed through Hargrett Rare Manuscripts Library, University of Georgia. Originally published 1733. Thomas Paine wrote in *Common Sense*, "We have it in our power to begin the world over again." *The Writings of Thomas Paine*, vol. 1, 118, Google Books, https://www.google.com/books/edition /The_Writings_of_Thomas_Paine/DTsPAAAAYAAJ (accessed April 14, 2022).

2. The list of grievances was informed by Tiffanie Drayton, "I'm a Black American. I Had to Get Out. The Racism Was Too Much. I Fled," *New York Times*, June 12, 2020.

3. Lafer, *One Percent Solution*.

4. Specific strategies to develop affordable housing in the historic core areas are discussed in the online supplement (https://ugapress.manifoldapp.org/projects /charleston-and-savannah/).

RESOURCES
Informed Respondents

Research for this book required contacting subject matter experts (informed respondents) for both contemporary and historic information of a tangible (quantitative) and intangible (qualitative) nature. Interviews and selective questioning were conducted in person, by email, and by telephone. A survey instrument was developed for those respondents informed about the comparative character of the two cities, although respondents were allowed to extemporize in order to pursue promising lines of thought. Subject matter experts in particular fields such as Lowcountry rice cultivation were asked more specific questions.

Informed respondents included David Anderson, Chatham County GIS; Judith A. Carney, associate professor, UCLA, author of *Black Rice*; Vincent Graham, developer of I'On in Mount Pleasant and infill projects in Charleston; Dorothy (Dot) Gnann, long-time public figure and icon in the Lowcountry; Billy Keyserling, mayor, Beaufort, South Carolina; Jacob Lindsey, director of planning, City of Charleston; Chris Miller, CEO, Illuminomics, cofounder of the Creative Coast; Ralph Muldrow, professor, College of Charleston; Jim Newsome and Jordi Yarborough, South Carolina Ports Authority; Michael T. Owens, president and CEO, Tourism Leadership Council, Savannah; Imre E. Quastler, transportation geographer and always the author's closest advisor; Beth Lattimore Reiter, Savannah preservationist; Patrick Shay, architect and curator of the Oglethorpe Resource Library; Christian Sottile, architect whose practice and family history involves both cities; James H. Tuten, professor of history, Juniata College, author of *Time and Tide*; Carolee Williams, retired planner retired, City of Charleston; Melanie Wilson, executive director, Chatham-Savannah Metropolitan Planning Commission.

A meeting at the studio of Patrick Shay, GMS Architects and Urban Planners, Savannah, was held on October 30, 2019, in which design and historic preservation professionals, among others, compared and contrasted the character of the two cities in a discussion led by the author. Attendees included Patrick Shay; Janice Shay; and GMS staff members Matthew Enering, Nick Gogal, Chelsea Jackson-Greene, Ana Manzo, Jessica Moeslein, Caitlin Moultroup, Meredith Stone, and Latoya Waters. Others who participated were Lissette Arrongante, City of Savannah; Ellen Harris, principal, Ethos Preservation; Sue Adler, Ryan Arvay, and Chassidy Malloy of Historic Savannah Foundation; Kait Morano, Chatham-Savannah Metropolitan Planning Commission; and Vaughnette Goode-Walker, independent scholar and an authority on Savannah history.

The author is indebted to the historian Christopher Hendricks of Georgia Southern University, Armstrong Campus in Savannah for a close reading of the manuscript and many illuminating comments. He is also grateful to those who steered the project through the review and development process, notably Patrick Allen and Melissa Bugbee Buchanan.

Others familiar with Charleston, Savannah, and the Lowcountry who provided useful insights included Teri Norris, former employee of the planning departments of both cities, as well as a friend, colleague, graphic artist, and contributor of maps and a photo to this book; Grace Cordial, manager of the Beaufort District Collection, Beaufort County Public Library; Nicholas Ashley Cooper, Twelfth Earl of Shaftesbury; and, last here but first in all other respects, my wife, Susan Townsend, who added her own insights on Savannah and the Lowcountry based on living there for twenty years.

BIBLIOGRAPHY

Adler, Lee, and Emma Adler. *Savannah Renaissance*. Charleston, S.C.: Wyrick, 2003.

Agha, Andrew. "Shaftesbury's Atlantis." PhD diss., University of South Carolina, 2020.

Ashley Cooper, Anthony, 1st Earl of Shaftesbury. *The Shaftesbury Papers*. Charleston: South Carolina Historical Society, 2000.

Badger, Emily. "Scientific Proof that Cities Are Like Nothing Else in Nature." *CityLab*. June 20, 2013. https://www.citylab.com/environment/2013/06/scientific-proof-cities-are-nothing-else-nature/5977/ (accessed May 30, 2019).

Bartram, William. *Travels through North and South Carolina*. Philadelphia: James and Johnson, 1791. Kindle.

Bell, Laura Palmer. "A New Theory on the Plan of Savannah." *Georgia Historical Quarterly* 48, no. 2 (June 1964): 147–65.

Berendt, John. *Midnight in the Garden of Good and Evil*. New York: Random House, 1994.

Bishop, Bill. *The Big Sort: Why the Clustering of Like-Minded America Is Tearing us Apart*. Boston: Houghton Mifflin, 2008.

Bloch, Matthew, Larry Buchanan, Josh Katz, and Kevin Quealy. "An Extremely Detailed Map of the 2016 Election." *New York Times*, July 25, 2018. https://www.nytimes.com/interactive/2018/upshot/election-2016-voting-precinct-maps.html (accessed July 25, 2018).

Bowne, Eric E., and Crystal A. Bowne. "Natives, Women, Debtors, and Slaves: Christian Priber's American Utopia." *Native South* 11 (2018): 56–80.

Brockwell, Gillian. "Before 1619, There Was 1526: The Mystery of the First Enslaved Africans in What Became the United States." *Washington Post*, September 7, 2019. https://www.washingtonpost.com/history/2019/09/07/before-there-was-mystery-first-enslaved-africans-what-became-us (accessed October 14, 2021).

Bull, Kinloch, Jr. *The Oligarchs in Colonial and Revolutionary Charleston: Lieutenant Governor William Bull II and His Family*. Columbia: University of South Carolina Press, 1991.

Butler, Christina Rae. *Lowcountry at High Tide: A History of Flooding, Drainage, and Reclamation in Charleston, South Carolina*. University of South Carolina Press, 2019.

Callahan, Patti. *Surviving Savannah*. New York: Penguin, 2021. Kindle.

Candler, Allen D., ed. *Colonial Records of the State of Georgia*. 26 volumes. Atlanta: Franklin Printing and Publishing, 1904–1916.

Carney, Judith A. *Black Rice: The African Origins of Rice Cultivation in the Americas.* Cambridge, Mass.: Harvard University Press, 2002.

Carrington, Sean, Henry Fraser, John Gilmore, and G. Addington Forde. *A–Z of Barbados Heritage.* 2nd ed. New York: Macmillan, 2003.

Cash, W. J. *The Mind of the South.* New York: Vintage Books, 1991. First published 1941.

Cashin, Edward J., ed. *Setting Out to Begin a New World: Colonial Georgia.* Savannah: Beehive Press, 1995.

Charleston, City of. "Century V Plan." https://www.charleston-sc.gov/285 /Century-V-Plan (accessed August 6, 2019).

———. "Century V Plan Review: Presentation to Planning Commission, December 7, 2016." https://www.charleston-sc.gov/DocumentCenter/View/12782 /Century-V-Plan-Review-Presentation?bidId= (accessed August 9, 2019).

———. *Vision | Community | Heritage: A Preservation Plan for Charleston, South Carolina.* Prepared by Page & Turnbull, Inc. for the City of Charleston and Historic Charleston Foundation, 2008.

Chastellux, Marquis de. *Travels in North America in the Years 1780–81–82.* Bedford, Mass.: Applewood Books. First published 1828.

Chinni, Dante, and James Gimpel. *Our Patchwork Nation: The Surprising Truth about the "Real" America.* New York: Gotham Books, 2010.

Clark, J. C. D. *The Language of Liberty, 1660–1832: Political Discourse and Social Dynamics in the Anglo-American World.* Cambridge, UK: Cambridge University Press, 1994.

"Clinton's Big Ditch." *The Erie Canal.* http://www.eriecanal.org (accessed February 11, 2018).

Coclanis, Peter A. *The Shadow of a Dream: Economic Life and Death in the Low Country, 1670–1920.* New York: Oxford University Press, 1989.

Cohen, Hennig. *The South Carolina Gazette: 1732–1775.* Columbia: University of South Carolina Press, 1953.

College of Charleston. *If These Walls Could Talk.* Video production by Charissa Owens and Michael T. Owens. Charleston: College of Charleston, Office of Institutional Diversity, 2021.

———, Pearlstine/Lipov Center for Southern Jewish Culture. "Mapping Jewish Charleston." https://mappingjewishcharleston.cofc.edu/2020/ (accessed October 13, 2021).

Conroy, Pat. *The Lords of Discipline.* Boston: Houghton Mifflin, 1980. Open Road Media.

———. *South of Broad.* New York: Doubleday, 2009.

———. *The Water Is Wide: A Memoir.* New York: Dial Press, 2002.

Cooper, Michael. *"A More Beautiful City": Robert Hooke and the Rebuilding of London after the Great Fire.* Phoenix Mill, UK: Sutton, 2003.

Corcoran, Paul. "John Locke on the Possession of Land: Native Title vs. the 'Principle' of Vacuum Domicilium." *European Legacy* 23, vol. 3 (May 2018): 225–50.

Courtenay, William A. *The Genesis of South Carolina, 1562–1670.* Columbia, S.C.: Privately printed by the State Company, 1907.

Coy, Peter. "The Creative Economy." *Bloomberg News,* August 28, 2000. https://www

.bloomberg.com/news/articles/2000-08-27/the-creative-economy (accessed December 22, 2019).

Crosby, Alfred W. *The Columbian Exchange: Biological and Cultural Consequences of 1492.* 30th anniversary ed. Westport, CT: Praeger, 2003.

Cutler, Harry Gardner. *History of South Carolina*, vol. 1. Chicago: Lewis, 1920.

Data Center (Greater New Orleans). "Historical Population by Race over 300 Years." https://data.datacenterresearch.org/Population/Historical-Population-By-Race -Over-300-Years/34pm-mf8u/data (accessed April 13, 2022).

David, Huw. *Trade, Politics, and Revolution: South Carolina and Britain's Atlantic Commerce, 1730–1790.* Columbia: University of South Carolina Press, 2018.

Davis, Burke. *Sherman's March.* New York: Random House, 1980. Kindle.

Davis, William C. *Rhett: The Turbulent Life and Times of a Fire-Eater.* Columbia: University of South Carolina Press, 2001.

Dawers, Bill. "Inaction on City's Ugly Past to Haunt Future." *Savannah Morning News*, March 2, 2021.

"The Declaration of Causes of Seceding States: Primary Sources." American Battlefield Trust. https://www.battlefields.org/learn/primary-sources/declaration-causes -seceding-states (accessed March 24, 2022).

Diamond, Jared. *Guns, Germs, and Steel: The Fates of Human Societies.* New York: W. W. Norton, 1999.

Dickens, Charles. *A Tale of Two Cities.* First published 1859. Kindle.

Dochuk, Darren. *From Bible Belt to Sun Belt: Plain-Folk Religion, Grassroots Politics, and the Rise of Evangelical Conservatism.* New York: W. W. Norton, 2011.

Doyle, Don H. *New Men, New Cities, New South: Atlanta, Nashville, Charleston, Mobile, 1860–1910.* Chapel Hill: University of North Carolina Press, 1990.

Dunn, Richard S. *Sugar and Slaves: The Rise of the English Planter Class in the English West Indies, 1624–1713.* Chapel Hill: University of North Carolina Press, 1972.

Edgar, Walter. *South Carolina: A History.* Columbia: University of South Carolina Press, 1998.

Elazar, Daniel J. *American Federalism: A View from the States.* 2nd ed. New York: Thomas Y. Crowell, 1972.

——— *The American Mosaic: The Impact of Space, Time, and Culture on American Politics.* Boulder, Colo.: Westview Press, 1994.

Elliott, E. N., ed. *Cotton Is King and the Pro-Slavery Arguments: Comprising the Writings of Hammond, Harper, Christy, Stringfellow, Hodge, Bledsoe, and Cartwright on This Important Subject.* Augusta, Ga: Pritchard, Abbott & Loomis, 1860. Project Guttenberg, https://www.gutenberg.org/ebooks/28148.

Ellis, Joseph. *American Creation: Triumph and Tragedies at the Founding of the Republic.* New York: Alfred A. Knopf, 2007.

Eltis, David, and David Richardson. *Atlas of the Transatlantic Slave Trade.* New Haven: Yale University Press, 2010.

Epstein, Kayla. "Revolutionary War Hero May Have Been Intersex." *Atlanta Constitution.* April 9, 2019.

Ettinger, Amos Aschbach. *James Edward Oglethorpe: Imperial Idealist.* Hamden, Conn.: Archon Books, 1968. First published 1936.

———. *Oglethorpe: A Brief Biography.* Edited by Phinizy Spalding. Macon, Ga.: Mercer University Press, 1984.

Farr, James. "'Absolute Power and Authority': John Locke and the Revisions of the *Fundamental Constitutions of Carolina.*" *Locke Studies* 2020 (October 20, 2020). https://ojs.lib.uwo.ca/index.php/locke/article/view/10310/8784 (accessed November 9, 2020).

Fausset, Richard, and Christopher Flavelle. "In Charleston, S.C., Saving Historic Homes Means Hoisting Them in the Air." *New York Times,* July 24, 2021.

Fields-Black, Edda L. *Deep Roots: Rice Farmers in West Africa and the African Diaspora.* Bloomington: Indiana University Press, 2008.

Fischer, David Hackett. *Albion's Seed: Four British Folkways in America.* New York: Oxford University Press, 1989.

Folke, Carl, et al. "Resilience and Sustainable Development: Building Adaptive Capacity in a World of Transformations." *AMBIO: A Journal of the Human Environment* 31, vol. 5 (2002): 437–40.

Foner, Eric. *Freedom's Lawmakers: A Directory of Black Officeholders during Reconstruction.* Baton Rouge: Louisiana State University Press, 1993.

Fraser, Walter J., Jr. *Charleston! Charleston! The History of a Southern City.* Columbia: University of South Carolina Press, 1989.

———. *Lowcountry Hurricanes: Three Centuries of Storms at Sea and Ashore.* Athens: University of Georgia Press, 2006.

———. *Savannah in the Old South.* Athens: University of Georgia Press, 2003.

Freehling, William. *The Road to Disunion,* vol. 2, *Secessionists Triumphant, 1854–1861.* New York: Oxford University Press, 2007. Kindle.

Fries, Sylvia Doughty. *The Urban Idea in Colonial America.* Philadelphia: Temple University Press, 1977.

Gallay, Alan. *The Indian Slave Trade: The Rise of the English Empire in the American South, 1670–1717.* New Haven: Yale University Press, 2002.

Garreau, Joel. *The Nine Nations of North America.* Boston: Houghton Mifflin, 1981.

Genovese, Eugene D. *A Consuming Fire: The Fall of the Confederacy in the Mind of the White Christian South.* Athens: University of Georgia Press, 1998.

———. *The Political Economy of Slavery: Studies in the Economy and Society of the Slave South.* Toronto: Vintage Books, 1967.

———. *The Slaveholders' Dilemma: Freedom and Progress in Southern Conservative Thought, 1820–1860.* Columbia: University of South Carolina Press, 1992.

Georgia Ports. gaports.com (accessed June 1, 2019).

Glausser, Wayne. "Three Approaches to Locke and the Slave Trade." *Journal of the History of Ideas* 51, no. 2 (June 1, 1990): 199–200.

Grant, Douglas. *The Fortunate Slave: An Illustration of African Slavery in the Early Eighteenth Century.* London: Oxford University Press, 1968.

Green, Jack P., et al., eds. *Money, Trade, and Power: The Evolution of Colonial South Carolina's Plantation Society.* Columbia: University of South Carolina Press, 2001.

Hagy, James W. *This Happy Land: The Jews of Colonial and Antebellum Charleston*. Tuscaloosa: University of Alabama Press, 1993.

Haley, K. H. D. *The First Earl of Shaftesbury*. Oxford: Oxford University Press, 1968.

Hammond, James Henry. *Secret and Sacred: The Diaries of James Henry Hammond*. Edited by Carol Bleser. New York: Oxford University Press, 1988.

———. *Selections from the Letters and Speeches of the Hon. James H. Hammond, of South Carolina*. New York: John F. Trow, 1866.

Hammond, John Craig. *Slavery, Freedom, and Expansion in the Early American West*. Charlottesville: University of Virginia Press, 2007.

Harrington, James. *The Commonwealth of Oceana*. Tutis Digital Publishing, 2008. First published 1656.

Harris, Christine, Margaret Collins, and Dennis Cheek. "America's Creative Economy: A Study of Recent Conceptions, Definitions, and Approaches to Measurement Across the USA." Oklahoma City: National Creativity Network in Collaboration with Creative Alliance Milwaukee, 2013. https://culturalheritagetourism.org/wp-content/uploads/formidable/Americas-Creative-Economy-2013.pdf (accessed July 20, 2019).

Hartz, Louis. *The Liberal Tradition in America: An Interpretation of American Political Thought since the Revolution*. Orlando, Fla.: Harcourt, 1955.

Herndon, Astead W. "Raphael Warnock's Win Is One for the History Books." *New York Times*, January 6, 2021.

Hicks, Brian. *The Mayor: Joe Riley and the Rise of Charleston*. Charleston, S.C.: Evening Post Books, 2015.

Historic Charleston Foundation. https://www.historiccharleston.org/.

History of the South Carolina State Ports Authority. Charleston, S.C.: SCSPA, 1991.

Hoare, Prince. *Memoirs of Granville Sharp, Esq.*, 2nd ed. 2 vols. London: Henry Colburn, 1828.

Home, Robert. *Of Planting and Planning: The Making of British Colonial Cities*. New York: Spon, 1997.

Jacob, Margaret C. *The Radical Enlightenment: Pantheists, Freemasons, and Republicans*. London: George Allen & Unwin, 1981.

Johnson, Samuel. "Taxation No Tyranny: An Answer to the Resolutions and Address of the American Congress." https://www.samueljohnson.com/tnt.html (accessed May 19, 2017).

Johnson, Walter. *River of Dark Dreams: Slavery and Imperialism in the Mississippi Valley*. Cambridge, Mass.: Harvard University Press, 2013.

Johnson, Whittington. *Black Savannah, 1788–1864*. Fayetteville: University of Arkansas Press, 1996.

Jones, Jacqueline. *A Dreadful Deceit: The Myth of Race from the Colonial Era to Obama's America*. New York: Basic Books, 2013. Kindle.

———. *Saving Savannah: The City and the Civil War*. New York: Vintage Books, 2009.

Jones, J. P., and Pauline K. Angell. "Birthplace of DeWitt Clinton." *New York History* 18, no. 1 (January 1937), 113–16.

Jordan, James. "Charles Augustus Lafayette Lamar and the Movement to Reopen the African Slave Trade." *Georgia Historical Quarterly* 93, no. 3 (Fall 2009), 247–90.

Jordan, Winthrop D. *White over Black: American Attitudes toward the Negro, 1550–1812.* Chapel Hill: University of North Carolina Press, 1968.

"Juliette Gordon Low: A Brief Biography". Girl Scouts of the United States of America. https://www.girlscouts.org/en/about-girl-scouts/our-history/juliette-gordon-low.html (retrieved December 10, 2019).

Key, V. O., Jr. *Southern Politics.* New York: Vintage Books, 1949.

Keyserling, Billy, and Mike Greenly. *Sharing Common Ground: Promises Unfulfilled but Not Forgotten.* Beaufort, S.C.: B. Keyserling, 2020.

Kolchin, Peter. *American Slavery, 1619–1877.* New York: Hill and Wang, 1993.

Lafer, Gordon. *The One Percent Solution: How Corporations Are Remaking America One State at a Time.* Ithaca, N.Y.: ILR Press/Cornell University Press, 2017.

Lane, Mills, ed. *General Oglethorpe's Georgia: Colonial Letters, 1733–1743.* 2 vols. Savannah: Beehive Press, 1990.

———. *Our First Visit in America: Early Reports from the Colony of Georgia, 1732–1740.* Savannah: Beehive Press, 1974.

Leng, Thomas. "Shaftesbury's Aristocratic Empire." *Anthony Ashley Cooper, First Earl of Shaftesbury 1621–1683,* edited by John Spurr, 101–25. Farnham: Ashgate, 2011.

Lesser, Charles H. *South Carolina Begins: The Records of a Proprietary Colony, 1663–1721.* Columbia: South Carolina Department of Archives and History, 1995.

Lind, Michael. *Made in Texas: George W. Bush and the Southern Takeover of American Politics.* New York: Basic Books, 2004.

Lloyd's List. "One Hundred Container Ports, 2020." https://lloydslist.maritimeintelligence.informa.com/one-hundred-container-ports-2020 (accessed December 10, 2021).

Locke, John. *Two Treatises of Government.* Edited by Peter Laslett. New York: New American Library, 1960.

The Lord Ashley Site. Blog maintained by the archaeological team. http://lordashleysite.wordpress.com/about/ (accessed September 30, 2013).

Marrs, Aaron W. *Railroads in the Old South: Pursuing Progress in a Slave Society.* Baltimore: Johns Hopkins University Press, 2009.

Martin, William R., Jr. *Classic Savannah: History, Homes, and Gardens.* Savannah, Ga.: Golden Coast, 1988.

Martyn, Benjamin. *Some Account of the Trustees Design for the Establishment of the Colony of Georgia in America.* Edited by Rodney M. Baine and Phinizy Spalding, eds. Athens: University of Georgia Press, 1990. First published 1732.

Mauser, Bruce L. *A Slaving Voyage to Africa and Jamaica: The Log of the Sandown, 1793–1794.* Bloomington: University of Indiana Press, 2002.

Mayle, Mary Carr. "Barge Delivers First Cargo up Savannah River in 40 Years." *Savannah Morning News,* June 11, 2016. https://www.savannahnow.com/business/bis/2016-06-11/barge-delivers-first-cargo-savannah-river-40-years (accessed March 29, 2019).

McCrady, Edward. *The History of South Carolina under the Proprietary Government, 1670–1719*. New York: Russell & Russell, 1897.

McIlvenna, Noeleen. *The Short Life of Free Georgia: Class and Slavery in the Colonial South*. Chapel Hill: University of North Carolina Press, 2015. Kindle.

McPherson, James M. *Battle Cry of Freedom*. New York: Oxford University Press, 2003.

Meinig, D. W. *The Shaping of America: A Geographical Perspective on 500 Years of History*, vol. 2, *Continental America, 1800–1867*. New Haven: Yale University Press, 1993.

Mellon, Knox. "Christian Priber's Cherokee 'Kingdom of Paradise.'" *Georgia Historical Quarterly* 57, no. 3 (Fall 1973): 319–26.

Meroney, Geraldine M. *Inseparable Loyalty: A Biography of William Bull*. Norcross, Ga.: Harrison, 1991.

Merritt, Keri Leigh. *Masterless Men: Poor Whites and Slavery in the Antebellum South*. Cambridge, UK: Cambridge University Press, 2017.

Mitchell, Margaret. *Gone with the Wind*. New York: Macmillan, 1936.

Moore, Francis. *Travels into the Interior Parts of Africa*. 2nd ed. London: D. Henry and R. Cave, 1738.

———. *A Voyage to Georgia*. St. Simons Island, Ga.: Fort Frederica Association, 2002. First published 1774.

Morgan, Edmund S. *American Slavery, American Freedom: The Ordeal of Colonial Virginia*. New York: W. W. Norton, 1975.

Morgan, Philip D. *Slave Counterpoint: Black Culture in the Eighteenth-Century Chesapeake and Lowcountry*. Chapel Hill: University of North Carolina Press, 1998.

Navin, John J. *The Grim Years: South Carolina, 1670–1720*. Columbia: University of South Carolina Press, 2020.

Oakes, James. *The Ruling Race: A History of American Slaveholders*. New York: Alfred A. Knopf, 1982.

———. *Slavery and Freedom: An Interpretation of the Old South*. New York: Alfred A. Knopf, 1990.

Oatis, Steven J. *A Colonial Complex: South Carolina's Frontiers in the Era of the Yamasee War, 1680–1730*. Lincoln: University of Nebraska Press, 2004.

Oglethorpe, James Edward. *The Publications of James Edward Oglethorpe*. Edited by Rodney M. Baine. Athens: University of Georgia Press, 1994.

———. *Some Account of the Design of the Trustees for Establishing Colonys in America*. Edited by Rodney M. Baine and Phinizy Spalding. Athens: University of Georgia Press, 1990.

Oldenburg, Ray. *The Great Good Place: Cafes, Coffee Shops, Bookstores, Bars, Hair Salons, and Other Hangouts at the Heart of a Community*. Boston: Da Capo Press, 1989.

Percival, John, Earl. *Manuscripts of the Earl of Egmont: Diary of Viscount Percival, afterwards First Earl of Egmont*. 3 vols. London: H.M.S.O., 1920–23.

Phillips, Kevin. *The Emerging Republican Majority*. New Rochelle, N.Y.: Arlington House, 1969.

Pocock, J. G. A. *Politics, Language and Time: Essays on Political Thought and History*. New York: Atheneum, 1971.

Post and Courier. Behre, Robert. "Despite Pushback, Charleston Historic Sites Expand Their Interpretation of Slavery." September 1, 2019.

———. Byrd, Caitlin. "Charleston Forum on Reparations." October 17, 2019.

———. Hobbs, Stephen, et al. "John C. Calhoun Statue Taken Down from Its Perch above Charleston's Marion Square." June 23, 2020.

———. Williams, Emily. "Has Tourism in Charleston Reached a Tipping Point? Local Experts Weigh In." June 6, 2019.

Poston, Jonathan H. *The Buildings of Charleston: A Guide to the City's Architecture.* Columbia: University of South Carolina Press, 1997.

Powers, Bernard E., Jr. *Black Charlestonians: A Social History, 1822–1885.* Fayetteville: University of Arkansas Press, 1994.

Pressly, Paul. *On the Rim of the Caribbean: Colonial Georgia and the British Atlantic World.* Athens: University of Georgia Press, 2013. Kindle.

Rahn, Ruby A. *River Highway for Trade, the Savannah: Canoes, Indian Tradeboats, Flatboats, Steamers, Packets, and Barges.* Savannah, Ga.: U.S. Army District, Corps of Engineers, 1968.

Ramsay, David. *The History of South Carolina, from its First Settlement in 1670, to the Year 1808,* vol. 1. Charleston, S.C.: David Longworth, 1809.

Reese, Trevor R. "Benjamin Martyn, Secretary to the Trustees of Georgia." *Georgia Historical Quarterly* 38, no. 2 (June 1954): 142–47.

———, ed. *The Clamorous Malcontents: Criticisms and Defenses of the Colony of Georgia, 1741–1743.* Savannah, Ga.: Beehive, 1973.

———. *Colonial Georgia: A Study in British Imperial Policy in the Eighteenth Century.* Athens: University of Georgia Press, 1963.

Reich, David. *Who We Are and How We Got Here: Ancient DNA and the New Science of the Human Past.* New York: Pantheon, 2018. Kindle.

Reinberger, Mark. "Oglethorpe's Plan of Savannah: Urban Design, Speculative Freemasonry, and Enlightenment Charity." *Georgia Historical Quarterly* 81, no. 4 (Winter 1997): 839–62.

Reps, John W. "$C^2 + L^2 = S^2$? Another Look at the Origins of Savannah's Town Plan." In *Forty Years of Diversity: Essays on Colonial Georgia,* edited by Harvey H. Jackson and Phinizy Spalding, 101–51. Athens: University of Georgia Press, 1984.

———. *The Making of Urban America: A History of City Planning in the United States.* Princeton, N.J.: Princeton University Press, 1965.

———. "Thomas Jefferson's Checkerboard Towns." *Journal of the Society of Architectural Historians* 20, vol. 3 (October 1961): 108–14.

Rivers, William J. *A Chapter in the Early History of South Carolina.* Charleston: Walker, Evans and Cogswell Printers, 1874.

———. *A Sketch of the History of South Carolina.* Charleston: McCarter, 1856.

Robertson, David M. *Denmark Vesey.* New York: Alfred A. Knopf, 1999. Kindle.

Rogers, George C., and C. James Taylor. *A South Carolina Chronology, 1497–1992.* Columbia: University of South Carolina Press, 1994.

Rowland, Lawrence S., Alexander Moore, and George C. Rogers Jr. *The History of*

Beaufort County, South Carolina, vol. 1, *1514–1861*. Columbia: University of South Carolina Press, 1996.

Roper, Louis H. *Conceiving Carolina: Proprietors, Planters, and Plots, 1662–1729*. New York: Palgrave MacMillan, 2004.

Rutherford, Adam. *A Brief History of Everyone Who Ever Lived: The Human Story Retold through Our Genes*. New York: Experiment, 2017. Kindle.

Salley, A. S., ed. *Commissions and Instructions from the Lords Proprietors of Carolina to Public Officials of South Carolina, 1685–1715*. Columbia: Historical Commission of South Carolina, 1916.

———, ed. *Narratives of Early Carolina, 1650–1708*. New York: C. Scribner's Sons, 1911.

Sasso, Michael. "Overrun by Tourists, American Cities Are Taking Aim at Hotels." *Bloomberg Businessweek*, October 16, 2019, https://www.bloomberg.com/.

Savannah, City of. "Civic Master Plan." Prepared by Sottile & Sottile, 2006.

———. "Chatham County-Savannah Tricentennial Plan" (the City-County Comprehensive Plan). Community Assessment (Volume 2) and Community Agenda (Volume 3). 2006.

———. "Downtown Master Plan." 2010 draft.

———. "Golden Heritage Plan." Chatham County-Savannah Metropolitan Planning Commission, 1958.

———. "Historic District Ordinance" (amendments). Prepared by Sottile & Sottile, 2009.

———. "Thomas Square Streetcar Historic District Neighborhood Plan." 2005.

"Savannah River Shipping." *New Georgia Encyclopedia*. https://www.georgiaencyclopedia.org/articles/geography-environment/savannah-river.

Saye, Albert B. "Genesis of Georgia: Merchants as Well as Ministers." *Georgia Historical Quarterly* 24, no. 3 (September 1940): 191–201.

———. "Was Georgia a Debtor Colony?" *Georgia Historical Quarterly* 24, no. 5 (December 1940): 323–41.

Schaub, Diana J. "Perspectives on Slavery: Beaumont's *Marie* and Tocqueville's *Democracy in America*." *Legal Studies Forum* 22, no. 4 (1998): 607–26.

Schneider, Keith. "The Charm, and Challenge, of Savannah." *New York Times*, August 7, 2019.

Shaftesbury, Anthony Ashley Cooper, 1st earl of. *The Shaftesbury Papers*. Charleston: South Carolina Historical Society, 2000.

Shuler, Kristina A., and Ralph Bailey, Jr. *A History of the Phosphate Mining Industry in the South Carolina Lowcountry*. Survey Report. Mount Pleasant, S.C.: Brockington and Associates, 2004.

Sieg, Chan. *The Squares: An Introduction to Savannah*. Virginia Beach, Va.: Donning, 1996.

Sinha, Manisha. *The Counterrevolution of Slavery: Politics and Ideology in Antebellum South Carolina*. Chapel Hill: University of North Carolina Press, 2000.

Sirmans, M. Eugene. *Colonial South Carolina: A Political History, 1663–1763*. Chapel Hill: University of North Carolina Press, 1966.

Slavery and Justice. Report of the Brown University Steering Committee on Slavery and Justice. http://www.brown.edu/Research/Slavery_Justice/documents /SlaveryAndJustice.pdf.

Smith, Henry A. M. "Beaufort: The Original Plan and the Earliest Settlers." *South Carolina Historical and Genealogical Magazine* 9, no. 3 (July 1908), 141–60.

———. *Historical Writings of Henry A. M. Smith, Cities and Towns of Early South Carolina*. 3 volumes. Spartanburg, SC: The Reprint Company (in association with the South Carolina Historical Society), 1988.

South Carolina Encyclopedia. https://www.scencyclopedia.org/sce/.

South Carolina Ports Authority. www.scspa.com (accessed June 1, 2019).

———. *The Economic Impact of the South Carolina Ports Authority: A Statewide and Regional Analysis*. Division of Research, Darla Moore School of Business, University of South Carolina, 2019.

Spalding, Phinizy. "James Edward Oglethorpe's Quest for the American Zion." In *Forty Years of Diversity: Essays on Colonial Georgia*, ed. Harvey H. Jackson and Phinizy Spalding, 60–79. Athens: University of Georgia Press, 1984.

———. *Oglethorpe in America*. Chicago: University of Chicago Press, 1977.

———. "Oglethorpe, William Stephens, and the Origin of Georgia Politics." In *Oglethorpe in Perspective: Georgia's Founder after Two Hundred Years*, ed. Phinizy Spalding and Harvey H. Jackson, 80–98. Tuscaloosa: University of Alabama Press, 1989.

———. "Some Sermons before the Trustees of Colonial Georgia." *Georgia Historical Quarterly* 57, no. 3 (1973): 332–46.

Starobin, Paul. *Madness Rules the Hour: Charleston, 1860 and the Mania for War*. New York: Public Affairs, 2017.

Stephens, William. *A Journal of the Proceedings of Georgia*. 2 volumes. [New York]: Readex Microprint, 1966. First published 1742.

Stone, H. David, Jr. *Vital Rails: The Charleston & Savannah Railroad and the Civil War in Coastal South Carolina*. Columbia: University of South Carolina Press, 2008.

Stoney, Samuel Gaillard. *Plantations of the Carolina Low Country*. Charleston: Carolina Art Association, 1938.

Stuart, Andrea. *Sugar in the Blood: A Family's Story of Slavery and Empire*. New York: Alfred A. Knopf, 2013.

Stubbs, Tristan. *Masters of Violence: The Plantation Overseers of Eighteenth-Century Virginia, South Carolina, and Georgia*. Columbia: University of South Carolina Press, 2018.

Sweet, Julie Anne. *Negotiating for Georgia: British-Creek Relations in the Trustee Era, 1733–1752*. Athens: University of Georgia Press, 2005.

Taylor, Thomas. *Memoir of Mrs. Hannah More*. London: Joseph Rickerby, 1838.

Thornton, John. *Africa and Africans in the Making of the Atlantic World, 1400–1800*. 2nd ed. Cambridge, UK: Cambridge University Press, 1998.

Tibbetts, John, and Chris Mooney. "Sea Level Rise Is Eroding Home Value, and Owners Might Not Even Know It." *Washington Post*, August 20, 2018.

Tuten, James H. *Lowcountry Time and Tide: The Fall of the South Carolina Rice King-dom*. Columbia: University of South Carolina Press, 2010.

Twelve Southerners. *I'll Take My Stand: The South and the Agrarian Tradition*. Glouces-ter, Mass.: Peter Smith, 1976.

U.S. Bureau of the Census. "Historical Statistics of the United States, 1789–1945." A Supplement to the Statistical Abstract of the United States, 1949.

——. "Historical Statistics of the United States, Colonial Times to 1970." Bicenten-nial Edition, Part 1, 1976.

——. "Population in the Colonial and Continental Periods." https://www.census.gov/history/pdf/colonialbostonpops.pdf.

U.S. Department of Commerce, National Travel and Tourism Office. https://travel.trade.gov/outreachpages/inbound.general_information.inbound_overview.asp (accessed June 7, 2019).

U.S. Department of the Interior, National Park Service. "South Carolina: Mother Emanuel AME Church." https://www.nps.gov/places/south-carolina-mother-emanuel-AME-church.htm.

U.S. National Weather Service. "Tropical Cyclone History for Southeast South Caro-lina and Northern Portions of Southeast Georgia." https://www.weather.gov/chs/TChistory.

Van Andel, Tinde R. "African Rice (*Oryza glaberrima* Steud.): Lost Crop of the En-slaved Africans Discovered in Suriname." *Economic Botany* 64, no. 1 (2010): 1–10.

——, et al. "Tracing Ancestor Rice of Suriname Maroons Back to Its African Ori-gin." *Nature Plants* 2 (October 2016): 1–5.

Weir, Robert M. *Colonial South Carolina: A History*. Columbia: University of South Carolina Press, 1997.

Williams, Chad, Kidada E. Williams, and Keisha N. Blain, eds. *Charleston Syllabus: Readings on Race, Racism, and Racial Violence*. Athens: University of Georgia Press, 2016.

Wilson, Thomas D. *The Ashley Cooper Plan: The Founding of Carolina and the Origins of Southern Political Culture*. Chapel Hill: University of North Carolina Press, 2016.

——. *The Oglethorpe Plan: Enlightenment Design in Savannah and Beyond*. Char-lottesville: University of Virginia Press, 2012.

Wood, Peter H. *Black Majority: Negroes in Colonial South Carolina from 1670 through the Stono Rebellion*. New York: W. W. Norton, 1974.

Woodard, Colin. *American Nations: A History of the Eleven Rival Regional Cultures of North America*. New York: Viking, 2011.

Wright, Gavin. *Old South, New South: Revolutions in the Southern Economy Since the Civil War*. Baton Rouge: Louisiana State University Press, 1986.

——. *Slavery and American Economic Development*. Baton Rouge: Louisiana State University Press, 2006.

Wyatt-Brown, Bertram. *Southern Honor: Ethics and Behavior in the Old South*. New York: Oxford University Press, 1982.

INDEX

Atlantic triangular trade. *See* transatlantic trade

Augusta, Ga., 184–91

authenticity (and authentic character), 275, 290, 294, 298; "diversity curve," 291

Bacon, Francis, 126

Bacon's Rebellion, 102, 203

Baker, Eleanor, 153

Baltimore, Maryland, 188

Barbados, 29, 48, 50, 52, 64, 87, 101, 131, 163–66, 169–70

Barbados Slave Code of 1661, 291

baronies of Carolina, 131

barrier and back-barrier islands, 32

Bartram, John, 33–34

Bartram, William, 33–34, 37

Battle of Bloody Marsh, 38, 98, 215

Beach Institute, 152

Beasley, David, 237

Beaufort, City of, 30, 136, 292–93

Beaufort County, South Carolina, 243, 292–93

Beaumont, Gustave de, 201-2

Bennett, Thomas, 65

Berendt, John, 20, 22, 25

Berkeley, George, 241

Berkeley, William, 203

Beth Elohim, 59

Biden, Joseph R. , 288

Bight of Georgia, 35

Blatt, Sol, 85

Bledsoe, Albert Taylor, 219

Bluffton, S.C., 292

Boston, Mass., 188, 192

Brailsford, Charles, 175

Brazil, 164, 171

Bridgetown, Barbados, 50

Briggs, Isaac, 186

Bristol, England, 174

Britain, 28, 41, 50–51, 58–61, 90–94, 96–98, 100, 102–3, 105, 164-65, 169, 175–76, 199–200, 207, 215, 228, 231

Brooks, Preston , 70

Broughton, Thomas, 97

Brown, John, 72

Brown, Morris, 66

Brown University, 58

Brown v. Board of Education, 82, 113, 239

Bryan, Hugh, 101

Bryan, Jonathan, 101, 212

Buckingham, James Silk, 256

Bull, Kinloch, Jr., 175

Bull, Stephen, 175

Bull, William, 94, 214

Bull, William, II, 175, 212

Bulloch, Archibald, 102-3

Burke, Emily, 106, 153

Burns, Ken, 204

Burton, John, 141

Butler, Christina Rae, 15, 276

Butler, Pierce, 72

cacique (class of Carolina nobility), 129

Cainhoy Peninsula, 138

Calhoun, John C., 61–71, 209, 221, 230; Calhoun monument removal, 86, 295

Callahan, Patti, 188

Canary Current, 26

Canary Islands, 164

Carib people, 165

Caribbean, 163–70, 232–33, 250

Carolina Colony (Province of Carolina): city and regional planning, 123–39; class structure, 128–34; origin of southern pretentions and manners in, 54, 58–59; Proprietary Period, 48–54, 123–39; religion, 129–30

"Carolina way," 101, 179, 203, 212, 216, 218, 222

Caroline (queen), 141

Cash, W. J., 231–32, 293–94

Castillo de San Marcos, 98

Catholic Church, 125

Cavaliers (English nobility), 200, 220, 233

Central and Latin America, 232

character traits of Charleston and Savannah, 9–36, 133, 274–83. *See also* authenticity

Charles I (king), 48

Europeanness, 275
Eveleigh, Samuel, 97
Evelyn, John, 123

Factor's Row (Savannah), 191
Federal Highway Administration, 263
Federal Housing Administration (FHA),
    137, 155, 239, 262
Ferguson, Leland, 173
feudalism, 41. *See also* gothic society
Fire-Eaters, 61–71, 194–95; Christopher G.
    Memminger, 63; J. D. B. De Bow, 62–64;
    John C. Calhoun, 63; Laurence M.
    Keitt, 63–64; Louis Wigfall, 63; Maxcy
    Gregg, 63; Robert Barnwell Rhett, 61–72
    passim, 75, 221, 230; William Lowndes
    Yancey, 63; William Porcher Miles,
    62–63
Fischer, David Hackett, 200, 202
Florida, Richard, 283
Floyd, George, 295–96
Foner, Eric, 74
Ford, Robert, 237
Forsyth Park, Savannah, 22, 153
Fort Frederica, 95
Fort Frederick, 91, 146
Fort Sumter, 71, 73
Forty Acres and a Mule, 110
France (and New France), 37–38, 150, 164,
    199, 202, 214, 268
Fraser, Walter , 106
Frederica, Ga., 94, 95–99
Frederick II , 286
freedom. *See* liberty
Freehling, William , 250
Freeport Doctrine, 70
French Revolution, 64, 230
Frost, Susan Pringle, 83
Fugitive Slave Act of 1850, 72, 221
Fulton, Robert, 177, 185
Fundamental Constitutions of Carolina,
    63, 124, 126, 128–34, 168; compared with
    the plan for Georgia, 141–48

Gaillard, J. Palmer, Jr., 18, 83–84, 236
Gallay, Alan, 51, 199, 202

Gamble, Samuel, 173
Garden City Movement, 154
genius loci, 7
Genovese, Eugene, 216
gentrification, 86, 245, 247, 254, 269, 278,
    289–90, 294–96, 299–300
gentry class, 129
George II, 54, 90, 142
Georgetown, S.C., 30, 136
Georgia Trustees, 141–50, 181–83
Georgia: becomes royal colony, 100–104;
    capital cities, 111; founding, 89–100; pop-
    ulation of cities, 11, 43, 93, 96, 111, 191, 193,
    242–43, 293; prohibition of slavery, 183;
    settlement by persecuted Protestants,
    96, 141, 182–83; Slave Code of 1755, 101;
    tensions with South Carolina, 95–100;
    Trustee period, 89–100, 141–50
German immigrants, 194
Gilbert, Ralph Mark, 115
Girl Scouts, 110
Glorious Revolution, 38
Golden Heritage Plan , 155–56
Gone with the Wind (Mitchell), 62
Goose Creek Men, 169–70
Gordon, Eleanor, 110
Gordon, Juliette, 110
Gordon, Peter, 93, 147
Gordon, William, 256
gothic society, 41, 55, 89, 124, 127–30, 140,
    148, 181, 217, 281; class reciprocity in, 164;
    gothic or medieval character, 250, 276
Graham, Vincent G., 265–66
Grand Model ("Modell") of Carolina,
    14–15, 49, 85–86, 121, 124–39, 141–48,
    163–64, 181, 281
Great Chain of Being, 233
Great Depression, 236, 238
Great Fire of 1666 (London), 123–24,
    132–33, 144
Great Migration, 52, 238
Great Recession, 157
Green, Charles, 110
Green, Nathanael, 60, 256
Greenberg, Reuben M., 84
Green-Meldrim House, 110

Greenville-Spartanburg industrial corridor,
42, 85, 244
Greer, Inland Port, 244
Grimké, Angelina, 58
Grimké, Elizabeth (Mrs. John Rutledge),
57–58
Grimké, Sarah, 58
Gulf Stream, 28, 30, 215
Gulfstream Aerospace Corporation. *See
online supplement*
Gullah people and culture, 30, 50–51
Gwinnett, Button, 103

Habersham, James, 101
Haiti, 65, 104, 165
Haitian Revolution, 202
Hales, Stephen, 141
Haley, K. H. D., 123
Haley, Nikki, 237
Hall, Lyman, 103
Hamburg, S.C., 68, 189
Hamilton, Andrew, 221
Hammond, James Henry, 66, 177, 217–19,
233
Hampstead (Georgia colonial village), 93
Hampton, Wade, 217
Hannover Square, 143
Harbor, The (Charleston nonprofit),
249–50, 284
Harney, John Milton, 106
Harper, William, 219, 223
Harty, Mary, 22
Haussmann, Georges-Eugene, 20
Hawkins, John, 38
Hayne, Robert Y., 67
Hicks, Brian, 138
Highgate (Georgia colonial village), 93
Hilton Head Island, 30, 243, 292
historic city core area, 24, 138, 241–44, 284,
289, 297–98
historicity, 275
historic preservation, 2–3, 115–18, 137, 245–66
H. L. Hunley (ship), 74
Hogarth, William, 144; paintings: *The Har-
lot's Progress* and, *The Rake's Progress*, 144
Holland (the Netherlands), 38, 165, 200

Hooke, Robert, 123
Hopkey, Sophie, 97
House of Stuart, 169, 200
Housing Acts of 1949 and 1954, 155
Houstoun, John, 102
Howard, Samuel, 186
Huguenots, 37, 51
Human Genome Project, 67
Hunter Army Airfield, Savannah. *See
online supplement*
hurricanes, 34–36, 80–81
Hutchinson Island, 191

ideal cities of the Renaissance, 143
Indians. *See* Native Americans
indigenous people. *See* Native Americans
indigo, 174–76
Industrial Revolution, 151, 178, 185
I'On (Mt. Pleasant, S.C.), 266, 291
Irish immigrants, 194
Izard, Ralph, 175

Jackson, Andrew, President, 177, 214, 221
Jackson, Edna , 248
Jacobs, Jane, 279–80
James II (king), 38, 126, 141
James Island, 138
Jamestown, 135
Jasper, William, Sgt., 256
Jay, William, 106
Jefferson, Thomas, 63, 90, 151, 203, 209, 214,
216, 218, 221, 229
jet streams and climate, 30
Jews, in the Lowcountry, 51, 59, 71
Jim Crow era and laws, 18, 42, 74, 75, 137,
194, 222, 235, 239; etymology, 77; in
Charleston, 77–85; in Savannah, 113–15
John Birch Society, 157
John Randolph (ship), 108
John's Island, 138
Johnson, Andrew, 78, 110
Johnson, James, 110
Johnson, Olin, 85
Johnson, Otis S., 116
Johnson, Robert, 55
Johnson, Samuel, 208

Johnson, Van, 248
Jones, Noble, 103
Jones, Noble Wimberley, 102–3

Kennedy, John G., 115
Kentucky, 178, 216–17
Key West, Fla., 9, 276
Keyserling, Billy, 265
Keyserling, Harriet, 254–55
King, Kristopher, 255
Knights of the Golden Circle, 219
Know-Nothing Party, 106
Knox, Henry, 214–15
Ku Klux Klan, 74

Lafer, Gordon, 298
La Florida, 38, 50, 90. *See also* Spain
Lamar, Charles Augustus Lafayette, 106
Lamar, Gazaway Bugg, 106, 188
landgrave, 62, 129
Landmarkism, 240
latitude and longitude, 29–30
Laurens, Henry, 57, 174–76
Law, W. W., 115
leetmen, 130
Leng, Thomas, 129
Lewis, Julius Curtis, Jr. , 247
liberty, 57, 62, 208–10, 233
Lincoln, Abraham, 61–71 passim, 109–10, 135
Lincoln, Benjamin, 60
Liverpool, 174
Locke, John, 14, 49, 63, 92, 100, 121, 123–39, 140, 142, 144, 164, 169, 208–9, 228–29; as planner of Carolina, 124–34; on slavery, 124–26
Long, Jefferson Franklin, 112
Longstreet, William, 185–86
Lords Proprietors of Carolina, 48–54, 62, 121; period of colonial administration, 48–54. *See also* Fundamental Constitutions of Carolina; Grand Model ("Modell") of Carolina
Lost Cause mythology, 51, 72, 84, 113, 218, 231, 237, 270, 294–95
Louisiana, 178, 215, 218–19. *See also* Mis-

sissippi Valley and Lower Mississippi region
Louisiana Purchase, 177, 215, 219
Low, Juliette Gordon, 110
Lowcountry: 14, 30–36; cities, 292–93; climate, 14, 30, 34; cultural blending, 12–13; defined, 25; ecology, 32–34; exports, 174; future prospects, 289; "grim years," 49, 169; as model for Deep South, 166–67; plantations, 175; rivers, 17, 33; religious dissenters, 170; settlement pattern compared with Virginia, 134–36; tides, 32–33
Lucas, Jonathan, 174

Mace, Nancy, 287
Maclean, Malcolm R., 247
Macon, Ga., 188, 190–91
Madeira Islands, 164
Madison, James, 3–4, 63, 72, 203, 209, 221, 229
Magnolia Plantation, 17, 175
malaria. *See* disease
Malcontents of Savannah, 96, 150, 183, 211
Manigault, Peter, 57
Marrs, Aaron W., 68
Marsh tidal ecosystem, 33 Maryland, 3, 39
Mason, George, 229
Mason-Dixon Line, 3, 216
Matthews, Maurice, 128
McConnell, Glenn, 237–38
McDonald, David, 265
McLean, Malcolm , 80
mechanic, 13, 70, 232
medieval character. *See* gothic society
Mediterranean climate, 14, 29-30
Meinig, Donald, 217
Menendez, Pedro, 38
Menotti, Gian Carlo, 18
Merritt, Keri Leigh, 23
Metropolitan Planning Commission, Chatham-Savannah, 155–57, 247
Michaux, Andre, 33–34
Middleton, William, 174
Miller, Chris, 284–85
Mississippi, 178, 216
Mississippi Valley and Lower Mississippi region, 18, 68, 166, 177–78, 215–19, 227

Missouri, 178, 219
Missouri Compromise, 219
Mitchell, Margaret, 62
Mobile, Ala., 243
monoculture, 166, 178, 203, 216, 218, 228, 271
Monroe, James, 63, 209, 229
Monticello, 135
Moore, Francis, 179
More, Hannah, 207
Mother Emmanuel AME Church. *See*
  Emanuel African Methodist Episcopal
  Church
Mulberry Grove Plantation, 186
Musgrove, John, 92, 94
Musgrove, Mary, 92, 94

Natchez, Miss., 217
National Association for the Advancement
  of Colored People (NAACP), 237
National Historic Landmark District. *See*
  Charleston: historic districts and neighborhoods; Savannah: historic districts
  and neighborhoods
Native Americans, 4, 150, 204; enslaved
  in Carolina, 51, 124–26; Mississippian
  culture, 37; trade in South Carolina, 170;
  Yamasee War, 213–14
Native American nations: Cherokee, 92,
  213–14; Chickasaw, 213, 215; Choctaw, 92,
  213, 215; Creek (Muskogee), 37, 92, 213,
  215; Kussoe, 213; in the Lowcountry and
  Georgia, 31–32, 36–37, 41, 92–95, 199, 268;
  Savannah, 31, 213; Shawnee, 213; Stono,
  213; Taino, 31; Westo, 213; Yamacraw, 92;
  Yamasee (Yemasee), 92, 213–14; Yuchi,
  92, 185
naval stores, 170, 174
Navin, John, 169
New Deal, 235
New Orleans, La., 9–11, 40, 166–67, 177, 188,
  194, 217, 220, 212, 276
New South, 238, 245–46
New Urbanism, 265, 291–92
New York City, 192
Newcourt, Richard, 123
Newport, R.I., 136

News and Courier, 82
Newton, Isaac, 140, 144
Nixon, Richard , 239
Nolen, John , 154
Norris, J. Frank, 238
North Atlantic Currents, 12, 26–28
North Atlantic Gyre, 12, 26–28
North Atlantic triangular trade. *See* trans-
  atlantic trade
North Carolina, 53
Nott, Josiah C., 67
nullification, 220–21
Nullification Crisis, 66, 72, 222
nullifiers, of South Carolina, 66–67. *See also*
  Fire-Eaters
Nutt, John, 175–76

Ocmulgee site, 36
Ocmulgee River, 36, 188
Ogeechee River, 107, 188
Oglethorpe, Eleanor, 141
Oglethorpe, James Edward, 20, 31, 38, 41,
  55–57, 59, 89–100, 105, 140–59, 179, 181–83,
  211–12, 256
Oglethorpe, Theophilus, 141
Oglethorpe Plan, 129, 136, 140–59, 194, 207,
  256, 260, 265, 281; compared with Grand
  Model of Carolina, 141–48; worthy poor
  as beneficiaries, 182, 184
Oklahoma, 215
Old South nostalgia. *See* Lost Cause
  mythology
oligarchy. *See* aristocracy and oligarchy of
  the Lowcountry
Owens-Thomas House, 106
Oxford, 123, 128, 141
Oyster Point, 134, 147

Paine, Thomas, 104
palatinate, government of Proprietary
  Carolina, 129
palatine, ranking noble in Proprietary
  Carolina, 129
Panic of 1837, 190, 232
Paris, ix, 20
Park, Mungo, 179

patriarchy, 58, 87, 233, 268. *See also* aristocracy and oligarchy of the Lowcountry
peculiar institution, 62–63, 207, 209, 222, 230
pelts, 174
Pennsylvania, 3
Pensacola, Fla., 192
Percival, John , 141–43
Peter Gordon map, 93, 147
Peter Tondee's Tavern, 102
Philadelphia, Penn., 66, 194
Philip II, 164
Phillips, Kevin, 239
phosphate mining, 78, 234
Pinckney, Charles, 72
Pinckney, Eliza, 174
Pinckney, Henry, 67
Pine, John, 141
Plant, Henry B., 193
plantation elite. *See* aristocracy and oligarchy of the Lowcountry
Plessy v. Ferguson, 82, 113
political culture, 3–4, 39, 107, 129, 134, 169, 200–204, 207–10, 217, 220–23, 227, 229, 233, 261, 288
political economy, 227, 229
Pope, Alexander, 7
Pope, John, 110
population and demographics: 39–40, 43, 49, 57, 76, 111, 135, 167, 193–94, 241–43, 293; comparison of Barbados and Carolina enslaved populations, 52; inward growth of cities before transportation innovations, 153; map of distribution of enslaved population in 1860, 168; Upper South vis-à-vis Lower South, 178
Port of Charleston, 33, 76–81 , 85
Port of Savannah, 33, 42, 78, 85, 108, 244
Port Royal Sound, 37, 91
Port Royal, S.C., 30, 265, 292–93
Portugal, and Portuguese, 26, 38, 164–65
Post and Courier, 83, 138, 246
Preservation Society of Charleston, 83, 137
Pressly, Paul M., 101
Priber, Christian Gottlieb, 98–99
Prince Eugene of Savoy, 141

Principia Mathematica (Newton), 144
Pringle, Robert, 174
prison conditions, 143, 144
Pulaski, Casimir, 103–4
Puritans, 200, 202, 205

Quakers, 200, 205
Quartering Act, 60
Queen Caroline, 141

racism: "peculiar institution" and, 62, 230; polygenesis thesis, 67, 87. *See also* white supremacy
railroads: 41, 68–69, 79, 85, 189–93; Amtrak, 191; Central of Georgia Railway, 108, 191; Central Rail Road & Banking Company of Georgia, 189; Central Rail Road and Canal Company, 108, 189–91; Charleston & Savannah Railroad, 192–93; csx Transportation, 85, 193; Illinois Central Railroad, 191; Louisville, Cincinnati & Charleston Railroad, 190; Macon & Western Railroad, 190; Norfolk Southern Railway, 85; South Carolina Canal and Railroad Company, 68; South Carolina Railroad, 69; Southern Railway, 191; St. Louis–San Francisco Railway ("Frisco" line), 191; Wilmington and Manchester Railroad, 69
Ravenel, Arthur, Jr., 237–38
Ravenel Bridge, 17
Reconstruction era, 42, 71–77, 109–12, 234, 269
Redeemers, 111–12
reinvention, ix, 1–3, 42, 47, 117–19, 267–68, 272–74, 294–96
Reiter, Beth Lattimore, 257
Republic of Letters, 228–29, 286
Republican Party, 42, 70–71, 237, 239–40, 287
Republican Southern Strategy, 42, 224, 239
resilience, 151, 173–74, 294, 299–300
Restoration period, 49
Rhett, Robert Barnwell, 61–72, 75, 82, 221, 230
Rhett, William, 62
Ribault, Jean, 37

Sept. 17th - 6:00 pm.
Sept. 24th
Oct. 1st

843-010-1522

9 780820 363196